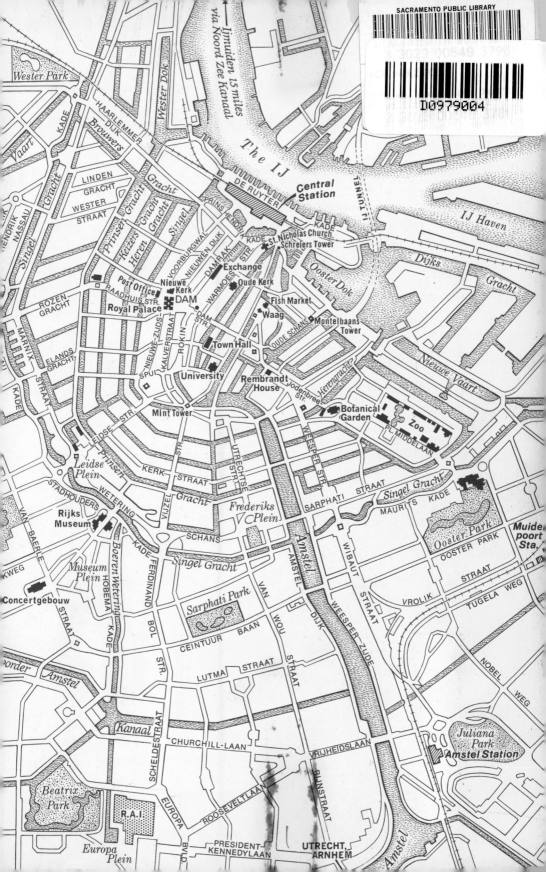

SACRAMENTO PUBLIC LIBRARY

3 3029 00549 3798

D0979004

Wester Park

HAARLEMMER DIJK

Brouwers Gracht

LINDEN GRACHT

WESTER STRAAT

HENDRIK

NASSAU

Singel

Vaart

KADE

Prinsen Gracht

Keizers Gracht

Heren Gracht

Singel

Gracht

ROZEN GRACHT

ELANDS GRACHT

MARNIX

STRAAT

KADE

Post Office
RAADHUIS STR.
Royal Palace

Nieuwe Kerk
DAM

PRINS HENDRIK

DE RUYTER

KADE

St. Nicholas Church
Schreiers Tower

Central Station

The IJ

IJ Haven

Wester Dok

TUNNEL

Dijks Gracht

Ooster Dok

Exchange
Oude Kerk

Nieuwe

DAM RAK

VOORBURGWAL

NIEUWEN DIJK

STR.

WARMOES

Fish Market
Waag

Montelbaans Tower

DAM STR.

ROKIN

NIEUWE-ZUIDS

KALVERSTRAAT

Town Hall

University

Rembrandt House

Mint Tower

Jodenbree Str.

Herengracht

Oude Schans

Nieuwe Vaart

Botanical Garden
Zoo

PL. MIDDELAAN

SPUI

LEIDSE STR.

Leidse Plein

PRINSEN

WETERING

KERK

VIZEL

STRAAT

Gracht

UTRECHTS.

STR.

Frederiks Plein

WEESPER STR.

Singel Gracht

MAURITS KADE

Ooster Park

Muide poort Sta.

STADHOUDERS

Rijks Museum

VAN BAERLE

KWEG

Museum Plein

Concertgebouw

HOBEMA STRAAT

BOERENWETERING

KADE

FERDINAND

BOL

STR.

SCHANS

Singel Gracht

Sarphati Park

CEINTUUR BAAN

LUTMA STRAAT

VAN

WOU

STRAAT

Amstel

SARPHATI STRAAT

Amstel

DIJK

WIBAUT STRAAT

WEESPER ZIJDE

VROLIK

STRAAT

OOSTER PARK

TUGELA WEG

NOBEL WEG

Kanaal

SCHELDESTRAAT

EUROPA

BLVD.

CHURCHILL-LAAN

ROOSEVELTLAAN

VRIJHEIDSLAAN

Juliana Park
Amstel Station

Beatrix Park

R.A.I.

Europa Plein

PRESIDENT KENNEDYLAAN

RUNSTRAAT

UTRECHT, ARNHEM

Amstel

Ijmuiden 15 miles via Noord Zee Kanaal

949.23
C847

Cotterell   1000
  Amsterdam
               c.2

McKINLEY

SACRAMENTO CITY-COUNTY LIBRARY
SACRAMENTO, CALIFORNIA

978

Books by Geoffrey Cotterell

GO, SAID THE BIRD

WESTWARD THE SUN

TIARA TAHITI

THE STRANGE ENCHANTMENT

STRAIT AND NARROW

ERRAND AT SHADOW CREEK

AMSTERDAM: THE LIFE OF A CITY

AMSTERDAM
The Life of a City

A view of Amsterdam Harbor in 1690
COURTESY OF THE AMSTERDAM CITY ARCHIVES

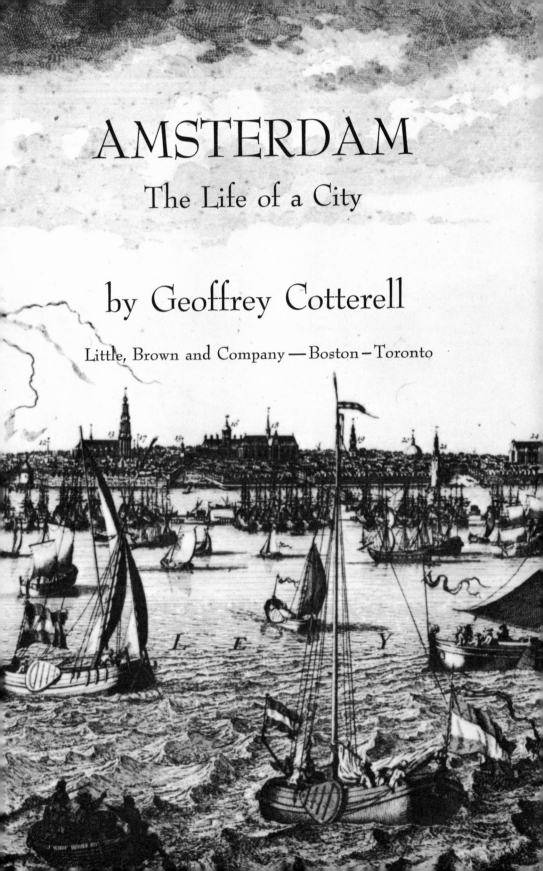

AMSTERDAM

The Life of a City

by Geoffrey Cotterell

Little, Brown and Company — Boston — Toronto

COPYRIGHT © 1972 BY GEOFFREY COTTERELL

ALL RIGHTS RESERVED. NO PART OF THIS BOOK MAY BE REPRODUCED IN ANY FORM OR BY ANY ELECTRONIC OR MECHANICAL MEANS INCLUDING INFORMATION STORAGE AND RETRIEVAL SYSTEMS WITHOUT PERMISSION IN WRITING FROM THE PUBLISHER, EXCEPT BY A REVIEWER WHO MAY QUOTE BRIEF PASSAGES IN A REVIEW.

LIBRARY OF CONGRESS CATALOG CARD NO. 78–183857

FIRST EDITION

T 05/72

Published simultaneously in Canada
by Little, Brown & Company (Canada) Limited

PRINTED IN THE UNITED STATES OF AMERICA

McKINLEY.

C.2

FOR HARRY SIONS
the patient begetter

In hac enim florentissima republica et urbe praestantissima omnes cujus-
cunque nationis et sectae homines summa cum concordia vivunt; et ut
alicui bona sua credant, id tantum scire curant, num dives an pauper sit,
et num bona fide an dolo solitus sit agere.

In this flourishing republic, this city second to none, men of every nation
and every sect live together in the utmost harmony; and all they bother
to find out, before trusting their goods to anyone, is whether he is rich or
poor and whether he is honest or a fraud.

— Spinoza

De Hoer aan't Y is voor elk geld te koop
Die vaart voor Paap en Heiden, Moor en Turk,
Die geeft om God noch't lieve Vaderland
Die vraagt naar winst alleen, naar winst! naar winst!

The whore on the Y can be bought with anybody's money;
She serves Pope and heathen, Moor and Turk,
She bothers about neither God nor the dear fatherland,
She is concerned with profit alone, profit alone! Profit alone!

— Bartens, a Seventeenth-century Calvinist

Prefatory Note

I SHOULD LIKE to express my gratitude to Dr. Simon Hart, deputy archivist, and the staff of the Amsterdam municipal archives, who gave me unlimited help and understanding, to Dr. C. Wegener Sleeswijk of the Town Planning Office in the Amsterdam public works service, who guided me on the somewhat tortuous path to the city's origins, and to the public relations officer of Amsterdam, Mr. B. C. Heinemeijer, whose efforts on my behalf were unstinted and invaluable.

I must also thank Meulenhoff Nederland n.v. and H. J. W. Becht's Uitgeversmaatschappij n.v. for permission to quote (in my own translation) from, respectively, "Schuldbekentenis van een ambassadeur" by Roel van Duyn and "Oproer in Amsterdam" by J. Fahrenfort, H. E. Janszen and F. Sanders.

Contents

Contents

Contents

Contents

Contents

[xvii]

Illustrations

Prologue

On the Dam

WHY, NOW, here is the Royal Palace and here come soldiers. They march into the great square, the Dam, from the street called Rokin, where an army bus deposited them half an hour ago, and where possibly they have just upset the ghosts of merchants and brokers as they passed by the site of the seventeenth-century Exchange. A crowd has gathered. An important visitor is in the city and there is to be a ceremony. The sun shines and the soldiers march well. Yet, somehow, they give the impression of not being overcareful about it, as if there might be someone around who will, at any moment, shout something rude; and the people who watch them, with pleasure, have also on their faces the look of persons mildly hopeful that a sword will be dropped or that one column will go the wrong way. The magnificent seventeenth-century palace looks down pretending to be a large post office. For how can a palace be a palace without a grand entrance — without, at least, a courtyard? Seven little doors are ridiculous. . . .

The consul's song

BUT HOW WELL they suit the city's mood.

This mood is a mixture of amiable mockery, unpretentiousness, unselfconsciousness and what the Dutch call *gezelligheid,* which is partly a sort of coziness and partly a living-togetherness. And it adds up to an intoxicant. The fact that no other city has had more sentimental songs written about it gives an idea of the potency. Though not too keen on the songs, I am an addict and understand. And now even the British consul has come out with one, which promises to be a hit, so this morning's paper says.

"Listen, the bells are ringing," it goes, "Amsterdam's carillons are swinging." The consul is right. Nowhere else is like Amsterdam. It is the most civilized and agreeable city in the world.

It is beautiful. Its great canals have been a wonder of the past few hundred years. So has the city's tradition of tolerance, which wobbled badly only for a few decades in the sixteenth century. This was the place where persecuted groups could live unmolested: Jews, Brownists, Mennonites, Catholics (rather secretly) and others were all in the same city with the Calvinists. It was a contemporary tourist fascination. Now the field has changed from religion to sex, drugs and anarchy. However, the tolerance is of a particular kind. It is an agreement to coexist. Variety is allowed within order. This is the essence of the civilized, free city. The sects used to understand; and today the Council gives a pamphlet to visitors it thinks may not.

Any place with such roots in freedom can erupt now and then. Amsterdam erupts now and then, and then goes back to *gezelligheid*. Naturally it has its proper number of murders (here on the Rembrandtsplein there was a savage one above the bar on the corner three nights ago — the atmosphere there was very hushed the next day). But the usual feeling is of security and comfort. Even the red-light district in the oldest part — brightly lit up bed-sitting-rooms with waxen figures looking out or resting on divans — is also the district of the lovely, venerable, fourteenth- and fifteenth-century Oude Kerk (Old Church) and the magisterial and historic headquarters of the burgomaster and the council. It is all part of the cozy mixture, and so are the hundreds of bars, to suit all tastes, where people talk and feel both "out" and "at home" — "*uit*" and "*t'huis*."

A marvelous city. No wonder there are songs about it. It is full of ghosts and full of a tantalizing conflict of doubts and hopes.

The faces seem familar

HERE on the Dam, which has seen everything — riots, burnings at the stake, hippies playing guitars — you could catch a taxi three hundred years ago. It was horse-drawn and mounted on a sort of sleigh, an invention to deal with the hump-backed bridges. You rang a bell and the assembled drivers had a little game of dice to decide who should be your driver. That also fitted the city's mood.

And is the Punch-and-Judy show in action in front of the palace? It started in the mid-seventeenth century, when Jan Klaasen and his wife Katrijn played themselves in a first satire show, directed against the authorities for their conduct of the war against England. The puppets remain and the same family also remains, still doing it. And are we across the square from the palace in the Hotel Krasnapolsky? Let us not miss the palm trees in the winter garden restaurant, an evocation of the late nineteenth century. Mr. Krasnapolsky was a tailor who began a café. When it was successful as a meeting place for businessmen, he wanted to stock it with wines; and he found suitable cellars close by, the cellars of a monastery. Stones thrown idly from a Hotel Krasnapolsky in the fifteenth century would have easily hit half a dozen cloisters. There are ghosts of monks in plenty on the Dam. And also of anti-Catholic Anabaptists who came sloping out of a little lane just behind on a night in 1535, in a fantastically bold conspiracy to take over the town — and soon met the grisliest of ends. And royal ghosts, too: Louis Napoleon frustrated and lonely behind the windows of the palace, and his brother the emperor slowly riding across the Dam, making his simple but magnificent entrance.

But the period that leans most heavily is always the seventeenth century, the time of Amsterdam's glory, followed by the eighteenth, the time of wealth if also of decline. The palace then was the greatest Town Hall in Europe. The black-hatted and black-suited earlier figures and the laced and bewigged later ones parade in the shadows, and they go towards two little streets, long since torn down, to make their way to the Exchange of Hendrick de Keyser, which for more than a hundred and fifty years was the unrivaled center of commerce and trading in Europe, and which taught all today's stock markets the rules of the game.

It was so wonderful then, the achievement so magnificent, the businessmen, the sailors, the builders, the painters — and the authors, who shared in the glory but whose niche in the fame gallery has always been diminished by the language difficulty. There was no difficulty to upset the fame of the others. In the first half of the nineteenth century the feeling in Amsterdam of living in a long-drawn-out anticlimax was almost too much to bear. And even in a dynamic late-twentieth-century economic expansion the golden era leans so heavily that the feeling is still there a little.

There are, after all, so many reminders — thank God — the great canals above all and their long lines of old patrician houses. Of course too many of the latter have gone and some of the smaller canals have been filled in. There was danger in the movement of the commonsense and cut-out-the-sentiment boys earlier in this century. But the great houses ceased to be lived in and they certainly couldn't all be preserved to make a dead museum city, an enormous ghost town. Fortunately it was discovered that they made splendid and impressive offices and showrooms, and so they survive alive — enough of them. As to any further destruction, Amsterdam vigilantes are aggressively vigilant — 114,000 out of a population of 836,000 signed a recent petition.

The other reminder comes from art. The effect of the great outburst of Dutch painting in the seventeenth century is that almost every native Amsterdamer is also a ghost. For visitors from abroad the impression has always been well known, since visitors, or at least tourists, automatically go to the Rijksmuseum, that fine example of nineteenth-century, railway-station Gothic. (They are mad if they don't.) Here the focal point of everything is Rembrandt's *Night Watch*, which is introduced by the guides as "the most valuable painting in the world." This guarantees the respect of all. It really needs no help, for it is surely more alive than the people looking at it. All day long parties of foreigners, youth groups and Dutch schoolchildren stand solemnly in front of the carpet which acts as a barrier. Captain Cocq is forever there with his company of musketeers. But the *Night Watch* is only one of the fruits of the compulsive desire of wealthy seventeenth-century Amsterdamers to see themselves in group portraits. There they are on the walls of the Rijksmuseum, the regents of the Lepers' House, the Guild of Surgeons, the "Corporalships" of fashionable militia companies, dozens of seventeenth- and eighteenth-century Dutch faces.

They are twentieth-century Dutch faces as well, and they follow you outside the museum and into the streets of Amsterdam in the most disconcerting way. You go into a café and there sitting opposite are two of the black-suited regents. These, of course, are middle-aged or elderly men. And this always used to be the form of the experience. When I first visited Amsterdam as a boy, it seemed to me to be a city of prosperous-looking men in dark suits, eating very large meals and smoking cigars. Even an errand boy on a bicycle had his cigar. The air was cigar-scented and all tables seemed to be covered with carpets. It was a kind of bourgeois heaven, and the regents were all around. And their fat wives as well, from the domestic "genre" pictures.

Nowadays this particular sensation has an entirely new dimension. Added to the regents are the background figures in the militia company pictures, the musketeers and halberdiers and pikemen. Youth has arrived on the scene. Often Amsterdam seems like a huge university city. It does have two universities, but thousands more students than they account for crowd the streets. In fact they are not all students, but they look like students. The hair-sex-clothing revolution of the sixties made this tolerant place a magnetic ground. So there are some strange sights — and some simple and beguiling ones, like a very tall, very thin youth who passes with an extra wide brimmed black hat like a bullfighter's perched straight on his head. He looks neither to left nor right and the hat continues along the street, never wavering. (It will end up in a café, where its owner will relax at last, sitting with friends in noisy pop-filled twilight, probably for hours. The splendid hat will stay on, dead square. As it would have in the seventeenth century.) And all around are cavaliers with pointed beards and colorful clothes, and Elizabethans whom the Earl of Leicester (an important sixteenth-century visitor) would have hired without blinking, and there are monks everywhere with long hair or cropped hair and drab clothes and steel spectacles — surely they are monks. But the harquebusiers and the cheerfully arrogant officers of the militia companies are in the so-called artists' cafés, where splendidly coiffed and moustached men are straight out of Van der Helst. Will they all go back onto the walls of the Rijksmuseum? Is Amsterdam some kind of Brigadoon? No. It comes as a shock to see them doing something unromantic, and nothing to do with the golden age, like catching a tram. (But the Amsterdam trams, little gray trains of three coaches, are also splendid.)

Variety with order. A number of the students in Amsterdam's universities are rather pointedly old-fashioned in a different way, that is, they wear neat suits and have short back and sides and can be seen with similarly old-fashioned girls filling half a theater audience. The hair styles and life-styles mix. All sects can survive in Amsterdam.

And the dark-suited businessmen are still there, of course. Their skyscrapers rise up. From my room in the evening I look straight across a dusky sea of elegant canal-house roofs to the miragelike Netherlands Bank, high and square and brilliant with lights. The businessmen still come out of the Rijksmuseum, but they seem to be not so fat as when I first saw them, and their meals not so large and the air not so cigar-scented. I miss that scent a little, it was a symbol of comfort.

A wedding incident

I DON'T MISS, but am a little sad about, the decline of the bicycle. There are plenty about still, far more than in most cities. But it isn't the same as it used to be. They used to swarm everywhere, ridden with dash, initiative and terrible confidence. It was a dance of death and for the inexperienced motorist to be caught in Amsterdam's rush hour was the sternest of tests. After a time you began to realize that you still hadn't hit a cyclist. They seemed to avoid cars as flies avoid a swat; it was as if air pressure forced them out of your way. But all that seems to be over. There are more motor scooters and more small cars. The important fact is that more Amsterdam-ers now live too far away for comfortable cycling — in the new suburbs, which one must not call suburbs, but independent garden cities, like Slotervaart and Slotermeer and Bijlmermeer, town planners' heavens and to some extent pre-glimpses of the twenty-first century. This old city is in places the newest of cities.

And it is a metropolis, going ahead efficiently in its corner of the Com-mon Market. But it is still graspable. People in bars sing songs about other districts as if they all feel the whole city belongs to them. The bigness is not too big. Crowded, trafficless Kalverstraat on a Saturday afternoon somehow gives the feeling of an enormous family reunion. There is no surprise element in meeting friends.

I was a guest at a wedding once. A civil ceremony came first and this happened at the Town Hall, which lies along one of the medieval canals, the O.Z. Voorburgwal. I listened to the harsh but attractive gutturals of Dutch and looked at the characteristic faces (all from the Rijksmuseum, of course) of guests sitting in rows as if in a classroom. The bridegroom wore the correct uniform, a sort of evening dress, and the bride was lovely. After "our" wedding was over, there was another one waiting, and that bride was lovely, too, an Indonesian girl. The air was full of happiness. Then we were on our way to the second wedding, which would be in a church — Dutch Reformed. I had no worries, the best man was taking me. We took some time to get going, there were many guests, and perhaps also the guests from the other wedding were complicating things. And once we were started, we were almost immediately in a canal traffic jam. These are a feature of Amsterdam life. The cobbled road is narrow and if somebody has to stop, so must everybody else. The patience shown is always rather remarkable, and the best man showed it. There was no sign of any of the other wedding cars. When we could move, the best man drove off briskly, around the other side of the canal, across to the Dam, behind the palace, and so to south Amsterdam, with a halt on the way when we had to back out of a one-way street. Soon we were hopelessly lost. The best man was not worried, even when the time of the ceremony passed, for he reasoned that it couldn't begin without him and furthermore, very much further-more, he had the key of the church in his pocket.

Then as we drove down a shopping street he noticed a cousin of his. She jumped aboard and guided us to the church, which seemed to be miles away. The crowd outside looked slightly impatient, but the best man, splendid fellow, was entirely pleased with himself. Before long we were all back in the center of town again, eating an enormous meal — as it happened, at the Hotel Krasnapolsky. The odd thing was that neither the best man nor his cousin, who was not a guest, nor anyone else at the wedding seemed to think that this chance meeting was very extraordinary. The reaction continues to baffle me. Amsterdam has over eight hundred thousand people, but you expect to see your cousin walking along when necessary. It can only be part of *gezelligheid.*

•

Ghosts

AMSTERDAM revolves round the Dam and a long straight street called Damrak, which was once a sea harbor, and is still a harbor, at least for sight-seeing launches. Three streets run parallel with Damrak, on either side of it, and the two outer ones extend a little beyond the Dam, and once made four canals as well, two of which have been filled in. Around all this went a circling canal, which still goes around it. And this was the medieval city. Around it in the seventeenth century the three great crescent canals appeared, the Herengracht or Lords' Canal, the Keizersgracht or Emperor's Canal and the Prinsengracht or Prince's Canal. Smaller streets and canals crossed them, making a beautiful spider's web. Round it all again went another circling canal. And so the city remained for two hundred years, offering the most attractive and noble example of town planning that ever had existed. What a fantastic achievement — the sheer size of it makes you catch your breath. If you stand at the end of the outermost canal, the Prinsengracht, and gaze down the straight line of the first section of the houses that go alongside it on and on into the distance and think of the available tools in the seventeenth century and that this was a city busy making its living — it is too much.

I like to look at dusk across the water from the bank of the River Amstel up the canal of the Kloveniersburgwal, which was the eastern boundary and moat of sixteenth-century Amsterdam. But the view in the half-light is that of the seventeenth century. Where the Doelen Hotel now stands on the corner of the canal's left bank were the drill hall and practice ranges of the militia companies and the old Utrecht tower — "*Swycht Utrecht*" or "Keep quiet, Utrecht!" — which was used as an officers' mess after it ceased to be a watch tower. This was where Rembrandt's *Night Watch* was first hung, and where Captain Cocq and all the others used to peacock in their uniforms. In the distance are the little pointed towers and turrets of the old St. Anthony's gate at the end of the canal, while to the left and quite close the river water goes towards the next old medieval gate, the Reguliers, now the Munt-tor, with its exotically charming spire built by Hendrick de Keyser in 1620. The date is firmly on it in large numerals and has a certain arrogance. (They knew *they* were something.) There had been a fire the year before and only the lower part of the gate remained. Under its arch a youthful anarchist is almost certainly selling the latest number of his particular broadsheet. Around the Munt-tor the traffic swirls, but here two or three hundred yards away all is quiet. Opposite the Kloveniersburgwal becomes a little dimmer. There used to be rich houses along there, one for example belonging to the Six family and another the great mansion of the Trips. . . .

There are ghosts wherever you go around these canals. The Trips and the Sixes . . . the Hoofts, the Pauws, the De Graeffs, the Bickers . . . the leaders of the "Magnificat" . . . their lordships . . . . Sometimes I gaze around from the end of the Leidsegracht, where it joins the Herengracht, for just here the latter canal has rather a sharp corner, so that the houses on either side go off at an attractive angle. Opposite is a narrow little street with smaller houses, which was all as laid down in the plan. This was the point where the first part of the scheme rested for a while, and there was still no Herengracht going off on the right. A quiet ghost appears and it is Arturus Quellin, the Flemish sculptor who was working on the decorative figures and bas-reliefs for the great new Town Hall on the Dam. He had his yard here. Later on, the canal was extended and made this beautiful scene. It is not perfectly preserved; there are one or two later intrusions, but they do not matter. At my back, the Leidsegracht — the Leyden Canal — is a smaller enchantment. The Herengracht is the grand scale. The gables and façades look down and are reflected with the trees in the water. You look from left to right and you can feel yourself at the high noon of it all.

I

A Special Situation
A.D. 50–1585

1.

THE DAM was originally a dam across the River Amstel. Then and long before, the surroundings were marshland. What a dreary place northwestern Europe used to be. Seven thousand years ago it wasn't even marshland, but under water, the lowland edge of the great plain. Then the Atlantic broke past the cliffs of Dover and swept up the sand which made the dunes; and the continental rivers, forced to find new mouths, deposited great quantities of silt, so that the land emerged, swampy and not too attractive. The Romans did not care for it at all. They had a fort on the dunes, close to the present-day Katwjk, where the Rhine then entered the sea. The remains of the fort can be seen when there is a very low tide. Pliny served there in A.D. 50 and described the scene with a total lack of enthusiasm.

There was nothing to enthuse about. The Frisians were the people in residence. They fished with nets made out of reeds and rushes. They kept cattle in the marshy area behind the dunes. They built mounds of earth called *Terpen*, on which they and their cattle could keep clear of floodwater from the sea or from the inland rivers and the hundreds of lakes that dotted the marshland. It baffled Pliny that they should have any regard for their own independence; slavery in a warm climate seemed to him distinctly preferable. But twenty years later there was even a successful uprising — in the tribe they called the Batavi, who lived on the land between the Rhine and the Meuse and were sufficiently advanced to be used as mercenaries. Tacitus wrote about it and mentioned the name of its leader, Civilis, who as a result became a folk hero of the Dutch people. (Rembrandt painted an imaginative portrait of him for the town councillors of Amsterdam. Like so many of his later pictures, it was not a success when delivered.)

Time passed on the marshes. As the land settled, its level became lower, so that floods became still more frequent and the sea tended to break down the dunes, forming islands. The comparatively small inlet the Romans called the Flevo Lacus assumed the shape of the Zuyder Zee, like a missing tooth on the European coast.

The Romans went. The Germanic Franks took over in France. The Frisians had a king, who in due course collided with the Frankish kingdom, which was expanding upwards from the south. On the marshland where Amsterdam would be built the inhabitants were tough and independent. It was a condition of survival. Christian missionaries protected by the Frankish king Dagobert received a very poor reception in the Zuyder Zee area early in the seventh century. A church was built on the site of Utrecht and was promptly destroyed.

However, the English east-coast missionaries kept coming and when the Frisian king was forced to give up the area to the south of the Zuyder Zee it was an Englishman, Willibrord, who became the first Bishop of Utrecht at the end of the seventh century. The Frisians, non-Christian in the north, partially Christian in the south of the Netherlands, had made some progress over the hundreds of years since Pliny's critical inspection. They had begun a commercial activity in the North Sea and the Baltic. They had gone on from terpen- to dike-building, that is, raising long embankments above the flood water level. They had learned to weave. The pagan north was finally subjugated under Charlemagne, and that marvelous man was able to send Frisian cloth as a gift to the Caliph of Baghdad, Harun-al-Rashid. One of the first great trade routes was from Cologne to Britain. The Frisians were automatically mixed up with it. Dorestad on the Rhine, not far from Utrecht, became the first Dutch port.

The Frisians were on the trade routes and they were also quite easily conquered. But it was not so easy to occupy the territory. They went on developing an independence of character which would not have been possible had they been constantly under somebody's tyrannical heel. The nominees of the Frankish kings formed a rough nobility, but the perpetual flood danger was common to everyone. (In the same way, hundreds of years later, the use of canals rather than roads with the resulting scarcity of aristocratic carriages was a factor in the lack of excessive pomp in Holland.)

After pleurisy killed Charlemagne in 814 the Vikings began to play in the territory. Dorestad, the river port, was destroyed; there was pillaging and general savagery. Then all was quiet, although events far away meant that the territory alternated in its nominal subjection to the new French and German kingdoms. The local lords, apart from having to make sure to whom they owed allegiance, went on fairly undisturbed. The nearest holder of real power was the Bishop of Utrecht and many of them held their land under his authority.

In 922 the King of France gave some church land in what is now northern Holland to Dideric, or Dirk, a Frisian count. Soon after, in the normal swing, he lost control of the Frisian territories to the German kingdom — which, owing to some faraway extensions in Italy, was about to become the German empire. The count was not affected. His son, Dirk II, founded an abbey, Egmunda, and received such enormous additional grants of land from the German emperor, who liked him, that he rivaled the bishop. Then in 1015 his grandson, Dirk III, having lost nearly all his great possessions to the neighbors when he succeeded as a boy, won them all back with his private army when he grew up and also a portion of the See of Utrecht. He built a castle on the bishop's land at a spot from which he could easily control the river traffic on both the Meuse and the Waal. And he then proceeded to levy tolls, which was a further irritation to the bishop. Not only to him. The grandson was astride the commercial link between Britain and Cologne. The Archbishop of Cologne complained to the German emperor, who sent a duke with an army to deal with the situation. Far from dealing with it, he was defeated easily. The Frisian count now called himself the Count of Holland, and not only he but the idea of Holland was established.

Now there continued a constant state of squabbling war between the Counts of Holland, the Bishops of Utrecht and the Counts of Flanders, all against all, all with an eye to the main chance — especially when a death left a child as an heir. In the second half of the century a particularly aggressive bishop was able to take exactly such an opportunity to rule Holland for twelve years. But intermarriage was helping the nobles towards a class solidarity, and owing to family relationships the Count of Flanders helped the Count of Holland back on his seat. Meanwhile the first really effective dikes were being built, the windmill was in use as a pumping engine, and the various trade skills developed, as the feudal system rooted itself. While it was preferable to be a great noble or even an insignificant lord owning some marshland in the See of Utrecht rather than one of the common people, nevertheless the system offered everybody advantages. In a rough world one needs protection, and the feudal lord gave that, even if the next problem was to protect oneself from him. The squabbling nobles and lesser lords were extremely independent. They were too far from the German emperor's power for him to be able to exert it to any effect; and at the same time he needed them as a barrier against the Norwegians and Vikings in the north.

The settlements which huddled close to their strongholds were growing larger. Timber, butter and cheese came down from the north. Fish, wine and metal came up the Rhine. Importing raw materials like wool and exporting salable articles like cloth became a natural order of things. Where the country had clearly no products of its own the crisscross of the trade routes, the water transport possibilities, the splendid accident of its geographical position would make up for everything.

2.

THE LORD who owned some of the Bishop of Utrecht's marshes at the beginning of the twelfth century was Gijsbrecht van Amstel. He had a castle of a rudimentary kind at Ouderkerk (which is close to and southeast of Amsterdam). Unkind neighbors destroyed it and Gijsbrecht is said to have built another on the left bank of the River Amstel, near to the present site of the Palace and Nieuwe Kerk. Not the slightest trace of this exists. Ruins of cloisters probably misled older historians. On the other hand he had to go somewhere and it would have been a sensible place to go. The river ambled north through his territory into an estuary which opened into the Zuyder Zee.

Some of the early diking which began after 1000 existed at the mouth of the river, following the line of the present winding honky-tonk street, the Zeedijk. This embankment continued in an easterly direction along the line of the future Jodenbreestraat, where Rembrandt lived. There was also some diking on the west side of the river, equally to protect the marshland from flooding. But the east bank had the firmer ground and it was here that fishermen's huts appeared, round about 1100. They fished in the IJ estuary and on the Zuyder Zee. During the twelfth century traders appeared to help distribute their catch and, no doubt with the permission of his lordship, put up the first exceedingly rough houses. This was the beginning of Amsterdam. The wood to build with had to be brought in, which was another beginning. They sold the fish to towns already existing, like Haarlem. This was in being because it was at the junction of a river and the one possible land route to the north — the strip of solid land which divided the sea from the marshes — and the Count of Holland had found it an obvious place for a headquarters. The town was growing round his castle. A little farther south there was Leyden, another favorite spot of the Counts of Holland. In fact most of the famous Dutch towns, as well as the Hanseatic towns to the northeast — Deventer, which was Dutch, was the closest of them — as well as the great towns of the southern Netherlands, Bruges, Ypres, Antwerp and Ghent, were well on their way.

Amsterdam would be late on the scene; it would be too late, really, to be one of the medieval great towns and when its marvelous days came there was a certain shame about it — the bourgeois's guilty shame that his ancestry wasn't anything very much. This feeling was assuaged every year until recently with an annual performance at the Stadsschouwburg, the city theater — usually on January 1 — of Vondel's classic tragedy, *Gijsbrecht van Amstel*. This gives the bourgeois answer to an unsatisfactory ancestry. It simply pretends that it *is* satisfactory. According to Vondel, writing in 1637 for the millionaire burghers, there was a large, prosperous, thirteenth-century Amsterdam. Everybody was pleased.

However, the settlement on the east bank grew. In the middle of the thirteenth century it was a village whose inhabitants were concerned with fishing and trade and cattle. A small brook almost certainly ran along separating the village from the peasant farmers' somewhat insecure land. A first version of the Oude Kerk (the Old Church) existed. Then and for a long time to come the church had many uses. Children played in it, women did their washing, traders did business, and the tower made a good lookout. The dwellings near to it ran along the line of the future Warmoes-straat, which is therefore the oldest part of Amsterdam. Sometime during the middle of the century the dam was put across the river, with a sluice on its east side, and so the village now had both a sea harbor and a river harbor. This is supposed to have happened under Gijsbrecht III of Amstel, but no records exist of his activity except a letter he sent to Lübeck in 1240 asking for the release of a ship.

With its two harbors the village grew fast. The dam was now its natural center and gave it a name. Gijsbrecht IV, a somewhat obstreperous character who quarreled with his own liege lord, the Bishop of Utrecht, was the local magnate when this name was first seen in writing. In 1275 toll exemptions were granted by the young Count of Holland, Floris V, to the inhabitants of Aemstelledamme — *"homines manentes apud Aemstelle-damme.* The Dam in the Amstel. Amsterdam!

That spelling would not be used for some time, but the city was born.

3.

THE TOLL EXEMPTIONS were of great value. The first Amsterdamers could now trade anywhere in Holland and Zeeland without paying duties on their way. Naturally they were extremely grateful to Floris V. He had intended them to be.

All the Counts of Holland had been successful and pushful, and the countship was growing in its stature. Floris V's father had even been elected as the German king during a twelve-year interlude between Holy Roman Emperors. And he would also have been crowned emperor by the Pope, but unfortunately in 1256, just when he was due to go, he was involved in a skirmish with some rebellious Frisians and he, his armor and his horse disappeared through some ice.

The new count, only two when he succeeded, showed himself as soon as he grew up no less pushful than the others. He had already achieved fishing rights on the English coast, promoting the wool business at Dordrecht, where he also dealt firmly with a still independently minded common population. Though the land did not offer much natural subsistence, it was never short of people — they were emigrating to England from Haarlem because it was so overcrowded. But he also dealt firmly with minor barons, balancing their power by offering charters to the growing towns which guaranteed a limited independence. His purpose with the toll privileges to Aemstelledamme was to make a first step towards pulling Amstelland away from the See of Utrecht and into Holland. Gijsbrecht van Amstel was probably far from pleased by the intrusion. Soon he was not only on quarrelsome terms with the bishop, but also with the count, who locked him up in Zeeland for a time, letting him free in 1285 in return for a partial renunciation of his possessions.

Gijsbrecht predictably found his new master a little too much to bear.

Ten years later he was one of a party of disaffected barons who ambushed him and took him as a prisoner to the turreted, fairy-tale Muiden castle ten miles east of Aemstelledamme. The count was on bad terms with England at that moment and they had a plan to ship him there as a present for the king. The big nobles, for whom minor wars were half sport and half business, were already much interrelated. The sudden coldness with England was due to Edward I's support of the Count of Flanders, who was quarreling with the Count of Hainault, who was the Count of Holland's nephew. But the ambushed count was popular with the common people, the news led to an angry mood, and the plotters lost their nerve. They murdered him and then had to disappear.

Aemstelledamme had not seen the last of its lord — or, at least, of his family. The murder had been in 1296. The late count's heir, whose wife was a daughter of Edward I of England, died two years later. It was the end of the direct line from Dirk I. A cousin from Hainault in the south took the title and at once found the new province troublesome. The long direct line of the Counts of Holland had been exceptional. There was no general tradition in Western Europe of heirs receiving their power easily. If there was weakness, through childhood, or any uncertainty, interested parties took the chance of grabbing what they wanted while the going was good. And this made sense, for the feudal overlord was a man's protector, and it was as well to find out if he was capable of protecting. The new count, Jan II, was therefore busy and the Bishop of Utrecht thought it a good moment, as soon as he could assemble an attacking force, to get back marshy Amstel-land into the See. A mistake: he invaded and was killed. The count was able to arrange for his brother, Gwy of Hainault, to be elected bishop and he also gave him Amstel-land. So it was Gwy of Hainault who gave Aemstelledamme its first charter in 1300.

This was of great importance to the inhabitants, who now became burghers of a town. The charter was a contract, giving them some independence in legal and trading matters in return for taxation, which incidentally included a tax on beer. They were organized as other towns, governed by the sheriff (the *Schout*) and magistrates (the *Scepenen*). Appeals could be made to Utrecht. The town could be fortified for defense by a wall, which was important for the security feeling of the new property owners. The wall was of wood. Outside it there was already a place for shipbuilding called "the Lastage."

While the new town was full of all this activity there was suddenly an invasion of the province — when the Count of Holland's back was turned — by the rival count from the south, Gwy of Flanders. It gave the Amstel family the chance to come out of hiding. The last Gijsbrecht was probably dead, but his son Jan arrived in "his" Aemstelledamme in May 1303. Other dissident minor nobles and knights were with him.

All went well for a time. The Count of Holland conveniently died and his son's first attempt at a battle failed. Jan van Amstel and friends were all laughing in Aemstelledamme. But everything changed in a week, from April 22 to May 2, 1304, when two Holland nobles, Witte van Haemstede and Nikolaas van Putten, destroyed the Flemish force. They set off promptly to deal with Amstel and besieged the new little town. This was the episode on which Vondel's play *Gijsbrecht van Amstel* was based — so he not only gave a false picture of the town but also chose the wrong name for his hero. In any case the town fell. Jan van Amstel escaped in the direction of Utrecht, passing out of the news for good.

It seems wildly unjust, but the burghers had to suffer for him. By an order of May 22, 1304, all their wooden defense works and bridges had to be torn down, and just to turn the screw the beer tax was doubled. They probably thought it worthwhile to get rid of his lordship. In any case the traumatic experience left its mark. Though the city was always capable of a good riot — "*lastige*," or troublesome, Amsterdam became a well-known phrase — its leaders always did their utmost to avoid its physical participation in wars, keeping it firmly to the less colorful but more deeply satisfying activity of making a profit. Perhaps the Amstels should be remembered with gratitude.

4.

WHEN the Bishop of Utrecht, Gwy of Hainault, died in 1317 Amstel-land belonged firmly to Holland. The town grew. The east bank was the Church Side and the west the Windmill Side, which became the Old Side and the New Side, the Oudezijd and the Nieuwezijd. The first canals were made out of the two little adjacent brooks, and the Nieuwezijd canal was connected with Damrak and Rokin, the sea and river harbors, by sluices.

These sluices were the responsibility of one of the oldest Dutch institutions, the Water Companies, which operated under the count. Their specialties were diking and flood control. Later they paid the council an annual fee to look after the sluices. Superintending the passage of boats through them — they were like tunnels, with houses built on top — was one of the duties of the Schout.

In 1342 the count agreed to another charter, which gave the town some more independence and for the first time defined its boundaries. (On a modern map: Zeedijk, junction Herengracht and Brouwersgracht, Herengracht at Koningsplein, entrance of Binnengasthuis.) This allowed some space, most of which tended to be filled by monasteries and nunneries. The burghers lived in narrow wooden houses clustered together, not very tall except for a house like Jan Witten's near the Oude Kerk on Kerkstraat (Warmoes-straat). He was one of the first of the rich Amsterdam burghers. But three years after the charter an event, or rather what was believed to have been an event, made the town attractive to the religious: the so-called Miracle of Amsterdam. This was the story: On the Tuesday before Palm Sunday, 1345, a man who lay ill, at death's door, in a house on what is now the city's most famous shopping street, Kalverstraat, sent for a priest and was given the Holy Sacrament. A few hours later, instead of dying, he vomited. The women who looked after him took what he vomited away and threw it in a fire. The next day one of the women raking out the fire saw the white Host in the middle of the red hot embers in the same shape and form as the priest had given it. She put her hand in and picked it out, feeling no pain. Other mysterious things happened. It was placed in a shrine. When a priest took it away in a box it disappeared and the next day was back in the shrine. It was taken to the Oude Kerk and women worshiped it, but it reappeared in the shrine. Then the town authorities were informed and it was taken in a solemn procession to the Oude Kerk again — while it was watched over there, there were "many wonders," probably of faith healing. The next year the bishop, Jan van Arkel, declared the whole episode to be a miracle and the house where it happened was broken up so that a chapel could be built in its place. By 1361 this was known as the Holy Place — the Heilige Stede. The fame of it went on spreading and later it became a place of annual pilgrimage — which goes on today in the form of the annual *"Stille Omgang"* or silent procession for which thousands of Catholics come to Amsterdam.

This kind of typical medieval story was the background of the over-

[23]

crowded life in the living quarters of the town. The surrounding water solved most sanitation problems, but people were certainly cooped up — which was also typically medieval. Three butchers, a cutler, a smith, a priest, a merchant's widow are all noted as living in one house on the Dam. Consequently as much time as possible was spent out of doors, which helped to make a convivial street life. The trade signs were coming out, a pot for a potter, scissors for a tailor, a red, white and blue pole for a barber surgeon. The tradesmen worked in the street under, if possible, a wooden awning. They drank beer and warmed themselves with peat fires, which were infinitely dangerous. The air buzzed with Dutch and Frisian dialects. Anyone with pretensions to culture spoke Latin. It was a small, sweaty, busy place, and at night, black and silent in the darkness.

Then in Zeeland in 1384 William Beukels discovered how to preserve herrings by salting them in barrels. The secret was degutting. They had been experimenting with salt, unsatisfactorily, as far back as the twelfth century. For Amsterdam traders and seamen it meant voyages to Portugal to get salt and to Baltic countries like Sweden to get wood for the barrels. Other goods came on board. The carrying trade began. From this moment the growth of Amsterdam accelerated. The Damrak was crowded with fishing boats that went to Norway and to England — East Anglian markets, as at Yarmouth, would be canceled if there were no Dutch fishermen around. In the Baltic the famous towns of the Hanseatic League strongly resented their new competitor. But the Dutch could not be thrown out. The Dutch sailors were tough and their spirit high.

With the increase of business the Town Hall on the Dam expanded continuously, taking over houses adjacent and behind. It stood between a hospital on one side, St. Elizabeth's, and the house of a rich Amsterdamer, Willem Eggert, the "Brillenberg," on the other — all houses had names and always did have until the end of the eighteenth century. By the end of the fourteenth century the present version of the Oude Kerk was under construction and in 1408 the Bishop of Utrecht gave permission for a second parish church, the New or Nieuwe Kerk. This was a formality; to some extent it was already built — it was in use by 1410 — on the site of an orchard belonging to the "Brillenberg" and given by Willem Eggert. Cloisters continued to go up. A lay order of nuns, the Beguines, had been established on land allotted to them in 1369 and their Beguinhof is there still, charming, peaceful and medieval, a few yards off Kalverstraat.

Like the rings across a tree trunk another line of canals was built (the

Oudezijds and Nieuwezijds Achterburgwallen — the latter is now Spui-straat), enclosing almost everything, but not the Carthusians, who were established slightly outside to the west, nor the leper house beyond the southern boundary. The combination of these institutions with the seafaring and trading interests made the town unusually interesting. The cloister industries were useful. The monks came begging on the Dam, which remained the center of everything with its Town Hall and weighhouse, or Waag, and all the markets, above all in fish, on and about the sluice, and in milk and cheese and butter and sheep and bullocks and all sorts of peddlers' goods, all of it making such a noise that before long the richer burghers who controlled the Town Hall felt that things were going too far.

Meanwhile the first elite militia company, seventy-five strong, had emerged from the old obligation on all burghers to take part in the defense of the town, guard duties, dealing with fires, and so on. They were equipped with crossbows and shields and had their own *schuttersdoelen,* a drill or artillery yard. They would take part in shooting competitions and the winner of an annual clay pigeon meeting called "shooting the parrot" was received with honor at the Town Hall and decorated with a silver collar and chain. The Count of Holland, the god they lived under and depended on, required military service from time to time. Amsterdamers were often fined for draft-dodging. The typical draft was a requirement of 1398, when the town had to provide 350 armed men, five carpenters, five smiths, five bricklayers, and twenty bowmen to join an expedition against the Frisians.

5.

DURING the first part of the fourteenth century the Count of Holland had become very grand. His countess was the King of France's niece. His daughter Margaret had married Louis of Bavaria, the Holy Roman Emperor. Edward III of England had married another daughter. These prestigious connections were of value to the burghers, for the count tended to help when they needed protection against envious landlords who felt entitled to their profits. (In the sometimes violent disturbances two factions emerged, the Hooks — a nobles' pressure group — and the Cods, who largely represented the burghers and the guilds.)

But in the long run it seemed nothing like such a good idea. The great princes, among them the Dukes of Burgundy, also became conscious of the profits. Enterprising marriages had extended their power from eastern France into the southern Netherlands. When the countship of Holland was inherited by a girl, the famous Countess Jacobaea, it seemed the moment to spread to the north as well. It took a dozen years of leaning on her to do it, but finally the Burgundians eased her out in 1432.

For the burghers it was like the world of mergers and takeovers, which disrupt small businesses and individuals but hold them to their contracts while changing the whole tenor of life. There was a loss by the Dutch towns of the independence they had won under the counts. Jacobaea had been able to lay down that the Schout of Amsterdam, whom she appointed, was responsible for collecting all fines and receipts, and could keep five percent for himself (an interesting system) — but now the town, like the others, was under the pressure of the Burgundian ambition to create out of the various provinces and dominions a unified and centralized country like France.

A first step in Holland was setting up a provincial Court of Justice at The Hague. Later on there was a still superior court at Mechlin for the whole of the Netherlands — greatly resented in Holland. There was the first meeting of the States-General at Brussels, with representatives of all the provinces. All these things implied authority over the towns.

The duke — until 1467 the brilliant Philip the Good — was patient, and some of his changes subtle. An old system had been that the Schout appointed the magistrates (the Scepenen) and they chose one or more burgomasters to administer the town. Since the appointments were more or less for life, this led to a few well-off families dominating affairs. The duke approved of this — a good number of strong councillors were a check on the development of powerfully militant craft guilds, which he did not care for. But he also ordered that at Amsterdam the three burgomasters, twenty-four council members and seven magistrates should submit to him annually fourteen names, from which he or his stadholder would select seven new magistrates. It was a simple way of ensuring control. Amsterdam, as it began to flourish in the fifteenth century, was very much conscious that it was part of a far larger concern than before.

However, like the Counts of Holland, the duke was quite ready to be helpful when there were commercial difficulties abroad — especially with the Hanseatic League of north German towns, led by Lübeck, which tried for years to freeze them and other Dutch towns out of the Baltic trade. The power of the Hansa was large and widespread and extremely complicated. The Dutch were forced to move their herring fishery into the North Sea, where, as it happened, it did much better. They had to agree that all piece goods which German merchants had been shipping in Dutch boats from Prussia must go through the "counter" at Bruges. But nothing could stop the big trade in taking salt to Danzig, and bringing wood and grain back. There was also good business in potash, hides, furs and hemp. The Dutch were welcome in Danzig and had their own bench in the *"Artushof."* At first their trips were mostly financed by foreign traders, like the Prussians, but gradually the Dutch themselves provided the finance, especially the new merchants of Amsterdam. They were unable to trade in the Hansa towns except under great disadvantages, but they used illegal and secret harbors, at their own risk, and made good profits — a competition which thoroughly upset Lübeck. They tried to prevent the Dutch trading between Lithuania and Russia — at Novgorod. What with these difficulties and the constant danger from privateers, things were never easy. Then the arrival of Burgundian power jerked the Hansa towns into taking stronger action. A three-year war started in 1438, fought entirely between scores of small boats, with heavy losses especially in trade on both sides. The Danes came into it, a new king made a treaty with the Hansa towns and the Duke of Burgundy helped the Dutch build a fleet to bring the old king back. That didn't work, but the new king then changed sides. Finally they all became tired of the loss in trading profits and an agreement was made at Copenhagen, initially for ten years, but it went on being argued about and renewed for the rest of the century. The Dutch were free to trade everywhere in the Baltic. Amongst those who caught a cold from their competition were the English, who lost most of their trade at Danzig. It all meant that good money was being made at Amsterdam.

Other things had happened. In 1421 there was a town fire — a constant danger with all the wooden houses — and the badly damaged Nieuwe Kerk had to be rebuilt. In 1425, worried that some cloisters built close to the town offered too easy an outpost to enemies — it was the time of the Hooks and Cods civil war around the Countess Jacobaea — they decided to build the first girdle canal, the Singel (the eastern part became the

Kloveniersburgwal). In 1442 there was a bad outburst of Hooks and Cods fighting actually in the town. And in 1452 another much worse fire destroyed hundreds of houses, including a good deal of the Town Hall — with a tragic loss of records — and once again the Nieuwe Kerk, which now had to be built in a third version. The Heilige Stede chapel also had to be rebuilt, but the story went all around Holland that the miraculous Host had come through the flames untouched. The fame of Amsterdam's miracle increased and by the end of the century, after some royal patronage, the annual pilgrimage began.

But Amsterdam's future was really being decided, indirectly, in the southern Netherlands, where great wealth and achievement were an old story. Bruges was already a continental center in the thirteenth century. Then the cloth business had raised Ghent and Ypres to such prosperity that these towns had been able to assert independence of the feudal overlords. But now feudalism was on the way out, and all around unified nations were emerging: France, with its new centralized tax structure, England recovering from the Wars of the Roses, Spain getting rid of the Moors — the Dukes of Burgundy, following the trend and trying to institute centralized government, automatically found themselves in conflict with the cities, which at the same time were suffering competition from England in the cloth business. Their populations, huge at the time, began to go down. At Bruges, which was also the center of the money market, there was the further complication that its approaches were silting up. Business went to Antwerp, whose day was beginning.

Medieval society was breaking down and the chief explosive factor was the change in commercial methods, the arrival of capitalism. Money was becoming important. And there was also more of it, silver from the mines of Germany, and of course the treasure of the just-discovered New World. Medieval Europe had really been a vast network of restrictive practices. The towns were jealous of their own particular area of business, and no foreigner or stranger could come in without being given a special privilege — as the Hanseatic League in London or the English "merchant adventurers" in Bruges. Trade had only been free at the city fairs. At these, restrictions had been eased, anything could be exchanged, and credits could last from one fair to another. They were exciting, useful, enjoyable, and short-lived.

But at Antwerp the conditions of a fair operated all the year round. Largely helped in the past by English trade and then becoming a center for the fish and salt of Holland, it had found itself faced with the hostility of the great Flemish cities. A successful fair showed that self-interest was best served not by the old restrictions but by promoting as great a volume of trade as possible, whoever did the trading. And they bought up the rights of landowners who were exacting tolls on the river, not to exact tolls of their own but to let things flow. So Antwerp grew magnificently from the end of the fifteenth century and on into the sixteenth. All the great spice business and other exotic cargoes of the Portuguese were distributed through Antwerp by Dutch seamen, and in exchange an immense market was found in Spain and Portugal for the fish, cloth and linen of the north. Hoorn, Enkhuisen, Amsterdam, all the Dutch ports, benefited from the new situation.

6.

WHILE many of the Dutch seamen sailed with the Portuguese and the carrying trade was dealing with its fascinating new cargoes, other unfamiliar worlds — printing, for example — had been opening up in the Netherlands. The Dukes of Burgundy had undoubtedly been a help. They were Renaissance men, they lived luxuriously, surrounded by lawyers, indulging in practical jokes and giving parties at which girls really did step out from under pie crusts — and they also employed painters like Jan van Eyck, who was able to work in the spirit of the Netherlands and to get away from the old Byzantine influence of the Crusades. The court writers on the other hand had been less helpful. Like Froissart they all wrote in French, which was the court language, and this contributed to a general debasement of the native language. A sort of bastardized French came into use, with Latin remaining for scholars.

But Dutch asserted itself — perhaps a subliminal reaction — in the extraordinary growth of the Chambers of Rhetoric. These were one of the great institutions of the fifteenth and sixteenth centuries and managed to flourish through the civil wars of the former and the religious upheavals of the latter.

They were, more or less, amateur dramatic groups. Moralities and miracle plays had always been part of the celebrations at medieval fairs (the annual *kermis*) — as well as being performed in church — and the Chambers took these over. The members became known as *Rederijkers* — the eloquent ones, the "rich in words." They met regularly, usually after church, drank, recited to each other, wrote verse, rehearsed. At the fairs they put on the plays, which gradually became less dominated by the church and more by the requirements of drama. As time went on, their verses unfortunately became more and more bound by rules, more and more artificial, and eventually lost in mythological references. Members had uniforms and marched in a separate contingent, whenever there was a procession, along with the guilds.

The movement caught on in an astonishing way; obviously it was a subsidiary part of the spread of humanism amongst scholars and religious in northern Europe of which Erasmus of Rotterdam (who wrote, of course, entirely in Latin) was the sublime example. There was a culture hunger amidst the up-and-coming bourgeoisie, the burghers who were everywhere scenting riches for the first time, and not only riches but the aspirations and feelings of independence which go with riches. A snobbery of knowledge grew up and was the most potent force behind the Chambers of Rhetoric.

Gradually they were adopted by towns and became semi-officially responsible for art and festivals. They were unconsciously rather vulgar, though well intentioned and very industrious. The country reverberated with the terrible verses of their members. If talent was lacking, energy was not. Competitions called "Land-Jewels" were organized between different towns. These took the form of a game of charades, a development of the old medieval folk moralities. Some phrase expressing a piece of moral wisdom would be the subject and each team would play it out, hoping to be judged the winner. What especially distinguished these splendid occasions was the feverish competition in turnout between the teams. Each Chamber projected itself with great pomp and circumstance. They entered with horses, triumphal chariots, banners, anything they could think of, all trying to outdo each other for the glory of their town and out of a general lust for life. The tedium of the performances, as well as the effect of the morality demonstrated, was neutralized by great quantities of food and greater still of drink at the feast afterwards. The Chambers often had striking names. Amsterdam's was "The Eglantine — Blossoming in Love."

7.

THE OVERHANGING AUTHORITY CHANGED. Charles the Bold, Duke of Burgundy, was beaten by the Swiss — they astonished themselves by winning three successive battles. The duke was found dead in a pond on January 5, 1477, and the Burgundian power fell to pieces. His nineteen-year-old daughter, Mary, succeeded and at once both the King of France, Louis XI, and the cities on the spot were out to make the most of it.

The States-General was called to Ghent and assembled on her twentieth birthday, February 3. This assembly of representatives from the provinces had been used by her father and grandfather as a convenient way of calling for taxes and loans. This time they were determined not to give her any help without getting everything they wanted — the French king's advance northwards providing a spur to fast decisions. Mary, forced to ignore the open delight at her father's death, had to sign a charter prepared in seven days. It was called the Great Privilege (*Groote Privilegie*) and brought back all the rights and privileges of the cities which the dukes in their modernist drive for centralization had taken away. It laid down that the States-General should meet when they liked, that Mary could not marry or declare war without their permission, and that government itself should be carried on by a representative council of twenty-four, under the sovereign. Mary signed. In return they would back her and raise an army, through militias in the towns and old feudal obligations in the country.

The members of the States-General might be full of triumph at their success, but they must have known that the power of princes was not avoidable for long. They may well have felt irritated. But the life of every burgher in Amsterdam, as in Bruges and Ghent and Antwerp, or in London and Paris and Madrid, was subject to the fall-out of major and minor family upheavals in the royal network. This was where the ultimate power had its quarters, and no burgher, however rich or rebellious, could ignore it. They had to accept it as a fact of life, almost *the* fact of life, and it remained so in all western European countries for the next few centuries. Moreover as time went on the network naturally became closer and more complicated. For three hundred years the death of a baby or an engagement or a marriage quarrel in some distant palace could affect you, and you, and you.

Certainly Mary of Burgundy knew all about the system in 1477. Her close advisers were pro-French, in accordance with the last policies of the late duke, and a secret embassy had been sent to Louis. At the same time her stepmother, a sister of Edward IV of England, was persuading her to rely on the English. Louis himself, as a result of the embassy — which had merely offered a deal, recognizing his sovereignty in certain territories — now suggested her marriage to the dauphin, who happened to be seven years old. Romance might be a little lacking, but by this means all the Burgundian possessions could be reincorporated into the French kingdom with that proper degree of legality, about which all the medieval and postmedieval monarchs and princes seemed to be surprisingly sensitive.

But Louis was a man who liked the minor pleasures of malice and at the beginning of March, at Arras, he could not resist letting slip to a deputation from Ghent some knowledge of the private negotiations. The result was fury at Ghent. Mary had to allow her pro-French advisers to be tortured and put to death. It was the end of the marriage plan (fate allowed the dauphin to become king and make his own arrangements in due course) and Louis now opened direct hostilities. It was already clear to the States-General, however much they might dislike it, that Mary must marry someone appropriately powerful; and fast.

There were two possibilities, the queen's brother, Lord Rivers, and the Duke of Clarence, either of whom meant the presence of England — but there was instantly so much disagreement and rivalry between them and their supporters that no decision could be made. And there was no time to wait for it. Fortunately there was one other suitable candidate, Archduke Maximilian of Austria, the eighteen-year-old son of the Holy Roman Emperor, Frederick III. When Frederick's envoys arrived on April 18, urging her acceptance, Mary accepted immediately. Maximilian arrived at Ghent a few weeks later, accompanied by eight thousand horsemen, and the marriage took place at six o'clock the next morning. It was just in time. The French were in Hainault and threatening Flanders and Brabant. But the marriage, as it had been hoped, made them pause.

Princes were not avoidable. And the Netherlanders were now irretrievably mixed up with the power and politics of the Hapsburgs.

8.

MAXIMILIAN was a Renaissance man, artistic, well educated, emotional and brave. But Austria was his main concern. He could only regard the Netherlands as a new and extremely valuable piece of property, especially the cities of the south, and a good source of money of which he was always in considerable need for his widespread military and power activities. So from the start he was not exactly popular, and neither were the German soldiers he had brought with him. On the other hand he did contain the French. But that was also a cause of unrest, for when Flemish merchants found themselves losing trade (especially with England) to Antwerp and the smaller but rising town of the north, Amsterdam, they wanted to keep their trade links open with France while Maximilian's Hapsburg policy was persistently anti-French. Above all after giving him a son and a daughter, Philip and Margaret, his wife, Mary of Burgundy, died. No longer a consort the young archduke could only hang on in the Netherlands — but he had every intention of hanging on — as the regent for the children.

It was not easy. Most of the Netherlands erupted. In Ghent they held the children as hostages and later he was forced to let the girl go to France, engaged, though a baby, to the Dauphin. He lost control of Gelderland. At Utrecht the bishop, a bastard son of Philip the Good, was thrown out in a Hook revolt and only restored after Maximilian had besieged the city with twelve thousand men. The Hooks versus Cods fighting broke out again all over Holland and Zeeland. At the sea town of Hoorn, Cods put Hook leaders to death and pillaged the town. They threatened to do the same at Haarlem, where later there was a peasants' uprising. There was a famous episode at Bruges where Maximilian was actually held prisoner for three months, and though they dared not touch him, he had to watch some of his supporters being executed. These things were here and there, and now and then — the *kermis*, the fair, could also take place, the *Rederijkers* could keep on reciting. However, these were rough years in the Netherlands.

[33]

Amsterdam kept out of trouble. But it was high time, under the circumstances, for the town to be walled in with a good thick wall; and this was done in the last two decades of the century. It offered a useful new punishment for the use of the magistrates; people could be ordered to provide bricks and also, of course, to work on it. The wall can be seen in Cornelis Anthoniszoon's famous map which appeared fifty years later. There are relics of it still in Amsterdam, the Schreierstor or Weepers' Tower — actually nothing to do with weeping girls waving sailors good-bye, but from a word meaning "astride" — the Waag on the Nieuwmarkt which was the St. Anthony's Gate, the bottom parts of the Montelbaans-tor and the Munt-tor.

The town was on relatively good terms with Maximilian. After his success with Utrecht he came as a pilgrim to the Heilige Stede chapel in Kalverstraat and he presented it with a stained-glass window. Certainly Amsterdam gave him plenty of funds. In return, in 1489, the astute Amsterdamers asked for something extremely useful, which was granted. They were allowed to add the imperial crown to the town's coat of arms. Every ship could carry it. It was an immensely impressive trademark and just what the town wanted to show the world it had "arrived." And it cost Maximilian nothing; an ideal arrangement.

He made other good arrangements, above all in the basic field of royal interest — marriage. However, a first one misfired when he married by proxy the fourteen-year-old Duchess of Britanny. Maximilian's eleven-year-old daughter Margaret had been brought up in France (she and her father spoke different languages), where according to contract she was to marry the king, Charles VIII, with Burgundy as her dowry. But the French were not standing for Maximilian's takeover in Britanny and the duchess was forced to marry the king instead. The proxy marriage and the fiancée were ignored, and furthermore the French said nothing about returning the dowry. An agreement took two more years. Then Margaret, aged thirteen, could happily return, crying out *"Vive Bourgogne!"* to a welcoming crowd. Maximilian, about to become emperor, had fresh plans. These, owing to a series of accidents, had incredible success.

A double marriage was arranged for his son and daughter, Philip and Margaret, with the younger daughter and son of Ferdinand of Aragon and Isabel of Castile. This link with the Spanish power would clearly be a good in itself and useful in containing the French. In August 1496 the Spanish princess, Juana, arrived by sea, splendidly, at Antwerp and was married to Philip. In April the next year Margaret went to Spain and was married to the Spanish heir, Don Juan.

But in October Don Juan and Margaret were on their way to the marriage of his older sister Isabel to the King of Portugal, when he caught a fever and died. Margaret was once more not going to be a queen, and the new Queen of Portugal was now first in line for the crowns of her parents. But a year later it was her turn to die, leaving a baby son, who became the heir. And then he died. So the heiress was now the younger sister, Juana, who was married to Philip. The Hapsburg marriage game could not have turned out better.

Charles, who was born to Philip and Juana at Ghent in 1500, was the heir to the Netherlands, all the possessions of the Dukes of Burgundy which the French had taken over, of the house of Austria, and also of Spain, Naples, and Sicily, an undreamed-of prospect. In due course the result would be the rule of the Spanish over the Netherlands, and terror and torture in all the Dutch towns — as well as automatically vast alterations in the whole course of European history. It was an outstanding example of how royal marriage ups and downs affected the lives of ordinary people.

Naturally enough Charles too was soon in the marriage business; when he married Isabella of Portugal at twenty-one, he had been engaged ten times, the first time when he was five. There was still a fourth destiny-making death, his father's. Philip died in Spain in 1506. Maximilian made the capable and ever-willing Margaret the boy's guardian, and also regent and governor-general of the Netherlands. Charles and his sisters lived with her at Mechlin in Brabant.

Under her and the new immense power behind her the Netherlands slowly settled down. Margaret tried to persuade the emperor to equip a fleet for the defense of Holland's interests in the Baltic, for there was another outbreak of hostilities with Lübeck. Amsterdam's new walls were almost in use in 1512 when the town was threatened by the magnificent, French-aided rebel, the Duke of Gelderland, who had not been at all subdued by the Hapsburg might. Something went wrong with the attack. The duke's ships suffered from fire and made off. The town sighed with relief. Elsewhere the Sistine Chapel was painted. Luther had become a professor at Wittenberg and had been to Rome as a delegate of his Order. The Fuggers were given the right to sell indulgences in Germany. The Spaniards and Portuguese were using Antwerp more and more, and at the same time thousands of Jews recently thrown out of Spain and Portugal were settling there. In England Erasmus was in full flood, a man deservedly famous though not perhaps for his famous joke about the wood piles on which Amsterdam's houses were built: "There is a city where the inhabitants are like rooks living in trees."

9.

THE DAM was busy enough now for traffic regulations. Wagons had a parking place. Various markets, especially the messier ones, had to move somewhere else. The bullock market had gone to the bottom of Kalverstraat. Booths and stalls were hired out to shopkeepers who week by week had to change places, to avoid unfairness. On the Damrak harbor there was a spot where ships had to put down their masts, on their way to the sluice. Five or six ships had to go through together — anyone trying to hurry the control, or go out of turn, was fined. The market on the square was reserved for people bringing goods in from out of town, nonburghers. Dam residents could and did sell fruit and vegetables, butter, kippers, eels, and brandy — but it all had to be done indoors. It was freedom within the bylaws, then as now. (But the Dam, incidentally, was much smaller.) The fishmarket around the sluice of course remained, with its dozens of shouting fishwives. They alone would have made the Dam a noisy place, but it was the center for everybody. When the bell was sounded from the tower of the ramshackle Town Hall opposite, which had a charisma all its own, the Schout would possibly appear to read out a new law or regulation. There was a good system for news announcements, which were preceded by someone blowing a horn — once for good news, twice for bad news. In spite of the firmly undemocratic, self-perpetuating oligarchy which ruled inside, the atmosphere was of liberty. It had to be for the sake of trade. The town was full of cloisters, but great business was done with Germans who came from the country of the now exploding Reformation. No one bothered about it on the Dam or on the New Bridge (which was not new) at the mouth of Damrak, where merchants and brokers were already using very sophisticated business methods. (When it rained they went into the nearby St. Olaf's Chapel.) It was here that Amsterdam was becoming wealthy.

Most of the Dutch ships in the Baltic came from other Zuyder Zee towns like Hoorn and Enkhuizen, but the proportion financed by Amsterdam merchants was increasing fast. Ships were cheap and quick to build. Each ship could have from eight to sixteen owners, all with a share. Since shareholders did not have to come from the same town and more loan capital was available in Amsterdam, its power had to grow. The Baltic carrying trade could be marvelously profitable. There were times when the cost of a ship and its equipment could be covered by two trips.

Royalty always found money attractive. Soon there was a royal visitor. In 1515 the Netherlands regent and governor, Margaret, handed over to the boy Charles, who was just sixteen. But she had to take up the job again a year later when Ferdinand of Aragon died and Charles became King of Spain. Soon his grandfather also died and he was elected emperor — and the extent of his dominions made him, at least outwardly, the greatest prince since Charlemagne. A few years before, one of his sisters, Isabella, had married the thirty-four-year-old King of Denmark, Christian II. Since the Hanseatic League was fading, Denmark was the most important Baltic power, with control of the passage of ships through the Sound, and the king's friendship with Amsterdam was vital. Fortunately there was a basis for it.

The king was a character. He was tough and clever — and in his portrait looks it. He was also cunning, suspicious, and pathologically cruel. He had a mistress whom he had met in Norway, of which he was also king (the Swedes, however, would not yet accept him). She was bourgeois and Dutch, and when she died Christian suspected a noble of murdering her, had him executed, and was from then on antinoble and probourgeois. He was especially influenced by the girl's mother, Sigbrit, born an Amsterdamer and a woman of brilliant ability. For the time being the king's main interest was to obtain the crown of Sweden, where his father's stadholder still ruled. A minor but also absorbing interest was that the Netherlands had not yet paid his wife's dowry. As a protest in 1518 he held up some Dutch ships for a time. In 1519, still unpaid, he sent Sigbrit's brother, Herman Willemsz, and a Dane, Van Metz, to negotiate in Amsterdam. They were to ask for a credit and from Brussels, the seat of Netherlands government, came a request to the town to offer four or five thousand gold guilders. However, Amsterdam was not keen. The negotiators, finding the going tough, reported back and Sigbrit now became tough, demanding the full payment of about a quarter of a million guilders.

Negotiations were resumed. The principal agent in Amsterdam was the immensely rich banker Pompejus Occu, whose house "The Paradise" in Kalverstraat covered all the ground between there and Rokin now occupied by the luxury Hotel Polen. Pompejus was also a scholar and art collector. (Later in the century, unfortunately, the collection had to be dispersed.) Agreement was signed on December 6, 1519. The sum would be paid in Amsterdam in four parts — on January 20, 1520, 100,000 guilders; and on June 24, 1520, 1521, and 1522, 50,000 guilders. Actually the first payment was not made until May, which was just in time to meet the expenses of Christian's final, successful expedition to Sweden.

He was crowned on November 4 in Stockholm, gave banquets night after night to the nobility, the church, and the rich, and then enjoyed himself even more on the night of November 7. Festivities were at their height when Danish soldiers entered the banqueting hall and began making selected arrests. By ten o'clock all the guests were locked up. On November 8 and 9 between eighty-two and ninety-four were beheaded. Executions followed in other Swedish towns and then Christian could go home to Copenhagen, feeling the satisfaction of a job well done.

He had had his second payment of 50,000 guilders but the next year when there seemed to be some slight doubt about the third he decided to come to Amsterdam himself. He left Sigbrit in charge of the three kingdoms and arrived by sea on June 29, 1521, disguised as a merchant, wearing a Spanish cloak, and with one page and a servant. He stayed the night with Pompejus Occu. The banker presumably told him that he had better see the emperor, for he went off the next morning without his money, first to Antwerp and then to Brussels, where he met his brother-in-law, just back from the celebrated Diet of Worms in Germany. Charles took him on a triumphal tour through Brabant and Flanders — at Bruges he met Erasmus and at Antwerp Dürer painted his portrait — but though Christian was easily able to persuade the younger man to an advantageous treaty, the emperor's ministers were able to make it null and void. In August Christian was back in Amsterdam, where he was also received with great festivity and given an escort of harquebusiers everywhere. But he still hadn't received his money. Giving up for the time being he went home, via Cologne.

But in 1523 he was knocked off his throne by rebellions in Sweden and

Denmark, where his uncle Frederick was proclaimed king, and he arrived once more in the Netherlands, with twenty ships, his wife, children, and Sigbrit. He was, happily, not at Amsterdam but at Veere in Zeeland. He could not reach the emperor, who was away making war against France. But of course he needed money and the Amsterdam burgomasters were highly nervous, for they did not want to offend the new king in Denmark, who had already announced that the continuation of all trade privileges depended on no help being given to his enemies. Though Christian himself stayed fairly quiet, to their relief, suddenly the emperor wrote to Brussels from Spain urging support for him, on the ground that the new king was introducing Protestantism. As a result Amsterdam was forced to equip a ship for him — they got rid of it, unfinished, as soon as possible, and hoped that they could forget about him.

That year they had more useful concerns. One of them was sewage. The council ordered the removal of privies and pigsties from the backs of houses bordering the Damrak. Next they ordered the removal of the privies which had appeared in large numbers round the new walls where many poor people lived, under the arches, in picturesque squalor. Wooden houses were no longer allowed, owing to the fire danger, but of course still existed in large numbers and as with the newly built brick ones were all apt to be overcrowded, with people upstairs emptying their slops of all kinds with a fine abandon out of the window — the council now forced everyone to put in sinks attached to lead soil pipes. In spite of all the progress the canals remained no doubt strongly scented, for years later when a meeting of the States of Holland was to be held at Amsterdam in the presence of the emperor, they held it at Haarlem instead "to protect his majesty's health and that of any of his party who want to drink the water, which at Amsterdam. . . ." Of course, if you lived there all the time, you didn't notice.

They hadn't, in fact, got rid of their friend Christian. He had waited for his moment and it came in 1531, when he was able to raise an army of five thousand in Friesland. Since he was still after his dowry money the news raised some panic in Amsterdam. An invasion by mercenaries was not very attractive. The burgomasters sent messengers to keep them informed of the king's movements. There were many rumors and alarms. When Christian and his force arrived at Amersfoort thirty-five miles away to the east, Amsterdam went into defense. The gates were shut and the walls manned by the militia, which now consisted of three companies and over seven hundred men. Bows and crossbows were now only for processions. One company was equipped with harquebusses and the others with muskets, plus of course pikes and halberds and broadswords. The harquebusiers or *kloveniers* had their headquarters in the "*Swycht Utrecht*" tower. The companies were rather more fashionable than they were militaristic. Nobody cared for the approaching guest. The emperor was at Brussels and they sent for help. None came.

On September 19, 1531, Christian and his private army arrived at Amstelveen — now the bright suburb close to Schiphol Airport — and then he himself rode up to the town. He saw the militia and rode round from gate to gate, ending at the Haarlem gate on the west. Even the monks at the Carthusian monastery outside were unfriendly. Inside, the town trembled. Then his demands came. "The king requires from Amsterdam and the water towns thirty or forty large ships well equipped for war: he will himself choose and indicate the ships. Holland must pay the cost against the debt still due to the king for the dowry according to the debentures he has in his possession."

Slightly relieved, they passed the problem to the States of Holland, who met at Haarlem. The king finally agreed to accept twelve ships. The Amsterdam shipyards worked like mad to be rid of the order — but naturally the news could not be kept from Denmark. The Danish king promptly closed the Sound to their ships. It was a good illustration of the sometimes infuriating power of princes to ruin the flow of business. The ban was removed after a time. At least Christian was off Amsterdam's back — his expedition failed and that was the end of him.

10.

THE NEXT PROBLEM, which had far greater impact, was religious. It was fourteen years since Luther had put up his protest against the abuse of indulgences on the door of the palace church at Wittenberg. The council at Amsterdam had done their best to take no particular notice of the immense convulsion now shaking so much of Europe, including the Netherlands. It was a commercial town, in spite of all the cloisters. Most people were automatically Catholic, or even profoundly — like Pompejus Occu. But with so many North German contacts the sacramentalist and Lutheran influence had naturally spread in the town. But no one had ever been put to death in Amsterdam for his religious belief.

However, after the Diet of Worms in 1521, the emperor, Charles V, had issued his "Placards" or directives against heresy and these were now supposed to be in force. But the Schout of Amsterdam, Jan Hubrechtsz, was a humanist and disliked persecution. Under him the magistrates did as little as possible. On December 19, 1522, a man had to make a pilgrimage because he had "sworn against God." In 1523 the town made an antiheresy regulation, from the point of view of "no scandals or commotions wanted here," without mentioning the emperor's placards, and in effect protecting the intelligent and humanist sacramentalists. But the Court of Holland at The Hague, an instrument of central authority, was leaning hard on them. In 1524 six Amsterdamers were charged with heresy before it. Amsterdam protested that all crimes must first be charged before the Schout and magistrates. The Hague replied that this did not apply to heresy. So they had to do a little more, reluctantly. (All this shows how deeply founded is Amsterdam's "tolerance.") When nine people were charged later in the year with taking part in "secret schools and gatherings" they were sentenced to eight days on bread and water in two of the gatehouses, and one had to go on a pilgrimage to Brabant and bring back twelve thousand Leyden bricks. This at least brought a little profit to the town. But the trouble went on. Catholic priests began to complain. Libels were sometimes posted up, monks insulted. The Old and New Testaments were being printed in Dutch in Warmoes-straat. Yet at The Hague there had already been a burning at the stake. At Brussels the Franciscans complained officially about Amsterdam's behavior.

Luther, of course, was conservative. He had no desire to upset the social hierarchy. But small and earnest and soon fanatical groups emerged who accepted what they read in the Bible as a basis for action as well as faith. The Apocalypse was attractive. Suddenly there were new preachers everywhere who did not believe in infant baptism, or the Trinity, or in celebrating saints' days. These were the Anabaptists. It was essentially a movement of the underprivileged and it did best where there was most poverty and unemployment. This at the time was in Leyden's textile business, and the most famous Anabaptist was to be a Leyden baker, Jan van Leiden. They were out for heaven on earth and, it followed, a revolution in society. Support grew in Amsterdam from about 1530. A man called Trijp-maker arrived from Emden and made a great many converts, and then there was another Emden man, Hoffman, a furrier, who was full of apocalyptic prophecies and had great influence. The Stadholder of Holland, Hoochstraten, was constantly urging strong measures on the liberal Schout, who still did nothing very much about it.

Then came the extraordinary episode at Münster in Westphalia, where Anabaptists took over the town. There was tremendous excitement everywhere. Prophets were sent from there to Amsterdam, where the unviolent and intelligent Jan van Campen was named "bishop" by the so-called "king" in Münster. There were thought to be at least four thousand followers in the town, but Hoochstraten could get no action from the authorities until March 1534, when there was a fiasco of a great march to Münster. The burgomasters heard about it in advance, and on the twentieth hundreds of Anabaptists arrived from the country around. Some were intending to march, others to go on by boat. It was all very disorganized. Suddenly that evening five men ran through the streets shouting, "The day of the Lord has come!" Hoochstraten was in the town and had them arrested and sent off to Haarlem for execution. As for the marchers in general, everybody was scattered and a few more arrests were made. Subsequently there were two beheadings on the Dam. But this was not so much for heresy as for law and order, and there had never been any doubt where the town stood on that.

Hoochstraten acted again in April. Weapons were found stored at a house in St. Joris-straat. All Anabaptists were now promptly ordered to leave the town; the Town Hall bell was rung, and the announcement read out on the Dam. Since, of course, they didn't leave, house-to-house razzias followed and about fifty were picked up. Some of these were burned at the stake. Hoochstraten had the stakes built outside the St. Anthony's gate, where he had his stadholder's lodgings in a cloister. He was able to watch.

Next Hoochstraten dismissed the Schout and appointed a tougher successor. The rest of the year passed without much trouble, although underground the movement was very much alive — helped by temporary unemployment in the port, due to a small war between Denmark and the Hansa towns which was upsetting the Baltic trade. Jan van Geel, a leader who had been deported but had secretly returned, was plotting an all-out revolutionary assault. Next, however, was the crazy event of the "naked runners" on February 11, 1535.

That evening there was a hot gospel group of Anabaptists at the house of a wool merchant, Jan Sylvaertsz, in the Zoutsteeg, a little street close to the Dam. Suddenly the "prophet" Hendrick Hendricksz went into a fit and cried, "I have seen God and heaven and hell, and the day of judgment come — and you are all judged for eternity, not even worthy of hell but only of the lowest depths!" His hearers exclaimed in alarm, "Heavenly father, have mercy!" Mercy was granted at once. Hendrick Hendricksz said, "The father will overlook you, your sins will be forgiven, if you are as a child of God." After some more prayers and preaching the prophet remembered the garden of Eden, tore off his clothes and threw them into the fire, and told them all to do the same. They did, men and women. The smell of burning brought down an anxious landlady. The prophet told *her* to take off her clothes. She could not refuse, apparently. The ecstatic group then went out of the house, running and shouting, "Woe! Woe! The wrath of God!" Those who came to their doorways or happened to be on the Dam were rewarded with a memorable sight. There were seven men and five women, and the new Schout knew just what to do with them. The women got off lightly, but the men were beheaded on February 25. Their heads were exhibited on spikes at a tollgate on the IJ. The unfortunate landlady was hanged in her own doorway.

Rumors of activity elsewhere kept coming in and the agitation remained on the boil. Underground an argument was going on between the militant Jan van Geel and the passive "Bishop" van Campen. But Geel's plan went ahead. May 10, the night of a Town Hall banquet, was chosen. All the burgomasters and other notabilities would be there and, it was hoped, the worse for wear. They had secretly installed harquebusses in the "Rhetorician's Room" in the old wooden weighhouse, or Waag, and from there they would occupy the Town Hall. They were to wear white sleeves. Women were to stay indoors. At eleven o'clock the Town Hall bell would be rung and the cry go round the town, "Who loves God, come with us!" — which would be the sign for the general rising.

The plan did not work out — a boy had seen and reported the harquebusses in the weighhouse. The party of forty left two houses in the Pijlsteeg by the fish market, reached the Town Hall, and cut down the sentries by sword. But they then found that the banquet was over early, the birds had flown. Next they found that the rope of the bell tower had been cut — so the all-important signal could not be given. They knew they were trapped. The battle was soon on. But the first attack failed and a burgo-

COURTESY OF THE AMSTERDAM CITY ARCHIVES

Hanging of Anabaptists in 1535

master was killed. The Anabaptists remained in command all night. The next day the attack was resumed under Burgomaster Reecalf, who had had the Dam barricaded, using sails and hopsacks. They came in from different directions, fired the Anabaptists' own weapons from the weigh-house, and finally broke in by the side door of the former St. Elizabeth's hospital. Inside they fought from room to room. It was said that the noise of the shooting was heard far away. Twenty burghers and twenty-eight Anabaptists were killed, including Jan van Geel, who fell off the tower onto the Dam.

The unfortunate twelve who were taken alive were soon dealt with. Sentences were delivered on May 14. They were "to be laid on a bench and cut up while alive and their hearts taken out of their bodies and they are to be quartered and the parts hung up at the town gates and the heads are to be placed on posts." Women who had sheltered the men were hanged in the Town Hall cellars or in their own doorways "as an example." The "Bishop of Amsterdam," Campen, who had taken no part in the assault and had advised against it, was speedily picked up. First he had to sit in ironical state on a scaffold in front of the Town Hall, wearing an imitation mitre, decorated with the town's arms. Then his tongue was cut out as a symbol of punishment for his preaching. Then his right hand, with which he had baptized people, was cut off. After this he was beheaded and his body burned. His head with its mitre and his hand were sent for exhibition at the Haarlem gate. The mother and son who had hidden him at their house, The Blue Angel in the Nieuwendijk, were hanged outside it.

The whole episode left a very heavy impression on Amsterdam. This town, which had been so free and tolerant, now became fervently Catholic. The most easygoing councillors had no time at all for social revolutionaries. Antipopery, yes, antiproperty, no. The Anabaptists had spoiled the market for every kind of Protestant position. From now on Charles V's placards were obeyed in full, and harmless, passive idealists were persecuted brutally. The stadholder appointed new magistrates. The burgomasters and council soon no longer included anybody tolerant. Menno Simonsz began a new baptist sect, mild, utopian, and pacifist. He came to Amsterdam in 1539 and managed to travel everywhere in Holland without getting caught, but his Mennonite followers suffered terribly — always treated when arrested as if they were militant Anabaptists. Men were beheaded, women drowned. After 1545 it was the stake. The next year two men tied to ladders were lowered into the flames on the Dam. On March 20, 1549, eight men were burned on the Dam and three women "executed with water" — that is, tied in a sack and dropped in a water-filled wine tub.

So it was a town that the twenty-two-year-old, serious, fervently Catholic Crown Prince Philip could look at with approval, when he arrived on a visit in September that year. The formal purpose was for him to be recognized as Count of Holland. The *"blijde inkomste"* or "joyful entrance" was a big occasion. He was rowed into the Damrak on a royal barge to the sound of firing and bell-ringing. All the bridges were decorated with allegorical pictures, ships were covered in flags, houses were hung with red cloth and the royal arms. The festivities included a sticking match, in which sailors armed with poles tried to push each other from boats into the water. Pieter Vloots, the rector of the Nieuwezijds school, received three guilders for writing some suitable verses on the gates.

That night torches blazed everywhere. The prince spent the night in the Warmoes-straat house of Burgomaster Buyck's sister. The next morning he went to the Oude Kerk for Mass and then to the Town Hall, where he swore to maintain Amsterdam's privileges; and the burgomasters, councilors, and magistrates took their oaths to him. There was a gate of honor on the Dam, decorated with an allegorical picture — "Faith holds down Error and Heresy." But the town retained its sense of proportion. Traders on the Dam who were inconvenienced by all the royal pomp could claim a compensation of two guilders.

11.

BURNINGS at the stake and beheadings were rare events and now became more rare. The worry about dangerous religious sects had died down — and people like the Mennonites knew that they had to stay strictly concealed. Though the town government remained rigidly Catholic, distancing itself from the radical poor and the more humanistic rich burghers, the Schout and magistrates had begun to lose their enthusiasm for persecution. They knew as well as anyone that the business of Amsterdam was business. For the time being religious controversy was confined to the jealousy between the Oude Kerk and the Nieuwe Kerk. The former had thirty-eight altars, the better organ and more beautiful windows, and a lovely tower was going up, while the latter had no tower, thirty-six altars, bigger windows, and the best pulpit. Bad feeling between the two parishes was strong.

On Sundays everybody went to church. Those who did not accept the "old faith" said nothing about it and in any case most people were also touched by older, more ancient faiths still. Magic, sorcery, ghosts, and spirits all belonged behind the neat gabled houses. It was a last link with the old Germanic tribes. Spirits were abroad in Amsterdam between Christmas and Twelfth Night. Hay was put out for Wotan's horse, and milk for the illusory snake which protected the hearth. When you were dying, you were given the last unction — the ghostly "white women" had already prepared you.

Odd thoughts, odd goings-on beneath the often outwardly dull façades of Amsterdamers. For a long time it was part of their makeup to seem duller than they were, which fooled many a foreigner. A whole caste of aristocratic burghers had now arisen, all of them very unostentatious in the town — though many had begun to maintain small castles and country houses outside, perhaps along the River Amstel (later along the Vecht). They did not know it, but everything was becoming set for the great push into the golden age. Meanwhile Antwerp was the city, the center of world trade and money exchange, and with a population of 150,000. Amsterdam's was 30,000 and a good, enjoyable life was on offer.

What was it like to be a burgher of Amsterdam in the mid-sixteenth century? A burgher was a citizen with full rights and to be one at all was an honor, only automatic if one was the legitimate or illegitimate child of a burgher. People coming to the town were investigated as to their wealth and also their morality, and they had to agree to stay for five years. Only then could the name be written down formally in the Town Hall. Loss of citizenship was considered a severe punishment.

The burgher was up early at about half past five or six. Even in the following century council meetings would begin at seven. If he were an average merchant, his house would have a cellar, a ground floor where he and his family lived and slept, an upstairs apartment which was probably his workroom but possibly included a bedroom, and above that an attic beneath the gable which was his private warehouse — goods went up and down by pulley. The street, whether it faced a canal or another row of houses, was an extension of his house. In fact it was like a large room belonging to all the inhabitants; they sat out in it, worked in it, and played in it. The air, though this was unnoticed, was a trifle stuffy. Their beds were in large, rather coffinlike affairs, attached to or recessed into the wall — a version of pullout beds in one-room apartments. Some houses had privies. If not, the matter had to be attended to with commodes and chamber pots. Washing was no problem. Nobody washed. Or, at least, very little.

During the night a rattle sounded once an hour to tell them the time. By day there were bells and horns — the baker would blow a horn to announce that bread was for sale. Breakfast consisted of various sorts of bread, butter, cheese, and beer. Milk, yes, a little, but it wouldn't be popular for a few more decades. The biggest meal of the day came at twelve and was mostly meat, venison, or fish. Vegetables existed but wouldn't be regarded as important for another fifty years at least. An Amsterdamer felt that vegetables were for animals. Perhaps some peas, for pea soup was to be and still is a great Amsterdam dish. More bread, more cheese, soup, and plenty of beer. A good, solid meal.

And at about half past three perhaps a few pickled herrings and some more beer. Forks were not yet in use, and didn't come in until the fashion for ruffle collars towards the end of the century made some mechanical extension of the fingers necessary. The merchant wore simple clothes, a dark jerkin, dark breeches fastened at the knee, dark stockings, and dark flat shoes along with his high dark hat. His lady was similarly dull, with a tight jacket, bursting after meals, a wide skirt, and a linen cap over her head.

Manners were free and easy. The young had a good time. Various ancient formalities endured, through which contact with the girl was made — one was tying some flowers to the doorstopper. If the girl could be seen subsequently with the flowers tied to her sleeve, a successful first move had been made. But once the first step had been taken there were no particular restrictions. Unescorted days in the country were all right and party games in the home, and there were many traditional ones with names like head-in-the-lap, offering possibilities for all tastes. There was a cheerful earthiness, combined with hardworking respectability, combined with good meals and lots of beer. Primness and similar virtues had not yet made much headway. In the air there were still traces of old Germanic customs, of times when one carried off a wife or bought one — hints of which survived in the handing over of earnest money by the bridegroom, or the traditional efforts of the bride's blood relations to prevent him making his way to her house.

Weddings were certainly for extroverts. Before the day itself there was a feast when the parents met to arrange money settlements, if they were well off enough for this to arise. Then the bride's friends would put up mirrors, flowers, and decorations in the house — and there was another feast on the Sunday of the first banns being read out when the couple received visitors together with their parents, and it was the friends who had to look after the guests, and see that the proper healths were drunk, verses recited, and also lead in the singing and dancing. A man would be hired to go round distributing sweets and spiced wine amongst all acquaintances. On the wedding day the friends had to do more decorating — usually with the trailing light blue periwinkle — and if possible manufacture a crown of rosemary and spangles. After the marriage they all sat down to a wedding breakfast. There was a whole collection of old east Germanic marriage songs glorifying sensual love to be gone through, then more love songs and marriage songs and drinking songs, folk songs and of course, in the land of the Chambers of Rhetoric, yards of poetry full of the pleasures awaiting the couple in bed and of the parenthood shortly to be expected. It was no place for sensitive brides, or bridegrooms. Shouting and playing around, overeating, getting drunk, telling obscene stories, dancing — into all this a wedding soon happily degenerated. Sometimes a little later on there was a traditional medieval "bride's play," a sort of charade; but the big moment came when the bride was danced to bed — the younger guests captured her and led her up to a festooned and decorated bedroom and bed and before he could get to her the bridegroom had to buy her back with the promise to provide the happy laughing company with another feast. Even so the guests undressed her a little. It was great if you liked it — and it was still going on a hundred years later — but it was the sort of thing people did like. In the morning the maid brought the "morning water" and was given a present, and the bride's female blood relations came to call. There was no honeymoon, but for a few weeks various gaieties went on. Then the bride became a housewife and, incidentally, remained legally underage for good. Her husband had the right to punish her and it was only if he did so quite barbarously that the law intervened — which it frequently had to. However, every visitor who left a report during the next hundred years found the ladies formidable and quite unbrowbeaten.

A lusty, agreeable life. There was skating in winter with iron skates — the whole population turned out when conditions were suitable, and there were various kinds of competitions and races — every one a good reason for a drink. In summer there were the fairs, or *kermises*. And there were many feast days. On Shrove Tuesday, for example, men would dress up as women, and women as men, and go round the houses demanding meat, bacon, and money; wearing black masks, they would bang on the doors and try to behave as if they were the devil come to call — and everything ended, needless to say, in drunken gaiety, a bacchanalia, in fact, as the Reformed Church was in due course to describe it, frigidly. There were dozens of holy days, and all of them involved the consumption of plenty of food and drink.

The more, the better for the Town Hall — for everything was taxed, except (as they said even in the fourteenth century) the air they breathed. Fish, meat, wine, beer, bread, everything was taxed at any point where tax was gatherable; and excise masters were not at all backward at entering private houses to make sure there was no black marketing. This led to a close control of people's lives, which in turn often led to excise protests. The burghers were always prepared to stick up for themselves and butchers liked to argue with butcher's knives in hand. But the Town Hall kept on intruding and taxing like any modern welfare state. If the burgher was a member of a craft guild this too looked after him with a sternly parental eye.

There were guilds for almost all the occupations — potters, tailors, hat makers, shoemakers, glove makers, chair makers, wheel makers, scabbard makers, armorers, coppersmiths, pewterers, drapers, weavers, fullers, dyers, bell tuners, and so on and on. The guilds laid down the rules for hours worked, for apprenticeships, numbers of employees allowed, examinations — for example Amsterdam barbers laid down in 1497 that a journeyman barber who wanted to become a master barber must make two lancets out of a piece of rough iron; demonstrate their perfect sharpness by tests on leather; then show his skill at bloodletting and finally prove himself knowledgeable about the three principal veins. If he passed, the new master had to provide a meal for his three examiners.

In general the guilds were colorful but restrictive. In 1527 Amsterdam carpenters and cabinet makers were limited to taking two apprentices or

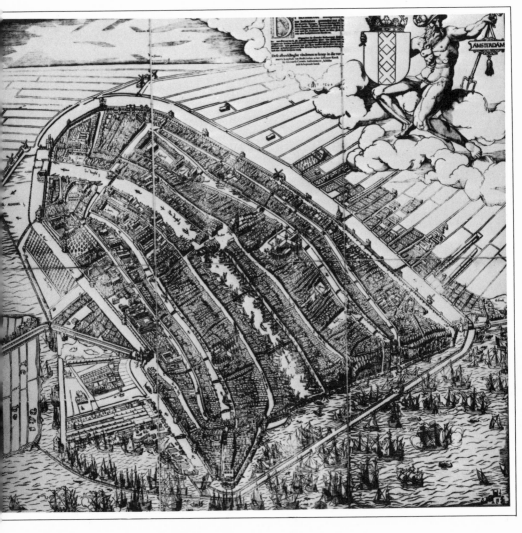

A bird's-eye view of Amsterdam in 1544

employees each. They were always trying to prevent the growth of organization and capitalism. But Amsterdam's merchants were moving her steadily into the capitalist world. The town was already the grain center of the Netherlands (Amstelodamum Belgicae horreum). Prosperity was once again making it come apart at the seams. There were protests about the rise in house rents "which rise is caused by the paucity of room and new building within the town and through the numbers of all sorts of people, including foreigners, who come to the town to be merchants and often to our inconvenience." Workpeople came in hundreds outside the walls, building themselves shacks. And the oldest canal, the Oudezijds Voorburgwal, parallel with Warmoes-straat, was nicknamed the Velvet Canal because so many rich people lived beside it.

The town, wrote a mid-century Italian traveler, Ludovico Guicchardini, "is one of the goodliest havens in the world, for you shall have at one instant five hundred sail of ships riding in the port. The town is so rich that though a fleete of three hundred sails, laden with all kinds of merchandize arrive there, the citizens within five or sixe days will buy up all their wares. . . ." (Translated in London, 1593, by Thomas Danett.)

In 1550 a German professor, Nicolaus Wimman, had coined the phrase, "a forest of masts," to describe his view of the harbor. Wood was a dominant feature. There were stacks of planks along the front and thousands of piles stuck out of the water to make jetties for the ships. There were the rope makers' and sail makers' yards. There were already warehouses five stories high, leaning forward to allow goods to be hoisted up. Behind it all was that peculiarly attractive sight offered by so many Dutch towns — the low brown line of clustered gables with an occasional spire reaching up into the sky.

But Amsterdam was not to be allowed to go on quietly and steadily becoming more prosperous. There was to be an interesting and unpleasant interval. For two things had happened. Calvinism had arrived and was proving to be highly attractive to all sorts of people throughout the provinces; the Emperor Charles V, worn out by immense responsibilities and gluttony-caused stomach troubles, had abdicated. The German empire went to his brother Ferdinand, everything else to his son, who became Philip II, King of Spain. At a magnificently staged ceremony in Brussels, in October 1555, Charles handed over the Netherlands.

The new king was not very attractive. Where his father had achieved some popularity because he spoke five languages including Dutch and could "get on" with people, Philip was reserved (though capable of a private night out), spoke only Spanish, and was surrounded by Spaniards at his Brussels court. Though his father had been a bigot, who had introduced the country to the Inquisition and the stake, Philip was an unspeakable bigot. His greatest and possibly his only interest was the suppression of heresy. One of his first acts was to reaffirm all the edicts and placards and one of his last, before leaving for Spain in 1559, was to have an instruction sent to all courts and councils in the country, reminding them that the decrees for burning, strangling, and burying alive must be carried out to the letter.

12.

SINCE the Amsterdam regents were fervently Catholic, all this did not worry them so much. But persecution was still out of fashion. The new stadholder of the province was the young, handsome, and highly civilized and liberal William of Orange, whom Philip detested and suspected. In the town itself the Schout, who had been so severe, had become so tolerant that he was to get himself into trouble for it. In any case the Calvinists were far less crude than the Anabaptists had been and did not invite arrest. Their supporters belonged to all classes from sailors to rich merchants and though the majority of the population remained unquestioningly in the "old faith" the ruling clique were aware of the underground and ready to look for support from Brussels. But there was no particular worry until 1562, when "Every day heresies are committed and heretical gatherings held all over the town." On February 19 the holding of all religious meetings or ceremonies outside the church was forbidden. In April a secretary was sent to The Hague for discussions. The trouble was that powerful trade interests were involved, like the Hooft family of grain merchants. Money always talked in Amsterdam.

Calvin's doctrines, which he was still revising in Geneva, had an extraordinary attraction in the Netherlands. They seemed to offer just what was required for the human predicament at this point, as the medieval world was slowly disappearing, especially in the towns of Holland and

Zeeland — although to begin with all the important action was in the southern Netherlands. Calvinism meant an all-powerful God, with man hopelessly corrupt except through faith in Christ. It offered a subtle, logical and apparently inevitable system of predestination for eternal life, which meant the selection of some and the rejection of others, combined with a certainty of personal salvation and a satisfactory relationship between divine and human will. For the church was God's instrument and its adherents were ipso facto being chosen as they maintained their faith and a pure life. There was a seductive infallibility about it. In addition people were expected to obey authority, both spiritual and worldly, which was pleasing to husbands, town councils, and merchants. But worldly authority could be rebelled against, provided the individual was not proceeding on his own and was backed by his spiritual organization. For the Netherlands cities and towns with their ancient charters and privileges so eaten away by the Burgundians and Hapsburgs, this was clearly a welcome message. As also for many of the lesser nobles. Calvinism, in fact, was an ideal fuel for the coming great revolt of the Netherlands against the power of Philip.

There were other fuels: the presence of Spanish and Italian troops, anti-Spanish feeling generally, taxation, hatred and fear of the Inquisition, hatred and dislike of the ministers around the king's regent, Margaret, Duchess of Parma — who was a natural daughter of Charles V, a good horsewoman and a fervent Catholic. Of course the Netherlands nobles, including the great grandees like William of Orange, Egmont and Hoorn, were all Catholics and continued to live a luxurious life. But they reacted with sympathy to the vast unrest stirring in the country. The grandees were not afraid to protest. The only result was a suggestion from the king to Margaret that heretics might be drowned in their cells to avoid martyrization, so long as their suffering was not reduced. Another suggestion for her from an assembly of bishops was that for people who were not heretics, but who through carelessness had got mixed up with the matter, whipping with rods was suitable. The ghastly death sentences had to be carried out everywhere, especially in the south, where so many Huguenots had infiltrated from France. However, the inquisitors wrote to the king in Spain complaining of the lack of cooperation they received.

Everything blew up in 1566 when a large number of nobles and some rich burghers signed a paper, the "Compromise," in which they professed loyalty to the king, but denounced the Inquisition. Resistance was now on at a higher level than that of the usual unfortunate heretics. The grandees took no part but held a watching brief. There were secret conferences and excitements. Then a petition was presented to the angry, somewhat nervous duchess; the deputation of three hundred was headed by the dissolute and aggressive Brederode, who was descended in unbroken male succession from a younger brother of the third Count of Holland and not lacking in self-assurance. There was great enthusiasm in the streets of Brussels and the next day the deputation went back to be told that the king would be informed and that meanwhile the inquisitors would show restraint. That night there was a triumphant banquet. When they were sufficiently lit up, Brederode rose and told them a story.

It was that during the presentation of the petition the day before one of the grandee nobles who was loyal to the Hapsburg master, the Baron Berlaymont, was heard to say to the duchess, "Madam, is it possible that your highness can entertain fears of these beggars?" His listeners, hearing that they had been socially insulted, were all furious. Then Brederode carried out the propaganda masterstroke of his life. He nodded to a page, who was ready with a beggar's leather pouch and wooden bowl. Brederode fitted himself with the pouch, had the bowl filled with wine, raised it high, and then swallowed it down noisily. "Long live the beggars!" he shouted. "*Vivent les gueux!*" The banquet erupted into a tumult of enthusiasm.

The marvelous cry was born and would last all through the years of struggle. Orange, Egmont and Hoorn turned up in the course of the riotous banquet and were compelled by the happy drunken nobles to drink the toast. The next day Brederode rode out of Brussels, with forty-three companions, firing pistols in the air to acknowledge the crowd's applause. He spent the night in Antwerp, where another large crowd came to his inn. Brederode, loving it, appeared at the window with his bowl and pouch. After this it became a fashion among nobles to wear the beggar symbols. A medal was struck which read, "*Fidèles au roy jusques à la besace.*" Faithful to the king even to wearing the beggar's pouch. Things were happening.

There was an immediate spread of "hedge sermons," or "*hage preken.*" When all meetings in houses had been forbidden, Protestants began to go outside their town walls. In Amsterdam this had been in the dock area called the Lastage (between Geldersekade and Oude Schans) and so many had attended that the regents had prudently done nothing about it. Elsewhere in the country as summer came there were gatherings, semiarmed, of thousands — often addressed by French, German, or Swiss preachers. Brederode, going about Holland, said he found as many beggars as sand on the seashore.

Wherever he went there were happy shouts at night from lighted windows, and a court of worthless hangers-on grew round him. In July he was at a noisy conference of his league of nobles, and Orange came to try to moderate him, without success. They sent more demands to the duchess, whose alarm was growing. The moderation she had promised that summer turned out to be, approximately, the substitution of strangling for burning (although she personally ordered the slow burning of one young man who dared, as a dissenting gesture, to throw down the Host). All the same she and the Brussels government could not cope with the "hedge sermons."

Soon there was a major disorder in Antwerp. The image of the Virgin being carried through the streets in procession was insulted by the crowd. The next day they were shouting at it in the cathedral. At night the mob broke in and there was an orgy of desecration and image breaking. After the cathedral the mob surged to other churches.

And suddenly the same thing was happening all over the country. Within a few days, almost in the same week of August, churches everywhere were sacked. Statues, gold and silver plate, jewelry, priceless embroideries were smashed, thrown around, destroyed where possible. In Amsterdam women hurried to the Heilige Stede chapel and defended it so fiercely against the image breakers that it was left alone. But a rabble got into the Oude Kerk and did great damage. Trouble was avoided at the Nieuwe Kerk, but various cloisters were plundered, including the Carthusians outside the Haarlem gate and the Franciscans outside the St. Anthony's gate. As elsewhere it was quite unorganized and simply a mass destructive impulse, not so much of Protestants as of the mob. The duchess was terrified and prepared to fly from Brussels. Persuaded to stay, she signed an accord ending the Inquisition — in return the nobles promised to keep order. And a thrill of hope went through the Netherlands.

No one, except the Prince of Orange, who prudently had his own spy service at Madrid, knew that the duchess was writing to the king wildly incriminating everybody, demanding help, demanding his presence, reminding him that she had agreed the accord on her own word and not on his. The king wrote back pretending leniency, while in fact planning the most draconian measures. Only Orange understood the nature of the monarch and of the possibly appalling future. He arranged a peace at Antwerp, where three churches were made available for various kinds of Protestant worship on the basis — as laid down in the duchess's accord — that it was allowed where it had already taken place. "I know this will nothing contente the King," William told Sir Thomas Gresham, the English financier. In the next two or three months he went round making similar arrangements, at Utrecht and in Holland and Zeeland. At Amsterdam he confirmed the worship which went on at the Lastage, after the duchess had suggested that Protestant sailors should go out in boats for the purpose. "I do not know who could have advised your highness to make such a proposition," the prince replied, and the duchess's answer was full of exasperation: "In the name of God, then, let them continue to preach at this Lastage." ("*Au nom de Dieu qu'ils ayent leurs presches au dict Lastaige.*")

The duchess could not do much with William, but in the other provinces the accord was very soon a dead letter. By the end of the year she was regaining confidence. For one thing the August outbreak had appalled many of the nobles, especially the strong Catholics. Egmont had gone to Flanders to do his law-and-order-keeping and had had no hesitation in hanging reformers. Hoorn, on the other hand, at Tournai, had given in too much to them and in October the duchess felt strong enough to recall him to Brussels and send a personal representative — by January the Tournai reformers had been suppressed. Nowhere were Calvinists more in evidence than at Valenciennes — and in December a siege began. A local amateur army of students and ex-soldiers tried to take on the government forces. They were destroyed and slaughtered, a further boost to the duchess's morale. The villages round Valenciennes — which still held out — were now given a taste of what was in store for a large part of the country; looting or property confiscation, terror, and, for the soldiers' amusement, selling the local girls by auction. (For the sadistically inclined readers of the future, the drinkers of torture and horror, the next few years in the Netherlands were to offer a banquet.)

The brave and noisy Brederode was now established to the south of Utrecht at the small town of Vianen, where he had seignorial rights and where life was one long drink-up with roaring parties, shouts of "*Vivent les gueux!*" and so on. But he was also assembling a rough army and a month later was trying to recruit troops for it at Antwerp, with the intention of mounting an attack on the island of Walcheren. The duchess was alarmed, and had the unprincipled nerve to ask Orange for more of his steadying help. But the highly civilized prince no longer thought there was any hope of a moderate solution. Egmont, on the other hand, backed her.

The Walcheren idea proceeded, but while one branch of the rebels, after failing to get a foothold at Flushing or some other port, landed along the river near Antwerp, Brederode was away in the north gathering support, with the intention of eventually going to the relief of Valenciennes. Close to Antwerp, in sight and hearing of the city, government forces appearing by surprise demolished the rough and raw army, professionally and cruelly — anyone who didn't get away was drowned in the Scheldt, burned alive in the barns where they tried to hide, shot, or in some other way cut to pieces. Inside Antwerp the tension grew and then uproar broke out. There were forty thousand Protestants in the city and large numbers of them now came storming towards the gates, armed with pikes, knives, old swords, sledgehammers. Orange, who was in Antwerp, rode to the gate and marvelously held them back. He prevented what would have been a suicidal venture. But within the city there was now a frightening situation, with mobs of Catholics, and of infuriated Calvinists and Lutherans getting ready for a bloody battle of their own. But again Orange managed to steady the atmosphere, going from one group to another at great risk.

Brederode was at this moment in Amsterdam. The confident but dissolute aristocrat was spending his time as usual. That is, when not recruiting, in uninterrupted, self-indulgent roistering which highly incensed the black-suited Catholic Amsterdam regents — however, his name and position, quite apart from his unruly private army of hangers-on, made him too much for them to control. But his time was running out fast and so was everybody's who had dared to show resistance to Brussels. Down in the south a few days later Valenciennes fell and its unfortunate citizens now experienced a plundering, murderous occupation, with weekly executions in the marketplace.

It was the end of the first chapter. Orange made a last attempt to persuade Egmont back to resistance but failing, left for Germany. So did Brederode. He had a last party on April 25 at his lodgings in Warmoesstraat. Then a disorderly crowd of his followers escorted him in a last noisy torch-lit procession, with songs, shouts, and music, and the great man sailed off to Emden. He died a year later and was luckier than some of his followers in another ship, who were arrested and found themselves (at least, the better born — the others were hanged at once) reserved for a new scaffold on the Brussels horse market. Everything was now hopeless for the Protestants. The day after Brederode's drunken departure from Amsterdam, Antwerp was forced to receive a garrison of the duchess's troops, which meant the end of any freedom there, and she herself arrived for a visit on the twenty-eighth. She had her troubles. Her brother was sending the Duke of Alva to replace her, which annoyed her intensely. In that early summer of 1567 the Netherlands waited in anxiety. The good and sincere Catholics, of course, were reasonably confident. The bad ones now became good. No rich Amsterdam table was without a priest to share the food and wine. In May the duchess proclaimed again, as a reminder, death for almost every possible offense, even singing a hymn at a funeral — and with whipping for children and servants who had attended a Protestant service even in their parents' or masters' houses. The king read the edict in Spain and thought there should be more burnings and less hangings. He wrote to her reproachfully.

13.

THEN ALVA CAME, bringing an army picked from the Spanish garrisons in Italy. This cruel, zealous, monstrous old man arrived in the Netherlands in August, sent troops to all the main cities, showed friendliness to Egmont and Hoorn, and then had them arrested along with the Burgomaster of Brussels. The duchess left the country in high dudgeon. The real terror began. Alva and two Spanish lawyers busied themselves with a tribunal which could try and condemn and confiscate at will. Commissioners were sent everywhere, informers encouraged, executions took place all over the Netherlands. A first attempt at invasion by the Prince of Orange was not a success. After a promising victory in Friesland his brother's forces were hopelessly beaten by Alva; and between the two battles Egmont and Hoorn, who could not find it in themselves to distrust the king, were beheaded on the town hall square at Brussels.

People in general were infuriated, for Egmont had been a hero, but were still more terrified. Orange, whose estates had been confiscated in lieu of his head, waited in Germany for another chance. Alva had a statue of himself put up at Antwerp. And the Inquisition and the terror went on mercilessly.

In Amsterdam the arrival of Alva had meant the exiling of dozens of people whose sympathies were with the Calvinists. Many of them were merchants who could carry on business at places like Emden and Enkhuizen. The property left behind was confiscated. The council had 170 empty houses on its hands and couldn't get rid of them, an extraordinary fact in a town which had been bursting a few years before. Business now was terrible. A gratuitous factor was a war between Denmark and the Swedes which at times closed the Sound, the priceless channel into the Baltic. There were also the Sea Beggars.

The Prince of Orange (whose nickname "the Silent" was due to the silence he had kept when he heard accidentally from the King of France about the French and Spanish intentions towards heretics) was increasingly involved with the Calvinist underground, especially in Holland and Zeeland. He had given his commission to a number of ships under the command of a Calvinist noble, the lord of Dolmain, who was served by two famous commanders, William de la Marck and William de Blois. They and their officers and crews, the Sea Beggars, were in fact pirates distinguished by their fanatical anti-Catholic feelings — "Sooner Turks than Papists!" — as well as recklessness and daring. They plundered any ships from Catholic ports — like Amsterdam — as well as churches and monasteries along the coast, and were able to sell the booty in English ports and also the Huguenot stronghold La Rochelle. The Amsterdam merchants wrote plaintively to the king accusing them of "piracy and plunder by sea and daily attacks not only on your majesty's good subjects, but on foreign merchants as well, associating your country of Holland with the ruin of good Catholics, who want only to earn their living going to sea and doing business." It was the bourgeois's cry of pain.

There were other cries of pain, rather more heartrending. On May 29, 1567, the first suspected Beggar had been arrested and in September hangings began on the Dam. After the executions the magistrates usually invited guests to a celebration meal. There were many victims over the next few years. In 1572 a Catholic priest wrote, "The town of Amstelredam is now called by the desperate Beggars and murderers and church defilers not Amstelredam, but Murderdam."

All the Netherlands lay under the terrible hand of Alva. The regents of

Amsterdam, ever mindful of the Anabaptist episode, collaborated happily, but the rest of Holland and the other provinces seethed with unrest. In Holland the countryside was terrorized by marauding bands of thieves, many of them out-of-work sailors. Just to make everything more unpleasant there had recently been the worst floods in memory. The outlook for William of Orange, the Calvinists, or any sort of Protestant was extremely dim. Early in 1572 the one successfully aggressive faction, the Sea Beggars, were up against it. The English had suddenly decided to listen to Madrid and forbid them the English ports. They could have been finished, but for the happy chance that bad weather drove some of their ships into the Maas estuary in April.

They found that the town of Brill was empty of Spanish troops. Their first natural reaction was to pillage it in the normal course of business. But then they decided, more or less by accident, to hold it in the name of the prince. At last they had had some luck. Urged on by William's brother, Lewis of Nassau, they made for Flushing, whose Spanish garrison was weak and whose position on the River Scheldt commanded the approach to Antwerp. At the sight of their ships the population rose, or at least enough of them did to overpower the garrison.

The news of this success of the Sea Beggars was sensational in Holland and Zeeland. Suddenly everywhere towns were in open revolt. A few weeks later representatives of twelve of them — Amsterdam, of course, was not one — met at Dordrecht as the Estates of Holland and recognized the prince as stadholder. As for the prince himself, he and his brother were now busy mounting a second invasion, with an army of German mercenaries and French Huguenots. But once again this failed disastrously — the St. Bartholomew's massacre at Paris pulled the rug under the French support. However, the revolt was now on, the prince set up in his province of Holland, and the Duke of Alva was determined to crack down on the wicked and dissident population.

The answer of the Dutch towns was romantically courageous. Not of Amsterdam, however. From a patriotic viewpoint the town under its Catholic regents behaved appallingly. As Alva's son, Frederick of Toledo, came north with his Spanish troops sacking and butchering on the way, Burgomaster Peter Ruysch of Amsterdam set out with a council-pensionary of the town to meet the duke. They found him at Nijmegen, where he was stuck with gout (one hopes not a light attack), and they offered their local knowledge and advice, which was to attack Naarden and then go for the Haarlem dike. The advice was taken. After Don Frederick had finished sacking Zutphen, he made for Naarden, where he superintended a famous and ghastly massacre. On December 1 Burgomaster Ruysch met him to emphasize Amsterdam's loyalty to Spain and to hand him a letter from his father, the duke, requesting that the Spanish troops should stay outside the walls of the town. Don Frederick agreed and came to Amsterdam with the Spanish Stadholder Bossu and other high-ranking officers on December 3. He stayed with Sybrant Occu — Pompejus Occu's son.

Amsterdam was already full of the war atmosphere. Owing to the heavy frost it was surrounded by ice. Though no one unauthorized was allowed to leave town — under penalty of whipping — people were slipping in and out, day and night, across the frozen IJ — even after they had cut a canal thirty feet wide. In November Bossu had sent a warning that a large number of Beggars were making for the town from the Leyden-Haarlem direction and several guerrilla-style attacks had taken place, usually on skates. The Carthusian monastery outside the Haarlem gate had been burned down one night. Thousands of skates were being made.

Haarlem was the next objective and Don Frederick's troops arrived, but camped in accordance with the agreement outside the walls of Amsterdam. Inside, however, was something utterly shameful, wagonloads of booty from poor, massacred Naarden. It was hardly possible to get into some of the houses on the Nieuwendijk and Kalverstraat. About twenty different merchants were dealing with it. On the Dam there were thirteen large Spanish artillery pieces, a large quantity of war materials, and Stadholder Bossu's personal baggage. Amsterdam had willingly become the Spanish forward headquarters, much to Dutch bitterness in general and William of Orange's in particular.

Between Amsterdam and Haarlem was the seventy-square-mile Haarlem lake (no longer there — a typical Dutch disappearing trick), divided from the IJ by a narrow strip of land. At the moment it was frozen and musketeers skated on it. In Haarlem itself a Calvinist force of four thousand waited grimly. They had no illusions. When three of the council came secretly to Amsterdam to treat with Don Frederick, two who returned with his answers were promptly tried and sentenced to death, while the third, who had prudently stayed in Amsterdam, sent a messenger urging surrender. The messenger was hanged. It was not nice, but it was the language Don Frederick understood.

The siege began. While the ice, and fog, lasted skaters could slip in and out of the town with supplies. In December and January the Spaniards tried assaults. Both failed. The defense included boiling oil and live coals. Heads were thrown over the walls in both directions. William sent a relief force of three thousand from Leyden, but they were defeated in a snow-storm — after which the Spanish indulged in a large-scale use of the gallows. Disease, cold, and boredom were now their enemy while for Haarlemers it was famine. Amsterdamers meanwhile were bringing food to the besieging trenches and also building a small fleet for the Spaniards. The lake became navigable in February and a series of small engagements took place. Amsterdam itself came under pressure from the Sea Beggars, for the dike road to Muiden on the east side was vital, and there were fights on the dikes and causeways and sluices. In March the Haarlemers managed an attack of their own, capturing cannon and provisions, but soon the Spaniards controlled the lake and the blockade had to win. After the failure of a last effort by the prince to relieve them they surrendered on July 12.

Whatever the Calvinist underground thought, there was relief and delight amongst the Amsterdam merchants. It seemed obvious that the Spaniards would now quickly overcome the rest of the rebellion and the shipping business could start up again. The business of Amsterdam was (still) business. The day before the surrender they were reminding Don Frederick of his promise to ensure the freedom of the seas for them. Then the burgomaster's party rode back from the Haarlem camp and set off at once for Nijmegen to meet the duke. It was at least to their credit that in offering their congratulations to Don Frederick they had asked him to show mercy to the Haarlemers.

In any case the duke's orders were on the way. The heroic garrison's leaders and some leading citizens were to be executed, and with them any Walloons, French, or Englishmen, but the Haarlemers, provided they renounced the Prince of Orange, might be spared. The duke hoped this would encourage other towns and he himself arrived in Amsterdam to enjoy the triumph on the evening of July 17. He stayed with Sybrant Occu and spent the next day looking at Haarlem, before going off to Utrecht. Alkmaar in the north was the next item and its surrender was now demanded. And the Amsterdam council found itself forced to offer a loan to pay for a new fleet being built. The duke wrote to thank them.

He had other troubles, which required more loans — but they paid, willingly enough, for they were backing the winner and expected to recoup when the northern towns were taken. One of the troubles was a mutiny of the Spanish troops quartered in Haarlem. Twelve thousand of them had died of wounds or disease during the siege and in addition they were unpaid. The prospect of loot had kept them quiet but now the generous terms to Haarlem prevented this.

Don Frederick had moved north to look after the siege of Alkmaar and the duke had to come back to Amsterdam. Equipped with a new loan, he went to Haarlem and managed to settle the mutiny (only just in time — Spanish troops had been secretly in touch with William of Orange, who was at Delft). The duke decided to stay on at Amsterdam, where he had been made so welcome. He lived in the Warmoes-straat and there waited for the good news. A brisk trade was done selling busts and portraits of him to the monasteries and the loyal burghers.

The good news did not come. Two thousand people inside Alkmaar were managing to resist sixteen thousand Spanish troops. The new fleet, manned largely by Spanish and German sailors, went to sea commanded by Bossu, whose ship, the soothingly named *Inquisition,* was the largest which had ever been on the Zuyder Zee. But the fleet was becalmed. The merchants waited impatiently, but instead of trade moving again by the *kermis,* September 20 to 27, as they and the council had hoped, nothing had happened. Then came disaster. The dikes were cut round Alkmaar and Don Frederick's besieging army was flooded out. The siege was raised on October 8. And on October 11 and 12 Bossu's fleet went into action and was overwhelmingly defeated. Bossu himself was taken prisoner.

There was deep depression in Amsterdam, with the prospect of a revival of trade ruined. As a Franciscan monk put it, "the fleeing captains who returned from the battle crept in like dog thieves." The unfortunate duke had another pay problem. He wrote self-pityingly to the king that there were two thousand men clamoring round him. The regents and the merchants — all too aware that they could kiss good-bye the loans they had handed out so happily — were now very tightfisted. The council sent to Antwerp for help, but no help came from the exchange there. The prestige of the tyrant in Warmoes-straat was falling fast. And the debts were accumulating. Even his landlord, Jan Persijn, was owed fourteen thousand guilders. In November the duke dealt with this problem in the spirit of a fine old tradition. He had a proclamation read out that all claimants must present their accounts on a certain day, when they would be met in full.

During the night before that day he and his staff discreetly faded away. Amsterdam had backed a loser and a welcher.

14.

EVENTS MOVED elsewhere, leaving the town in its depressed state, still tied to Spain by the regents — always, of course, strongly backed by the priests and monks. In any case it seemed inevitable that the sheer power of Spain would win in the end. But now Leyden endured a long-drawn-out, Haarlem-style agony and was rescued by the purposeful use of flood water and the arrival of the Sea Beggars. The prince's brother, Lewis, trying to attack Maastricht, was killed and the battle lost; but again the Spanish had a mutiny problem owing to pay shortages. They mutinied elsewhere when forbidden to loot or when, as after their failure at Leyden, they were unable to loot. Three thousand Spanish soldiers marched into Antwerp and billeted themselves on unlucky households; the citizens were blackmailed into providing three years' back pay for them. Possibly it was some compensation that Orangist forces had a naval victory in the Scheldt while this was going on. But the great city was becoming accident prone.

Meanwhile the Prince of Orange was still controlling only a small section of the country, without resources, constantly trying for help from abroad (Elizabeth of England was giving a little but was not keen, for professional reasons, on aiding rebels). And in the second half of 1575 the Spaniards suddenly had success in Zeeland. William was nearing desperation when luck stepped in and Requesens, the Spanish governor who had replaced the Duke of Alva, quite unexpectedly died. The Council of State in Brussels was paralyzed and the prince had his chance. The situation roughly was that Holland and Zeeland (except for Amsterdam) were Protestant and Orangist, while the other fifteen provinces were largely anti-Spanish but (the Protestant minorities being cowed) pro-Catholic. This was the moment when the common hatred could lead to something — if one forgot everything else, the economic position of the country after all the horrors was catastrophic. Moreover the Spaniards had had one last victory in Zeeland, at Zierikzee; but as in other recent victories the only result was that their troops promptly mutinied. Thousands of them marched across the country and settled at Alost, or Aalst, in Brabant. Throughout the summer the mutiny spread. The prince met delegates from all the provinces at Ghent in October. While they were still at it the mutinous troops arrived in Antwerp, easily crushed the Walloons and Germans the government had sent to protect the city, and treated themselves to a few days of bloody enjoyment, murdering, looting, raping, burning. The callous orgy became known as the "Spanish Fury" and it had the effect of concentrating the minds of the delegates at the prince's conference wonderfully.

By the Pacification, which was signed on November 8, all the seventeen provinces agreed to press for the expulsion of Spanish troops and meanwhile that all the antiheresy placards were to be suspended, that the reformed religion could be practiced in private in the fifteen Catholic provinces and would be the official religion in Orange's own domain, which was more or less Holland and Zeeland; and that Catholic cities in a Protestant area should be given a "Satisfaction" about their religious security before they need join. With this settled and a new hope throughout the country, they waited to deal with the arrival of the new governor — the glamorous young Don John of Austria, a hero of battlefields elsewhere, a bastard son of Charles V. The new governor traveled through France disguised as a Moorish slave.

He had to wait for some months in Luxembourg, for he dared not concede what was demanded, and at the same time the unity resisting him was too much. Finally he agreed to withdraw all the Spanish troops and in April 1577 happy crowds everywhere watched them go.

Don John, wearing a green cloak, was received in triumph at Brussels. But the honeymoon did not last long. He took the first opportunity of resuming hostilities and set himself up at Namur. So the Prince of Orange then made *his* triumphant entry into Brussels — but that didn't last long either, for the Catholic nobles of the southern Netherlands couldn't bear his predominance, and invited instead the twenty-year-old Austrian archduke Matthias, who made *his* entry into Brussels in January 1578. However, he accepted that the prince kept most of the power.

Highly irritated by the invitation to Matthias and still more by its acceptance, King Philip now sent the brilliant Alexander Farnese, Duke of Parma, who was both a subtle diplomat and a highly efficient general, to

help Don John. He began right away, on January 31, with an easy victory
at Gembloux — too near to Brussels for comfort. The States-General took
themselves off hastily to the comparative safety of Antwerp.

Meanwhile things had been happening at Amsterdam. Since the withdrawal of the Spaniards there had been increasing pressure on the town to
come over to the Orangists. The regents remained obstinate. Though it
was intensely annoying to the prince, he refused to use force — he wanted
the town, whose potential he understood very well, to be preserved intact.
But he had a job to stop the constant schemes of angry Hollanders and
Zeelanders to starve the town or take it by surprise. There was an unsuccessful raid in November 1577 — but the commander was killed at once
and the raiders had to get out fast.

However, a visit to Utrecht, where the prince had a great welcome,
resulted in a "Satisfaction" to protect the Catholics there, as agreed at
Ghent, and this was the breach. An agreement was negotiated at last and
signed on February 8, 1578. There was jubilation among the Calvinists,
who could now show themselves, and of course throughout Holland and
Zeeland. But the Amsterdam regents had given away extraordinarily little.
Protestants were now allowed to worship *outside* the walls, but could have
their dead buried inside on unconsecrated ground. The garrison which
had replaced the militia companies was to be paid off, and a burgher
guard of five or six hundred raised to man the gates. Burghers could again
be given weapon training and people exiled for religious reasons could
return and reclaim their property. But the Catholics retained their
churches, and the magistracy and the monks remained.

With the Calvinists now feeling triumphant, however, such an arrangement could not last very long. (In fact, no "Satisfaction" did.) They were
soon leaning on their former oppressors, and were further stirred by news
leaked to the prince's representative in Germany that the Swedes had
been approached by Don John to provide ships for an attack on Amsterdam. In May a coup was organized. On the twenty-eighth, William Bardez, a Calvinist, with four others, went to the Town Hall, in order
ostensibly to discuss with the council certain grievances, such as the unsatisfactory provision of burial grounds. At midday one of the five went to a
window overlooking the Dam and raised his hat. Instantly a sailor ran
across the Dam shouting, "All who love Orange do what your heart says!"
Within a few moments armed men appeared everywhere. A party rushed
into the Town Hall, where Bardez proceeded to tell the council they were

all under arrest. Then all over the city the monks were hunted down and marched to the Dam with the mob shouting happily, "To the gallows!" and, perhaps prescient of late twentieth-century demos, "Out — Papists — out — Papists — out out out!" The arrested regents waited in fear and resignation, locked up with the monks in the beautiful weighhouse, or Waag, built only thirteen years before, while excitement and cheerful tumult reigned round them on the Dam. They were ready for some hideous fate, and in view of what had happened to their enemies in this same square it was not unreasonable. Mevrouw Dirckzoon, wife of an arrested burgomaster, pathetically sent him two shirts — he sent them away with the message that he would never need shirts again. Later in the day, to shouts of derision, they were all embarked in two boats on the Damrak. But then what happened could not have been more civilized. Outside the walls they were disembarked on a dike and left to get on with it, unharmed. In due course most of the regents prospered elsewhere.

Inside Amsterdam a new and non-Catholic council was appointed, by the authority of the restored militia. The Calvinists took over two churches at first but in September — after zealots had burst into the Nieuwe Kerk to do a little image breaking — all of them. The best of the priests disappeared from view and continued to officiate in private, others earned surreptitious livings casting out devils, sprinkling holy water, and so on; five or ten percent managed the changeover to the new church, and another five percent who were willing to make the change were turned down as being insufficiently educated. But although Catholic power was now so summarily ended, enough of the old oligarchy remained to ensure continuity and efficiency of government. Another great asset was the use to which the empty or emptying cloisters could be put, which naturally included some of the most substantial buildings. They became hospitals, sugar factories, warehouses, old people's homes, orphanages, prisons. St. Cecilia's cloister on the Oudezijds Voorburgwal became the Prinsenhof (Prince's House), which would be used to house important visitors — and, with additions, is the present-day Town Hall. On the other side of the old canal a meat market appeared in St. Pieter's Chapel, and the upstairs apartment was given to the Amsterdam *Rederijkers'* Chamber, "The Eglantine — Blossoming in Love." Here the *Rederijkers* could rehearse for a big occasion, the arrival in March 1580 of William of Orange.

Like the Crown Prince Philip in 1549, William arrived by boat on the Damrak. The procession included two barks with oarsmen, three sloops, six yachts, and three galleys. The ships were decorated with shields and on deck were orange tents with scarlet coverings. That evening the Town Hall, the weighhouse, and the fish market were all lit up. Close by William visited his friend Dirck Graeff, a Protestant exile in 1564 and a burgomaster since 1578. (The high-backed chair the prince used is in the Rijksmuseum.) And the *Rederijkers* had their moment when they recited panegyrics to him on the Dam. After which at ten o'clock a firework blazed, a crown set with oranges filled with gunpowder and two standards with the seven Pleiades, on which all ninety-eight points were fixed by pots of tar. It made a great spectacle and William's presence was the final symbol that the town had joined the revolt.

The change from the arrangements of the "Satisfaction" was always referred to, with tasteful restraint, as the "Alteration."

15.

By 1579 the split between the northern and southern Netherlands had become firmer, although Antwerp and the major Flemish cities remained Orangist. But the Catholic grandees could not take the tolerant and determined prince; and some of the French-speaking Catholic provinces were now tied, more or less willingly, to the Duke of Parma and Spain. In the north, where an agreement between provinces at Utrecht had unconsciously founded the Dutch Republic and where — the Spaniards having gone — the population in its private mind was still probably for the most part Catholic, the Calvinists had been helped by an announcement of the Pope that any supporter of the Prince of Orange was an enemy of the church. And the prince was further helped when Philip offered to pay for his assassination. However, the first coin minted for the Orangist provinces showed a ship at sea without sails or oars, and the inscription: *Incertum quo fata ferant* — It is uncertain where the fates will lead. It could not have been put better.

The state of affairs was confused and complicated. The Archduke Matthias not having been a success, the Catholic Duke of Anjou, brother of the French king, was invited by the States-General to take over and was later asked by the prince to be the "Defender of the liberties of the Netherlands" — it never occurred to anybody that it was possible to exist without a sovereign, least of all to Orange — and there had been a brief intervention by John Casimir, a fanatically anti-Papist German prince from the Palatinate whose troops swept across from the east and committed excesses at Ghent, which had helped to antagonize the south against the Orangists. The Duke of Anjou, after resting in England, where he was the current official suitor for Queen Elizabeth's hand, arrived in 1582 at Antwerp, and he was instantly unpopular.

He and the prince stayed in Antwerp for the rest of the year, playing a poker game — for Orange wanted him to be sovereign in name only, and that was not Anjou's idea at all. The prince, who already owed his survival to his distrust of royalty, considered with some care an invitation he received in person from Anjou early on the morning of January 17, 1583. Would he care to attend a review of the French regiments in camp outside the city? He declined with thanks, and how wisely, for at midday the troops were storming into the city. "*Ville gagnée! Tue! Tue!*" they shouted.

However, the Antwerpers were not taking it. Infuriated, they put up such a stout resistance that the French were driven out, leaving fifteen hundred prisoners and many dead. It was a victory, but a bloody one, and like the "Spanish Fury" of '76, it was not the sort of thing that helped a commercial city. The duke, not unnaturally, soon left the Netherlands, but it says everything for the Prince of Orange's view of the priorities, that in spite of this episode his wish for French help in the main struggle kept him still backing Anjou as his sovereign. However, time was running out for him, as it was for the duke, who died in June 1584. A month later Orange was assassinated at Delft, at a time when the affairs of the northern Netherlands were looking extremely dim, for the Duke of Parma was slowly but relentlessly advancing, hampered only by money difficulties. But one by one the towns of Flanders and Brabant were being regrasped by the Spanish power.

Ypres, Bruges, Ghent. Brussels in the spring of the following year. And now Antwerp was threatened. At Delft they kept their nerve, but knew that they had no hope without big-power support. They offered themselves to the King of France. He refused. They offered themselves to Elizabeth, and she also refused, for she was still averse to rebels. But she was also afraid of the Spanish and therefore inclined to help. Nothing happened, however, until the news came that Antwerp had fallen to Parma

Procession of lepers on the Dam in the early seventeenth century,
as depicted by A. van Nieulandt

and was in Spanish hands again. Elizabeth promptly agreed to send troops and a governor general. The northern Netherlands felt themselves saved. The Earl of Leicester arrived with fifty ships at Flushing on December 19 and was installed in February, accepting the title "Excellency." Hearing about this Elizabeth was highly annoyed and sent Lord Heneage over to forbid it. And she did not allow Leicester to be called "Excellency" until July.

16.

BUT ANTWERP HAD FALLEN. The greatest city in Europe, with its population of over 150,000, with its thousand foreign merchants, the original Bourse, was finished. The Spanish fury, the French fury, and now defeat at the end of a long siege were damaging enough in themselves. But the Sea Beggars controlled the approaches of the Scheldt. Therefore, Antwerp was no longer a port. Moreover, its immense international trade had made it a center of freedom and a haven for minorities. Now with the Duke of Parma imposing the strict Catholic rule of the Spanish, there was a huge exodus of Protestants and all anti-Spanish elements from the city, taking with them money, skill, and know-how. The foreign merchants had been gradually leaving over the past ten years. Depression, to put it mildly, had set in over the same period in the textile industry. Antwerp did remain important; it was still the focal point of the great continental land routes, and of course the chief commercial city of the southern Netherlands, but its old position was gone.

Forty-four percent of the new burghers at Amsterdam between 1580 and 1589 came from Antwerp. Fourteen percent of all Amsterdam bridegrooms in the last twenty years of the century were born in Antwerp. But the refugees did not only go to Amsterdam. Middelburg, Haarlem, Rotterdam, Utrecht, all were swollen. They went also to Cologne and Emden and England. And refugees did not come only from Antwerp. Liège metalworkers, for instance, appeared in the northern Netherlands. Whatever happened, it was all a potential profit to Amsterdam. Suddenly there were Huguenot textile workers in the town. Suddenly there were merchants

deeply experienced in the most refined and subtle Italian business methods. Suddenly there was the diamond trade of the Jews, who had been
thrown out of Spain and Portugal at the end of the fifteenth century, and
now out of Antwerp at the end of the sixteenth. And there were the German Jews, safe from centuries of hounding. There was never a moment
when a town had so much to gain.

Moments of great opportunity are not always grasped. The Amsterdamers, however, grasped theirs. Inside twenty-five years the town of the
northern Netherlands had become one of the great cities of Europe.

17.

KALVERSTRAAT, the Nes, Nieuwendijk, Warmoes-straat, all the narrow
main streets swarmed with antlike figures in somber black and high hats.
The Dam, of course, was the center for promenading and the exchange of
news and gossip. It was not generally called "the Dam" until the seventeenth century. The part in front of the Town Hall was still the "Plaetse"
and the easterly side from the weighhouse to the fish market was the
"Middendam." This section, with the Damrak — "the Water" — and the
stalls and the fish-women and the fish auction on the square and the taverns by the sluice, supplied the old-style lustiness about which the English
Mr. Peschem complained in his *Complete Gentleman* (1622): "Within
these fifty or three score years it was a rare thing with us to see a drunken
man . . . but since we had to doe in the quarrel of the Netherlands . . .
the custom of drinking . . . was brought over into England. . . ."

The new world of the ambitious city, bursting with Protestant refugees,
was on the Town Hall side. Here all was puritan severity. Leading burghers now were elders and deacons in the church, and as the Synod at The
Hague in 1586 laid down, deacons must be "upright, honorable, irre-
proachable as to manner of life, not miserly nor hard-hearted, and in no
danger of being devoid of means." This was certainly how the black-suited
gentlemen thought of themselves on the Plaetse.

II

The Glory Time
1585–1669

1.

MEANWHILE the war against the Spaniards continued, and Amsterdamers did business with both sides, as they had done all along and would often do in the future. The Earl of Leicester, one of the earliest guests at the Prinsenhof, protested, as later on Napoleon would protest. But the regents and the merchants insisted that unless they supplied the enemy they could not afford to fight him. It was a point the earl could never understand. Nobles and the common people were his cup, not the bourgeois, however patrician. But all the Dutch seaports and the province of Holland itself were upset by his attitude. The province had made money for years from a system of licensing goods directly intended for the enemy — it had been worth half a million guilders in 1573, the year of the siege of Haarlem. The earl's departure in 1587 could not have been more welcome.

He left the new Republic mixed up and full of factions, without a powerful ally and with the forces of the Spanish Netherlands leaning hard;· everywhere south of the Scheldt and Waal was in their hands; but fortunately it was 1588, the year of the Spanish Armada against England, and the Duke of Parma could not give his attention to the seven united provinces. The following year the Protestant Henry IV came to the French throne, and the resulting civil war in France was another distraction for the duke. In the circumstances the Republic had a chance to breathe.

There emerged a country whose political arrangements were quite extraordinary. It was like a national *Kon-Tiki*. But just as Mr. Heyerdahl was able to make his trip, so were the administrators of the United Provinces able to make theirs. Not, of course, that it was clear who the administrators were. The Council of State, once the most powerful instrument, was gradually weakened because the English ambassador had a treaty right to sit on it — a right which was used until 1626. There were twelve councillors, three from Holland, and two or one from the other provinces. The stadholders belonged — which meant the late Prince of Orange's son Maurice — twenty-one in 1588 — and the latter's cousin, William Lewis of Nassau, who was Stadholder of Gelderland. The Treasurer-General and the Clerk of the States-General also belonged. Once a year the Council of State applied to the States-General for the next twelve months' military expenses. How much each province should pay was suggested in petitions sent to the Provincial States. Holland always paid more than half, and for naval requirements as well; which established the predominance of Holland's opinion — and equally of Amsterdam's, since the city was the biggest contributor inside Holland.

In the States-General sat representatives of each province, and each delegation, or each province, had one vote. The States-General controlled foreign, military, and naval affairs. Their title was splendid: "Their High and Mightinesses of the States-General." But all seven votes had to be unanimous. And no delegation could cast a vote about anything possibly controversial without having had instructions from its province, which of course meant fantastic delays while somebody rode back, say, to Gelderland. In the Provincial States representation was on behalf of towns, or certain towns, each of which had a vote. In the case of Holland there were eighteen towns with a vote, and the nobles also had one, which was supposed to cover the voteless small towns and the countryside. The other provinces each had their States with slightly different arrangements — in Utrecht owners of former church lands formed a State, since the deposed church could no longer supply a representative. In Friesland there was actually an elected assembly, but nobles had more influence in administration. Groningen was different. Overyssel was also different. And not only did all the seven provinces regard themselves as more or less sovereign, but so did the towns. And then there were separate councillors in each province whose function was to see that the rulings of the Estates of their province were carried out; and these men, being in action all the time, developed great influence. In Holland there existed the Advocate, who was the lawyer to the States of Holland and was in charge of the other councillors, and at the same time headed the Holland deputies to the States-General; this clearly offered a chance of power to an exceptional man, and that man was Oldenbaarneveldt, one of the two great statesmen of the Republic; the other, who held approximately the same job later in the seventeenth century, was John de Witt, the Grand Pensionary. (Both were murdered, the former judicially, the latter by the mob.)

Then there was the stadholder, or stadholders. This was the title of the regent of a province under Burgundian and then Hapsburg rule. William of Orange had been Philip II's stadholder in Holland, Zeeland, Utrecht, and Burgundy. Now the stadholder was appointed by the States of a province — it was done firstly to put a check on the Earl of Leicester. The stadholder was responsible for the administration of justice in the province, for the appointment of magistrates, and for military and naval defense. The magistrates appointed the members of the States of the province, who appointed the stadholder, who therefore, once in, became the source of his own authority. But he also had to be accepted by and take an oath of allegiance to the States-General. When Prince Maurice, the stadholder of Holland and Zeeland, also became stadholder of Utrecht, Gelderland, and Overyssel, he automatically achieved semisovereign status; his cousin William Lewis, ancestor of the present Dutch royal family, was stadholder of Friesland and Groningen.

All this was fantastically involved, especially for a small country newly and shakily independent. But the method of running the navy, the absolute core of their existence, was equally remarkable. There were five Admiralties of seven members each, one for Amsterdam, the others for Rotterdam, Veere, Hoorn and Enkhuizen together, and Harlingen and Dokkum together. The States-General appointed the Commander-in-Chief, and chose the captains from a list supplied by the Admiralties. The Provincial Estates chose the Vice-Admirals of Holland and Zeeland, and also the Lieutenant-Admiral of Holland. The five Admiralties chose the lieutenants. It was the *Kon-Tiki* method of running a country and running a navy. The extraordinary fact was, it was a great success.

2.

ALTHOUGH the spectacular new trades, skills, capital and financial know-how which arrived as a result of the fall of Antwerp were the essential feature of the rise, a very large proportion of Amsterdam's wealth would still be due, even for most of the seventeenth century, to its original Baltic trade. Grain was the basis of many a great fortune, like that of the Hoofts. They bought the grain cheap, stored it in the marvelous, high, gabled, leaning warehouses and sold it when the price went up. What could be pleasanter? And in the last decade of the sixteenth century there was widespread famine in Europe, especially in the south. Nothing could have been better for the Amsterdam merchants. Enormous profits came in. (But incidentally, having mentioned the name of Hooft, one should also say that the contemporary head of the family, Cornelis Pieterszoon Hooft, was a delightful man. He was one of the Protestants who returned after the "Alteration" in 1578. He was a success in business and politics, many times a burgomaster, the owner of a large house on the Singel and a country estate. But he was also a humanist and spent his life in conflict with the strict Calvinists. He fought for religious freedom, he fought against corruption, of which there was plenty, and he was the father of a great poet and historian. The portrait of him in old age, by Cornelis van der Voort, shows a kindly man with white moustache and white pointed beard, with a black suit, of course, a black skullcap, and the high white ruff. He was everything that was good about the Amsterdam merchant.) But, to repeat, fortunes were made out of European famines — and of course there were lean years for the city when continental harvests were good.

Grain, herring fishery, fish oil — these were the roots of wealth. They began to build cargo ships, called flutes — or *fluiten* — in great numbers in the last twenty years of the sixteenth century, and this increased their proportion of the general carrying trade. It was first of all a growing commodity market, and this meant more shipping, and the two led to the development of a money market — and nothing was more natural than to supply both sides in a war, even one they were not involved in themselves. For years hardly anything could happen in Europe which did not mean money for Amsterdam. For example, sea battles and privateering led before the end of the sixteenth century to the establishment of marine insurance and before very long ships of Amsterdam's enemies were actually being insured in Amsterdam; the States-General felt this to be going too far and put a clamp on it.

Add to this all the new trades brought by the Antwerp exiles, the glass-making and diamond-cutting, the refinement in textiles, the silk and damask makers, the jewelers and goldsmiths. But without any doubt the most glamorous and important development of all was that of the Dutch East India Company.

In 1595 Jan Huyghen van Linschoten, who had spent thirteen years in the East, published a book, *Itinerario,* describing his experiences, which caused a considerable stir in Amsterdam. His picture shows a squat-looking man, rather like James Cagney, with fairish hair brushed back, wide but wispy moustaches, a pointed beard, and the end-of-the-century ruffle. An adventurous boy, he had left the Netherlands when he was barely seventeen, made his way to Lisbon, and joined the Portuguese service which took him to the Indies. Many other Dutchmen did the same and even held responsible positions in the outposts. Some also served with the Spanish and made the trip to America. But Linschoten's book not only described Portuguese commercial methods in detail but showed that the state of Portuguese government in the Indies was precarious. The idea of a Dutch entry into the Far East trade became highly tempting.

What increased the temptation still more was Philip II's behavior. Throughout the century the Portuguese had brought their cargoes back from the Indies to Lisbon, and from there Holland and Zeeland ships brought the luxury goods, largely to Antwerp, for distribution to western and northern Europe. And it was such a deeply imbedded and vital part of the Holland and Zeeland commerce that a good reason had to be found to justify a switch of resources to making the Indian trip on their own, with all the risks involved, physical and financial. (Although the fugitive Brabanters who had arrived with their bigger ideas and distinctly more speculative attitude to investment were an influence towards risk taking.) So long as Lisbon was open for business there could be no sense in the Dutch trying for any regular direct trade with the Indies. But in 1580 the Spanish king took over Portugal, and Lisbon became a Spanish port.

Since Spain and Portugal were hopelessly dependent on the Dutch shippers both for imports and for the distribution of their exotic Oriental cargoes, the change of sovereignty made no particular difference; they went on sailing in under their own flag. But King Philip finally could not bear it, and suddenly had all Netherlands ships in Spanish or Portuguese harbors seized. Their cargoes were confiscated, the crews died a lingering death in the dungeons of the Inquisition or else were forced to serve in Spanish galleys. In spite of this episode the Dutch kept on with the trade under different flags. In 1595 it happened again. Archduke Albert, the governor of the southern Spanish Netherlands interceded and some ships were returned, but by now even the profit-conscious Dutch shippers felt they had had enough and turned their eyes on the possibility of direct trade with the Indies.

They knew the way round the Cape of Good Hope perfectly well, but they had no enthusiasm for fighting the Portuguese on the way, if it could be avoided, and so to start with there were great efforts made to find a northern passage. Balthazar de Moucheron, a Huguenot refugee from Antwerp, now of Middelburg, was the enthusiast behind three expeditions which tried and failed to get round the north of Asia. He was already doing trade with the Russians and had built a factory at Archangel in 1584. But while the third expedition were wintering in Spitzbergen after terrible sufferings, nine Amsterdam merchants had already formed a company and sent out four ships, commanded by an ex-Lisbon resident, Cornelis Houtman, to follow the Portuguese route. The author Jan van Linschoten, whose book was inspiring the merchants, gave them an itinerary (he himself had been on the Arctic trips). They left the Texel to cheers and an artillery salute on April 2, 1595, reached Bantam (W. Java) on June 22, 1596, and were home minus one ship and ninety out of two hundred and fifty men in July 1597. This trip did not in fact make a profit, but the cargo they brought back was rich enough for bourgeois excitement; and in any case it had been shown to be practical. Hendrik Hudde, Reinier Pauw, Pieter Hasselaer, and their other colleagues who had promoted the trip for 290,000 guilders were delighted. Their company was called the "Compagnie van Verre" — the Far Away Company. They promptly set up a new expedition, this time of eight ships. But now everybody was wanting to get into the act. Capital was offered from all sides. A second company was formed and the *Compagnie van Verre* prudently amalgamated with it; the name of the combination was now "de Oude Compagnie" — the Old Company. But other companies sprang up in Amsterdam, and not only there — one was formed in North Holland, two in Zeeland — the famous Balthazar de Moucheron was in one of them, and in another at Rotterdam. One ship was financed by merchants at Delft. And there was also a company formed down in Brabant in the Spanish Netherlands. Twenty-two ships went to the Indies in 1598, all intent on trade — no privateering, and no force to be used unless they were attacked. But the companies were all in the most frenzied competition with each other, with no holds barred. The danger that this might ruin the whole enterprise was obvious and in the same year the States-General sent a warning to the directors of the companies that whether their ships were on their own or amongst the enemy their mutual affairs should be conducted with wisdom and unity. This excellent advice was totally ignored; the rivalry became almost insane. This was an instruction given to three Amsterdam ships in 1599: "It should be remembered at all times that Zeelanders are our trade enemies and are therefore not to be trusted." Hardly a very useful attitude when it is remembered that Holland and Zeeland were the two most prosperous provinces in a new small break-away country still at life-or-death war with Spain.

The consequences soon showed. No one had the time to establish a settlement of any size and what they did manage to put up remained unfortified. All the rival ships turned up at approximately the same spots, with the result that there was an enormous rise in the cost of the Indies products such as pepper, cloves, nutmegs — and the prices were readily paid in the hope of preventing competitors from getting a cargo at all. And some ships returned home with gigantic supplies, which were as yet too much for the capacity of the home market. Prices fell and the new trade looked set for disaster. In any case they were bound to be snuffed out of the Indies by the Spanish and Portuguese before long. The Amsterdam council, in spite of its deep-down devotion to the idea of free trade, advised the companies to amalgamate. Then at Middelburg they did the same. This got nowhere, for suspicions and jealousies were far too imbedded. Finally the States-General had to invite all the companies to The Hague and after long and difficult negotiation masterminded by the great Oldenbaarneveldt, unity was achieved and the East India Company born in a States-General charter of March 20, 1602. This granted the company the sole right to trade in all the lands east of the Cape of Good Hope and west of the Straits of Magellan for twenty-one years. It was also given sovereign powers, could make treaties with local rulers and potentates, set up administrations and defense systems, wage war on Spain and Portugal, enlist troops — although any oaths taken were to the States-General first and the company second. It was run by directorates set up in the towns of the various former companies and on top of these was a principal authority, the Chamber of Seventeen, the members determined by the amount of the original capital their towns had supplied. So there were eight members for Amsterdam, which had supplied more than half the six and a half million guilders, four to Zeeland (Middelburg), one each to Delft, Rotterdam, Hoorn, and Enkhuizen — and the extra one could be chosen by the other chambers in turn, excluding Amsterdam, whose position in the affair was now very dominant. There was soon a market in the shares.

The original company directors now belonged to the local chambers. When there was a vacancy the States of the province set up a board of three to make the choice — and in practice this became the choice of the local burgomaster, and as a result the Burgomasters of Amsterdam developed, inevitably, great influence in the company.

Trading and fighting the war against Spain were the dual purposes of the company, for which the States-General had handed over, temporarily, its sovereignty; but trading was what interested the company, and the war came very much second; so, to begin with, did any attempts at colonization or empire building which the governors they appointed might energetically support — there was no enthusiasm for that sort of thing from Amsterdam. Fleets of thirteen to seventeen ships went off to the Indies and met with the greatest success. Large dividends began to be paid to the shareholders, at least on paper — there was a certain amount of showmanship going on for credit purposes; this was still the time of promise, the days of real wealth were still ahead. The 1602 trip under Van Waerwyck included visits to Ceylon, Malaya, Java, and even Siam and China — from time to time he sent back a rich cargo and returned himself in 1607. Van der Hagen, setting out in 1604, was equally successful, taking over Molucca and setting up factories in the Spice Islands. But the war now intruded. On his way back two years later, at Mauritius, Van der Hagen met another Dutch fleet coming out, a naval expedition of eleven ships commanded by Cornelis Matelief. They were on their way to Malacca, which was held by the Portuguese. De Castro, the Portuguese Viceroy of India, got there first with a larger fleet which was too much for the Dutch; but then he went off, leaving only a small detachment, and Matelief, returning on the scene just in case, was able to destroy it completely, every ship sunk or burned. From now on the Spanish and Portuguese treated the presence of the Dutch seriously. The East India Company ships were in danger from Portuguese forces based in Goa and Mozambique, and from the Spanish in the Philippines, and also from both Portuguese and Spanish attack as, full of rich cargo, they had to slip close to the West African coast on their way home. The tension was considerable. Each trip was an adventure, and surely would have been without an enemy to bother about. It is marvelous to think of those large, squat, beautiful, shallow-bottomed, three-masted, wooden sailing ships and their cocky independence and their grandeur. In 1607 rumors reached Amsterdam of a large Spanish fleet intended for the East Indies and the directors of the company were highly alarmed. The States-General, some of whose members incidentally were shareholders, gave Jacob van Heemskerk, leader of the unsuccessful arctic expeditions, the command of twenty-six ships and sent him off to deal with it. Heemskerk found the Spanish fleet at anchor in Gibraltar Bay. There were twenty-one ships and ten of them were large and powerful galleons. Both the opposing admirals were killed on that April day, but the Spanish fleet was destroyed for trivial Dutch losses. They could breathe again in the States-General; but it was still more important, for it made the humiliated Spaniards consider the idea of a truce in the long war more favorably. In any case the trade could go on. Nothing could stop the new and dazzling wealth of Amsterdam.

3.

THE TWELVE-YEAR TRUCE was signed on April 9, 1609, and on May 5 the Amsterdam *Rederijkers* offered a show of allegorical scenes in celebration. An elaborate stage was put up on the Dam, with carved dragons and Neptunes and torches flaring. The burghers watched happily, wearing their tall black hats and cloaks. At the end of the month, on the twenty-ninth, there was a far greater symbol of success. Hooft's youngest son laid the foundation stone for the new Exchange. Up to now, it may be remembered, merchants and brokers had done their business on the Nieuwe bridge over the entrance of the Damrak, and in bad weather in the nearby St. Olaf's Chapel or even in the Oude Kerk. This was obviously not on in the new situation, and two years before the council had set up a committee to consider a proper building. Its chairman was Franz Oetgens, a rich regent, many times a burgomaster and especially famous for his ability to cover avarice with a fine layer of Calvinist piety. Other famous names were on the committee, like Jan Huydecoper, whose vast interests included war material and South American merchandise. By September they had recommended a place and the design, which along with the construction, was the work of "mastersculptor" Hendrick de Keyser, assisted by "town-mason" de Rij and "town-carpenter" Staets.

The site of it was on the river-harbor side of the Dam, called the Rokin. Boats therefore had access to it. It was not exactly on the Dam; one got to it through one of two small streets. Great preparations had to be made in the two years before building began, for the sluice under the Dam — and under the fish market, and various taverns — between the Damrak and Rokin, had to be lengthened. The building was 200 feet long and 124 feet wide. An inner courtyard was surrounded by an arcade with forty-two pillars, above which was accommodation for 123 offices or shops. A clock-tower with a carillon stood at the southeast corner, overlooking the water.

Soon there were more institutions: an exchange bank, which was on the ground floor of the Town Hall so there was a constant flow of merchants from there across the Dam to the Exchange, and then a lending bank and a special corn exchange. All these together offered trading facilities unequaled in the world at that time. Drafts could be written instead of the old cumbersome exchange of coin.

Meanwhile the East India Company was beginning to declare glittering dividends, 50 percent in 1606, 329 percent in 1609. Speculation in the shares now began. One of the great investors in the company, Isaac le Maire, a southern Netherlander, organized highly developed "bear" operations, selling shares they hadn't got to depress the price. The game caught on. Everything caught on. It was the boom city atmosphere. No wonder the quaysides and islets of Amsterdam seemed to be a seething mass of net knitters and ships' carpenters and rope makers. It was a heady, intoxicating time, the first flowering of the successor to Venice, Genoa, Lisbon, and Antwerp. Or it should have been; but in fact the Amsterdam merchants reacted with a proper Calvinist restraint. The white ruffs round their necks were the only gaiety in their appearance; the old gloomy black cloth remained. But still there were signs. The first heavy luxurious carriages had appeared in the streets and were at once an unmitigated nuisance. By 1617 there were one-way streets and traffic regulations. And more merchants were planning country retreats.

Meanwhile the vastly increasing population — over 100,000 by 1620 — had forced the city to expand outside its walls. Already in 1585 the Lastage in the northeast was built up — the ancient ship-building area where the Protestants had been allowed to preach for a time. On the other side to the northwest 1593 saw the digging of the Brouwersgracht (Brewer's Canal) — which offers today some of the most attractive and untouched views in the city — and in this area building went outside the Singel as far as the first digging of the Herengracht (Lords' Canal). Two years later there was an expansion outside the walls to the southeast and the "Jewish quarter" came into being. But the great and marvelously imaginative plan of the three concentric crescent canals, largely the work of Hendrick

Staets, was passed by the council in 1607 and took off in 1611. It proceeded in stages, and the full half-moon effect was not achieved until the last decades of the century. But to pass it, to lay down the proper rules and to get on with it as they did was to the lasting credit, possibly the greatest credit they ever earned, of the "Magnificat" of Amsterdam — which was the name given to the group of rich and closely, ever more closely connected families who between them shared all the key jobs for most of the next two centuries.

Not that the matter went entirely smoothly. Franz Oetgens, mentioned above, and his brother-in-law Cromhout, who like himself combined an outer layer of Calvinist piety with an inner layer of avarice, could not resist the temptations offered by their knowledge of the expansion plans and they bought up land they knew the city would have to buy. The liberal and utterly upright Hooft fought them, and in this matter actually had an ally in a man soon to take over power in Amsterdam, the famous Reynier Pauw, who was in every way Hooft's opposite. At the age of thirty he had been one of the nine Amsterdam merchants who financed the first trip to the East from which the East India Company developed. His father had fled Amsterdam in 1568, and Reynier Pauw carried on the hard "Reformed" line of the "Old Beggars." He was intolerant, passionate, immensely rich, a master of rude interruption and scornful tirades. Quite unlike the classically reasonable Hooft. But they both had big houses on the Singel. In 1612, between the reigns of Hooft and Pauw, Oetgens became burgomaster (there were always four burgomasters, of whom one took precedence) and was able to push his deal through, making for himself a quiet 112,000 guilders.

In spite of this background of corruption and intrigue the plan, which increased the city area from 450 to 1,800 acres, was a triumphant success. It was a remarkable mixture of private enterprise and socialism, in the shape of municipal interference and control — or the traditional Amsterdam freedom within order. Along the three great canals frontages were allocated for business houses and for the town houses of the rich. There were intersections by radial canals and streets of more modest dimensions, suitable for more modest people. There were plans for churches, markets, even a city park — and, of course, a new ring of fortifications. The plots were sold on the open market, and buyers had to enter into heavily restrictive covenants. Only four kinds of brick could be used for outside walls (Lekse, Leytse, Vechtse, and Rijnse) and one kind of stone (Bremen) for the drains. Along the three great eighty-feet-wide canals sizes averaged twenty-six feet in frontage, 180 feet in depth. There was a minimum distance of 160 feet between the backs of houses; accordingly each plot allowed for an eighty-foot garden. In obedience to the 1565 building ordinance — which lasted until the nineteenth century — municipal officers had to inspect the foundation piles, sixty feet deep, before a brick could be laid, but all the building was by private enterprise. It went on for decade after decade. Frontages were kept for warehouses in the harbor and along the Brouwersgracht, areas were reserved for industry and for charitable foundations. The only mistake was not extending the council's supervising authority to the large district beyond the outermost of the three canals, the Prinsengracht, on the west side. This was left to speculators, with the interesting result that streets followed the lines of the paths that can be seen in sixteenth-century maps coming up diagonally from the southwest to the walls of the city. The streets here were narrow and the district became known as the Jordaan — a semislum, gay, overcrowded, cheap area where immigrant workmen lived, and some of the poorer Spanish and Portuguese Jews. Yet, on reflection, it was a happy mistake, possibly even the most remarkable touch of the "Magnificat's" genius, for the contrast the busy, overcrowded, underprivileged, exploited Jordaan area made with the city's sublime example of Baroque planning added life to Amsterdam, a necessary touch of dirt and untidiness.

4.

THAT CIVILIZED OUSTING of the Catholic burgher regents from the power of government at Amsterdam had left some of them with a gap in their lives which could be filled by the quiet pursuit of literature. If they remained Catholics there was, generally speaking, no persecution, but they could hold no public office. Two such men, well-to-do merchants, were Hendrik Laurensz Spieghel and Roemer Visscher, both of whom in turn held literary salons to which the talented made their way in due course. The link was Amsterdam's splendidly named old Chamber of Rhetoric, The Eglantine — Blossoming in Love. A third Catholic associate was Dirk Volkertz

Cornheert. He was a poet whose best-known work was called *Zeden-kunst, dat is Wellevenskunst* — The Art of Morals is the Art of Manners — a suitable title for a man fanatically devoted to moderation. He was sixty-eight when he died in 1590, and had therefore been a spectator of all the troubles, in which he had taken a fairly stormy part; and his fierce advocacy of moderation had guaranteed him poor treatment from both sides. He was suspected of free-thinking, and though Amsterdam was becoming famous for toleration, this was really reserved for sects, properly organized — free-thinkers remained highly unpopular. When Cornheert died, Spieghel was forty-one and Visscher forty-five. What all three had in common was a determination to restore life and importance to the national language, so debased, formalized, and corrupted in the terrible verses of the old Rhetoricians.

"Serious" work was written in Latin, and so were most lectures at Dutch universities for another two hundred years. The prosperous classes of Amsterdam were well educated in the classics, and the carrying trade had promoted the facility which the Dutch still have for speaking foreign languages. Their own was the poor relation, merely useful for common intercourse. The three wanted to return to the simple Dutch of earlier medieval writers and in 1584 they published their manifesto — which no doubt, at that moment, was the quintessence of the nonevent. The book, *Twaespraek* (Dialogue), was produced by Spieghel and was in the form of a dialogue with Roemer Visscher in the garden of the former's charming house, Meerhuyzen, which stood outside the city, close to the Utrecht gate. He had a famous summer house built in a large old linden tree where people came for literary conversation — the atmosphere was wealthy, cultured, civilized, somewhat precious (London's Bloomsbury comes to mind). The theme of "Dialogue," for which Cornheert wrote a foreword, was that the classics must be used to purge Dutch literature of its second-hand Burgundian extravagances and impurities. The message was sound, and soon made all the more appropriate, for the disasters at Antwerp meant the arrival in Amsterdam of two fugitive Chambers, "White Lavender Bloom" and "The Fig Tree" — and they, being exiles, were not unnaturally concerned with preserving themselves as they were, complete with all the old rhetorical flourishes. With these rivals on the scene the crusade of the leaders of Eglantine — which now began to be known as the Old Chamber — became still more meaningful. Spieghel and Roemer Visscher had great influence. Both wrote verse, without achieving anything memorable. What they did do was to lay the foundations for a marvelous out-burst of plays and poetry which owing to the curious inaccessibility of the Dutch language have never had their due — as Shakespeare no doubt would not have had his, if he had written in Welsh. (In fact they did not produce a Shakespeare — but a Milton, a Ben Jonson, a Webster, all of these, certainly.)

Spieghel's second wife, as all nonliterary persons can understand, forced him to break up the salon, the summer house in the linden tree, and the conversation, and move to Alkmaar in North Holland in 1602. Roemer Visscher took over. He, with his wife and three young daughters, also lived just outside the city but on the west side along the Singel, and on the road to Haarlem. Between them and that city was the great lake on which battles had taken place thirty years before, during the terrible siege. Now all was peace and culture. The girls were eighteen, twelve, and eight, and all three, but especially the charming eight-year-old, Tesselschade, when they were not busy skating on or swimming in the canal that ran beside their garden, were busier still on a wide range of artistic activities — the girls were clever at everything; music, painting, embroidery, poetry. And such is life's unfairness, all three were attractive. Especially Tesselschade, whose remarkable name celebrated the fact that the day she was born her father was in a shipwreck off the island of Texel at the mouth of the Zuyder Zee. The atmosphere of civilized wealth made a pleasant back-ground for members of the Old Chamber to exchange verses in pure Dutch.

The first great name produced by the Old Chamber was Hooft, eldest son of the famous and liberal burgomaster (who would have preferred him to go into the family grain business rather than be a poet). He had been admitted as a member of the Eglantine when he was seventeen. The same year his tragedy *Achilles and Polyxena* was played before the Cham-ber. Although as a play it was very much what a seventeen-year-old play-wright might be expected to turn out, that is to say formless, plotless, and unseeable, it was an attempt to meet the requirements which Spieghel and Roemer Visscher had laid down. The boy was rich, considered to be a genius by his elders in the circle, and very good-looking. His was and would remain a golden life. Now his father sent him off on a three years' grand tour. He went to Paris and then to Venice, Florence, and Rome. The whole scene of the Renaissance intoxicated him. No more charming letter-writer ever lived. From Florence he wrote one in rhyme addressed to the Old Chamber which was received with enthusiasm. He wrote another play, *Theseus and Ariadne,* and came back through Germany to Amsterdam in 1601, where he very soon fell in love with Anna Visscher, the eldest daughter. But he got no response, in spite of or perhaps because of the fine Renaissance moustache he had developed on the trip.

It was a good time to be young, privileged, and talented, when the country itself was new and bursting out of its old provincial clothes. A few miles to the southwest, at the university and textile town of Leyden, Hugo Grotius was already famous at twenty, and would go on to upset James I of England with his views on national sovereignty at sea before he was twenty-six. For Grotius there would be a great European reputation, a dazzling prison escape, and illustrious exile. For Pieter Corneliszoon Hooft everything would go on smoothly — except that death was always round the corner and now two nieces of Hendrik Spieghel with both of whom he became involved died one after the other. In 1605 he had his first real triumph with a pastoral play, *Granida,* performed before the Old Chamber, which now had the use of a hall (formerly monastic) in the Nes. To know what kind of an occasion this was one has to imagine an amateur dramatic society performing before an enthusiastic and opinionated public in a booming city where this is the only entertainment available, for the Calvinist authorities were certainly not out to encourage the theater. Dramatically, not too much happened. The audience was happy with a fairly statuesque recital of verse from the different characters. Laurence Oliviers were not expected and not available. So Pieter Hooft's quiet and lovely play made a deep mark. It was too delicate and artificial and Italianesque to have a lasting effect, but it made its author's reputation and also enchanted Tesselschade Visscher.

This lovely girl was now sixteen, and that year the Visschers moved to a house in the center of the city on the Geldersekade (then the Engelsekaai), the canal street which runs south from a famous tourist spot, the Schreierstor, the Tower of Tears, where, quite mythologically, weeping women said the last good-bye to their men who were setting sail for the other side of the world. Anyhow there was no time for sadness in the Visschers' house, where the young ladies were hard at it perfecting their accomplishments and entertaining the guests. The house was comfortable, narrow and tall, built of red bricks which looked as if they had been scrubbed clean every day. When they went out they saw ships everywhere, big and small, and hundreds of masts, like a forest of television aerials.

Pieter Hooft left their company for a while, went to Leyden to study at the university, and in 1609 was rewarded for his own brilliance and for having the right father. Prince Maurice made him the Governor of Muiden, which post included a large income, some mild administrative duties, and Muiden castle, a rather forbidding-looking turreted establishment (visited a few hundred years before, it may be recalled, by Gijsbrecht van Amstel), about ten miles east of Amsterdam, where the River Vecht joined the Zuyder Zee. He also became the bailiff of Gooiland and the lord of Weesp. It was one of the richest plums the stadholder could hand out and the recipient was twenty-six years old. From now on he lived there and set about making the castle a new center for the Amsterdam literary circle. Meanwhile there was a marriage in the Visscher house, when Gertruid, the middle daughter, and the least sparkling, or the most normal, became the wife of Nicolaes van Buyl, the son of rich Amsterdam brewers and, unlike the Visschers, a Protestant. The following year their affable and good-natured mother died, a bad loss for Roemer, and Anna had to take over as the hostess of the salon. New faces began to appear, and one of these was the newly married twenty-three-year-old Joost van den Vondel.

He was a quiet, agreeable young man who lived in the busy, fashionable, narrow Warmoes-straat. His father had been an Antwerper who left as a Protestant fugitive and settled first in Cologne, where Joost was born, and then finally at Amsterdam. He sold stockings for a living, a business which Joost had taken over since his death two years before. The young man had therefore a background considerably more humble than the gracious living atmosphere of the Visschers. He was, however, highly cultured and a very good classicist, which made him attractive to Roemer Visscher, who was known in the Eglantine as a "second Martial." Another new visitor was the brilliant scholar Daniel Heinsius from the university at Leyden. At thirty he had a European reputation, not least for three volumes of Latin poetry which he had produced in his early twenties. The girls were the great attraction. He fell for Anna. Other famous Latinists from Leyden came to the house, and Tesselschade was now beginning to enjoy her glory. It was a decorous scene, although the street outside was busy and round the corner were the sailors' taverns and the brothels, and

everywhere in the city money was being made, new houses and warehouses going up, and the old trades being carried on by the craftsmen on
the pavements. Soon patrician burghers would live in stately mansions
along the great crescent canals about to enclose the city so luxuriously, but
not yet. It was still the springtime, the marvelous springtime of the city. In
the Visscher house Anna and Tesselschade played and sang and talked to
the brilliant gentlemen. Everybody talked, everybody recited at the drop
of a hat — which, incidentally, gentlemen kept on indoors. They all wore
white ruffs and were dressed in black.

5.

ONE DAY Gerbrand Adriaenszoon Bredero arrived. He was the new name
in the literary circle for 1611. His romantic play *Rodderick and Alphonsus*
had just been performed. He was twenty-six, and compared to the Latinists of Leyden or to someone like Hooft, who was now settling in his castle
with a wife, Christina van Erp, he was uneducated. Unlike the rest of
them he had no Latin and Greek. He had started out as a painter — a
trade which was rapidly becoming the glory of the new country, filling the
houses of the poor as well as the rich with pictures that colored and lit up
the gloomy clothes of their owners. Bredero remained a painter in his
outlook. He saw people and he saw things; he was the one writer who was
fully possessed of the immense new consciousness of the material world
which inflamed the Dutch painters, and satisfied them all — except the
greatest one. He was attractive. He had an intense face with high cheek-
bones, he moved about and spoke quickly, his eyes were wide apart and
saw everything. He had none of the calm wisdom of Vondel and Hooft,
but plenty of wisdom — all his works were full of it, and full of some
curious quality of human agreeableness; Bredero was and remains forever
likable; though he was not the man to go with for a quiet evening out.

His father came from a peasant background, but he had been able to set
up a successful business as a shoemaker and Gerbrand Adriaenszoon had
been brought up in a comfortable house in the Nes, close to the Dam.
When he was seventeen they moved to the old canal street Oudezijds

Voorburgwal, a sign of prosperity. His father had the portrait of the "Great Beggar," Brederode, hung up as a house sign; and this was the origin of Gerbrand's name. His father liked art and the young man learned to paint from Francisco Badens, who came back from a four-year stay in Italy in 1604, and was known by the young artists as "the Italian painter"; nude figures with some historical or mythological background were his usual subjects, and Gerbrand did the same and with some success. He claimed that he made a "sweet profit" with his pencil. But poetry and then plays attracted him more and more, and provided a more substantial outlet for his energy. It was not that his poetry was good. Most of it was extremely bad, because most of it was humbly imitative — but it poured out of him. This energy, this prolific aspect, combined with a sort of sublime normality, is what makes him so compellingly attractive.

His first achievement was to be an ensign or standard bearer of the Militia — in which his father was an officer. It meant that he was accepted as a good type, a desirable young officer, and he was pleased about it. He drilled with them, attended the fencing school, and on parade there he was marching along, Gerbrand Adriaenszoon Bredero, with ostrich feathers in his wide-brimmed hat, the green sash across the buff jerkin, high boots and wide breeches, rapier at his side, and of course the colors held high. He liked that, just as he liked all the sports — *kaatsen,* a sort of tennis with a hard leather ball — rather dangerous for passers-by, though there were courts built for it; and *kolf,* a form of hockey played on land or on the ice. He skated, of course, and took girl friends for sleigh rides and had other rather different girl friends in the taverns; he knew the taverns as enthusiastically as he knew the tennis courts. Gerbrand Adriaenszoon did it all, and painted his pictures and wrote his poems. And apart from being energetic, in this genius-for-life way, he was also, it is needless to say, highly mercurial. From hour to hour he was up in heaven or down in the mud. He was an entirely open person. He had no secrets. If he liked you he told you so.

"My dear Charles," he wrote to a young man of his own age, in March 1611, "you are the friend of my heart . . . ever since knowing you my heart, my senses, my thoughts, all my powers have been determined to love you to the last gasp of my life . . . perhaps I shouldn't admire you so much — do you think it indecent? Oh, no, for as Bias, the philosopher and prince of Priene says: it is not forbidden to prize a man for his virtues. . . ."

[94]

On he wrote, with more and more quotations about friendship, from the Bible and from classical writers; as Periander of Corinth says, as Pythicus says, as Cleobulus says, Marcus Aurelius, Plautus, Seneca. Gerbrand was somehow like Gatsby, working away at his self-improvement like a terrier, marvelously determined now that he was becoming a writer to keep his end up among the Rhetoricians. It was the year that they put on his first play. It was based on a chapter from one of the Spanish novels of chivalry (the four books of Amadís de Gaula) which had been the favorite reading of the Netherlands nobility during the sixteenth century — William of Orange himself was an admiring reader. They were translated into French and then into Dutch. The prosperous burghers became keen. They were used to princes and princesses in their old medieval books, but these knights and their beautiful and glamorous ladies, though living in the imagined world of chivalry, were all behaving and talking with what seemed to be the most enviably sophisticated manners. Gerbrand, the romantic, ate it up. Three of his plays were taken from the same novel, *Palmerijn van Olivje*, and the first was about two chivalrous knights, Don Rodderick and Don Alphonsus, who were both in love with the beautiful and gracious Lady Elisabeth at the court of Ferdinand and Isabella. Elisabeth was captured by pirates and at the end of act five all was death and tragedy. There were two small parts for a servant and maid who produced some irrelevant comic relief in low-class language — which was Gerbrand's unforced, original writing, unlike the imitative grandiose stuff of the tragedy.

But all went well with the Old Chamber audience and the next year, 1612, he wrote his second play, *Griane* — based on other chapters from the Amadís novel. It was about a noble foundling left in the care of peasants and a princess forced to marry the wrong prince. This time the comic relief was still more successful. His real talent was bursting out quite naturally, as if he were unaware of it himself. The play has some similarities with Shakespeare's *The Winter's Tale* which had been produced the year before and was probably seen by Gerbrand when the English players came to Amsterdam earlier in 1612 (though *The Winter's Tale* was not based on the same source). Anyhow he overwrote and hammed to his heart's content with his emperors and queens and knights and ladies, often allowing a down-to-earth line from the Amsterdam streets to slip into the noble air by mistake. But he made no mistakes at all with the peasant farmer and his wife, and let the former bring out the motto which the author claimed to be his own on which the play was based. "*'t Kan ver-keeren.*" *Things can change.* A splendid motto, incidentally, and he explained it in his own note on the story of the play — "showing clearly how all temporal things are subject to change, so that a man must never let himself be too certain, never be too puffed up when things are going well, nor too downcast when they're not — but must always remember . . . things *can* change." And he was so delighted with this motto that from now on, except when he was being formal or writing to exalted persons, he always used it after his name as a sort of trademark. *Griane* was an advance on the first play. He used his peasants to make contact with the audience right away: "You lot, you ought to be ashamed of yourselves, spitting and dribbling and smoking — this air's so stifling people are almost cooking in it — you're no benefit to us with your coughing and your stinks — go to a tobacco house if you want to smoke and drink. . . ." How they all laughed, on that Sunday, the day before *kermis*, in 1612. Then at the end, when the royal servant told the farmer that as a reward for looking after the infant prince, "The Emperor makes you one of his greatest Lords," the old farmer cried out jubilantly, "Well, would you believe it? Then things *can* change!"

Gerbrand Adriaenszoon was encouraged now to expand his comedy production and he wrote some short playlets which he called farces — *Kluchten*. The first was the *Farce of the Cow*, which was put on at the Old Chamber, also in 1612. It was about a smooth-talking trickster who swindled a peasant farmer by selling him back his own cow — the idea, as usual, was taken from a medieval story, but everything else was his, the dialogue, the freshness, the observation, the picture of life — and incidentally the cow-thief, changing the conversation when the poor farmer is getting suspicious, gives us a view from the country outside Amsterdam: "How this dike winds and turns and what a lot of boats there are — all these young sparks putting out in their yachts! But how charming the city looks, with all the new houses — I hear all this land is being cut into dikes and sluices — it's wonderful, isn't it? What a good view of the South Church [the Zuiderkerk, which at that moment was almost built] with its white stone towers — it's really an elegant piece of work! How all the glazed roofs and all the new buildings glitter and shimmer in the sunshine. . . ."

The two are walking alongside the Amstel. Last night the countryman sitting outside his simple rustic dwelling farther along the river, offered a

night's rest to the confidence man, who said he was on his way from Cologne to Amsterdam to do some business, and was too late to get into the
city. (The gates were closed every evening at half past nine.) The peasant
had talked about his wife's cooking and how people came out from the
city on holidays, and how gay it was then. He had promised to wake him
early.

"You'd better undress or you'll be too hot."

"Oh, no, people who sleep in their clothes are dressed nice and early in
the morning," said the confidence man, a view which was acceptable to a
good many in the audience.

Bredero was particularly good with his coarse character studies of low-
class women barmaids and tarts, and there is one in the next scene, Frisian
Gerty, the hostess of the Black Horse, who has her hands full repelling,
not too ardently, a late customer.

"Who's that?"

"It's me, Gerty, open up, darling, and draw me a beer."

"The clock says eleven, and we don't draw so late. It's night!"

"Sweetheart, open up, be nice, I'm on the guard, honestly, I've come to
get a pot of beer to take to the patrol. Let me in, you'll get paid. For
friendship's sake, open up — ah, that's it, good evening, love —"

"Is it, monkey?" she says, letting him in. "Here, now, stop messing
about. Oh, lord, what a rogue you are — *listen,* where do you think you
are? Keep your hands to yourself! Now, do you want beer or wine — or if
you don't want to drink, get out —"

"Hey, hey! Be reasonable, you were looking so friendly, it made me
think you were pretty —"

They bicker on until the sound of the two o'clock rattle — the night
patrol which, in the absence of alarm clocks, let any citizens who were
awake know the time.

Laughter in the Old Chamber, and on comes the confidence man out
walking alone in the night, followed by a theatrical cow. He tells the audience that the countryman had talked so much about his cow that it had
kept him awake, so he got up and made off with it — he'll just tie it up
safely in the grounds of this house — and hurry back to bed. . . .

Morning, and here the two are walking along beside the river, the trickster and the innocent victim, who talks in a good-natured bragging way
about the local characters, the young men who like having a fight, and
about his own love life.

"Me, I don't go for fighting, I like to do my fighting naked, I mean — it's a fact, Joosje, I've made many a kid over in the fields — get the girls happy and have a lovely fight and no umpire required. But take my brother, that's a different type. Show him a girl and he disappears. . . ."

The confidence man leaves him to go into the house where he left the stolen cow, pretending that he is going to get a bill paid. He comes out with the victim's own cow and says he was given it instead of the money. And our friend goes off to sell his own cow in return for a commission in the form of drinks at the Black Horse. Here the confidence man goes to wait for him and the attack on Frisian Gerty's virtue is resumed. Can we not hear the hilarity in that stifling Old Chamber? We can. With this sort of material Gerbrand Adriaenszoon's touch was exact and his position as a popular writer of farces was established.

Accordingly his social life flourished. Having reached the Visscher Circle he became a regular visitor to the house on the Engelsekaai, and what happened then was inevitable. He fell madly in love with Tessel-schade. It was equally inevitable that the ending would be disastrous for him. In that happy haze of culture and high life, certain aspects were apt to be clouded over, such as that rich burghers tended to marry rich burgh-ers, that liberal hosts to fiery and impecunious young playwrights were not necessarily enthusiastic fathers-in-law of the same. In addition the Vis-schers remained Catholics and Bredero was a Protestant. So he was lost before he began, but pressed his suit with all his natural fiery passion, accompanying it with hundreds of poems and dedications; and to start with the lovely Tesselschade was encouraging. She adored him, but after all, almost everybody who came to the house was half in love with her.

6.

TWO MORE NEW NAMES. There was a seventeen-year-old English boy, Jan Starter, about to become a charming lyric poet — his parents had brought him over when they escaped from James I's persecution of the puritan Brownist sect — one of the Separatist sects which had begun to settle in Amsterdam in the 1590's, among whom were some of the American

Founding Fathers (but these left Amsterdam for Leyden). And a physician, Dr. Samuel Coster, appeared on the scene. He was an energetic, managerial sort of man, a natural organizer and showman. He wrote some farces, knockabout, vulgar stuff, the sort of thing which had always done well on the Dam at *kermis* time, but he was keenest on the blood and thunder department, modeling himself on the goriest Elizabethan dramatists. Geniuses or not — and he was not — almost all these people had a share of one quality common to geniuses; they were extraordinarily prolific. Dramas and farces were poured out, and if a play was printed the dramatist thought nothing of adding a dozen poems, as well as long introductions — and there might be a few poems from friends as well — as there were, also, on any private occasion of note. At births and weddings the verses gushed away, like a cottage industry for the greeting-card business. And if, instead of plays or poetry, one wrote history, it was not considered abnormal to produce several volumes, each of which would be about eight hundred pages long, each page a double column and closely printed — and when you got to the last volume, you were able to include long panegyrics in verse from your friends. These were the end manifestations of the old Chambers of Rhetoric, which died out in the first decades of the new century, as the printing and publishing business took root.

But Bredero was still extremely honored to be received, in 1613, as a member of the Eglantine. He took the Brothers Blossoming in Love very seriously and he burned with enthusiasm for the Dutch language, in the spirit of Coornhert and Spieghel and, of course, Roemer Visscher. He sent the Eglantine a long letter attacking the bastardizing of the language with Latin, French, Spanish and Italian. He told the story of the wine cooper who would spit the wine through his teeth and say: *"Par dieu il est bon."* Someone who kept on hearing him do this asked him reproachfully if he knew what he was saying. "No," he said, "but the French always say it when they taste their wine." The cooper then heard that he was swearing by the Almighty that the wine was good and, shocked, he said, "Forgive me, Lord, I've been trying to put on style in my ignorance. . . ." Bredero's tone sounds vaguely like that of a Chinese Red Guard chiding someone caught with bourgeois feelings. The same thing was happening daily, he wrote on, among supposedly learned merchants, above all in the windy speeches of puffed-up lawyers, among young doctors — "Wake up, Netherlanders!" the new member cried. He was very earnest.

But it was his touch in rough comedy that made him wonderful, his eye for reality and the kindness that shone through — while his private life went on not giving him satisfaction, always cheating him of what or whom he wanted, for he was always the impetuous, romantic young man aiming for the impossible. Tesselschade was only one example. There was a widow he fell for. "I beg and pray that Almighty God gives you pleasure in reading what follows. . . . God, who knows everything and stirs men's hearts after His own will, knows that I love you deeply and sincerely, and have loved you since shortly after the death of your saintly husband — but opportunity and courage have been lacking, I have been keeping it secretly in my heart and thinking how wonderful you are and how unworthy I am. . . ."

Not long after he was writing her another letter.

"Perhaps it puzzles you that I should be so sparing and reserved in writing —" (what remarkable delusions people can have) "— and yet be so expansive and reckless in life, or why I should write so wisely and talk like a fool. Respected and sagacious lady, think of a calf bursting out of its pen on to the fresh green grass and how it jumps and springs about. It's just the same with me, for most of the time I'm a hermit in an isolated hermitage . . . my respect for my parents makes me avoid all frivolity at home, but when I come to Haarlem for a good time I'm so bursting out that I get stirred up and disagreeable, which does me harm in fact as I know when I think about it. But there you are, careless youth never thinks about the end. I beg you, treat my great follies with your usual wisdom, and remember, oh child of Adam, that we are all children, who daily eat and taste the forbidden fruit . . ."

Poor Gerbrand. But his unrestrained nights out gave him better background than the cultured talk at the Visschers, and the sort of rough humor that the audiences loved — as when he had a servant comment, confidentially, on a prince who has failed a test to prove his moral purity, "It's clear you've pissed out of the pot. . . ." He wrote a little masterpiece of bawdy humor, the *Farce of the Miller*. The monstrously earthy Slim Pete, the miller, is accosted by a respectable young wife from the town who wants a night's shelter because (the gate being shut as usual) she is too late to get home. The miller's wife agrees willingly and for a while there is an almost Harold Pinterish scene as Pete finds himself highly attracted to the guest and determines, as we might put it, to know her carnally before the night is out. It ends in farce with the two women changing clothes and tricking him — and his servant, whom he invites to join in the fun and games — into mistaking the target. This farce, like the *Farce of the Cow,* was to be popular for years.

Vondel, his quieter contemporary, had also had his first success — with *The Pasha,* a drama about the freeing of the children of Israel from Egypt, which was produced by the rival exiled Brabant chamber, the White Lavender Blossom. Vondel, the greatest Dutch poet, and their nearest equivalent to Shakespeare and Milton, was above all a good man. His face was kind, his outlook serious and benevolent. He never had any money and he never wanted any, he had no pride, no conceit, only an absolute determination to be and to write what he liked. He was already married and lived a calm, sober life. He had none of the gay Bredero's wildness nor any of his genius for the comedy of the streets — his dramatic works have the ponderous and noble rhythms of a Corneille (who would soon be a contemporary playwright); they appeal to the sense of beauty but they don't touch the human comedy very intimately.

Vondel had arrived, Bredero had arrived. The elegant Hooft came out with a historical play set in his own castle at Muiden, which he was busy turning into a comfortable and attractive place in which to entertain his friends. The "Muiden circle" would take over as the principal literary center from Roemer Visscher's house, as this had taken over from Spieghel's. The latter had now died in Alkmaar and Roemer Visscher decided to have his old friend's works and his own printed. Belles lettres was their field and the two books went down well. These quiet events were taking place while the country was becoming more and more gripped by a theological controversy. Amsterdam was fortunately a little less affected by it than elsewhere, or the literary circle might have been more worried; for they were certainly all on one side, and it was not the side which in due course the Amsterdam regents, led by Reynier Pauw, were going to back.

The quarrel had begun at Leyden between two professors — Gomarus, the strict Calvinist (they were all Latinists, wrote in Latin, and were usually known by Latin names) and Arminius, whose views on predestination, election and grace, and other vital Calvinist interests were more moderate. In 1610 the Arminians had drawn up a petition, the *Remonstratie,* defining their points of difference. The Gomarists promptly produced one of their own, and the two parties became known as Remonstrants and Counter-Remonstrants. Every week the row thundered out from the pulpits. People in general took religion seriously; many ships' companies, for example, were strongly Protestant — as the Sea Beggars certainly had been — and did not at all share the attitude of Prince Maurice at The Hague who laconically asked if predestination, that highly important part of the Calvinist creed, were red or green. It was all one to the prince until his political interests suddenly made him feel more strongly. Meanwhile Amsterdam remained tolerant of its sects and subsects — as long as you belonged to a church, you were all right, though you might not be able to worship in public. But everybody was interested in theology. Down at the Beguinhof, that peaceful courtyard off the Kalverstraat, the small chapel of the sisters had been given by the city for the use of the English Reformed Church, within the body of the Dutch. It was perfectly all right for Ainsworth, the Separatist preacher, to produce a pamphlet, "An Arrow against Idolatrie, taken out of the Quiver of the Lord," which attempted to prove the minister, the Reverend Paget, an idolator. That congregation was rather humdrum — one or two merchants but mostly small tradesmen and craftsmen — but equally, over in the privileged house on the English Quay, the Visschers had no need to conceal the fact that they were Catholics. They could still, though conscious of the Remonstrant controversy, stay primarily interested in literature.

In *Lucelle* Bredero found a French play to adapt in which he could see himself as the clerk Ascagnes who marries secretly the Princess Lucelle. Lucelle, of course, was Tesselschade, to whom he dedicated it. "As to whether it succeeds I leave that to those whose minds are pure and rich in judgment and to those who are least full of conceit and arrogance —" — it was a sign of success that there were now constant allusions to envious enemies. "Your name," he said, "will be a protection and shield against the arrows of the bitter slanderers." Tesselschade had seen the play and had wept, a sight that transported the author to ecstasy. Unfortunately for poor Gerbrand he did not wake up like Ascagnes and find himself really a Polish prince, and socially okay; in the reality of Amsterdam he was accepted as a playwright and poet, but not as a prince-consort — he was welcomed and even cherished in the Visscher and Muiden circles, but still as an outsider. He was still Gatsby.

But his writing was beginning to touch the heights. In the greedy Lecker-Beetje in *Lucelle*, who never stops talking about food and drink, he produced a comic character of Rabelaisian size. He had set out to write a romance, representing his heartfelt desires and hopes, but he had to give in to the power of his own genius and let the minor character dominate, even giving him the last scene. It was as if Bredero finally recognized the nature of his talent. *Lucelle* was the bridge between the farces and the two great comedies by which he lives and always will live.

7.

THE FIRST was *The Moor,* performed before the Old Chamber in 1615. It was based on a French translation of Terence's *Eunuch* (produced in Rome about 160 B.C.). Bredero found it an immensely attractive challenge, in the midst of all his classically educated patrician friends, to see what he could do with a classical work. Later, when it came to be printed, he wrote a heavily ironical foreword, entitled *An Address to Those Learned in Latin.* "Most respected and honored masters of the well-known Latin language, here — if you please — you observe a simple Amstelredammer, with just a little kindergarten French stuffed into his head, having the colossal nerve and impertinence to take Terence — whom you all so admire — into his own hands and to force this most pure Latinist to prattle and babble not just in Dutch but in what is thoroughly despised by all neighboring cities — Amsterdamish."

In a separate piece about the plot, he explained that although the comedy had been written hundreds of years before by the witty Carthaginian, under the title *The Eunuch,* he had taken the liberty of changing the person of the title into a Moor, since most people nowadays were unfamiliar with eunuchs. "At the time when Spanish haughtiness was most humiliating the lowly Netherlands," our friend wrote on, "Katrijntje, a young girl from The Hague, was taken by a Spaniard to Spain, where she was entrusted to the mother of Moyaaltje (not the chastest of girls). . . ." And so on. The plot involves Moyaaltje's sea-captain lover accidentally coming across Katrijntje, lost and in danger of being sold into slavery, bringing her to Amsterdam to be Moyaaltje's maid, but refusing to deliver her until his mistress has got rid of her other lover, a young gentleman of Amsterdam, who agrees to stay away for a day or two and to send over a Moorish girl to look after Katrijntje — a conversation which is overheard by his brother, who has seen and fallen for Katrijntje and so what is more natural than that he should enter Moyaaltje's house dressed as the Moorish girl? It was a fine plot for a Mozartian opera and it was also rather too much, it must be admitted, for Gerbrand Adriaenszoon's powers of construction. *The Moor* is not a well-built play, to put it mildly. But where genius showed was in the sudden interludes in the action when a character takes off on his own and describes a stroll through the Amsterdam markets, or a grizzled midwife conjures up the old days, or in the description of young men on the Dam discussing what to do with the next ten minutes, or the conversational battle of wits between the hero's father's agent and Kackerlack, the sponger — and for the Old Chamber's audience it was all a marvelous evocation of the colors and sounds of the city around them.

"The lessons to be learnt from the play," Bredero said, "can easily be grasped by a reasonable man — the idiotic folly of lovers, the foolish fawning and flattering of the crawling Kackerlack, the worthless love of immoral women, who are under no circumstances to be trusted. . . ."

The text was printed in 1617 and reprinted again and again throughout the century — 1621, 1622, 1633, 1638, 1644, 1646, 1662, 1663, 1678. In 1694 Casparus Commelin, the Regent of the Oudezijds Almshouse, wrote a *Description of the City of Amsterdam* and said about the play, "Beyond all doubt he managed to do for the spectators and audiences of Amsterdam what Terence in Latin had done for them in Rome. There are old people today who testify that whenever they see the play or hear it read, they at once feel fifty years younger and in the Fish Hall or the poultry and fish market, hearing the shouts of the old sales women and being enticed to buy because of the prices. . . ." Incidentally, the word-production industry was still strong at the end of the century — Mr. Commelin's note about *The Moort* came in Part Two of his book, *page 863*. (The pale author in the autumn of the twentieth century can only bow respectfully.)

With *The Moor* Bredero was really established on the Amsterdam scene and the next year, 1616, his works began to be published by Cornelis Lodewijcksz van der Plasse, "Bookseller on the Corner of the Exchange," starting with his first play, *Rodderick and Alphonsus*. It was a mark of arrival that he was able to dedicate it to one of the great celebrities of the Republic — and of Europe — Hugo Grotius. "Oh, ornament of the Netherlanders!" Gerbrand wrote, no doubt using restraint. And he was able to sign it, "Your humble Servant and Friend." He was an opportunist and somewhat naïve pusher of himself — he had had to be — and when he met Grotius he at once wrote to his other grand acquaintance, the Governor of Muiden: ". . . on Sunday and Monday at the wedding . . . I had the pleasure of seeing and also of talking quite freely with the learned and very respected Grotius, the Pensionary of Rotterdam. While on another subject we came to speak of you, Sir, and this most agreeable man asked me after your health and well-being, and I answered him to the best of my knowledge. I also said that Muiden was not far from Amsterdam and that if he pleased we could come to see you together; the idea seemed to appeal to him and he did not turn it down. If I have gone too far, forgive me (for I know I have done you an agreeable service) and let me know if I am to carry on and bring him over, or let it drop and remain in Amsterdam, from where with heartiest greetings, my lord, I am . . . Your willing and devoted Servant, G. A. Bredero."

Thus Gerbrand, gently making his number with the great. For Grotius himself famous and dramatic moments were approaching. The great religious debate was now on the boil, turning into a battle between Prince Maurice, the power of the state and strict Calvinism on one side and the veteran statesman Oldenbaarneveldt, moderate thought and the independence of the provinces (especially Holland) on the other. Amsterdam's councillors under Reynier Pauw backed the prince and went against the rest of Holland. But for the Visscher circle there was a different excitement — an absolute fissure in the Eglantine between the old-fashioned members and themselves. As a result the energetic and ambitious Coster led the break away and built a wooden theater, the First Dutch Academy, on some land leased by the city council on the Keizersgracht. It was known as Coster's Academy, which was able to produce Bredero's new play, the second of his great comedies, *The Spanish Brabanter.*

He wrote it at the beginning of the year, using as his base the Spanish novel *Lazarillo de Tormes* by Mendoza. It is a marvelous play, like *The Moor* with hardly any construction, and unlike *The Moor* with hardly any plot — in fact some of *The Moor,* the stroll through the markets, for example, would have been rather better placed in it. But who cares? The scenes, the characters, the atmosphere are what matters. The idea itself was superb. The Spanish novel was about a young beggar servant and his proud, boastful, but poverty-stricken master. Bredero turned them round in importance, and made the knight the main character and the servant the feed — and at the same time made the place Amsterdam and turned the

COURTESY OF THE AMSTERDAM CITY ARCHIVES

't kan verkeeren

Gerbrand Adriaensz Brederode Amsteldammer
is gheboren in 't Jaer 1585, den 16.en Maert,
gesturven den 23.en Aug.ti des Jaers 1618, op d'uer
zyns gheboorte, tusschen 9.en 10.uren 's Voormiddaghs.

Bredero

knight, Jerolimo, from a Spaniard into a Brabanter. The servant, though
for some reason Bredero said he came from Emden, was a perfect type of
Amsterdam layabout youth.

The change to a proud but bankrupt Brabanter was highly amusing and
suitable to an Amsterdam audience. This was indeed a well-known sort of
exile — among, of course, the vast number of the rich and productive ones
who had contributed so much to revolutionizing the city's position. But
the southerners from Brabant and Flanders had for so long been the
richer, the more cultured, the more fashionable of the Netherlanders, and
the northerners in Holland for so long had felt slightly provincial. So
when, inevitably, Brabanters arrived without money or anything but the
old air of effortless superiority they were a great source of scorn, irritation
and derision to the honest native Amsterdamers. All that happens in the
play is that Jerolimo appears, picks up the servant, Robbeknol, discusses
his allegedly splendid past, talks royally to a couple of tarts who laugh him
off when they find he is all wind and no cash, and does a bunk in the night
leaving creditors behind. But the atmosphere of Amsterdam is everything,
as in *The Moor* — and one contributory factor to this, incidentally, is the
importance in the play of the word "bankruptcy"; this could only be in a
city that was above all a bourgeois place, rapidly becoming, in fact, the
world's bourgeois capital.

With this brilliant, loose, ambling, lively comedy Bredero reached his
height. Only one more year remained for him. It seems likely that he
would have written greater comedies; that was certainly his intention.
Meanwhile the usual despair in his private life, the usual unsuccessful love
for a princess was going on and he was busy with a new play expressing it,
the pastoral *Angeniet* — and then gave it up, unfinished, when his mood
changed. For his last love had appeared, Magdalena Stockmans. She was
a nineteen-year-old Dordrecht girl, who was in Amsterdam from September that year — she had come for her sister's marriage. Poor Gerbrand!
The usual thing happened. That winter there also arrived in Amsterdam a
Mr. van der Voort, an Antwerper from Naples, about Gerbrand's age and
no doubt with a good deal more to offer — in any case he was the cause of
the usual agony.

The unhappy lover wrote to her at the end of December. "Downcast,
Gerbrand greets his gay, clever and beloved M. S. with a broken heart and
wishes her, in the Lord, all happiness and blessings of soul and body, and
a good and agreeable New Year. Fire cannot exist without heat and I

cannot exist without dreaming of you day and night. . . ." On Monday evening he had been to a party and they insisted on him staying to eat, which evidently meant that he missed seeing her, and if God pleased he would excuse himself to her at greater length by word of mouth — but meanwhile on the Tuesday morning he had to confess that he was persuaded to go off to Haarlem to a funeral — and that was more trouble, for he forgot to tell his parents, who consequently feared an accident — and, of course, Bredero being Bredero, there had been an accident. "Furthermore I must (unwillingly) tell you that I am sick and not in good health, because I went through the ice with my sledge and sat up to my waist in the water — so you can imagine I caught a fearful chill and must keep to my room — where my unspeakable vexation is that I am banned from your charming society. And moreover my terrible jealousy of the dark Brabanter troubles me, I am terrified of losing what little hope I have, so my hours seem to be days, and the days years and the nights centuries. So dearest love, for humanity's sake, or if your maidenly breast is pierced with loving rays of compassion, or if you have ever known what it is to be forced to choose one before all others to love, then let your lover not pine away hopeless, but comfort him with the kindly favor of a little letter, so that in life or in death I shall remain your always loyal servant and slave — G. A. Bredero."

Poor Gerbrand. No doubt he was too much to take. The tragicomic aspect seems inevitable. He was doomed to be thwarted in this as in all his love affairs — upon which his usual procedure was to go off to the stews for comfort, to drink and go wild, and then to find the cure worse than the disease, and then to write poems of depression and shame, asking God for strength, bitterly despising himself. "Venus and the drinking cup, or even the devil, have led me often to a head full of wind and wine, a heart full of suffering and pain, a body full of distempers. . . ." But then he would forget it all and remember: it can change. However, his body was sick. He cheerfully helped prepare *The Spanish Brabanter* for publication, with a dedication to the Swedish ambassador and a letter and a poem to the reader. The poem was written on June 6, and twelve days later Magdalena Stockmans was married to Van der Voort. She went off to live with him at Naples. But Gerbrand's days were almost gone. He died in August in the arms of his devoted parents, aged thirty-three, in the house on Oudezijds Voorburgwal.

They had all been fond of him. Dozens of poems praised him. Tessel-

Tesselschade

Vondel

COURTESY OF THE AMSTERDAM CITY ARCHIVES

COURTESY OF THE AMSTERDAM CITY ARCHIVES

schade, still unmarried, felt grief. Cornelis van der Plasse began a small industry issuing his plays and also collections of his poems, which went on profitably for years. In doing so the bookseller gave Gerbrand his perfect memorial, for he printed on the title pages of the two collections of poetry:

G. A. Bredero, Amsterdammer.

8.

A FEW WEEKS after Bredero's death the Amsterdam rhetoricians put on a show which was not to the taste of the Visscher circle. Prince Maurice was visiting the city and the show was in his honor, a series of allegorical mimes in the old manner, processions of chariots, all heavily symbolical and representing the homage of the provinces. He was on a whistle-stop, strong-arm political tour of the country after having brought off the fall and the arrest of the statesman Oldenbaarneveldt, which meant the defeat of the moderate Remonstrant side in the great religious controversy.

The strict Calvinist side, backed by the Amsterdam regents under the burgomaster, Reynier Pauw, had won. In the previous year they had refused to raise levies demanded by the States of Holland (which were to back Oldenbaarneveldt's attempt to defend the independence of the provinces in religious matters). But many towns had agreed, and so had Utrecht, which allied itself with Holland in the matter. Now in summer 1618, the prince had actually marched on Utrecht to demand the disbandment of its force. The great Hugo Grotius got there before him to stiffen their resistance. While the commanding officer of the Utrecht force was wavering and hesitating news came that Amsterdam was also sending a force on the prince's side. On this the colonel saw that resistance was hopeless, and the next day the prince entered the city, while Grotius and his friends hurriedly departed. Now they, like their leader, had been arrested and the prince was going round the towns, bulldozing the councils into acquiescence.

In Amsterdam, of course, this was not necessary and the visit could be all celebration. But Hooft's splendid father, who had lost power years before, was not afraid to get up in the council chamber and face the prince with strong, liberal, reasoned criticism of his policy. He was greatly respected, but no one was taking notice of him anymore. The prince told him kindly, "Dear father, it has to be like this. The country's need and service demands it."

Reynier Pauw took the opportunity of having seven enemy council members replaced by reliable relations and friends. Three months later the West India Company was launched by permission of The Hague, a project which Oldenbaarneveldt had opposed but which had been dear to the hearts of the Amsterdamers, thus showing once more that politics motivated by religion could also have a commercial aspect. Fortunes were made out of this (and among those besides Pauw who had a finger in it was Isaac le Maire, the "bear" operator in East Indian shares). For two years Reynier Pauw was at the height of power — in Amsterdam, at the side of the prince, and in the States of Holland.

But many of his supporters were very lukewarm on the hard Calvinist line, and when they had got what they wanted commercially Amsterdam's normal tolerance was reasserted — especially after the appalling treatment of Oldenbaarneveldt. The unfortunate elderly statesman, who had done more than anyone to preserve the Republic, and even to found it, was allowed no defense, not even books or writing material. Every incident of his long administration was mercilessly probed, as well as his private life. Reynier Pauw was one of the interrogators, the bullying bigot par excellence. Of the four distinguished prisoners one committed suicide (Ledenburg), two were sentenced to life imprisonment in Loevestein Castle (Hoogerbeets and Grotius, who two years later made a famous escape in a trunk supposedly full of books). But the old man had his head removed before the windows of the prince's residence at The Hague. William of Orange's widow, Louise de Coligny — whose carriage had been the first ever to appear in the streets of Amsterdam — was so appalled by her stepson's ruthlessness that she left to settle in France. Many others were unenthusiastic and Reynier Pauw now found the political atmosphere in his city distinctly cool. The first sign was a failure to get his son appointed as the Schout. He lost the support of everybody but the strictest Calvinists and the possibility of the church dictating affairs in Amsterdam was over. In February 1622 he failed to be elected burgomaster and that was the end of him politically.

Sir William Temple, an English ambassador, writing later in the century described the system operating at the Town Hall. "The Soveraign authority of the City of Amsterdam consists in the Decrees or Results of their Senate, which is composed of Six and thirty men. . . . When anyone of their number dyes, a new one is chosen by the rest of the Senate, without any intervention of the other Burghers. . . . By this Senate are chosen the chief Magistrates of the Town, which are the Burgomasters, and the Eschevins [*Schepenen* or sheriffs]. . . . The Eschevins are the Court of Justice . . . they are at Amsterdam nine in number; of which Seven are chosen annually; but two of the preceding year continue in Office. . . . The Burgomasters are chosen by most voices of all those Persons in the Senate, who have been either Burgomasters or Eschevins. . . . This office is a Charge of the greatest Trust, Authority and Dignity; and so much the greater, by not being of Profit or Advantage . . . the salary of a Burgomaster of Amsterdam is but five hundred Gilders a year. . . . They are upon all Publick Occasions waited on by men in Salary from the Town. . . . At other times, they appear in all places with the simplicity and modesty of other private Citizens. . . ."

It was all true, but the power and the opportunities were there, too, and they were beautiful. The power now gradually went to a combine of two great families, the Bickers and the De Graeffs and they kept close to it for years. The times were wonderful for astute and thrusting businessmen. Reynier Pauw, resigned to his exit from power, concentrated on making an immense fortune, surviving on the way a charge that he and his sons had diverted large quantities of the Zeeland butter and cheese output to the enemy. (For the truce was over and the war against Spain had begun again.) After Prince Maurice died and Pauw saw himself lampooned in a play by Vondel he made one more attempt to stir up Calvinist passion in politics. But the prince's successor, his brother Frederick Henry, was theologically liberal and stamped on the former burgomaster. He returned to business. So much was happening in this new and tiny and booming country. There was plenty for the Dam promenaders to talk about in the 1620's and to read about in the elementary newspapers or broadsheets that were becoming wildly popular, with their snob gossip from The Hague, the first printed advertisements, and news from the various campaigns.

They could talk about the winning of Java by Jan Koen, the Amboina incident in the Moluccas, where some Englishmen were executed, the Dutch treaty with Persia, the Dutch trade in Formosa, the Dutch trade with mysterious Japan and, who knows, the Dutch purchase of Manhattan

Island from the Indians for sixty guilders, surely the all-time real estate bargain. There were glamorous new names, San Salvador, Rio de Janeiro; there was Vice Admiral Piet Hein, hero of the Brazilian coast, burning and capturing Portuguese ships, storming islands, spiking guns and sending the booty home. There was the marvelous capture of the galleons of the Spanish treasure fleet off Cuba — the fleet which for years had been bringing the riches of Mexico and Peru home to Spain. This last episode brought vast profit, through the West India Company, to Cornelis Bicker. He was one of four brothers, sons of a rich merchant, who all made fortunes while becoming part of the new power structure in Amsterdam. Andries, the eldest, was in the spice trade from the East and had a monopoly of the Russian fur trade. Jacob was in grain in the Baltic. Jan, the youngest, sent ships to the Mediterranean and was also a shipbuilder — he is remembered today by the district Bickers Island, near the West Dock. Two of this formidable quartet were married into the De Graeff family — whose grandfather was William of Orange's friend — and so the combine began, encouraged in due course by more marriages. It was Andries Bicker's political function to lead Amsterdam's opposition to most of Prince Frederick Henry's military demands, especially because the prince was ambitious to recapture Antwerp — the last thing Amsterdam merchants wanted.

One of the outstanding Amsterdam success stories was Louis de Geer's. He was a perfect example of the way the city was able to profit from other people's needs and difficulties — as distant famines helped the grain market or the bookselling and printing business, crippled in Germany by the just-started Thirty Years War, was exploding delightfully in Amsterdam and Leyden as a result. De Geer's father had been a rich iron master at Liège and at the end of the last century had gone to Dordrecht, as a Protestant refugee, and set up in business there. On his father's death Louis de Geer moved to Amsterdam; and there in 1615 he set up as a merchant in all iron and copper goods, but particularly in the armaments business. He could not have been more ideally placed for it, not only because of his own background but because his wife was the sister of Elias Trip, who was the head of a very large ironware concern. The combination made them supreme. De Geer, whose talents were outstanding, was sent by the States-General to Sweden to negotiate the supply of iron and copper ore. During his stay there the Amsterdam merchant-industrialist became conscious of the immense reserves of ore that Sweden possessed and also of the fact that the mines lacked both capital and skilled workers.

His chance came a year later when the Swedish king wanted to raise a loan on the security of the copper mines for one of the earliest of his military excursions (which were to make Sweden a great power for several decades). Louis de Geer was a principal contributor and in return Gustavus Adolphus granted him a lease to a rich mining area. De Geer took his chance and went in with both hands, investing heavily. He imported iron workers from Liège and built factories and foundries. Already in the early 1620's he was not only exporting vast supplies of his own goods to his own warehouses at Amsterdam but satisfying the armament requirements of the Swedes. The young, brilliant and aggressive king now treated him as an intimate, and also as a quartermaster for his armies — he was even required to raise troops for him. In 1626 he became the acting manager of the royal copper mines and was given the rights of Swedish citizenship. His power and property in the country kept on increasing, he was able to loan immense sums to back the expeditionary forces, he was the king's confidant and financial adviser.

When Gustavus Adolphus was killed in 1632, De Geer's position was untouched. Oxenstjerna, the Swedish chancellor, who was now the most powerful man in the country — and in northern Europe — was equally friendly with him, and even invested his own money in a Swedish-Dutch company De Geer started for trading on the West African coast. The Dutchman became a Swedish noble and all his loans were repaid by the grant of the lands on which his mines and factories stood — as a result he became one of the greatest landowners in Sweden. And still his greatest moment was to come when during a war with Denmark, the Swedes were frustrated by the refusal of the Dutch government to honor an agreement to give them naval help. De Geer went ahead and supplied them with a navy on his own. Yet he remained through all this, first and foremost, an Amsterdam merchant with a large, highly decorated, orange brick house on the Keizersgracht. (It is still there — number 123.)

But more famous and more important for the city than any particular merchant were its two great institutions, the Exchange and the Bank of Amsterdam. There was a story of a Spanish plot to blow up the former in 1622. A young city orphan was supposed to have found a small boat full of gunpowder in the sluice which ran from the water of Rokin to the Damrak, under the Exchange and the Dam. He informed the Town Hall and in celebration annually, during every September *kermis*, children were allowed the run of the place. Normally it was open for business from twelve until two and for the two hours was packed out with merchants, brokers, clerks and spectators. There they were in their black hats and black breeches — something like old-fashioned golfer's plus fours — and black cloaks and black shoes. The brokers were mostly in the courtyard, unless it was raining, and the merchants set up in their various kingdoms along the arcades, the Russia merchants, the East India merchants, the Levant merchants, timber merchants, shipping merchants and so on, all in a proper Exchange atmosphere of masterly confusion.

When a deal was done the parties to the contract, payer and payee, were able to carry it through by a simple adjustment of their balances at the Bank of Amsterdam — the exchange or *wisselbank* below the Council Chamber in the Town Hall. One of the most famous admirers of this institution was Adam Smith, author of the eighteenth-century economics classic, *The Wealth of Nations.* "Before 1609," he wrote, "the great quantity of clipt and worn foreign coins, which the extensive trade of Amsterdam brought from all parts of Europe, reduced the value of its currency about nine percent below that of good money fresh from the mint. Such money no sooner appeared than it was melted down or carried away, as it always is in such circumstances. The merchants, with plenty of currency, could not always find a sufficient quantity of good money to pay their bills of exchange; and the value of those bills, in spite of several regulations which were made to prevent it, became in a great measure uncertain.

"In order to remedy these inconveniencies, a bank was established in 1609 under the guarantee of the city. This bank received both foreign coin, and the light and worn coin of the country at its real intrinsic value in the good standard money of the country, deducting only so much as was necessary for defraying the expense of coinage, and the other necessary expense of management. For the value which remained, after this small deduction was made, it gave a credit in its books. This credit was called bank money. . . ."

And from then on all bills of exchange drawn on or negotiated at Amsterdam had to be paid in it. Consequently every merchant had to keep an account at the bank. Apart from being superior to currency, bank money had other advantages, Adam Smith pointed out, and by doing so illustrated the sort of difficulties merchants had operated under before the Amsterdam era: for bank money was secure from fire, robbery and other accidents; the city of Amsterdam was bound for it — it could be paid away by a simple transfer, without the trouble of counting, or the risk of transporting it from one place to another.

Finally: "At Amsterdam . . . no point of faith is better established than that for every guilder, circulated as bank money, there is a correspondent guilder in gold or silver to be found in the treasure of the bank. . . . each new set of burgomasters visits the treasure, compares it with the books, receives it upon oath, and delivers it over, with the same awful solemnity, to the set which succeeds. . . ."

When he wrote, the system had lasted for a hundred and sixty-six years. (But it came to its end after the French Revolution had broken out.)

9.

ALTHOUGH the power of the church had been controlled, it still had a very large influence on the lives of most burghers. No one could belong to a guild or take city office without belonging to it. And there was great interference in private and even in business life. This did not worry the burgomasters, for they paid the ministers (and eventually later in the century controlled their appointment) who belonged to the assembly, or *classis*, which had authority over the churches, each of which had a consistory, of its minister and elders, with authority over church members. This authority leaned on people in multifarious ways. Attendance at church, a priority concern, might be checked by the minister going round the houses of his congregation and leaving little lead disks which they had to bring the following Sunday. Matrimonial troubles and scandals were dealt with very thoroughly. If a child was born rather too soon after marriage, the happy couple were liable to have this even announced publicly from the pulpit — which was a help, perhaps, in developing the national trait of unselfconsciousness. Or there was the case of Mr. Webster over in the affiliated English church at the Beguinhof, off the Kalverstraat.

A maid in his household had produced a bastard and he was accused of being the father. He was a well-to-do merchant in business between Amsterdam, Yarmouth and Norwich. There were a good many servants in this household, men and maids — though menservants as such were frowned upon in Amsterdam as a somewhat decadent luxury; in this case they were more likely to be young men doing a stint from England, or else apprentices or workers in the offices and warehouse which adjoined the house. (Mr. Webster dealt, amongst other things, in salt.) Mrs. Webster, whose name was Jannetien, was Dutch. This brought both the English and a Dutch consistory into the case and enables us to see that the Dutch were amazed that it was Mr. Webster who had all the details about all the members of his household — in an all-Dutch Amsterdam family this would not have been the case; the wives had very few legal rights but their word was law in the household. But Jannetien was no archetypal Amsterdam housewife. It came out at the enquiry that it was her rather kinky pleasure to lie in bed and scatter sugar around on the floor of her bedroom, and watch the maids and young men scramble for it. And she took two maids off with her to live for three months in their country house. The girl in the case, Clara, had the duty of waiting up for her master to come home and the still more interesting duty of helping him to take off his doublet and hose. No wonder that it was disclosed to the consistory that Mrs. Webster had murmured her anxiety to one of the maids who accompanied her to the country (though with her sugar habits, one would have thought, the less she said the better). No wonder that a daily help, employed apparently in addition to the indoor staff, reported seeing Clara embraced by Mr. Webster on his way from the house backyard. No wonder also — thank God, thought Mr. Webster — yet another daily help reported seeing Clara slipping out of the young men's quarters.

But Webster, incidentally himself a former deacon, finally got out of it simply by swearing his innocence before the magistrates — and an oath to the Dutch was so serious a matter that they accepted what was sworn as the truth. Not to discredit Mr. Webster — for something that happened or did not happen four hundred and fifty years ago (not so long, really) — it's possible that an English merchant's attitude to an oath on a matter of sexual morality might well have been that it was the only convenient way out. And Jannetien is reported to have been urging him, "As you are innocent, why do you not swear?" Why not indeed, it would seem, he finally decided.

The consistory's powers against those they considered guilty ranged from, at worst, anathema, then excommunication, and for more humdrum matters suspension from participation in the Holy Supper or forced public acknowledgment of your sin, or being named from the pulpit. (No wonder the churches were packed.) Suspension, apart from whatever its effect might be spiritually on the victim, also meant that he could get no grant from any church charity fund, very important if he were poor, and in any case he could go nowhere else — for a demission certificate was required to move to another congregation. And for the faithful there was the danger of dying while under suspension and possibly missing salvation as a result. Not everybody was worried by this, especially as the century wore on, but a great many were and it was a real weapon of discipline. Among those who suffered suspension (unless an arrangement with their creditors could be made) were fraudulent and involuntary bankrupts, and sometimes also their unfortunate wives. As Bredero had shown in *The Spanish Brabanter*, bankruptcy was a basic sin to Amsterdamers — though, as with other things, less so later in the century.

But the general moral behavior of the congregation was looked after with a very sharp eye. People were only too keen to report each other's misdemeanors. A public sin had to be confessed publicly, a private sin could be dealt with privately by a stern person-to-person talk, and if the accused didn't accept this lesser humiliation, it became public. Humiliation was really the great weapon. As for examples of sins, a woman seen to drink too much was reported, a woman who wasted good meat until it stank — she threw it into the canal *and* then shamelessly went off dancing — or someone known to have received charity who had been seen in a tavern, or a neighbor suspected of being a witch or a whore. Then there were complaints by servants against masters, and, more commonly, by masters against servants.

For it was one of the most important moral duties to work as hard as possible in the job God in His wisdom had allocated to you. What an asset strict Calvinism was in the rise of Amsterdam — no wonder employers backed the church. When profit and the right go together, it has always been an awesome combination. Neither servants nor wives could be beaten, or at least not very hard (a fact quite surprising to English members of the church). Servants and apprentices, however, usually got the worst of it. The consistory would also act as an arbiter in business disputes between members, and their enquiries about these as about all the other matters could be very far-reaching — if some woman accused her neighbor of having been a whore in the past, the consistory would spend months unraveling the details, if necessary sending someone all over the country or even abroad to check up. They were protective and paternal as well as disciplinarian. If a husband stayed away on business for too long, the consistory would go after him to ask why, not only with a prurient interest in what was going on, but to help keep the couple together. In marriage affairs there was a close linkage with the burgomasters and the council. Where adultery or fornication was involved, the matter had to be resolved, as with Mr. Webster, by swearing before magistrates — there was a department of matrimonial affairs in the council, and most of the careers of the patrician regents included a stint in it.

And so Calvinism firmly, humorlessly (if a deacon made even a semblance of a joke at a meeting, he was fined six stuivers on the spot) leaned on the citizens; and of course on the interiors of the churches, too, which remained bare of all the old ornamentation, without color, in most cases without music except for the bell ringers, who added tunefully to the noise of the city — although Sweelinck, the organist and composer, was able to stay on at the Old Church until his death in 1621; and on the architects, causing such curiosities as the empty niches for statues in de Keyser's Zuiderkerk (South Church) — the half-medieval, half-Renaissance building which the thief and the victim saw under construction from the banks of the Amstel in Bredero's *Farce of the Cow*. But the puritanism of church decoration was now showing an indirect result of sublime splendor, God working His will mysteriously as ever. Frustrated in their traditional direction the painters found another one and there took place in these two or three decades one of the most extraordinary upsurges of talent in history. What they painted were scenes of ordinary life, landscapes and numberless groups of civic worthies — all of it adding up to a marvelous picture of their nation, glowing, living, but devastatingly silent. (Only Bredero breaks that silence a little.) Painters of high quality seem to have been born in dozens approximately at the beginning of the century. Not all of them lived in Amsterdam, but certainly most of them worked there at some time. The greatest of them, who was to live in the city for most of the rest of his life, Rembrandt Harmens van Rijn, stayed for six months under the vigorous and romantic Peter Lastman in 1625. The Dutch Reformed Church could claim a certain accidental credit for all this.

10.

AT THE VISSCHERS' HOUSE on the Engelsekaai there had been developments. There was a new friend, the brilliant Constantyn Huyghens. This
glamorous young man, who once nearly killed himself trying to climb the
tower of Strasbourg Cathedral and who would live to be over ninety and
one of the great ornaments of the Republic, was brought up in the highest
circles of The Hague — his father was the Secretary of the Council of State
— educated in Italy, France and England and equipped with both literary tastes and talent. He was also a first-class Latinist and a painter. And a
gymnast. And a musician. In England he played the lute to James I, who
was far from averse to personable young men. He was also friendly with
John Donne.

The golden youth was naturally made welcome by Tesselschade and by
Hooft at Muiden. He was employed in diplomacy when he was hardly out
of his teens, and was at Venice when he heard the news of Roemer Visscher's death. He sent Tesselschade a long poem (so did everybody). A
period had ended. The clever sisters were on their own, conscious more
and more of time and death. They stayed with Hooft at Muiden, where
the medieval castle was now comfortable and elegant, surrounded by gardens and woods. Vondel also, leaving his house and business in Warmoes-
straat in the care of his wife, was a constant guest. Then Anna went off to
Zeeland, where she was made much of by the famous "Father Cats" — Jacob Cats, the middle-aged statesman and author of celebrated homespun
verses, whose books could be found in every seventeenth-century Dutch
home — one of them sold fifty thousand copies, which would be splendid
now, but was fantastic then. This was a slight break-up. It was not really
surprising that within two years both sisters had married. Both left Amsterdam and moved to the north, where Anna's literary interests began to
fade. But the lovely Tesselschade remained firmly in the Muiden circle,
though she would now have to travel from Alkmaar to visit it. After all the
adulation she had received, and would go on receiving, from besotted
playwrights, poets and professors, it was a little odd that she fell in love at

last, at thirty, with a middle-aged widower, a sailor by profession. He was called Krombalgh. Poems poured out from Amsterdam to celebrate the marriage.

Tesselschade at Alkmaar busied herself translating Tasso from Italian to Dutch. A year later at Muiden, Hooft's wife died, leaving him alone and miserable in his castle. (They had had four children, but none had survived.) It seems possible, for they were intimate friends, that if Tesselschade had not met Mr. Krombalgh she would most suitably have taken over the castle. But possibly not. There seems to have been something a little passionless in Tesselschade's friendships. The one she had with Vondel, for example, was intimate, lasting, deep — but in no way, the feeling comes, earthy. Though one would like to think of orgies at Muiden, there were none. Vondel was too honorable, Tesselschade too cold and Hooft, as a matter of fact, soon had his eye on somebody else. But one effect of Vondel's friendship with Tesselschade was to buttress, if not to cause, his attraction to Catholicism. He had not yet "gone over," but there were hints in his work. As yet he had made no great mark. He had his stocking business to keep him going, and would always need it — as long as it lasted. But he was a late developer, as well as an intelligent, kindhearted and extremely honorable man, and such a person is unlikely to find life entirely easy. In any case he had to wait until he was thirty-eight, and Prince Maurice had died, before his play *Palamedes* was produced — in which the nauseating tragedy of the old statesman Oldenbaarneveldt was shown up, thinly disguised by the classical characters, one of whom was clearly Reynier Pauw. There was an immediate uproar. The Calvinists would have had Vondel hanged from a Town Hall window — like an ordinary rioter or criminal — but when he was brought before the civic authorities, they, full of Amsterdam's wisdom, merely fined him three hundred guilders. His real danger had been the attempts to make him face a charge of treachery at The Hague. That it was all dealt with coolly and summarily at Amsterdam was due especially to the influence of Harmen van der Pol, who spent most of his life in high offices at the Town Hall. He was born in 1559 and served in a typical patrician career from 1593 on as Commissioner of Marriage Affairs, as Magistrate, as Master of Orphans, as Commissioner of Minor Offenses. He had been out in the cold since the Oldenbaarneveldt affair and was now back in the warm after Prince Maurice's death. Vondel was also looked after, during this crisis, by a rich family, called Baeck, with whom he was very friendly. (Jacob Baeck, a lawyer, is buried in the Nieuwe Kerk). He was able to use their country house, Scheybeeck, as a hiding place.

When it was all over, and the fine paid, Vondel all at once had become famous. His name was suddenly known everywhere in the country; he was the hero of all moderate opinion. He felt free to write satirically about the Calvinists and did so. He became associated with the magnificent, but still exiled, Grotius. At this time the dazzling Huyghens — who had been knighted when he was twenty-six by James I — became Secretary to the new prince, Frederick Henry. He married Susanna van Baerle, who was a beauty — it was she on whom the widower Hooft had had his eye. He married Leonora Hellemans instead. The Muiden circle retained its prestige. It always seems vaguely reminiscent of the Bloomsbury of Lytton Strachey and Virginia Woolf, open but inbred, and with the same sort of deep relationships between the members, the same sort of real accomplishment, and the same eye for talent. It was this last which made Huyghens commission a portrait of himself before his marriage from a young Leyden painter, Jan Lievens.

The portrait shows him looking mildly surprised or skeptical, dressed in the normal puritan black, with a white collar and a highly unsuitable hat. Years later the painter was said to be extremely conceited, and Huyghens' expression is certainly that of someone listening to a young man talking too much. In any case he liked the picture and a year or two later he was sufficiently interested to visit Lievens in Leyden and also the fellow painter with whom he shared a studio. They were both very young, a little over twenty. The partner, who already had a slight if local reputation, was Rembrandt.

He was, like Lievens, of humble, but not absolutely humble, background. He was an extraordinary mixture of toughness and refinement. Both of them fascinated and no doubt were fascinated by their patrician visitor. Lievens was slim and good-looking, but Rembrandt was stocky and pale, rather plump, with a big coarse face not so much peasantlike as earthy. The fastidious Huyghens was impressed by them both and he gave them some advice which came naturally from an all-round Renaissance man, firstly that they should improve their health by taking some exercise and secondly that they should go to Italy — a study of the Raphaels and Michelangelos would bring out all their potential, and he did not think too much of their artistic education. The young men told him, more or less, what he could do with his advice. As far as Italy was concerned, they hadn't the time. Huyghens was not upset and wrote about them, praising Lievens' inventiveness and his bold choice of subject and Rembrandt's discernment and his vigorous treatment of human emotion — a very creditable summing up, it must be conceded. Huyghens was especially sold on a Rembrandt biblical picture, *Judas Returning the Thirty Pieces of Silver*.

Lievens' father was an embroiderer, Rembrandt was the fourth son of a miller. His parents looked after him well; he was sent to the Latin school and at fourteen enrolled at Leyden University. But his real talent was soon so evident that it was pointless to go on with the law and theology, and they apprenticed him to a local painter, Jacob van Swanenburg, who taught him the basic tricks of the trade. Then he had his six months, when he was about nineteen, with Pieter Lastman in Amsterdam, who had also taught Lievens — which had probably brought the two together in Leyden. Lastman was a considerable artist. Rembrandt had told Constantyn Huyghens that he had no time to go to Italy, but he was very much aware of Italy. Swanenburg had been there and had an Italian wife. Lastman had been to Rome where he was influenced by the German Elsheimer and Caravaggio — which led to a great emphasis on chiaroscuro, the treatment of light and shade. Lastman gave this to Rembrandt and also a taste for historical and biblical subjects.

After his months in Amsterdam Rembrandt returned to his home town and his parents' house, where he set up a studio. Lievens, an ex-pupil of the same master, worked with him. They did well at once and worked ferociously. Lievens had his commission from Huyghens. Rembrandt was mentioned by a Utrecht lawyer, van Buchell, who was made aware on a visit to Leyden of "the miller's son's" reputation. He was twenty-two and coming into possession of his marvelous talent. He was an absolute master of his craft and instinctively he was universal in feeling. There was no need for him to go anywhere; he saw the universe in everything and everyone around him. His delight in the old, his reverence for them, his incredibly subtle understanding of them — at twenty-two, at twenty-three — were part of this. He knew that age and decay and loss and bewilderment were all in the human comedy, and did not run away from it and hide from it in fear, like so many of the sad young — like so many of the sad young in today's Amsterdam — but accepted it and celebrated it, in the scenes and faces of his own family, and in his own face which he studied and reproduced again and again, with a sublime lack of vanity, with an immense objective interest in what it meant to be a man. There was nothing morbid about it, it was simply: here it is, this is how it is. And nothing depressing either; he had an almost theatrical delight in exotic costume and loved to paint his family models and himself dressed up. He was always a child-man in the grand Churchillian style.

Nothing went wrong for him in the early years. He already had pupils, his reputation advanced, and probably as a result of Huyghens' visit to Leyden an English earl visiting the stadholder at The Hague took back two Rembrandts, a self-portrait and a portrait of his mother, for Charles I. Everything now pointed in one direction, to Amsterdam. Not only were the newly rich Amsterdamers the best possible customers of the moment, but there were two other attractions — the colorful and cosmopolitan nature of the city, which made it an ideal background for Rembrandt, and the fact that it was now the center of the European art trade. All the important sales took place there, even the Italian collections. It justified still more his telling Huyghens that there was no need to go to Italy. To be in Amsterdam was to see everything. He made the move in 1631, when he was twenty-five, and stayed with an art dealer, Henrik van Uylenburgh, who had been acting for him and selling his work, in St. Antonies-Bree-straat.

11.

ON THE OTHER SIDE of the city, the west, someone else destined for immense and lasting fame, and also interested in direct acquaintance with or observation of facts, had recently settled in. This was the French philosopher and mathematician Descartes, then thirty-five years old. He was of independent means, had traveled extensively, and was looking for a place where he could work undistracted. He lived in a typical three-storied gabled house on the Westermarkt, facing Hendrick de Keyser's almost completed, magnificent West Church (Westerkerk). Descartes loved Amsterdam. That year he wrote to the French littérateur Guez de Balzac: "I suggest Amsterdam for your retirement . . . it is preferable to all the monasteries. . . . A country house may be very well run, but there are always all sorts of things missing which can only be obtained in a town, and even the solitude you are hoping for is never total . . . whereas in this great city everybody except me is in business and so absorbed by profit-making that I could spend my entire life here without being noticed by a soul. I go for a walk every day in the Babel of a great thoroughfare as freely and restfully as you stroll in your garden. . . ."

It is pleasant to think of this highly contented and exceedingly shrewd young philosopher quietly picking his way through the mass of black-clothed, black-hatted Amsterdamers — listening happily, he wrote, to the bustle and noise, as if it were the murmur of a country stream, and reminding himself still more happily that all their toil and hurry was merely helping "to adorn the place where I live, and to supply my needs." And as for the pleasure Guez de Balzac might have watching the fruit grow in his orchards, what about seeing the ships come into Amsterdam with all the produce of the Indies and all that was rare in Europe? It was clearly the place for an intelligent man to be.

But while Descartes, with the self-assurance given by his French properties, used Amsterdam as a lively and interesting and well-equipped place for the solitude he needed, it was for Rembrandt quite the reverse. He was going into the world, or rather, taking on the world. So far he had shown a fantastic capacity for work and for using his immediate family and surroundings to satisfy all his needs, but now that he was in Amsterdam as an independent painter, it was part of his all-embracing nature that he must now see and be involved in all the sides of life around him, to be passionate and ambitious — to make for success, like any careerist, and to bring it off like a genius. The commissions for portraits that began to come in almost at once he carried out with absolutely no intention of displeasing the sitters. They wished to look rich, distinguished and respectable; and that was how he made them look.

His first great opportunity was a commission to paint one of the group portraits which were so popular with all institutions, boards, military companies and so on. But this was particularly testing. He was to paint the fashionable physician, Nicolas Tulp, a very important Amsterdamer, and a member of the Muiden circle, giving a demonstration of dissection to a group of colleagues. Dissections were rare occasions and treated as a rather special public entertainment, and the body was usually a recently hanged criminal, in this case, coincidentally, a Leyden man. In fact it was not long since permission had first been granted to the Amsterdam hospital for corpses to be dissected at all and the study of anatomy was really the latest fashion; there was probably an offstage audience in Rembrandt's picture, which was a masterpiece.

Or at least it seemed to be a masterpiece. For it was certainly a revolution. The whole trouble with group portraits was that everybody had to face the front, and previous attempts on scenes of this kind had been distinctly statuesque and lifeless. But in Rembrandt's effort something was happening. Dr. Tulp was commenting on the ligament he had delicately raised, with forceps, from the corpse's left forearm, and some of his associates were staring at it, while another merely listened and two more had their attention caught by something out of view. Dr. Tulp, who became Rembrandt's friend, was particularly well done — which was fortunate. In due course he became burgomaster four times, visited his patients in a carriage — this was very unusual and grand, and no doubt expensive for the patients — and had a house on the Keizersgracht. He was in fact exactly the sort of man Rembrandt had painted. Everybody was delighted. It was done in the Anatomy theater which the Guild of Surgeons, the owners of the picture, had in the south tower of the old Antoniespoort (now De Waag on the Nieuwmarkt) and its success made it a fundamental breakthrough for him.

Now he was flooded with commissions for portrait after portrait of burgher after burgher — sometimes, though not often, with the wife along too. A dazzling example of this period is the *Shipbuilder*, whose wife has interrupted his work to bring him a note. Both of them are elderly and in the usual black, he white-bearded and vaguely surprised, she full of energy and happiness — a sumptuous, wonderful picture. Rembrandt's work always had an extraordinary capacity to leave the viewer with some lasting though perhaps uncertain impression, partly because there were minds behind the faces, which often became character studies on a Shakespearean level, and partly because of a dramatic ability, which made for instance the pose of the man with the large ruff at the back of the *Anatomy Lesson* something that could haunt one indefinitely. But the people who really intrigued Rembrandt more than anyone were the Jews.

Amsterdam was full of and already famous for the number of sects that flourished there. The freedom of worship was wonderful. As Sir William Temple explained, even Catholic worship, though outlawed, was "as free and easy, though not so cheap and so avowed, as the rest." As for the other religions "every Man enjoys the free exercise in his own Chamber, or his own House, unquestioned and unespied: and if the Followers of any Sect grow so numerous . . . that they affect a publick Congregation, and are content to purchase a place of Assembly, to bear the charge of a Pastor or Teacher, and to pay for this liberty to the Publick; They go and propose their desire to the Magistrates . . . who inform themselves of their Opinions and manners of worship; and if they find nothing . . . destructive . . . and content themselves with the price that is offered for the purchase of this Liberty, They easily allow it. . . ." Buying religious freedom was really the most brilliant of bourgeois ideas.

And so almost all sects had public meeting places, including "some whose Names are almost worn out in all other parts, as the Brownists, Familists, and others. . . ." There were the Arminians, or Remonstrants, who were "more a Party in the State than a Sect in the Church" and the Anabaptists, "very numerous, but in the lower ranks of people, Mechanicks and Sea-men. . . ." As for the Jews, like everyone else they were free burghers, there was no ghetto, no poll tax, no badge, no limitation on numbers. They were excluded from guilds and city office, but only like any other non-Calvinists. They had their own school for Hebrew and Hebrew literature — called "The Tree of Life." The area they lived in began more or less in Rembrandt's, or rather van Uylenburgh's street, the St. Antonies–Breestraat (part of which later became known as the Jodenbreestraat). It was here, incidentally, that Rembrandt had come on his first short stay, for his master, Pieter Lastman, now at the end of his life, also lived in it. There were some rich houses, a few of them owned by Jews (tax returns, by the way, showed no Jews amongst the richest Amsterdamers). Further into their quarter the scene became extraordinary. It was overcrowded, poverty-stricken, there was luxury, squalor and exoticism. The diamond business itself had a certain glamour. Here more Spanish, Portuguese, German and Yiddish were spoken than Dutch. Here were strange clothes and strange food, and often the shops seemed more like Oriental bazaars. It was all entirely fascinating to Rembrandt. In the synagogue, which the magistrates had permitted twenty years before, he was able to see what (to go forward a little to 1641 for an eyewitness) young John Evelyn, the English diarist, saw: "The women were secluded from the men, being seated in galleries above, shut with lattices, having their heads muffled with linen, after a fantastical and somewhat extraordinary fashion; the men, wearing a large calico mantle, yellow coloured, over their hats, all the while waving their bodies, whilst at their devotions." For Rembrandt the Jews had everything: character, color, immensely interest-

COURTESY OF THE RIJKSMUSEUM, AMSTERDAM

Saskia — Rembrandt

ing faces, and above all the fact that they came straight out of the Bible, which was and remained a fundamental mainspring of his life. They asked to be treated in paint with rich colors and extravagance. They asked to be drawn and etched. Working furiously as always he indulged himself in this while he went on with his commissioned portraits.

And he fell in love. The girl was Van Uylenburgh's cousin, Saskia. She was twenty, quite attractive, with light brown hair and brown eyes. She had a simple charm. She was also well bred and well connected. Her parents were dead, which possibly was as well for the bridegroom. Her father had been a wealthy burgomaster of Leeuwarden in Friesland, her brothers and sisters were, or were married to, lawyers, theology professors — and they too had good connections. Saskia also had some money. It was an ideal marriage for him. The rise in social status was something that Rembrandt understood, enjoyed, used, and was entirely above. He was engaged to her in 1633 and was her husband a year later. It was springtime for him. He reveled in playing the part of the highly successful, extravagant, socially acceptable young painter. He would be more dramatic than Rubens, more life-loving and lusty than Franz Hals and more downright and coarse than Brouwer. Self-portraits of this time showed him in one looking much older than his age, with careful hair and moustache, looking the part of the distinguished burghers he was painting, and in another as a quite handsome young man with a cloak slung elegantly over one shoulder, a sprig of some patrician or princely family — in fact the latter one is so strongly like pictures he would be painting and drawing of his son Titus twenty years later that this is what he probably did look like in the first year of his marriage. In any case happiness comes through all his activities. This was the time of success in his career, continuing achievement in his art and, alone with Saskia, bliss. He adored her. He used her again and again as a model, decorating her with lush velvets and jewels, or with flowers, or putting himself in the act as a sort of podgy laughing cavalier, wine glass in his hand and Saskia on his lap and a sword attached to his belt. He was twenty-eight or twenty-nine and on top of the world.

COURTESY OF THE NATIONAL GALLERY, LONDON

Self-Portrait — Rembrandt at thirty-four

12.

SOMETHING RATHER ODD was happening in the city. On the Dam, ignoring perhaps the musicians who came to play there every morning, they were talking about tulips. A general enthusiasm for flowers had been on for some time. There was a florists' guild and a flower market. There was a public garden on the Herengracht, a small, very artificial and ornamental affair, with carved figures and urns on the surrounds and neatly designed paths. The gardens behind the tall canal houses all formed this sort of pattern; everything was terribly neat with the blooms drawn up like soldiers on parade, reds here, whites there; and the grander the garden, the more likely it was for there to be high yew hedges, box trees in fantastic shapes — ships or even biblical scenes. But apart from the rich, hundreds of Amsterdamers kept a small garden or allotment of their own outside the city walls, and used them for pleasure or to sell what they grew.

The tulip, which grows wild amongst other places in the north and eastern Mediterranean, had arrived in the Netherlands, via Germany, from Constantinople and the Levant, at the end of the previous century. It became the flower above all others as a result of a fashion starting in France, and had caught on sufficiently in Amsterdam for Bredero to have a character in *The Moor* say, "I'm not such a fool as the people who give a lot of money for a tulip. . . ." But ten years after that, in the mid-twenties, the flower was becoming widely popular in Europe — and nowhere could it be grown so well as in the sandy soil between Amsterdam and Leyden, and especially round Haarlem. It became a flourishing business. And now dozens of tulip variations began to emerge, to be named and to hit an ever rising market. The best known was and remained a white one with red stripes called the "Semper Augustus." And the more varieties there were, the more expensive the bulbs of the successful or particularly exotic ones became. And they were so easy to grow. Gradually it began to dawn on thousands of people that there was a fine way of making easy money.

Suddenly in 1634 the whole thing burst into a widespread gambling fever. For now the pleasures of speculation had been discovered by Calvinist schoolmasters and butchers and students and barber-surgeons, by everybody, in fact, especially those with the least business aptitudes. It was a sucker's night out — horribly reminiscent of certain later fevers elsewhere. So why not with tulips? Bulbs were bought and sold and resold a dozen times, were bought and sold unseen. Growers had to take tremendous precautions to protect their beds — and there were men angry at the whole affair — like Professor Vorstius, a Leyden botanist, who was a compulsive tulip destroyer. An "Admiral Liefkens" sold for 4,400 guilders. The peak price for "Semper Augustus" was 5,500 guilders. One Amsterdamer made 60,000 guilders in four months (the burgomaster's annual salary, it may be recalled, was 500). Horror stories abounded; typically one of the ship's quartermaster who was sent for by his owner and while waiting in the office noticed a few onions on a desk. A slice of bread being available, they made him a nice little snack. Those onions had cost 17,000 guilders, and included an "Admiral of Enkhuizen," a "Vice-Roy of the Indies" and a "Semper Augustus." Most of the stories were variations of this. The fever went on, getting wilder and wilder, until suddenly at the beginning of 1637, the market cracked. Suddenly bulbs bought for one or two thousand guilders in the confident expectation of a quick profit could not be sold at all. The speculators panicked. In a few days hundreds were ruined. The losses were such that the whole credit system, and not merely for tulips, was in danger. There was a meeting of florists in Amsterdam on February 24 at which it was decided, as a rescue measure, that all contracts made after November 30 the previous year were null and void, on payment of ten percent and the return of the bulb. The provincial government, the States of Holland, supported it, and tulip mania was over, with a good many households saved from total disaster. Among the casualties left out in the cold was Jan van Goyen, the Leyden painter. It was remarkable that Rembrandt was not involved. Perhaps he didn't notice it.

But the whole affair had something chilling about it. It was a reminder of fallibility. It was a little sign of the decay that may always accompany prosperity. This small country and this wonderful city had been expanding so fast and had been achieving so much, and were still on the way up, and would be for years — it was still the glory time — but the tulip disaster was a very small danger-ahead signal. Things could go wrong.

They had been going wrong, at last, for Tesselschade.

Though living at Alkmaar she was still the queen of Amsterdam's literary world, and all the more so when the rival Chambers of Rhetoric to the old Eglantine, like the White Lavender, which had come from Antwerp, and of which Vondel was a member, all agreed in 1630 to merge in Coster's Academy. It was a triumph for that vigorous doctor. In celebration Hooft offered a prize for a poem. Vondel suggested a subject for it and — surprise, surprise — Tesselschade won. However, there was no doubt that she was very talented as well as attractive. The next year there was a house party at Muiden, including Coster, Vondel sans Madame Vondel and Tesselschade sans Mr. Krombalgh — and she was treated to another admirer, Barlaeus, or van Baerle, a professor of Latin of forty-seven, a brilliant man who had spent years as a village pastor and was now enjoying himself. At Muiden they enjoyed themselves exchanging witticisms and elaborate puns, and were full, like their letters, of classical allusions. Tesselschade sang and played the organ, klavier, viol, guitar and cithern or lute — equally divinely, according to Barlaeus, who also later praised the pictures she had painted in her house at Alkmaar — from which she also sent goblets she had engraved to Hooft. She was an accomplished lady, and indeed it seems rather tediously so — but what can't be denied is the high quality of her admirers. Tesselschade undoubtedly had something.

But in 1634 Hooft became conscious of a long silence from Alkmaar. He sent somebody to find out what was wrong, and the news came back that the elder of Tesselschade's two daughters was down with smallpox. Soon it was learned that the child had died, and the father had died, too. The death of children, though awful, was common enough — Hooft had lost all four of his children by his first wife. Death anyway was always around in force, if only because of the epidemics which hit all the cities regularly — Amsterdam had one every two or three years; occasionally the burial grounds had been bursting, unable to take any more bodies. But the loss of child and husband was a bad blow. He had been and remained the one man Tesselschade loved. She settled down with her other daughter and her relationship with Vondel became closer — he, in his turn, lost his wife and this increased the pressure he felt to turn to Rome, spurred on by Tesselschade's own Catholicism. It was a mild scandal in the Muiden circle — Huyghens and Hooft were critical and encouraged Barlaeus to pay court to her. The professor wrote poem after poem, but got nowhere.

In Amsterdam Rembrandt and Saskia had a taste of this kind of loss, spoiling their first happy ardor, when their first child, a boy, Rumbartus, survived only a couple of months. Otherwise the sun was still shining for him. They now had a house in the N. Doelenstraat. He had so many pupils that he had to hire an extra room and partition it. He had commissions from the stadholder at The Hague — through Huyghens, the prince's secretary. Possibly under this influence he indulged at this time in some Baroque tendencies, full of emotion and movement, crowds and sometimes cruelty, which was Huyghens' taste. His price for these pictures was 600 guilders each — he tried to raise it to a thousand, but found Huyghens tough to deal with. It was at this time also that he began to be interested in landscape and his walks outside the city produced drawings and etchings. In some of his drawings of the late thirties there were signs of the great late development whereby reality of line, light and darkness became subsidiary to other needs — which necessarily lost him his fashionable popularity. But for the moment he was making money and spending it. His tastes were extravagant, and he was a constant buyer at the art sales. He bought a Rubens, he bought Venetian glass and Chinese porcelain. He indulged in an unsuccessful slander action — angered by rumors that he was wasting Saskia's inheritance.

Baroque is a word not easily definable, but if one takes its definition from the late Professor Huizinga, who spoke of "its rounded forms and luxuriant draperies" or from Irving Wardle, who called it in the London *Times* the "combination of the ornamental with the overripe," it seems to suit Vondel. He was a Baroque writer and a very suitable playwright to start off the first real brick-built Amsterdam theater.

This was also Baroque, and designed by Jacob van Campen, later famous for the new Town Hall. It was financed by the wealthy Regents of the Orphanage and it was on the same Keizersgracht site (the gateway remains, at number 384) as Coster's Academy, which had been a small wooden building. The new theater offered two tiers of boxes, Roman-style pilasters and an impressive stage, with painted wings and a central pavilion and balcony useful for big effects. They could manage angels floating down from the air, very impressive on a late winter afternoon with a stage lit by flaring torches. Bills remain for the hiring of shrubs and trees used in forest scenes.

Vondel not only wrote the first play, but also the lines carved on the architrave above the entrance, and above the boxes, and on the ceiling rafters and anywhere else that could take a few suitable words, such as the mantelpieces in the Regents' room and the Actors' room (there were still no actresses — it would be seventeen years before the first one appeared in Amsterdam). "The world is a stage — each plays his part and gets his share." "Playacting is the most instructive of diversions, it surpasses all other games or royal inventions, it imitates the world, stimulates mind and body, stirs us to happiness, wounds us pleasantly, shows on its little stage all of man's vanity, at which Democritus laughs and Heraclitus weeps." A notice in gold letters was next to the entrance to the lobby where the tickets were sold, warning in Vondel's verse against nuisance from tobacco pipes, beer pots or any sort of licentiousness — "Those who do otherwise will be led out." In fact, nobody took much notice of it. All the nuisances would be freely committed.

The opening — not an opening night but an opening day, for the first performance was at midday on a Sunday — took place on January 3, 1638. In proper theatrical tradition it did not happen without a few difficulties. It had been intended to open on December 26, but a week before that the Reformed Church decided to send a deputation to the Regents of the Orphanage to urge them not to allow "performances of Papist superstitions like the mass and other ceremonies." Vondel's proclivities were, of course, well known and his many anti-Calvinist satires guaranteed plenty of enemies. Pastor Laurentius and his assistant Claes Visscher (definitely no relation of Tesselschade's) got nowhere with the Regents and they took themselves to the burgomasters requesting them to look carefully at the play and take care that "nothing scandalous should be given." They were answered that "Their lordships the Burgomasters had decided that neither the Church nor society were injured or traduced, and were of the opinion that it was more likely to have the effect of mocking popery than of dishonoring the Christian religion." The Church retired for the moment, but they had at least managed the partial success of postponing the opening.

They tried again. A Mr. Wachterdorfius went to the burgomasters on December 31, to thank them for their trouble but once more "earnestly and seriously" to demand the "withholding of this comedy" because the Consistory had learned "that various persons not well disposed to the Church had conspired to ask their lordships the Burgomasters for permission to put the play on." The minister tried to show once more that the work "tried to make popery attractive." The burgomaster to whom he spoke promised merely to communicate everything to his officials. So the play finally went on. It was fortunate that at least two of the burgomasters were known to Vondel — Geeraert Schaep was one; he performed in all the high offices of the city from 1624 to 1665, and became burgomaster for the first time on February 2, 1637. His wife was Maria Spieghel, related to the old Spieghel who was Roemer Visscher's early associate. Another Spieghel, fifty-five years before, a member of the Council, had refused to swear allegiance to William of Orange. So Vondel's known Papist tendencies did not denude him of supporters at the Town Hall. Then again Harmen van der Pol, now seventy-seven, who had helped him in 1625 when he was in danger of being tried for treachery for his play *Palamedes* was having his fourth spell as a regent of the Orphanage. The burgomaster who actually had to read the play was Jakob de Graeff, the sixty-seven-year-old head of the family now so linked up by marriage with the Bickers. (A typical rich patrician, he lived on the Herengracht and had a princely country house. He was born in 1571 and had studied at Leyden and traveled abroad. He came back to Amsterdam in 1597, married his father's best friend's daughter, and the next year became a magistrate, and five years later joined the Council, and eight years later was chosen to be a burgomaster. He couldn't be, for he wasn't quite forty, the qualifying age. But he was doing it for the fifth or sixth time when "Gijsbrecht" came up — and ten months later he died, after a pleasant patrician career.)

The Schout himself (the Sheriff), who acted as the ceremonial head of the city, was present at the first performance. (The church tried once more, fourteen days later, but again with no success.) As for the play, it was intended to be a grand celebration of Amsterdam's success and Vondel brought it off magnificently — his Baroque style and outlook being ideal for the purpose. He also equipped the citizens with an entirely spurious past, and no one bothered that the city he described did not exist in the play's supposed period of 1304, but instead bore a close resemblance to the one shown in Cornelis Anthoniszoon's famous map of 1544, and even had an Exchange. The play began with a 162-line prologue spoken by the hero, setting the scene — he is back in his city, from which he has been exiled. Enemies surround them, especially the Haarlemers and Waterlanders. Gijsbrecht, foolishly merciful and trusting, is easily taken in by a planted prisoner, and because of this at the very moment — it is midnight at Christmastime — when all the citizens are in the churches, a ship, secretly full of armed men in the style of the Trojan Horse, is able to come up to the Haarlem gate. The walls are set on fire. Enemy noblemen and their forces, hidden in a nearby monastery, pour through. A friar brings the news to Gijsbrecht and his wife. The hero rushes to the Dam.

We follow a story line full of bishops, abbesses, heroics, burning walls, a romantic husband and wife, but a losing battle. In the end an angel appears to prophesy the future greatness of Amsterdam, and also to put in a few anti-Papist words, which the burgomasters had insisted on. They were all in the audience on January 3.

Three days later the learned G. J. Vossius, who was the professor of history at the city's five-year-old university (or athenaeum or "illustrious school"), wrote to his friend Grotius in Paris, where the great man was acting as the Swedish ambassador, "You will certainly have already inspected Vondel's *Gysbreght van Aemstel,* which he has dedicated to you? Some people, in the name of the Consistory, if I'm not mistaken, were against it being put on. In the end it was given to Burgomaster de Graef to read through carefully. He found nothing in it to irritate anybody; the fact that the whole piece has a slightly Romish tint, like the writer himself, is of no concern — the people in it have to be in tune with their time, not with that of the Reformation. Anyhow the day before yesterday it was played for the first time and to great applause. . . ."

And played again and again, usually around January 1, all through the century and on into the future, until Amsterdam in the late 1960's had had enough — at least, for the time being.

Was Rembrandt there on that January 3? I hope so. He certainly saw *Gijsbrecht,* for he made sketches from the box next to the stage on the right. Was Tesselschade? There is no record — but of course she was. And she certainly came in September for another and bigger show, which like Vondel's play had the effect of confirming the citizens' feeling of self-esteem. It was their first visit from a queen.

The queen was Maria de' Medici. She was the widow of Henry IV of France, the mother of the present king, Louis XIII, of the Duke of Orleans and the Duchess of Savoy, and of the Queens of Spain and of England (Henrietta Maria, the wife of Charles I). She had become the regent of France in 1610, after the murder of Henry IV, and had then tasted the heady delights of intrigue and power for the first time. Unfortunately she had suffered the penalty of those who play with fire without full qualifications. Her son, the king, had rebelled against her in his teens, her chief adviser was murdered, and his wife, who was her childhood friend, tried for sorcery and executed. She had known exile once or twice and above all had found herself an enemy all too qualified to play with any sort of fire — the Cardinal Richelieu (a discreet arms customer of Amsterdam).

But the Queen Mother of France was still hooked on intrigue in 1638, and traveled around in the hope of using her exalted position to find help in the fight against the cardinal. She was in Amsterdam on Wednesday, September 1. And the bourgeois city was thrilled.

She arrived on the outskirts, accompanied by the Prince of Orange and a distinguished retinue of nobles and ladies. Here she was welcomed by a mounted guard of honor commanded by Cornelis van Davelaer, Lord of Putten, and by the sound of bell-ringing and gunfire from inside the city, where twenty companies of militiamen lined the streets she would pass through. At the city gate she was received by Andries Bicker, former burgomaster and commandant of the city; by Peter Reael, Gerbrand Pankras and Jacob Bicker, representing the citizens; and was addressed by the pensionary, Cornelis Bloom.

The procession, with the mounted guard ahead and a section of militia behind, came slowly along the Nieuwendijk to the Dam, coming into it through an arch of honor, where, under the seal of the city, there was a picture of the wedding of the queen to Henry IV, together with some explanatory lines in Latin by Tesselschade's admirer, Barlaeus. From the Dam the procession went along Warmoes-straat, turned into the Niezel, and down again to the Oude Doelenstraat, where there was another arch of honor, highly decorated — when its curtains were raised one saw the queen as Berecynthia in a chariot, and her princely children, and four girls representing the four parts of the world. And again there was a little Latin poem by Barlaeus.

At the Prinsenhof the queen was greeted by the four current burgomasters, Pieter Hasselaer, Abraham Boom, Antoni Oetgens van Waveren and Albert Conrad Burg, accompanied by two pensionaries, Willem Boreel and Cornelis Boom. She went inside while the prince continued to the house of the merchant Elias Trip (Louis de Geer's brother-in-law). The prince's view of the visit must have been interesting, for not only was the queen's enemy Richelieu his own Great Power ally, but this was a period, a year after his triumph in recapturing Breda from the Spaniards, when he was finding the Estates of Holland, led by Amsterdam and Andries Bicker, totally noncollaborative in his war effort. There was a state of cold war between him and the city and he was reported to have said, "If I could take Antwerp, it would bring them to their senses." Indeed it would. Amsterdam preferred Antwerp to stay bottled up, and it was only prudent

COURTESY OF THE AMSTERDAM CITY ARCHIVES

The entrance of Marie de' Medici into Amsterdan in 1638

A watershow performed in honor of Marie de' Medici's visit

for Bicker and other merchants to ensure that the southern city received plenty of defense material.

However, on the surface, the ball continued. The watchword for the guard on the walls that evening was given by the queen: "Maria." The next day the burgomasters took her on a tour of the city, which included a banquet at East India House, entirely composed of East Indian dishes. And more Latin verses from Barlaeus accompanied it. Overnight an artificial island appeared on the Rokin water between the Doelen bridge and the Long bridge. Here on the third day more tableaux were offered the queen. The royal company were in a boat with the Schout and the burgomasters — as it appeared in the canal, Neptune greeted them from a craft shaped like a shell, and he was followed by Mercury in another suitable craft, in the front of which sat a girl representing the city, the Amsterdam Maid, who recited a Latin verse of welcome. The happy crowds watched from the banks while the boat circled the island stage, on which various scenes were presented, such as a representation of the marriage of the queen's parents — Francis, Duke of Tuscany, and Joanna, an Austrian archduchess — five tableaux showed the sufferings of France under Henry III and the good times under Henry IV, and there was also the Emperor Maximilian presenting Amsterdam with the crown in its coat of arms. And after all this, as a light relief, there was a water fight between ten sailors, all dressed in white with red caps, using sticks to try to knock each other from their boats into the water. Finally the queen named an East Indian ship, the *Maria de' Medicis.*

On Sunday, September 5, she said good-bye to the burgomasters and left the city, amid applause and excitement, in the same way as she had come in. That day, it so happened — in the same hour as her departure, it was claimed — she became a grandmother with the birth in France of a dauphin, the future Louis XIV. In due course this also was a subject for a few appropriate Latin lines from Barlaeus. He added them to his "book of the visit" which was published with great success the following year.

As for Tesselschade, she had, naturally, been in the party. She had come down from Alkmaar to sing for the queen, with another member of the Muiden circle, Francesca Duarte. And she also presented her with a poem she had written for the occasion in Italian.

13.

A TIME OF DESOLATION, perhaps necessary for the peaks of human achievement, was approaching Rembrandt. The first child, Rumbartus, had died in 1635. A daughter, Cornelia, died in 1638. The next year he bought the house, for 13,000 guilders (1,200 down and the rest over six years), which is now the Rembrandt museum in Jodenbreestraat, although its outward appearance is not quite as he knew it — the top story did not have its classical façade, but was gabled in the normal way. Here in 1640 a second Cornelia died after a few weeks. He began at this time to produce some etchings of landscapes just outside the city — often looking back towards it, a low roof line with the windmills and spires showing against the sky, seen across marshland or the Amstel. Another favorite scene was the bend of the river near the ruined country house, Kost-Verloren, where Bredero's cow-thief hid his cow. His success continued; he was the "name" to mention among the artists of Amsterdam. The portrait commissions kept coming in and his pupils each paid him one hundred guilders a year plus a commission on anything sold. He was proud of his house and kept on filling it with treasures he bought at sales. But his mother died in Leyden and then his sister-in-law, a constant visitor and friend, and Saskia's comfort. As these shadows fell his art deepened and gradually changed its form, the beginning of the process whereby his obsession with light and shade and his obedience to the demands of a picture as opposed to any other consideration could only mean the end of him as a fashionable painter.

Happiness came back with the birth of a son, Titus, who survived. His acquaintance with the illustrious Six family began — they had been rich Huguenot refugees, and now owned dye-works and silk mills, and lived in state. The son and heir, the twenty-three-year-old Jan Six, was to become for a time a close friend of Rembrandt's, and also of Vondel's. They were all interconnected — which must naturally happen amongst those at the top, socially and professionally, of any society. Jan Six, an arts and literature lover, would dedicate his first poem to Hooft — who incidentally be-

Titus — Rembrandt

Night Watch — Rembrandt

came a burgomaster — and he would marry the daughter of a burgo-master, Rembrandt's fashionable Dr. Tulp, and go on in fifty years' time to be a burgomaster himself.

Another rich acquaintance during Titus's first months of survival was the self-made merchant Frans Banning Cocq, a tall and stately man, who had married into the immensely rich Overlander family and had thereby become a brother-in-law of Jakob de Graeff's brilliant eldest son, Cornelis. He had been ennobled as the Lord of Purmerland, he had a grand house like a palazzo on the Singel, and he was the captain of a company of the part-time civic guards. All this was a remarkable achievement for the son of a Bremen laborer. But this was the time of achievement for the Dutch. A year or two before there had been a remarkable naval victory, more or less under the cliffs of Dover, in which the Spanish fleet had been thoroughly clobbered. The fact that it had taken place in what the English regarded as their territorial waters had annoyed Charles I, but he could do nothing about it, in view of his domestic troubles, and in fact he married his daughter to the Prince of Orange's son. The Spaniards were now very much on the way out — Portugal had become independent again, which meant that the sea war against Spain in the Far East was virtually over. In fact the one touch of anxiety for the Amsterdam business world was that if the war itself should come to an end, it would also be the end of some very good pickings from both sides. The burghers' prosperity had been steadily rising for years. In August 1641, the twenty-year-old John Evelyn wrote, "Prodigious it is to consider the multitude of vessels which continually ride before this Citty, which is certainly the most busie concourse of mortalls now upon the whole earth, and the most addicted to com'erce."

All in all it was an ideal time for Captain Banning Cocq and his company to think about having a group portrait. They chose Rembrandt, agreed to pay one hundred guilders each — and so there came about the *Night Watch,* that strong contender for today's most famous and valuable picture. What is it all about? It is, to start with, of magnificent size, though cut down a little from the original. It shows a crowded scene with a dim building in the background, and not night but day — that is, a little sunlight and a great deal of darkness. Official words of the time stated that the captain was "ordering his lieutenant, the Heer van Vlaerdingen, to march the company out." It doesn't look much like that. Instead there is a general state of agreeable confusion as a procession, indicated largely by the raised pikes in the right background and led by the captain, in a typi-

cal rich burgher's black suit enlivened by a red sash, and his lieutenant
dazzling in a smart yellow uniform, is moving into the center foreground.
There is a dog running around, barking at a drummer, a musketeer in red
inspecting his weapon, a little girl in yellow there to watch, the cornet
looking up at his flag (the job Bredero did in his time), and a dozen or so
other members of the company, with assorted hats and weapons, standing
at the side and perhaps waiting to join in at the rear. It has probably been
a wet afternoon; there are still heavy clouds about, but the sun is breaking
through. As for what Captain Banning Cocq is saying to the lieutenant, it
is possibly (for he is holding his hand out), "I think it's stopped." The
truth must be that they are not really going anywhere, there is no alarm or
practice alarm, they are not off to man the walls or even to go to target
practice or a shooting competition. They are simply in a picture. And the
light gives no clue as to the time of day or night or the weather; it is
simply the light Rembrandt wanted.

Everything has a price, especially self-indulgence, and it is hardly surprising that he was not asked to paint another group portrait (except for a
second *Anatomy Lesson* in 1656) for twenty years. And when it did happen (the *Syndics of the Drapers' Guild*, 1662), the sitters clearly made
sure that there would be none of the master's experiments in chiaroscuro
to shade their faces from history. But the *Night Watch* was not, as is
occasionally suggested, derided and resented at the time, even if its pre-
eminence as a masterpiece was not appreciated — it was too startling for
that. But it was hung with the former portraits in the Great Hall of the
Kloveniersdoelen, and stayed there until the eighteenth century when it
was moved to the Town Hall, and there the cutting down to the present
size was done, to fit it to the available wall space.

Certainly Banning Cocq and his lieutenant had no cause to complain,
although they probably paid more for their prominence. Of course, if they
liked it, that was it, and maybe some of the junior ranks were less enthusiastic about their hundred guilders' worth. But the *Night Watch* does not
so much represent the moment when Rembrandt began to fall from grace
— four years later he was commissioned to paint more pictures for the
prince and for more money — as it does the moment when he himself lost
interest in being a fashionable painter. All the famous money troubles
which dogged the rest of his life were brought on by himself, or by this
loss of interest. He could have been rich, if he had chosen. But he was not
the man to make that choice. He seems to have been in some way bent on

self-destruction, as if he were all too eagerly embracing grief and disaster as a means of understanding the universal sorrows of humanity, and as if he needed them to enter the great dark territories known to Shakespeare, known to Beethoven, known to a very few. When he was a young man he had reveled in painting or drawing the old; he reveled all the more, with a sublime creative satisfaction, in the self-portraits he produced to the end of his life, showing changes brought about by age and grief and tragedy that were his own.

The move on from being fashionable was accelerated in the year of the *Night Watch* by the worst blow he ever suffered, Saskia's death. At that time motherhood was the most dangerous of occupations — it was the ghost at every marriage feast. Not long before he had done an etching, a view from behind of an elegant young couple, with the husband gently assisting his wife to step into a grave waiting for her — death in the shape of a skeleton sits there, a welcoming host with an hourglass in his hand. It was prophetic. Her four children had destroyed poor Saskia and after the birth of Titus she became progressively weaker and died, probably from pulmonary tuberculosis, on June 14, 1642. Rembrandt bought her a tomb in the Oude Kerk. A week before, she had made her will, leaving her money to Titus, with his father holding it in usufruct, subject to his remarriage. Devastated, he faced life with the ten-months-old baby. A nursemaid joined the household. She was a trumpeter's widow, Geertje Dircks.

Sixteen forty-two was also the year that Tesselschade came back with her surviving daughter to Amsterdam to live at the house of her sister Gertruid van Buyl. Vondel no doubt was pleased to see her, for having finally "gone over" to the Catholics — on November 17, 1641 — he found himself cold-shouldered by Hooft. The attitude seems unfair, in view of the highly Papist tinge of others of Hooft's friends, like the late Roemer Visscher, and of course Anna and Tesselschade — but they had at least been born and brought up in it, and no doubt it seemed to the civilized lord of Muiden tedious to go to unnecessary extremes. Tesselschade had an unlucky accident soon after her arrival — she lost the sight of an eye which was hit by a spark from a smithy she was passing. Poetical sympathy came from all the Muiden circle, naturally — she took the misfortune well and went on with her Italian translations, wearing a patch. But her time and the Muiden circle's as well was running out, just as the time of the Spaniards was running out.

The French beat them at Rocroi in 1643, and in the Netherlands in 1644

Frederick Henry took Sas-van-Gent from them, cutting Ghent's communication with the Scheldt, and the next year took Hulst, gaining territory south of the Scheldt. It was the peak of the prince's career and it was the end of the first great period of the Dutch republic. Frederick Henry's court at The Hague was glittering, his incredibly small country was accorded equal status amongst the European great powers. But he became ill and died, after some months of suffering, a year before the peace with Spain was concluded. So he did not take part in the vastly alcoholic national celebrations of January 3, 1648 (the Treaty of Münster).

And there were no celebrations at Muiden. Hooft had died two months after the prince, his great history of the Netherlands unfinished. Barlaeus was dying. All Tesselschade's old friends were gone or on their way off the stage — except for Vondel and Huyghens, who both lived to more than ninety, and still had years to go. She had maintained her old regal position in the Amsterdam literary life and, one-eyed, had been in at the birth of the new playwrights, Vos and Brandt. But nothing was the same. Her world was really centered now on her daughter, who was attractive and almost grown up. Death however was now in constant attendance. The means used may as well be left to the seventeenth-century view of Sir William Temple: "The Diseases of the Climate seem to be chiefly the Gout and the Scurvy; but all hot and dry Summers bring some that are infectious among them, especially into Amsterdam and Leyden: These are usually Fevers, that lye most in the Head, and either kill suddenly, or languish long before they recover." Tesselschade lost her daughter, as she had lost her other child and her husband. All the pleasures of her celebrity, all the hours of talk at Muiden, all the privileged happiness, all the brilliant accomplishments had ended in a private, terrible sorrow. She died of grief on June 20, 1649. Huyghens wrote:

> *This is Tesselschade's grave.*
> *Let no one presume*
> *To measure her immeasurable quality in words:*
> *Everything one can say of the Sun is true of her.*

14.

PEACE WITH SPAIN, the only official enemy, having been achieved, the regents of Amsterdam had no doubt at all that it was a good time to reassert the independence of the provinces, and in particular of themselves, in relation to the nationalism and constitutionalism for which Frederick Henry had stood. Secondly they saw no reason at all to waste good money on the armed forces. Taxes, direct on the rich and indirect on everybody, were very high. Amsterdamers paid about seventeen million guilders a year. Fewer expensive troops and fewer warships seemed very desirable. The new prince had taken over at the age of twenty-one, and had so far been chiefly noted for having a good time. It was a matter of some irritation when the young man turned out to be aggressive and militaristic, and in addition, brilliantly capable.

William II did not approve at all of the Treaty of Münster, though the process of making it was too far advanced for him to scotch it. But he was already busy negotiating secretly with the French for a joint conquest of the Spanish Netherlands. Another idea was an expedition to England to help his relations. His wife was Charles I's daughter, and also in The Hague were her aunt, the Queen of Bohemia and an exile of long standing, and her brothers, the Prince of Wales and the Duke of York (the future Charles II and James II). The French, under Cardinal Mazarin, were however not too interested, and though the prince himself had great popular support, most of the Dutch were on the side of Cromwell and Parliament. But the trial of the king changed everything and there was great indignation. The aged and distinguished Amsterdamer Adriaen Pauw, the council pensionary, was sent to London to plead for Charles's life. The execution was badly received in the Netherlands. The English, as if blithely unaware of the ill-feeling, sent an envoy to The Hague with hopes of drawing the two countries together. Three days later he was assassinated in his hotel. The assassins escaped.

Cromwell's government, though outraged, sent another envoy. The States-General refused him an audience. He was recalled, and a month or two later the Dutch envoy in London was also recalled — a situation of perfect breach which suited the Prince of Orange very well. But now the Estates of Holland, the government of the province, largely ruled by the power of Amsterdam, stepped in — they received the English envoy themselves before his departure and later on sent one of their own to London. Their purpose was the commercial one of avoiding war at all costs. But both actions were appropriate to a sovereign power, and not a province in the Republic. Next there was the question of the disbandment of the foreign troops who were the basis of the army — when the States-General refused to do anything, Holland went ahead and discharged the 600 who had to be paid by the province — another illegally sovereign action, for there were not seven armies but one, and the commander was the prince.

He was biding his time, and still negotiating with the French, although his cousin William Frederick, the Stadholder of Friesland, warned him that the Amsterdam merchants were endangering the Republic and should be dealt with. Next there was an order from the States-General, ordering the provinces that though the number of troops in the army were being cut down, the officer-cadres must be kept at full strength. Holland disagreed again and ordered all the colonels of regiments in the pay of the province to disband. This was on June 1, 1650. A week later the prince, authorized by the States-General, began to visit the various towns of Holland at the head of a deputation, in order to iron matters out. But he didn't do very well, for the States-General were as much out of order in interfering directly with individual towns as the Estates of Holland were in behaving like a sovereign power. So one town after another informed the prince that they were answerable only to the province. And at Amsterdam, where the greatest influence was now held by the brothers Andries and Cornelis Bicker, the Council refused to receive either the prince or the deputation. William returned to The Hague, livid, and with his mind made up that force must now be used.

Just over a month later he invited six distinguished members of the Estates of Holland to visit him, had them arrested as soon as they arrived, and sent them off to Loevestein Castle. That was move one. Move two was in action that night — July 30–31 — with an army, secretly assembled, marching towards Amsterdam under the command of his cousin, the Friesland stadholder, Frederick William.

The plan was a surprise attack at dawn, followed by the easy overrunning of the city. But something went wrong. It was, in a way, the old style of life tripping up over the new bourgeois world. Amsterdam had a very good postal service. Originally hired out to individual carriers, it was now becoming a big business. A letter to Paris took four days. There were four depots in the city for the various routes. The mail was taken to catch the stagecoaches or ships. Late deliveries on busy routes went with solitary riders through the night, and it was one of these night postmen on his way to Amsterdam who caught up with the prince and his army moving silently and glamorously in the darkness. He talked to some soldiers who had lost their way, learned what was happening, and galloped off hell for leather to warn the city.

At Amsterdam there was at once furious activity. Cornelis Bicker summoned the Council, the militia were called out, the walls were manned, and the gates, of course, remained closed. William Frederick was disconcerted when on arrival at the appointed time he found this state of preparedness. He decided not to attack, but merely to surround the walls and cut the city off until he had conferred with his young cousin. The latter no sooner heard the news of the fiasco than he was on his way from The Hague to take over. He arrived in the afternoon fully prepared to use the army to the utmost. Meanwhile inside the city the Council, in spite of the apparent triumph earlier in the day, was steadily losing its nerve. It was logical. Their opposition to the prince's policies was based on the fact that war was bad for business (in general if not in particular). They were also anxious, as usual, about any idea of trying to retake Antwerp — which must involve the possibility of its being restored as a competitive port. But it was equally clear — and much, much clearer every minute — that any kind of heroic resistance to attack or to siege would do still more damage to business. It was chilling to consider it. The new houses and gardens along the canals were not made for war. Not only were there the huge investments in money and time which had gone into their businesses, but great sums were being spent on the city — there was the great new Town Hall designed by Jacob van Campen, now being erected on the Dam to replace the one they were sitting in, which would be a headquarters worthy of the new Venice (and the stones for which had been imported from Scotland — from Boswell's great-grandfather, the Earl of Kincardine, as it happened). Building was going on everywhere and the capital at risk was enormous. The next day, after an unhappy night, they opened negotiations, which turned almost at once, under the implacable eye of the young prince, into an acceptance of total defeat. Groveling in the dirt their lordships had to agree that both the Bickers must resign and never accept office again and that there would be no further opposition from Amsterdam to the demands of the States-General.

While the burgher-regents licked their wounds, William contentedly spent the rest of the summer hunting and carrying on his secret negotiations with Cardinal Mazarin — the intermediary was the Governor of Dunkirk. He would almost certainly have led the Republic into adventures supporting the Stuarts in England and into the Spanish Netherlands — and perhaps with great success, for he had shown himself to be masterful as well as ambitious. But it did not happen. As Bredero had kept on saying, " 't Kan verkeeren" — "Things can change." The prince was in the country at Dieren near Arnhem at the end of October when he suddenly went down with smallpox. Ten days later he was dead. He was twenty-four. A week afterwards his wife gave birth to a son.

People everywhere in the country were stunned, although the regents of Amsterdam bore the news with equanimity. The members of the Estates of Holland, where the city's influence was paramount, could hardly wait to propose a Great Assembly which must meet to consider the new situation; and they immediately abolished the office of stadholder. Four other provinces followed them; Orangist supporters everywhere were hopelessly confused. Only Groningen and Friesland kept William Frederick on the job. The effect of this and the decisions of the Assembly which went on at The Hague for most of 1651 was that the position of the provinces was strengthened, especially in relation to the armed forces they had to pay for; and that without a strong prince as a leading figure power in the Republic now lay with the city oligarchies — Amsterdam's, of course, being preeminent.

Across the Channel the republican English under Cromwell were also out to make use of the situation and were annoyed when their attempts to bind the Dutch to them, and under them ("one people, one republic"), were coldly received. To start with, when the envoys arrived at The Hague during the early days of the Assembly, shouts of "Regicides!" and ruder words came from a hostile, largely Orangist crowd in the streets. The English government struck back with the Navigation Act — all imports must be carried in English ships, a hard blow aimed straight at the Dutch carrying trade. Envoys led by Adriaen Pauw now went to England for more useless negotiations. There was consternation in Amsterdam —

and still more when the news came that an English squadron had seized Dutch vessels in the West Indies. But here was a lesson for the burgher-regents (which they soon forgot), for their economies in defense had already hopelessly weakened the Dutch fleet. In February a panic rebuilding program started. In May it was possible to risk an unofficial naval battle in the Channel, with no conclusion but the heightening of anger on both sides. War was declared on June 30, 1652.

Perhaps it was symbolical that soon afterwards — July 7 — the half-demolished old Town Hall of Amsterdam, the center of the city for 250 years, went up in flames. According to Vondel's account in the long poem he wrote for the inauguration of the new Town Hall, the watchmen were asleep, the peat fuel kept in the loft caught fire mysteriously, and destroyed the rafters and roof. It was about two in the morning. The flames reached the gunpowder kept in the tower, and by then everyone in the city was out of bed. Ladders and buckets were still the main fire-fighting devices. People tried gallantly to rescue letters, books, money, and the bank's gold and silver, and succeeded to some extent — because the fire stayed up above long enough for rescue work. However, some silver coins were melted down. According to Adam Smith, writing in the next century, gold and silver paid out by the bank twenty years later had obviously been scorched by the fire. As the flames licked out, the Dam was hidden in smoke, Vondel said. Naturally there was a tragic loss of old archives and pictures. Looters got away with 51,000 guilders. But the regents showed great resilience. The next day the exchange bank opened for business two streets away, the burgomasters moved to a tavern on the Dam, "The Prince" (the town bell was hung from a window as the sign of authority), and the Council went to the Prinsenhof — which is, it so happens, where it is now.

Rembrandt made a drawing of the ruins immediately afterwards. They had more attraction and meaning than the oversize pile of Italianate, non-Dutch grandeur which was slowly arising behind them (and whose scaffolding, although so close, had somehow escaped damage). Age and decay had lost none of their compelling interest for him.

15.

HE WAS STILL LIVING in his splendid house. He looks out from the wonderful self-portrait of 1652, a sturdy, thick, middle-aged man with an expression that implies readiness for anything. Whatever you say to him next, or do to him next, it won't surprise him. He is defensive, wary, skeptical and confident. The ten years since Saskia's death had been a time of withdrawing into himself more and more, without however becoming solitary — the process would go on until his death, and so would his development. He had friends, but he certainly did not cultivate the better society of Amsterdam. He tended instead to find comfort with more common people, although he still saw the young patrician Jan Six, and had other high acquaintances, like Cornelis Witsen and Dr. Tulp, both about to be burgomasters. He was not wholly forgotten. And the pupils kept coming. After leaving him they often became fashionable and were better paid than their master — as, for example, Ferdinand Bol and Govaert Flinck. He went his own way — not quite approved of for his queer, obstinate individualism. His country excursions, never very far — Arnhem and Amersfoort seem to have been the farthest — affected him deeply. He produced dozens of almost miraculous drawings and etchings of what he saw. He often went to Jan Six's house on the Diemerdijk, between Amsterdam and Muiden. More and more he became pervaded by a religious feeling of the kinship of all nature, landscape, animals, things, people. Whatever subject he was dealing with received and reflected the glow of this humble, beautiful universalism. The *Slaughtered Ox* comes to mind — it is more than a carcass hanging in a butcher's cellar, with a woman looking round the door, it is the martyrdom of all animals, and more than that, the martyrdom of flesh itself, the martyrdom involved in all life.

Rembrandt had some domestic happiness, for Saskia came alive again in Titus, who was growing into a particularly attractive boy and was a center of his interest. He painted him constantly. And there was Hendrickje Stoffels, a plumpish good-looking girl, probably an Amsterdam orphan rather than a peasant, whose arrival in his household as a servant upset Titus's nurse, Geertje Dircks. The latter had been with Rembrandt from 1642 on, when she was about thirty-five, a homely middle-aged widow. She had been of great service to him and he, extravagant and kind as always, became close to her — reaping a whirlwind when a young girl came into the house. Titus's nurse suffered the tortures of jealousy. Rembrandt was in many ways a Christlike figure, but there are disadvantages to universal loving kindness, where the general unfairness of life makes the recipients themselves liable to feelings of hate and revenge or simply misery; the loving kindness can begin to seem pure callousness. Poor Geertje Dircks had been in her own eyes the mistress for three or four years — she loved the painter and loved Titus, and she had put the boy in her will. He was the co-legatee with her mother, with the one condition that he should give one hundred guilders and her portrait, obviously a Rembrandt, to the child of some relation. But the main point about the will was that Rembrandt had made gifts to her, including a diamond ring — probably Saskia's — and the idea, possibly his, was that these should return to Titus. Hendrickje turned up first as an eighteen- or nineteen-year-old model, came more often, and finally was in for keeps. In June 1649 Geertje blew up, threatened to go away to make a scandal and also to alter the will. (Servants in Amsterdam were a fairly privileged class — their lordships on the council had laid down strict regulations. Very unsatisfactory behavior could land them in the pillory or even get them an official whipping, but if an employer beat them he would be heavily fined. They could give notice when they liked, but couldn't be sacked except for thieving. Except in the grander houses they lived on equal terms with the family.) Rembrandt, faced with this crisis, offered to pay her 150 guilders to redeem some of his gifts — which she had pawned — and then to give her 160 guilders a year, to guard against a sort of breach of promise action. But Geertje brooded, her relatives stirred her up, and the matter came before court. Rembrandt was summoned in September, and on October 1, Hendrickje, making her public debut, gave evidence that the first offer had been agreed. A few days later, in the kitchen of Rembrandt's house, his lawyer was trying to persuade Geertje to accept a down payment of two hundred guilders — but she refused to listen and refused to sign. Then there was another summons and they were both in court again on October 23 — the judge decided that he must pay two hundred guilders a year, but ruled otherwise in favor of the June arrangement. And that was not the end of it, for the poor woman broke down completely the next year and her relatives sent her to a home at Gouda — they asked him to advance the expenses of this, which he did.

The lily that festers smells far worse than weeds, and it was no wonder that Rembrandt, who had been so fashionable and so ambitious, as it seemed, in the best bourgeois style, should not have been one of the six artists chosen by Frederick Henry's widow to celebrate different aspects of the late prince, or that not Rembrandt but the highly respectable and dependable and fashionable Van der Helst, who would die quite rich, was commissioned to paint the *Banquet of the Civic Guard to Celebrate the Treaty of Münster.* No wonder, either, that the interest shown in him by the fastidious Constantyn Huyghens apparently lapsed. Rembrandt had gone a little to seed to all outward appearances, which included a certain indifference to the state of his clothes. Three or four weeks before the burning of the old Town Hall he had buried a child he had had by Hendrickje. It was a new taste of sorrow for him — equally it was not the sort of event, in the highly religious, Calvinist-run city, which won respect and favor. And the war which had begun would very soon add to his troubles with its effect on the credit situation. In February 1653, the bill came in for the money owing on the house — with interest accruing, it amounted to 8,470 guilders. It was naturally a time for old debts to come up, for Amsterdam was in a state of financial depression — the successful English blockade of the coast threatened every kind of business prospect. Rembrandt managed to borrow 4,000 guilders each from Cornelis Witsen and Isaac van Heertsbeeck, and 1,000 from Jan Six, and was able to meet the bill. But he still owed the money. Obviously the air was full of portents. Vondel was also heading for financial disaster. He needed to concentrate in order to achieve his colossal output of poetical dramas and celebratory odes — in spite of the chilliness about his religion he acted as a semiofficial Amsterdam laureate and no important wedding or funeral went by without inspiring a dozen or even several hundred Baroque lines. Accordingly he had handed over his hosiery business in the Warmoes-straat to his son, and the latter was now making a mess of it. However, this was still hidden from the poet, who had gone to live with his daughter in a house on the Singel. In the autumn of that year — with Amsterdam feeling a little better, for the blockade had been broken in August — everything still seemed splendid. Now sixty-six, a most benevolent-looking, white-haired little man, rather like a kindly general, he was in the middle of writing his masterpiece, *Lucifer* — a precursor by thirteen years of *Paradise Lost,* which it possibly influenced; Milton, who had learned Dutch, certainly read it. On October 20 he was a guest at a banquet for "painters, poets and lovers of the arts" in the hall of the St. Joris–Doelen. This was to inaugurate the Amsterdam painters' guild — the Guild of St. Luke — which had been organized by Van der Helst and Nicolaes de Helt Stokade, two organization men. About a hundred people were there, possibly including Rembrandt — emphatically not an organization man — who would of course, from now on, be subject to the professional control of the guild, a fact that would cost him plenty.

Certainly the most important guest was one of the burgomasters, Joan (Johan) Huydecoper, who was immensely rich and an enthusiastic patron of the arts and artists. Brought up to great wealth he had married a daughter of Balthazar Coymans, possibly the biggest merchant and banker in the city. Vingboons, the fashionable architect, had built him a sumptuous house on the Singel (by the present Carlton Hotel), with a large garden full of fountains and sculptures. He kept his own poet, Jan Vos, who exaltedly described all his possessions. He was expansive and popular. When he became captain of a militia company Jan Vos said that all Amsterdam was buried in a sea of smoke and flame from the happy shots in the air. He loved being painted and dressing up and social occasions, and the current leader of the Amsterdam "Magnificat," the most splendid and powerful of all the burgomasters throughout the two centuries of the Republic, Cornelis de Graeff, was glad to send him on embassies. Once he took four patrician youths, including his own and De Graeff's sons, to Berlin, with an entourage of servants and soldiers all dressed in Amsterdam's livery. One of the boys, Pieter de Graeff, described with high amusement how the great man lost his nerve when he had to make a presentation speech in German. But they were welcomed back with a procession of seventy extravagantly dressed riders. That was Huydecoper, and naturally the St. Luke's Guild was crazy about him.

However, this was Vondel's night. On his arrival he was paid homage in a poem read out to him by a guild member dressed up as Apollo. He was given the place of honor at the head of the table, and there he listened to poem after poem eulogizing him. Banquets were among the major Amsterdam amusements. They could last for hours, with courses being served from two o'clock in the afternoon until eleven at night — roasts, pies, chickens, geese, and of course always a great amount to drink. Toast followed toast — everybody was toasted. In a country dependent on the carrying trade every import was likely to be reexported: but not wine. (Rotterdam, however, not Amsterdam, had the best of the wine trade.) So Vondel enjoyed himself. He wrote an ode of thanks, which was read out at next year's banquet.

Lucifer was performed at the theater on February 2, 1654, and for the second and last time on the fifth. It wasn't quite the run Vondel hoped for, but in between the performances his old Calvinist enemies had stepped in. "Yesterday," said a Protocol published on the fifth, "the Consistory was informed that a tragedy has been produced by Joost van den Vondel, called *Luisevaer's Tragedy*, about the fall of the angels, dealing in a humanly sensual manner with the exalted subject of the profundities of God, offering scandalous and unbridled stories, and that this same tragedy is to be played again today. The Consistory is of the opinion that this is wholly irregular, and has ordered Dr. Ruleus and Dr. Langhelij, with Brother Elyson, to remonstrate with the Burgomasters and persuade them to use their authority to prevent the playing of the tragedy and to this end to salute their lordships. The Brothers report that they have carried out this duty at their lordships' houses and at places where they were meeting, and have brought back the answer that their lordships were unable, owing to the pressure of business, to take any action this evening, but will forbid it tomorrow and give an order that it will not be played again. . . ."

They pursued him further, because the ban, as bans do, made the printed version a best seller — and the first edition was gone in a week. On February 12 the Consistory sent Drs. Ruleus and Langhelij back to the burgomasters to ask for the withdrawal of the book and the forbidding of its sale. On the nineteenth they reported that the burgomasters "had difficulties, saying that people would be all the more eager to buy it." No flies on the burgomasters. The persistent Church kept trying and in the end "out of respect for the Consistory" the burgomasters agreed that the book should be withdrawn. Withdrawn or not, however, six editions of the play were brought out in the year, so Vondel was able to get some satisfaction out of the wreckage.

The same year, during which Rembrandt painted two wonderful pictures of Hendrickje — in one she was a model for *A Woman Bathing* and in the other for a nude *Bathsheba at Her Toilet* — the Consistory investigated their relationship with predictable disapproval. They were summoned to appear together, and ignored. Then in July another summons arrived, for Hendrickje alone. Presumably they had now realized that

Rembrandt was not a member. There is a possibility that he belonged to the Mennonites, a sect which flourished in Amsterdam — their insistence on the sanctity of human life and the authority of the Bible fitted his philosophy. Hendrickje went through the ordeal alone. She made no attempt to deny the situation — in any case she was pregnant — and received the penalty of being forbidden Holy Communion. She was not bothered. Her first loyalty then and always was to Rembrandt. He would probably have married her, except for the complication that his usufruct of Titus's inheritance from Saskia would lapse on remarriage. They went on living in sin and their daughter, Cornelia, was baptized on October 30. The child survived and so now there were four of them.

16.

ANOTHER AMSTERDAMER now beginning to upset his religious superiors was a brilliant young man of twenty-one, Baruch Spinoza, destined to be, in Bertrand Russell's words, the noblest and most lovable of the great philosophers. But how different these two were, though living, as it happened, a stone's throw from each other. The painter was a big wine, full of romance, intuition and passion. The youth was pure, crystal-clear water.

His family were Portuguese Jews who had escaped from the Inquisition in 1593 and found safety in Amsterdam. They were merchants, not rich but respected. Their background had some distinction. There had been famous Galician "Espinosas" in the fourteenth century. But in Amsterdam they had had to start from scratch. Baruch was born in 1632 in a fairly modest dwelling in the narrow Houtsteeg — in the crowded Jewish quarter where Rembrandt loved to stroll — and lived his first years among the sights and sounds of the largely poverty-stricken Portuguese, German and Polish Jews. Then his father bought a superior house on the site, later, of Waterlooplein 41. Illness and death struck them. One daughter remained from his father's first marriage. Baruch was the child of the second. His one brother died, and so did his mother, when he was six. Another girl survived.

Life in the Jewish quarter was full of psychological and social complica-

Benedict Spinoza
COURTESY OF THE MANSELL COLLECTION

tions. Poverty was worse amongst the Germans, whom the more sophisticated Portuguese and Spanish "Sephardi" rather despised. Many of the latter had been forcibly brought up as Catholics and they or their parents had been used to pretending a religion, which led to a wider viewpoint — which led also to conflict within the Sephardi. The Germans disapproved of the Portuguese habit of bringing their tobacco into the synagogue and about their casual attitudes to prayer. Again, while German children were kept much more under guard, so that they should not "see anything evil," the Portuguese and Spanish could play their traditional "El Castillo" in the street. They could wander into the rich city.

In fact there was a certain liberalism in the Portuguese tradition, and this was something their own rabbis, in the synagogue and in the newly founded school, were very wary about.

When he was eight Baruch was given a close-up view of the synagogue's power. He saw what happened to Gabriel da Costa. This was a Portuguese Jew who had been brought up in Portugal as a Catholic. He had even taken lay orders, but burdened with a highly sensitive character he had run into spiritual difficulties. He was in fear of eternal damnation and began to yearn after the law of Moses. He fled with his mother and sisters to Amsterdam, where he was circumcised but also soon disillusioned. He went back to his old beliefs and was finally excommunicated. Six years later in 1624 he wrote a "scandalous" book questioning the immortality of the soul. The pendulum swung again and overcome by his loneliness in 1632 he was trying to rejoin the community. But he still openly expressed some outrageous views and a nephew of his passed these on to the synagogue. The rabbis suggested a suitable exorcizing punishment and Da Costa, hearing about it, preferred to go on as he was. But the matter was pursued within his family for years, until the poor fellow was broken, and so on a certain Sabbath in 1640 he went through with it. First he had to read out a statement of his errors to the synagogue congregation, and promise never to make them again. Then, half undressed, he was tied to a pillar and lashed on his back thirty-nine times, while the congregation sang psalms. Finally he was laid on the ground at the threshold and everybody trod over him. Now it was permissible to welcome him back. But there was no happy ending. Humiliated and enraged, he hurried home and tried to shoot his nephew. Having failed, he shot himself.

Baruch's father held various honorary administrative posts in the community, which hints that he was probably no scholar. The rabbis preferred business to be carried out by businessmen. The kind of advice he gave to Baruch shows in a story (told by the philosopher's French friend, Jean Maximilien Lucas) of the boy being sent by his father to collect a debt from an old woman. He found her deep in the Bible and had to wait. When she finally paid him the money she told him, "Be as honorable a man as your father — he has never strayed from Moses' Law — be like him and you will receive Heaven's grace." Baruch was instantly conscious of his father's warnings about such fulsomeness, and insisted on counting out the money again; upon which he found that the old woman had managed to slide away two gold pieces. His father was delighted.

Baruch, however, was made to be a scholar and not a merchant. At school his life was spent with the Pentateuch from eight to eleven every morning and two to five every afternoon. Spanish was the vernacular of the children, but they were taught Hebrew thoroughly and of course they all picked up Dutch. Other subjects, like mathematics, had to be learned in private lessons. There were seven classes to pass through and the Talmud was dealt with in the sixth and seventh. Baruch was engrossed by it all and his brilliance pointed inevitably to a life as a rabbi. As he grew up he developed into a handsome, pale, slim youth with glowing eyes and dark curling hair.

His teachers — who were elected by the community and paid enough for independence — included two who were especially well known. Manasse ben Israel, an Amsterdam rabbi at eighteen, had begun a printing press and was on correspondence terms with many famous Europeans, such as Grotius, and he was to do great service for the Jews in England by his negotiations with Cromwell. But though full of knowledge he was a naïve believer in every word of the Cabala, and in every new Messiah rumor, or in any semiconfidence man like Aron Levi, who was in Amsterdam in September 1644, telling tall stories about American Indians whom he claimed to be descendants of the Jews. Unlike him, the other eminent teacher, Rabbi Morteira, who was also the presiding rabbi of the community, had no outside reputation. He was a clever polemicist, a great scholar of the Talmud and the Cabala, buried deep in old Jewish lore and blind to any other viewpoint. He was magnificently painted by Rembrandt. The portrait shows a white-bearded man full of intellect and dignity and arrogance. Rembrandt also etched Manasse — who was painted by Govaert

Flinck — and this was a man more cheerful, lively and rotund. Both teachers, but especially Morteira, idolized their gifted pupil, Baruch Spinoza.

Unfortunately for the rabbis' peace, a pupil could be too good. He might think so thoroughly and well that he came to unpalatable conclusions. Baruch was asking philosophical and theological questions. There was no question of arguing in the school — that was emphatically not done. But for the enquiring scholar there was a vast tradition of criticism and Baruch was soon deep in it. The Cabala's mysteries struck him as ridiculous. Twelfth-century religious philosophers of Moorish Spain like Abraham Ibn Ezra and Moses Maimonides, and in the fourteenth century Gersonides and Crescas, all of them were apt to point out disconcerting biblical inconsistencies and to provoke almost heretical ideas, including the pantheistic notion of God in all things and all things in God — an idea abhorrent to the orthodox.

Apart from this there was the influence of Spanish literature. He read the greatly admired contemporary satirist Quevedos. He was learning Latin from a German student. Politics touched him in the Sunday gatherings where the news that had come in during the week to the Amsterdam Jewish quarter from London and Venice was freely discussed. But his most intense reactions were to the philosophical-theological ferment of the Renaissance, which owing to the multitude of sects had a firm grip in Amsterdam. Descartes was being discussed. There was much confidential passing round of "hot" manuscripts and discreet conversations about the revolutionary ideas of people like the heroic Italian Giordano Bruno. Hobbes had recently been published in Amsterdam. All this was outside the closed Jewish world. Searching for his answers the embryo rabbi read and overheard everything he could.

Two jealous friends among the synagogue students provoked him to talk about his new and dangerous opinions, such as that God had a body because He could not be separated from nature, that angels were fantasy figures, that soul meant no more than life and so on — and reported to Rabbi Morteira. He, of course, was appalled. The brilliant youth was put on the mat, but remained calm, while Morteira beseeched him to stay loyal to the beliefs he had been taught and then, enraged, threatened excommunication.

For the time being Baruch seemed quiescent, but his mind stormed with ethical, religious and philosophical crises of doubt and uncertainty. He became conscious of more and more voices in the great and fascinating city. He would certainly not become a rabbi now, but while the synagogue authorities watched him reproachfully he found a temporary way to peace in mathematics.

He had already made friends outside the Jewish community, with Christians whose views approached the philosophy he was developing — especially among a group called the Collegiants. These had begun as a breakaway movement from the "Remonstrants" thirty years before. They met at Rijnsburg, a village near Leyden — simple people, farmers and craftsmen — and they played at being prophets and advocated peace and love. Descartes was once curious enough to go and inspect them. Towards the end of the 1640's they turned up in Amsterdam, in a more sophisticated guise — forming a discussion group. They were one of many "Ethical" societies or circles in the city, existing more or less unseen in the midst of the commercial bustle, all of them brimming over with godliness and good intentions.

Among the Amsterdam Collegiants were many Mennonites, who shared with them a dislike of church organization, dogma, oath-taking, sacramentalizing the Lord's Supper — and also a taste for simplicity and pacifism, and for the striving for knowledge. All this tended to attract Baruch. His knowledge of Hebrew made him an asset to them in return.

His new friends, mostly young, included Simon Joosten de Vries, who was related through his mother to Vondel, and became a well-to-do merchant; Pieter Balling, who acted as an agent for Spanish business interests and was interested in mysticism; and Jarig Jelles, who had given up being a spice merchant to devote himself to the pursuit of knowledge. They were helpful to him in his struggle — he said it was a struggle — to live in the manner he had decided was a condition of happiness. This was to seek only enough money or pleasure which was necessary for health, and to be wary of fame.

That the struggle had been partially won was shown by his conduct in 1654, when his father died and he was suddenly alone. The only other survivor of the family was his half-sister, Rebecca. Aided by a brother-in-law, she tried to get the inheritance away from him. Baruch contested it firmly and won. Having won, he kept for himself one bed and one bed-curtain, and handed everything over to her.

To keep himself now he learned how to grind lenses. At the same time he joined a school run by a fifty-two-year-old Antwerper called Francis van den Ende at a house in the center of the city, in the street called the Nes. Baruch taught simple Latin and advanced Hebrew in return for lodgings and the chance to go on studying his own Latin. His employer had formerly been a Jesuit, but he had had to leave the order owing to "errors." He had married, and become the father of two daughters, and settled in Amsterdam — where his first venture, a bookshop, was a failure. His Latin school, however, was a success. Van den Ende was a remarkable character. (In due course he went to France, practiced as a doctor, and ended as a failed conspirator on the scaffold.) He managed to combine free-thinking with the Catholic faith — which he conveniently called "the second truth." He could teach Cartesian, Stoic and Scholastic philosophy, and his house was full of students, all to Baruch's benefit — not only youths learning Latin but pantheistic so-called Libertines, much more revolutionary than his Mennonite friends.

In this atmosphere he lived and worked for two years, while naturally enough his relationship with his own community became more and more strained — especially when he refused an extraordinary offer by a group of leading Jews to pay him a pension of a thousand guilders a year, if he would stay and work within the community and at least go to the synagogue. Obviously they did not underestimate him. It could also be that they were oversensitive to the relationship between the community and the protective city and did not want a scandal. In any case Baruch was made very thoughtful when a man leaped on him with a dagger as he left the theater. (Or, by another account, it could have been the synagogue.) This probably helped him make up his mind that it was time to leave Amsterdam. Either way his enemies in the community were out to get him and in July 1656 he was at last excommunicated, as Morteira had threatened:

". . . With the judgment of the angels and the sentence of the saints, we anathematize, curse and cast out Baruch de Espinoza . . . pronouncing against him the malediction wherewith Elisha cursed the children and all the maledictions written in the Book of the Law. Let him be accursed by day and accursed by night; let him be accursed in going out and accursed in going in . . . hereby then are all admonished that none hold converse with him by word of mouth, none hold communication with him by writing; that no one do him any service, no one abide under the same roof with him, no one approach within four cubits' length of him, and no one read any documents dictated by him, or written by his hand."

While these awesome words were read out, candles in the synagogue were gradually extinguished to represent his spiritual death. But Baruch was not present. He was already out of the city. Rabbi Morteira had been to the authorities and demanded his banishment for blasphemy — and this was ordered, after consultation with the Calvinists, though only for a few months. Baruch went a few miles south to Ouderkerk, the village where the Jewish cemetery lay. There he probably stayed at the country house of Coenraad Burgh, an Amsterdam magistrate, a son-in-law of Hooft and a Collegiant. This was the family which had helped Vondel. Rembrandt's Dr. Tulp had married into it, and later the doctor inherited the house — though, as a stern Calvinist, he was quite out of sympathy with the Collegiant outlook. Rembrandt had also been there and made some sketches.

Ahead of Spinoza was a quiet, collected and virtuous life. He could show courage when necessary, but his motto was caution. Whether or not he was shattered by what had happened, one of his first acts in "exile" was to write a defense of himself in Spanish, which he sent to the synagogue. For the next three or four years — after the banishment period — he would often be in Amsterdam, seeing his friends, and Van den Ende, one of whose daughters he possibly contemplated as a wife — however, she married a German student instead. And afterwards he came back to the city occasionally. But the excommunication was the watershed. It was the end of his life as an Amsterdamer and the end of his youth. Now could begin the mind's journey which would be a treasure of mankind.

Oddly enough, the day before the ceremony, and only a few hundred yards away, Rembrandt had been meeting disaster.

17.

THE UNCERTAINTY of his income due to the personal character of his painting, the continuing extravagance in buying whatever objets d'art he fancied, and the debts that ran on and on, all this suddenly pointed to the Amsterdamer's nightmare — bankruptcy. Already in May, in a desperate attempt to save things, the house had been transferred to Titus. Rembrandt had appeared before the Chamber of Orphans to transfer the deeds. The move did not succeed, for the house was, after all, the principal security on which he had borrowed. His friend Jan Six — or former friend — had already seen the red light, and shown that although he loved art, he also loved — as an Amsterdamer should — his guilders. The thousand he had loaned had been guaranteed by Lodewijk van Ludick, a friend of Rembrandt's. No doubt about it, it could be expensive to be a friend, for Jan Six prudently sold his bill to a merchant (losing only the discount), and when the crisis came, the latter made Ludick pay up. To be fair to Jan Six he was possibly short of cash, for he was just about to get married to Margarite, daughter of Rembrandt's Dr. Tulp — who was now one of the burgomasters. However, in July 1656, Rembrandt was forced to ask for his insolvency to be declared. The city Commissioners in Bankruptcy moved in, a receiver was appointed, and on the twenty-fifth and twenty-sixth an inventory of his property was drawn up.

There were 363 items, including paintings by Raphael, Van Eyck, Bassano, Palma Vecchio, Giorgione, Brouwer, Seghers, etchings by Michelangelo and Titian, Rubens, Van Dyck, Brueghel the Elder, Carracci, Holbein, Cranach, busts of Roman emperors, a Michelangelo head, and the porcelain and the fans, the medals, the glasses, the stringed instruments, the weapon collection, the pieces of coral, the shells, the Japanese helmet, the Spanish chairs, all these and more in all departments, except, perhaps, books. The Bible and sales catalogues seem to have been Rembrandt's only reading, but that was right and proper — he did not need words. If he wanted, unconsciously, an occasion for bitterness and despair, a private crucifixion, here it was. More creditors appeared. Worry and humiliation were the daily diet. He had to wait for the sale, which took some time to organize and was done in three parts — all the while he went on living in the house, and working as usual; but he was allowed to keep only a minimal amount to cover living expenses. The 1657 self-portrait shows him taking all the blows but staying defiant — and one reason is shown in the portrait of the sixteen-year-old Titus, who gazes beautifully and lovingly out. He was growing up in a world falling about him, but like Hendrickje he remained steadfast. The first sale did not come until December — paintings and objets d'art — and the second in the following February, when the house and furniture were sold. The house went for 11,218 guilders, but owing to objections lodged by creditors the sale was not authorized for twelve months. The third sale, of drawings and etchings, was in September

The Jewish Bride — Rembrandt

Officials of the Drapers Guild — Rembrandt

Self-Portrait — Rembrandt at sixty-five

1658. The notice advertising it read: "The Trustee of the insolvent estate of Rembrandt van Rijn, skilful Painter, shall as authorized by their lordships the Commissioners in Bankruptcy of this city, sell by order the paper art of the above estate consisting of the etchings of various eminent Italian, French, German and Netherlands masters, collected by the same Rembrandt van Rijn with remarkable care. Together with a large number of drawings and sketches by Rembrandt van Rijn himself. The sale will take place on the day, hour and year as above at the house of Barent Jantz Schuurman, Innkeeper of the Keysers Kroon (Emperor's Crown) in the Kalverstraat. . . ."

It was at least a splendid-looking inn, with a crown over the entrance, and imperial crests decorating a façade largely composed of windows with a classical pediment crowning the gable. But the knock-down prices were the cruelest blow. The Guild of St. Luke was largely responsible, for in the fine old tradition of professional organizations it helped in the persecution of its greatest member by laying down at this time, perhaps from a fear of the market being saturated, that any selling up by a member must be done speedily. Secondly, having sold up, he could not carry on his business in the city. The proceeds of the sales, of possessions valued at 17,000 guilders, were less than 5,000. This plus the house, did not add up at all to the 20,000 guilders he owed his creditors. But not surprisingly the man who was paid in full and first was Dr. Cornelis Witsen, who had loaned him 4,000 guilders to pay off the debt on the house, and who just happened to be a burgomaster. Isaac van Heertsbeeck, who had also loaned 4,000, had to die with it unpaid. A legal battle went on about Titus's share of the estate — Rembrandt could no longer be his trustee — and their friends tried to prove how much Saskia had been worth, by giving evidence about jewelry and so forth, while the creditors did their best to knock the sum down. It was all squalid and humiliating — and not too agreeable for the unpaid creditors.

Four years after the inventory had been taken some sort of settlement was reached at last. The purchaser took over the Breestraat house and the battered Rembrandt moved with his household to the Rozengracht on the other side of the city, a long quiet canal street in the unfashionable but colorful Jordaans district, leading up to the Westerkerk. Not far away, just over 280 years later, a young Jewish girl would hide, week after week, month after month, and win her own immortality — Anne Frank. Here Rembrandt settled down. A way out of the Guild of St. Luke's rule preventing him from carrying on business was found — Hendrickje and Titus formed a company and employed him.

Amsterdam's greatest painter was insolvent. So was its greatest poet. In his seventieth year, 1657, poor Vondel had suddenly been informed that his son, having ruined the Warmoes-straat hosiery business, was departing hastily for the Indies, leaving him to face the (that word again) creditors. Unlike Rembrandt, whose ruin had been more or less self imposed by his own extravagance, Vondel had always lived simply — in spite of his associations with the great and noble — and his troubles had come through his desire not to be preoccupied by trade. But either reason was ground enough to earn disgrace in the city, for the true Amsterdamer of at least the first half of the century was both unextravagant and devoted to trade and trading. Vondel's behavior in his crisis was heroic. Though far from strong he went to Denmark to face the more important creditors. He had a modest but comfortable capital of 40,000 guilders, on which he lived. It all went into the disaster. Left with no assets at all he took a clerk's job in the city bank, although he was now over seventy. And still he went on writing his verse dramas. He produced four biblical tragedies during 1659–1660 — *Jephta, Samson, King David in Exile, King David Restored* — and finished his translations of *Oedipus Tyrannus* and the *Aeneid*. Is it any surprise that he was told off at the bank for writing poetry in working hours? The official who told him off has earned a black name for himself, but in Amsterdam of all places his attitude was surely reasonable. It was not even as if his venerable clerk had the sense to be earning good money on the side by his activity — unlike the painters, writers had to put up with being, largely, amateurs paid by fame rather than cash.

18.

IN ANY CASE, insolvency is properly and naturally the artist's companion. Two more Amsterdamers of the time who knew about it were the landscape painters Jacob van Ruisdael, a Haarlemer who at thirty-one had just been admitted to Amsterdam citizenship, and his young friend and pupil

Meyndert Hobbema, who was in the city all his life. Ruisdael's *Jewish Burial Ground* has the reputation of being the greatest landscape ever painted, but all the same he died in a Mennonite almshouse. Hobbema had, but should not have had, a similar fate. His production of exquisite country scenes was cut short by his marriage to a burgomaster's cook, and his bride's influence gained him an establishment job that should have made his fortune. He had to gauge the casks in which wine was imported and estimate their contents in the Amsterdam measure. How could he have *failed* to make a fortune? But both he and his wife died as paupers. He is supposed to have painted no more after his marriage. Poor Hobbema. And poor Mevrouw Hobbema, too.

But Amsterdam was not full of bankrupt artists and poets. The business of the city was business. Amsterdam was rich. Its population was now 200,000. Naturally, there were downs as well as ups. There had been the English blockade in the '52–'54 war. The brilliant young John de Witt, now the Council-Pensionary and the most influential man in the Netherlands, had forced through a drop in the interest paid to investors in government funds to four percent (from five percent — nobody liked that). There was always nervousness about what the French were doing or planning in the southern Netherlands. In 1657 war broke out with Portugal. Like all wars it kept well away from Amsterdam, but it reflected some of the troubles of the West India Company. Already some empty warehouses, empty because of the loss of Brazilian trade, had been turned into a workhouse for poor children (later it was also used for beggars and loafers who were picked up and forced to work there). Admiral de Ruyter had now become one of the country's great names; his squadrons dealt with French freebooters in the Mediterranean and helped blockade the Portuguese by seizing their merchant ships at sea — all of which was beginning to stir up bad relationships with England again, but fortunately Cromwell's death eased the strain. The Portuguese affair ended well, with the Dutch totally leaving Brazil — though many independent Dutch merchants remained there, and all along the northeast South American coastline — with compensation; and in the East, which was far more important and profitable for the Amsterdam business community, the hold on the old Portuguese possessions was solidified. What really worried Amsterdam, however, was the danger to the grain trade caused by Charles X of Sweden, who was being aggressive in the Baltic. His siege of Danzig caused the Amsterdam merchants to break out into a flurry of warlike demands, and the States-General was pressured into sending a fleet through the Sound to raise the siege. This was done and a garrison left there, with the agreement of the Poles.

Obviously the Swedes would not let it go at this, and though John de Witt was anxious for a peaceful settlement, Amsterdam, touched on its sensitive grain market nerve, remained most unusually bellicose. The Council-Pensionary had certainly every means of knowing their attitude, for he owed his job in the first place to the influence of Cornelis de Graeff and now he had just married the great burgomaster's niece, Wendela, daughter of Jan Bicker. (Vondel, of course, had written a poem about the wedding.) So De Witt was entirely mixed up with the "Magnificat" and the relationship between The Hague and Amsterdam was never closer.

But however much De Witt wanted peace, another important Amsterdamer made it impossible. This was the brilliant and talkative Van Beuningen, who was the ambassador of the States-General in Copenhagen. (In a few years' time, Sir William Temple, who admired him, warned another diplomat, "He'll talk you to death.") Van Beuningen urged the Danish king to fight and rely on the Dutch, and was popularly believed to have told the Swedes, when they threatened to close the straits, that they would fail because "The oaken keys of the Sound lay in the docks of Amsterdam." The boast turned out to be justified, though it was expensive to make it good. There was a naval battle, with considerable casualties, followed by an expedition sent to the Baltic under De Ruyter —with 12,000 troops and 3,000 guns. In November 1659, he took the Swedish-occupied town of Nyborg in Denmark by storm, and became the master of the Baltic. De Witt was able to make a magnanimous peace.

He and De Ruyter were praised by Sir William Temple for the simplicity and modesty of their way of living. "I never saw (De Ruyter) in Cloaths better than the commonest Sea-Captain, nor with above one Man following him, nor in a Coach: And in his own House, neither was the Size, Building, Furniture, or Entertainment, at all exceeding the use of every common Merchant and Tradesman in his Town." The town was Amsterdam — he lived on the Buitenkant, near the wharves and not far from the Weepers' Tower and the Engelsekaai. Sir William also noted approvingly that De Witt's private establishment at The Hague was merely the same as any minister's, that he had only one personal servant and that he could be seen on foot in the streets "like the commonest Burgher." But the rich of Amsterdam as well as of The Hague had for some time been losing their outward simplicity of behavior. The Six family in the picture painted by Barent Grant for the betrothal of Jan Six and Margarite Tulp are all dressed simply enough, but they give an impression of complete opulence. The big money was beginning to be spent more openly. The new house of the Trip family going up on the Kloveniersburgwal was large enough to serve in due course more or less as the national art gallery, until the Rijksmuseum appeared at the end of the nineteenth century. Designed by Justus Vingboon — who with his brother Philippe was responsible for many of the loveliest houses in the city — it was really a small palace, complete with Corinthian pilasters, elaborately decorated windows and a very grand cornice and pediment.

So there was none of the old simplicity for the Trip family. Sometimes, however, the conscience of the rich could be pricked. There was a merchant who had a house built on the most elegant of the canals, the Herengracht. Expense was entirely disregarded. The architects, the builders, the stonemasons, everybody had a field day. The magnificent house soon rose and looking at it, the merchant burst with pride. He thought how he had started at the bottom, and how with shrewdness and with years of hard work he had accumulated a great fortune. He had done it alone and now he was a leading citizen of the leading commercial city in the world. His parents had existed in a hovel, and his children would live in a palace. It was something to make the heart sing. But the merchant had no sooner enjoyed these reflections than they were followed by others which sobered him. How did he know that his fortune would last? How could he expect his children, living here, to understand the world? He saw that it was essential for them to know that poverty was always possible, to remember their modest origin and to be aware that their forefathers had known privation, cold and hunger. He felt quite ashamed for his moment of exaltation.

Fortunately there was a way out — as, indeed, there usually is for people like the merchant — and he turned to his architect, who stood beside him. There happened to be some empty building land on the other side of the canal and he pointed to it. "We shall buy that plot tomorrow and you will build some small, narrow little houses there which I can let to poor people — build them so that they can be seen from every window of my house." The astonished architect accepted the commission, and what was more the merchant did not move in himself until they were built. His children were able to grow up with the poor constantly in view.

19.

"THE MIGHTY enlargement of the City of Amsterdam," Sir William Temple said (disapprovingly), ". . . must have employ'd a vast proportion of that Stock which in this City was before wholly turned to Trade. . . . There seems to have been growing on these later years, a greater Vie of Luxury and Expence among many of the Merchants . . . than was ever known." One height of luxury at this time, incidentally, the surest sign that a family was rich and trendy, was to have a torch-lit funeral at night. It was natural that funerals should be an important part of the fashionable round, when death was so frequent. Afterwards relations, friends and neighbors came to pay their respects and to drink toasts to the departed. Tradesmen who had supplied the deceased also turned up. The custom of having a banquet and a singsong was dying out, but not the drinking; in rich households, however, they were tending to give the poorer mourners money so that they could go off to the taverns.

The real center of the new expenditure was on the Dam. Jacob van Campen's Town Hall now stood there, proclaiming the greatness and wealth of the city. Owing to a superstition that Antwerp's glory began to dim in the year its Town Hall was finished, there was no anxiety to proclaim the finishing of Amsterdam's; and it was not really complete until the beginning of the eighteenth century. Imposing outside, it was magnificent inside, above all because of the immense "burgerzaal," the great hall which burghers were free to use. In its present form as a palace all the rooms used by the "Magnificat" — the Council chamber, the burgomasters' room, the commissions for matrimonial affairs, bankruptcy, minor offenses, and so on, the courts, including one for death sentences — remain much as they were. What there is now, but was not then, is a doorbell at the rear entrance which has a suitably deep, luxurious and royal sound. But possibly the horn they still used before announcements to the Dam of good and bad news was of equal quality.

A new Town Hall had been discussed as early as 1625, for the old one was becoming very unwieldy. But a committee of regents was not set up until 1639. They reported in 1640, in grandiose terms, and Andries Bicker for one was nervous at the cost implications of the houses and ground that would have to be bought, let alone the building. As an example, a shrewd and informed businessman, Mr. van der Wiere, was able to buy a house on the Dam in 1639 for 16,400 guilders, which he sold to the Council very soon afterwards for 25,500. Over 600,000 guilders had to be spent in this way. Constantyn Huyghens was responsible for bringing in Van Campen (who had designed the theater) as architect, and introduced him to the Muiden circle. But when Cornelis de Graeff laid the foundation stone in 1648 the plans were still very much under discussion, and Van Campen in the end was so upset at various alterations made by the "town-master-builder" Daniel Stalpaert, that he refused to attend the opening. In 1652 there was a crisis owing to the war situation, when they decided only to build one story, and in addition there was the question of the proposed tower on the Nieuwe Kerk, also designed by Van Campen and involving enormous expense. Both projects could not be managed and a Calvinist burgomaster, Willem Backer, was insistent on the church tower's priority. "God's wrath must fall on a city, when such treasure is spent on the outward appearance of a worldly building." But he died and that was the end of that view. The street which now lay between the two buildings was called Moses and Aaron, nicely symbolizing the distinction between the spiritual and the worldly. In any case the "Magnificat" preferred their Town Hall not to be dwarfed by any tower, even God's. And with the war over it went up with all stories, as planned.

On July 29, 1655, after an early service in the towerless Nieuwe Kerk, there was a splendid procession from the Prinsenhof to the Dam, halberdiers first, then the beadle with the city standard, then the Schout with his attendants, and then the burgomasters and the Council and all the staff. Cornelis de Graeff made the inaugural speech inside the Town Hall and outside festivities went on all day on the Dam. The pastors and elders of the church arrived to offer congratulations, and each pastor received a cask of Rhine wine, delivered to his home — which must surely have soothed anyone still upset about the Nieuwe Kerk tower.

The inauguration was also celebrated, naturally, by a long poem from Vondel and by the striking of a medal. This showed Mercury, the God of Trade, flying over the Town Hall with his snake staff and a hat bearing the Virgilian motto: *Omnibus idem* — To everybody the same. A crowd stood before the building, but in the foreground Amphion sat with his lyre (which once had caused some stones to rise up and form themselves into the walls of Thebes). At his feet was a stone tablet bearing the names of the burgomasters, Huydecoper, Cornelis de Graeff, Jan van der Poll, Spieghel, along with (but of course) Dr. Tulp and Cornelis van Dronkelaar, who were city treasurers that year. The Town Hall itself, filling most of the medal's face, stood shoulder to shoulder with a reticent Nieuwe Kerk — emphasizing a some-are-more-equal-than-others equality. Nobody doubted that the quotation from Horace encircling the medal was appropriate: *Fuit haec sapientia quondam* — This was the wisdom of the old days — that is, to build Town Halls like this.

How magnificent it was. Over the vast and solid base — including the modest entrance, which was like seven back doors (probably due to space shortage, but possibly a crowd-control precaution) — four lines of twenty-three windows stared down, and two rows of twenty-four pilasters. The higher row covering two lines of windows were Corinthian, while the lower row were Composite. In each of the two lines of windows the upper row were half the size of the lower. Somehow the building had to be thought of in these mathematical terms, it was all so solid, so uniform — and it was also as if instead of building a Town Hall with two wings, instead they put one wing on the other, making for seriousness and strength. On the central pediment Neptune and his attendants had been elaborately sculpted by Arturus Quellin (much more of whose slightly ponderous work was to be found inside), and on the summit of the pediment stood three allegorical figures. Behind them against the sky was the campanile supported by eight columns, and bearing a clock face. Above was a weathercock in the form of a ship. Up there, of course, the great spire of the church at Haarlem could be seen, and the Haarlem lake and all that great flat countryside, full of windmills and spires, even the distant ones of Utrecht. Every quarter of an hour a bell tune could be heard from the campanile — as it could be from the Oude Kerk and other churches, pleasant tunes that added to and were lost in the noise of the city.

But, however little anyone noticed, there was something sad about the Town Hall. After all, the architecture of the first part of the century had been very Dutch and very attractive. There had been the curious, remaining touch of Spanish influence. All sorts of fantastic and picturesque effects were somehow absorbed naturally in the northern air — the crooked lines of the gables, the pinnacles and scrolls on some of the

Herengracht and Keizersgracht houses. There was the slight exoticism about the Exchange and the East India Company headquarters and in some of the little streets around the St. Antonies–poort. Exotic, but Dutch-Amsterdamish. And there were the quite Oriental and Slavic campaniles they put up over the old towers and clocktowers — like the Montelbaans-tor, which used to be merely round and solid and all at once became like something out of Scheherazade. As for the North, South and West Churches — Noorderkerk, Zuiderkerk, Westerkerk — which were the same mix-up of influences, they violated all the classical laws with vulgarities and somehow ended up miraculously — they had the same touch of the slightly exotic, and yet were as bare and uncompromising as the Church could wish, and stood out with grace and elegance, Dutch as Dutch in the great Dutch sky. What a pity, then, that the architect Van Campen had now to express authority and grandeur — and rather heavily — in order to please his clients. His Town Hall was magnificent and imposing, but it was not Dutch. Up to now they had absorbed, but Van Campen's masterpiece was a sign of a growing compulsion to imitate. From now on the architects — often French already — would keep their gaze firmly abroad. The great houses on the Herengracht would be Louis XIV French. Culture in general would go abroad, too. In a few more years francomania would take over. The word that comes to mind increasingly is decadence. But it was still in 1661 a whisper, for the Republic was still approaching the peak of its power and influence, De Witt was in control at The Hague and his friends — the Bickers and De Graeff — in Amsterdam. And in his new house on the Rozengracht, as if his financial disasters had fed his soul, Rembrandt reached that awesome development of his work comparable to Beethoven's late quartets and the Shakespearean tragedies.

It was accompanied by more squalid money troubles and petty litigation, none of it particularly to his credit. It was in the sixties that Titus's share of the proceeds of the house sale was acknowledged. Isaac van Heertsbeeck, who had helped to save Rembrandt ten years before, actually had to hand back the 4,200 guilders he had been repaid — when he died, the debt was listed as irrecoverable. And now that the devoted son, Titus, had some cash, what did the loving old father do? Very soon, he was offering 1,000 guilders for a Holbein that appealed to him — he was the greatest Amsterdamer, but he was not, repeat not, an admirable citizen, and the bourgeois virtues definitely eluded him. In justice, he had suffered from plenty of sharp practice himself — the ruinous sale at knock-down prices, the activities of shrewd gentlemen who knew how to exploit artists' debts — such as Mijnheer Jan Bicker, who bought the bill of the original loan from Jan Six. He was quarrelsome, too. He had, like Shakespeare, no doubts about his capacities. He suffered certainly — the succession of self-portraits hauntingly prove that. But he was also at heart an actor, or an opera singer — he suffered and painted his suffering, and once or twice in the last self-portraits you seem to hear *Pagliacci*. A touch of the tragic clown, a touch of ham — but what a voice. The sixties soon brought him a humiliation. Vondel — who did have the bourgeois virtues — had chosen the theme of the Revolt of Julius Civilis against the Romans for some pictures to decorate the gallery of the Town Hall. Govaert Flinck, the former pupil of Rembrandt, was given the commission but died when he had merely made a few sketches; so they decided to divide the commission between several artists, and Rembrandt was to paint the scene where the oath to conspiracy was taken at a banquet. What was wanted was something pompous and Baroque — and what they received was a disturbing masterpiece full of grandeur and barbarism. It lasted in the Town Hall for a few months and then was taken back to the Rozengracht, where the master cut it down to its small central scene in the hope of being able to sell it. In the Town Hall a second-rate but dependable artist, Jurriaen Ovens, worked up a Govaert Flinck sketch and filled the space more to their lordships' satisfaction.

It was not all humiliation. That year he painted *The Syndics of the Drapers' Guild,* to everyone's satisfaction — five wonderful faces, with long hair and black hats, a heavy orange tablecloth, a servant at the back and evidently something interesting, but unseen, at the front. He still had half a dozen years of life — and it was the transcendental nature of that life with which every picture was now concerned. The self-portraits, the pictures of Homer, the love of the young couple in the *Jewish Bride* (which was just possibly of, or concerned with, Titus and his bride, Magdalena van Loo), *The Return of the Prodigal Son,* in all these light and shade and color were used to express the inexpressible. He could always make a living, if not a good one; though it was a long time since he was fashionable in Amsterdam his fame was widespread; his clients — with whom he usually had rows — included a Sicilian nobleman, Don Antonio Ruffo; he was visited in 1667 by Cosimo de' Medici, later the Grand Duke of Tuscany, who probably bought one of the self-portraits. There was always a market for his etchings, although he didn't do any after 1661 — earlier on his subtlest and deepest effects had been in etchings and drawings, but now he could do everything with paint.

There were two more blows to come. Hendrickje became ill. She was "sick in appearance" when she went to a lawyer to make her will in August 1661 and made Titus her heir after her daughter, Cornelia. She died and was buried in the Westerkerk in 1663. He lived on with Cornelia and his son, who managed his affairs. There was the time of financial relief — and a last chance to spend — when Titus was granted his money. But in February 1668 Titus married Magdalena, the daughter of an old friend of Rembrandt's, Jan van Loo, a silversmith. The couple went to live on the Singel near Magdalena's mother, and the old painter was left with Hendrickje's child, who was fourteen. That September his beloved Titus died. It was the most shattering blow of all. The last self-portrait shows a plump old fellow, punch-drunk, who has taken everything. Squabbles began again about money, now with Magdalena, who was anxious to safeguard the interest of her daughter, born after Titus's death; the sublime and the squalid were with Rembrandt to the end. But he had done enough and he did not survive the next year. When he died, on October 4, 1669, there was an unfinished picture on his easel — the old man Simeon recognizing the infant Jesus. Like Titus and Hendrickje he was buried somewhere in the Westerkerk. No one in Amsterdam bothered or cared.

III

How to Decay Richly
1669–1795

1.

A FEW YEARS BEFORE, across the Atlantic, New Amsterdam had been seized by the English. It was part of the general worsening of Anglo-Dutch relations which had begun when the republican Commonwealth in England came to an end and Charles II was able to return to his kingdom. The burgher-regent regime, presided over on a tightrope by the devoted and brilliant John de Witt, was not enthusiastic about the Stuarts, who were so closely related to the Orange family. Charles II returned the hostility with interest. The Navigation Act was enforced; the English arrived not only at New Amsterdam but at Guinea on the West African coast, where they seized Dutch settlements. The second Anglo-Dutch war was soon going strong. It was a good deal bloodier than the first one and except for a brief and unsuccessful intrusion by the Bishop of Münster's forces it was fought at sea. In spite of the seven Admiralties De Witt had been able to ensure that the navy was first-class. So were its admirals, Tromp and De Ruyter.

The war was expensive on both sides, with great battles in the Channel in 1665 and 1666. The French, acting as De Witt's allies, gave token but useful support in the Atlantic. Charles had his difficulties, among them the plague and the Great Fire of London — which led to the minister of the English church in the Beguinhof at Amsterdam being sharply reprimanded for offering prayers for the Londoners. The way was open for the great episode of De Ruyter's spectacular and daring raid up the River Medway in the summer of the second year, which deeply shocked and humiliated the English. The raid was a great help to De Witt in the peace negotiations already begun. England kept New Amsterdam, which became New York. (But you could still have a passage from Amsterdam for 50 guilders, with free food and drink on the upper deck.) The Dutch took Surinam and the Navigation Acts were relaxed.

It was a very good outcome, but almost at once there was another problem. Pursuing his dynastic interests, Louis XIV, the supposed ally of the Dutch, was advancing into the Spanish Netherlands with a large army.

All De Witt could do to appease the great alarm felt in the Republic was to make a treaty — on which he worked with Sir William Temple — with the recent enemy, the English, who were themselves not too keen on seeing the French in Antwerp. This was brilliantly achieved and Louis XIV was halted, by discretion. In terms of political power it was the high moment of the Dutch Republic.

In that same year, 1668, the eighty-year-old Vondel was summoned to the Town Hall and told that he would be given a pension. So he was able to give up his job as a clerk. The poet, ever productive, spent his time translating Sophocles and Ovid. But the Amsterdam cultural scene for which he had lived was no longer pleasing to him. All his friends had died, even the younger ones like Jan Vos, and as in architecture French influence was taking over. Almost a hundred years before the members of the Eglantine, Spieghel, Coornhert and Roemer Visscher, had begun their campaign to revive the cultural use of Dutch and get away from the Burgundian French extravagances — and that effort had resulted in the wonderful upsurge of Vondel himself, and Hooft, and Bredero — but now, when the Republic had achieved such heights (in effect a small group of break-away provinces being treated as a Great Power amongst the Great Powers), it was going back to square one.

The French themselves had always been busy cultural as well as diplomatic propagandists in the city. There was already a French theater at The Hague. In 1669 a society called Nil Volentibus Arduum (Nothing is difficult for the willing) was founded at Amsterdam to propagate the French classics and French classicism. Racine, Corneille and Moliére were all translated and put on at the Keizersgracht theater which had begun with Vondel's *Gijsbrecht*. So were many inferior French writers. Though many rich Amsterdam merchants maintained the old simple appearance (which disguised their wealth), many were also dressing like upper-class Parisians. Expensive wigs were worn. Coffee houses — where news was now discussed instead of on the Dam — were all part of it.

It was also no comfort to John de Witt, fully aware that Louis XIV, irritated by the way he had been thwarted in the Spanish Netherlands, was now secretly planning to crush the Republic. And in spite of his achievements for the country De Witt's own position was precarious. There had been too many jobs for the boys and enough time had gone by for resentment against the power structure to solidify. Moreover Cornelis de Graeff had died and his younger brother Andries, rather a pompous-looking man, had not found it easy to take over his position. The new man of power in Amsterdam was Gillis Valckenier, a fleshy-looking, self-confident man. He was a great-nephew of Reynier Pauw and he was like him in manner — outspoken, rude and aggressive. He was also very capable.

And all the time there was the problem of the boy prince, who was reserved and forbiddingly intelligent — and growing up. The holiday the regents had had from the influence of the house of Orange must soon be over. De Witt worked with Valckenier and Andries de Graeff to make the prince a "Child of the State," to give them control over his upbringing — which the Orange family willingly accepted, since it confirmed the boy's position — and the next year Valckenier again seemed to be working with him in promoting in the States of Holland the "Eternal Edict" which washed out the conception of stadholder from any town in Holland for good. But nothing stopped the boy's growing up and an Orangist faction growing up round him, with De Witt as their natural enemy. It only remained for Valckenier to choose the right moment to desert. In 1670 he openly changed sides and supported the Orangists.

This was also the year of a famous and extravagant party held for the wedding of Valckenier's son, Wouter, with the enormously rich Anna Maria Trip. The firework display arranged outside the bride's home, the palatial Trippenhuis, greatly alarmed the owners of nearby houses, including the directors of the East India Company, who had the walls of East India House covered with wet sails as a precaution. But the luxurious feast went on as planned. One would like to know what Dr. Tulp thought of it, for in spite of his role as a fashionable physician, he had always been a rather puritanical Calvinist and had fought in the Council against extravagance with some success — through him a regulation had been passed in 1655 which had laid down strict limits to wedding festivities — the number of guests, the time they must leave, the amounts allowed to be spent on food and drink and even on the bridegroom's presents of jewelry. (The purpose of it, apart from puritanism, was possibly that any excess meant a fine, which had to be paid to the Charity Orphanage.) In fact not very long after the Valckenier-Trip wedding Dr. Tulp himself gave a party at his Keizersgracht house to celebrate his fifty years of membership on the Council. Everybody was naturally hopeful that the great doctor would be seen overstepping his own regulation. But his party stayed strictly within the limits. The guests found a large decorated tent in his garden and here they were served with a two-course meal. Then they all retreated to the house, where pipes and tobacco were ready. After a time back to the tent, where everybody received a plate of fine preserves and sweets, and then the healths were drunk, some Latin poems were recited, and the doctor's son-in-law, Jan Six, presented him with a silver medal — with his portrait on one side and a cedar tree on the other, symbolizing a long and happy life.

Gillis Valckenier was not at this decorous occasion. At this moment he was out in the cold as far as Amsterdam was concerned. There were two reasons. As soon as the open move to the Orangists had been made De Witt pulled every string he could to upset the election of Valckenier as a burgomaster in February 1670. Added to this Valckenier's own behavior antagonized too many of the voting councillors. He went round publicly insulting his rivals. He snarled at Andries de Graeff, insulted the Schout, accused people of intrigue and threatened to "ruin them and their stupid sons," told Vondel's friend Jan van der Poll that he was an idler and Dr. Tulp's son Dirck that he was "an ignorant flatterer." He annoyed too many people and he and his supporters were defeated. So there was a return to power for the De Graeff faction and in The Hague John de Witt could breathe again.

But as he knew all too well, the pressure was on. The danger from an aggressive and powerful France remained and De Witt's only hope was still his treaty with England. He could keep the navy in good order, but any attempt to persuade the regents to go to the expense of building up an army was useless — and they did have the reasonable fear that an army was always likely to be pro-Orange. Meanwhile Louis XIV negotiated and intrigued and finally, by means of the Duchess of Orleans, persuaded Charles II to join him. (An underlying suspicion that everyone is going to let them down has been with the Dutch ever since.)

Suddenly, at the beginning of 1672, the Republic realized what was happening and in the general panic De Witt could go to work raising an army, largely of mercenaries. But throughout the country people were blaming him for the mess and turning desperately towards the now twenty-one-year-old and ice-cool prince. In February, in spite of De Witt's lack of enthusiasm, he was appointed to the command of the armed forces. On March 28 Charles II declared war and a week later the French invaded with an army of over a hundred thousand, helped by the forces of the Bishop of Münster and the Archbishop of Cologne. The invasion succeeded at great speed, and very soon all that could be done was the old trick used against the Spaniards (and they would try it again in 1940 against the Germans), the opening of the dikes. Muiden castle, ten miles from Amsterdam, only just missed enemy occupation. The one good thing that happened for the Dutch was a successful naval action against the English, which enabled De Ruyter to protect the coastline. Prices on the Amsterdam Exchange, it need hardly be said — especially of East India stock — were falling fast. An attempt was made to assassinate John de Witt — and, a few days later, his brother Cornelis. Nobody minded. In July the prince was made stadholder.

Amsterdam had agreed to it and poor Andries de Graeff, leaving for The Hague with the documents to endorse this, found his coach surrounded by an angry crowd who thought he was about to surrender to the French. He got out, trying for shelter in a building where there were some militiamen, but a woman pulled at his wig and another one hit him in the face with her cap and he just missed a sword-thrust. Then the militia appeared and escorted the battered regent back to the Town Hall. He left again a little later, this time with a substantial guard. But it was too late for the De Graeff party to support the prince. Their day was over. The mood in the streets worsened, helped by floods of anti–De Witt pamphlets.

He came to the city in August and did nothing to calm it. Two or three days later John de Witt and his brother (who had been arrested and tortured) were murdered by a mob at The Hague. When the news reached Amsterdam there was at once a mood to try the same thing on some of the regents. Viciousness, spite and hysteria prevailed and the mob, automatically doing the wrong thing, arrived in the street called Buitenkant in the naval area on the east side, and stopped in front of De Ruyter's house, shouting treachery and accusing him of selling the fleet to the French. The admiral was at sea, busy protecting them from the English, and poor terrified Madame de Ruyter had to come out with a letter to prove it — fortunately the militia arrived with pikes and halberds to disperse them.

The Amsterdam regime was hopelessly on the defensive. All this time Valckenier had been on close terms with the prince, and De Graeff was now forced weakly to ask him to collaborate. He accepted, with characteristic venom, accusing De Graeff and his dead, famous brother of manipulating the finances. Andries resigned and gave way to him on September 11. Sixteen other councillors also went, with the stadholder's backing, and

Father Hooft leaves the Town Hall

Valckenier replaced them with friends and supporters. Typically he amused himself in the next few years persecuting the unfortunate Andries with arbitrary and unfair taxation demands.

2.

BACKED by a German general and an army De Witt had largely raised, and with De Ruyter brilliantly protecting the coastline, the young prince was a great success. He raised morale everywhere and was both calm and aggressive. The French could not overcome the water line. They were in any case too stretched out, and then Austria and Spain came in against them. Soon the prince was able to make peace with England. The house of Orange had done it again, and his stock in the Republic was sky-high. He could have had anything he wanted from them. Valckenier's happy city suggested the province of Holland taking over his personal

Gillis Valckenier — Burgomaster (1623–1680)

debts of two million guilders and it was done. The stadholdership, against which they had recently been signing eternal edicts, was now declared hereditary.

There was one snag. The prince's own ideas rose above the affairs of the Republic. He felt himself to be the standard-bearer of Protestantism. He wanted to bring Louis XIV down and his great aim was to form a grand coalition against the Sun King. He was also very sensitive to the situation in England, where the heir to Charles II was his bigoted Catholic brother James and where he himself, as a grandson of Charles I, had growing support. All this was not at all in line with the more material concerns of Amsterdam merchants. The prince soon lost Valckenier's support and the city regents were back in their traditional anti-Orange posture, demanding peace negotiations with France — and having them privately — while the prince went on trying to make war. As it happened, though a brave and inspiring leader, and loved by his men, he was no strategist. Lack of success made the Amsterdam case for peace all the stronger.

In the city Valckenier had met his match in a member of the great Hooft family. Hendrick Hooft, a nephew of the poet-historian of Muiden, had become a burgomaster in the sixties. During the power struggles in the Council, unlike Andries de Graeff, he was open about not being able to stand the loudmouthed Valckenier — who managed to have him put out of harm's way with a job in the Admiralty. When he became a burgomaster again in February 1672, Hooft returned the compliment by sending Valckenier off to The Hague — which, however, gave him his chance of establishing a close relationship with the prince and getting his support for throwing out the De Graeff regime later in the year. Hooft survived this upheaval, but flatly refused to work with "the scoundrel" Valckenier, "the man who put riff-raff into the [city] government by improper practice and sacked honorable men." But out of loyalty to the city he finally made an alliance with him, for the sake of a common front.

Sir William Temple met him in 1678, when Hooft was sixty, and the ambassador both admired him and was amused and fascinated by him. He was in Holland for the peace negotiations which had finally been forced on the highly irritated prince. He spent some time in Amsterdam and talked to Hooft every day, in French. Sir William described a dinner where the guests discussed the great authority Dutch women had in their houses and the fetish for cleanliness. He was told the story of the dignified visitor at a house almost opposite (Hooft lived on the Herengracht), who asked to see the mistress and was promptly hoisted on to the back of a sturdy maid who took him through two rooms and dumped him at the bottom of the stairs, where he had to change his shoes for soft slippers — all this in order not to spoil the shining floor. As for the authority of Dutch women Hooft told Sir William that, while it was true, no man could wish for a better partner than his own gentle mistress (*"douce patronne"*).

The ambassador accepted this little sentimentality as the truth, and it is somehow typical of many exchanges between sophisticated foreigners and leading Amsterdamers, who always succeeded in appearing more ingenuous than they were. In fact at this moment Hooft and his wife, his second, were parted. The first, who died, after giving him eight children, belonged to the rich Hasselaer family. Through his second wife, the widow of a Haarlem magistrate, he became lord of the manor of various places, but the marriage, when he was fifty, was a failure. A year later in 1668 at the annual dinner of the Haarlem-Amsterdam roadway, attended by high municipal representatives of both places, Hooft caused great hilarity when he suggested suitable epitaphs for her, such as:

[190]

"Here lies a lady, which is all very fine — it's not only for her rest, it's also for mine."

The lady cannot answer, and so we don't know. Anyway, when Sir William came to dinner she was in Rotterdam. But what impressed him most about his host, apart from his honesty and knowledge, was a remarkably cheerful philosophy. A man was a fool, Hooft told him, who didn't get everything possible out of life. And a man was a fool who bothered to live beyond the age of sixty. He, of course, was sixty and quite ready to die. According to Sir William on the day he did die — which was quite soon after this — he was chatting with friends around his bed. When he felt himself going under he sent them away, but then he was bored by the silence and sent for them to come back, because "he was just strong enough for another half hour of conversation." That was the character of Monsieur Hooft, said Sir William, admiringly.

There were some other notable deaths. The city's greatest war figure was dead. At seventy, given no rest after his successes against the English, De Ruyter had been sent to help the Spaniards, who were in the process of losing Sicily to the French.

"I won't come back," the old admiral had said, when he left his house on the Buitenkant, which the mob had attacked three years before. He was quite right. He was wounded and died at Syracuse. The body was embalmed and brought home for a state funeral in Amsterdam on March 18, 1677. Great crowds watched the long procession wind slowly through the streets, everywhere was packed and silent, all windows and doorsteps and the leaning upper stories filled with people. They saw first companies of militiamen, civic guards, led by Major Witsen, slowly marching to the somber roll of muffled drums, their flags and pikes trailing. Then came half a dozen "Aansprekers" — undertaker's men of a specialist kind, whose job on normal occasions was to take the news of a death to friends and acquaintances — like everyone from now on, great and small, they wore wide hats with crepe attached and long trailing black cloaks. After them came the trumpeters, then a man by himself with the admiral's flag, then more men in single file each bearing a heraldic device, the quarterings, the blazon, then a man with the admiral's spurs, another with his gloves, another with his sword, and finally the coat of arms. Now came the admiral's horse, and then the bier with its coffin, surrounded by sea captains. Then by himself behind the coffin, in

Admiral De Ruyter's funeral

the place of honor, there walked slowly the prince's representative. He was eighty-one. Long years ago he had climbed Strasbourg Cathedral's tower, he had visited the young Rembrandt in his Leyden studio, he had been Tesselschade's friend — it was Constantyn Huyghens. He was followed by members of the Republic's seven Admiralties. Then came De Ruyter's son, and after him his grandson, Thomas Potts, a quaint little figure in the same uniform of wide-brimmed hat and long cloak. Everybody walking, everything quiet except for the muffled drumbeats. No women. Now came relations and close friends, then — but now the cloaks ceased to be trailing — a group of their "high and mightinesses" of the States-General, honorable members of the Provincial Estates, honorable members of the States of Holland, their lordships the magistrates of Amsterdam, the directors of the East and West India Companies, the directors of trade with the Levant. Then it trailed off into professors, pastors, church council members, high and low sea officers. All marched through the streets, across the Dam and into the Nieuwe Kerk. As an aftermath to the great funeral that evening the Westerkerk was packed to hear Professor Wolzogen preach on the text from the second book of Kings: "And Elisha saw it and he cried, My father, my father, the chariot of Israel and the horsemen thereof." (*Ruyter*, or *ruiter*, means horseman.) The congregation listened "with stricken hearts and tearful eyes."

There were two other notable deaths. A month before the admiral's funeral Spinoza, lying ill with consumption at his lodgings at The Hague (in the house of an artist, Van der Spyck), sent to Amsterdam for a young doctor friend, Georg Schuller. A few days later on Sunday, February 21, Schuller was at Spinoza's bedside when he died, aged forty-four.

It was just over twenty years since his excommunication. He had lived them simply, as he intended, always in one room and with hardly any possessions but books. From 1660 he was at Rijnsburg, where the Collegiants met. Then he moved to Voorburg near The Hague and finally to this lodging. He had spent his time grinding his lenses (the dust had done no good to his lungs), studying and writing (always in Latin — and he called himself Benedictus instead of Baruch), and keeping up a large correspondence. He had stayed in contact with his friends in Amsterdam, Simon de Vries, Balling, Jelles and Lodewijk Meyer — who became the director of the Amsterdam theater and started the francophile "Nil volentibus arduum" society — and Johan Bouwmeester, a doctor who was also associated with the theater, and Jan Rieuwertsz. In return they had revered him and served him.

In 1663, Rieuwertsz, who was a bookseller, published the one book which came out under Spinoza's name during his lifetime, his geometric version of Descartes' *Principles*. Bouwmeester wrote a poem for it, Meyer the introduction, and Jelles paid the production costs, while the next year Balling translated it for a Dutch edition. At other times De Vries tried to give him money, but Spinoza always refused. He was always obedient to his own logic. He took what was to his purpose.

His acquaintance was wide. In his last few years he saw a good deal of Leibniz, who was deeply impressed by him. He was in touch with the Royal Society in London, through Oldenburg, its first secretary; he knew Vossius and Constantyn Huyghens' wonderful son Christiaan (who discovered Saturn's rings and invented the pendulum clock), he discussed the mathematics of chance with the most eminent man in the country, John de Witt. He lived in great simplicity as a very ordinary person, but he was not treated as one.

He did not know fear (his philosophy had dealt with it) and when De Witt and his brother were assassinated by the mob the Van der Spyck family had to use force to stop him sallying out in protest. The following year, 1673, there was the famous episode when he calmly went to Utrecht, by invitation, to meet the invading Prince Condé. A hostile crowd gathered on his return to The Hague. No harm came to him. Philosophy won. But though he was fearless, his motto was caution — "Caute" — and he ensured that he always had some patrician supporters. These had included, apart from Conraed Burgh at Ouderkerk, two other prominent Amsterdamers, the sometime burgomasters Van Beuningen and Hudde. Powerful friends were necessary, for though he was the most God-conscious of men, a vague and dangerous reputation for wickedness and atheism clung to him.

Caution had seen him through. The second book which appeared, the *Tractatus Theologico-Politicus,* in which he discussed the scriptures critically in the interests of freedom and reason, was published in 1670 without his name, and he asked that there should be no Dutch translation. Equally in 1675, when he was seeing his friends in Amsterdam about the publication of his masterpiece, the *Ethics,* he suddenly postponed everything because he had heard of complaints about him being laid before the authorities by enemy theologians (as he wrote to Oldenburg in London). He was too wise to have a taste for martyrdom.

But now he was dead, leaving a book on politics unfinished. Schuller saw that all the papers and manuscripts went back to Amsterdam to the care of Jan Rieuwertsz. The next year all the works were published. But the name Spinoza would remain shrouded in distrust and hostility for over a century, until Lessing brought him to the attention of Goethe. From then on he could take his place among the gods.

Had he grown up normally and become a devout merchant in Amsterdam he would now have been able to share the pride of the rabbis in the new Portuguese synagogue. This great monument of the Sephardi, dedicated in 1676, remains one of the most splendid buildings of the city. Outside it is magnificently simple, even severe, even forbidding, but inside with its immense stone pillars and the great women's galleries and the heavy shining brass everywhere you feel at once that this might have been Solomon's Temple. Incidentally many of the Amsterdam Jews had hardly got over a bitter disillusionment of a few years before. Sabbathai Zevi, a Spanish Jew born at Zevi, then the chief trading city of the Levant, had turned to mysticism and proclaimed himself the Messiah. He had great personal charm and success, myths rapidly formed about him, and excitement and rumors — and faith — spread to Jewry everywhere in Europe. At Amsterdam in 1666 — which was supposed to be the apocalyptic year — books had been published describing what would be the coronation ceremony, the prayers and even the rules of etiquette. Alas, alas, when he went to Constantinople in that year he was arrested and months later, when brought before the Sultan, was forced — or, in any case, agreed — to become a Moslem.

The other death — at long last, in his ninety-second year — was Vondel's. This was in February 1679. The great old poet had never been ill. Though it was a few years since he had written a play, he had not lost his intellectual faculties in the least. He died simply because he had lived so long and the warmth was going from his thin body. He explained it himself, with amusement, when he wrote a suggestion for his epitaph:

> *Here lies Vondel, still and old,*
> *Who died — because he was cold.*

3.

THE REPUBLIC was still at its high tide; no one knew how long it would last, or whether it would last forever. The peace forced on the prince allowed the Amsterdam merchants to concentrate on business and possibly to think about commissioning Italianate landscapes in their houses — painted rooms were coming in, the paint on velvet or leather. But the prince, the frigid, always scheming Protestant crusader, remained obsessed with his view that Louis XIV's overpowering ambition and aggressiveness had to be contained. He soon looked to be right. The Sun King was busy working out little legalistic aggressions — such as taking over Strasbourg in October 1681.

In 1682 he demanded Luxembourg from Spain, and nobody wanting to give it to him, the next year he marched into Flanders. Once again the tiresome crisis was on, the fate of the Spanish Netherlands. In The Hague the prince and his supporters considered the Republic's allies without rapture. The Austrian emperor could do nothing — he was at war with the Turks, and at that moment Vienna was under siege. Charles II, who had been bribed by the French, was clearly passive. Meanwhile the Spanish had asked for eight thousand troops to be sent by the Dutch, under a treaty obligation. This could be done without making war and the prince insisted that it should be done. The Amsterdamers conceded it, and troops were sent after the invasion of Flanders — but they refused to support the prince's suggestion to bring sixteen thousand more into service. For this did mean war — and they were very alarmed by the mood at The Hague, where young bloods at the prince's court were tipsily shouting for it.

It was now 1683. Valckenier had died almost three years before, after a reign in Amsterdam about which an English ambassador, Henry Sydney, said, "I promise you that the Sultan of Turkey does not have more power. . . ." The power had been handed to two highly intelligent, admirable but unpushful men, Hudde and Witsen, who had worked together on sluice problems. They were a great relief, even a holiday, for the prince. But now suddenly a strong burgomaster appeared again, Coenraad van Beuningen. He was an Amsterdamer of the greatest distinction. Brilliant, ascetic and religious when young, he had been a secretary to Grotius in Paris and had developed into a diplomat of the first rank. Valckenier, who had a very good eye for picking people, took advantage of his coolness towards De Witt and pushed him into a burgomastership. He had retained high city positions while acting as ambassador for the Republic — for the last few years in England. Back in the city he at once dominated Hudde and Witsen. He was all against the prince's policy. In Van Beuningen's view, if Louis XIV had to be contained, it should be done by someone else — certainly not by the Dutch.

When the French ambassador, d'Avaux, brought a compromise message from Louis that he could do without Luxembourg, provided somewhere else was substituted at Spain's expense, Van Beuningen informed the States of Holland that this was a much better idea than providing more troops at Amsterdam's expense. The prince blew up. He would not be tyrannized by Amsterdam. If Van Beuningen were investigated, he would be in danger of losing his head. It was like listening to the French ambassador. And so on. Recovering, the prince then made a further effort. He came himself with a deputation from the States-General to plead the case for the extra troops at Amsterdam.

It was quite reminiscent of his father's more threatening arrival thirty years before (which led to the temporary fall of the Bicker brothers), but this visit was less successful. A spokesman in the Council, believed to be Van Beuningen himself, announced that Amsterdam would not alter its views, if only to show the next generation that "even the presence of a Prince of Orange could not stop the free deliberations of the Council." It

was a great moment for the city and the prince was, predictably, infuriated. *"Ces coquins d'Amsterdam!"* (The French were the enemy, but
French culture, fashions and the language were more and more in use by
the upper classes.) And he refused to have anything more to do with
Van Beuningen. According to d'Avaux, the French ambassador, there was
a further failure chalked up by the visit. He said the prince was accompanied by a band of hardy drinkers, whose function was to soften the
Amsterdamers during the round of banquets that accompanied the proceedings. But by the second day the prince's courtiers were all pale and
hung-over, while the burgomasters and councillors remained hale and
clear-eyed. (It may be, of course, that the ambassador was prejudiced.)

Three months later, in February 1684, there was a greater outburst
when the prince was able to cry treason and show intercepted cipher letters between the Amsterdam regents and d'Avaux. He demanded the on-
the-spot indictment of the two Amsterdam delegates at The Hague, Gerrit
Hooft and Pensionary Hop. They were allowed to return, but their
papers were sealed up. With no representatives now in The Hague, and
memories of 1650 very much alive, the city prepared for action. It was
still important to have good walls. Outside them the burgomasters ordered the ice to be broken. The people were on the Town Hall's side.
Pamphlets came out reminding everyone how much Amsterdam had
to pay towards the cost of the Republic's troops and deriding some of the
lesser nobles now showing off as officers, who a few years before were
"too poor to keep a horse."

But Amsterdam's defenses were not tested. The prince could do nothing. The Council's attitude inspired other towns and when the French
took Luxembourg and overran Flanders, he was forced to agree to make
peace. Van Beuningen's city had triumphed. It was at least a comfort to
the prince that Van Beuningen then took the opportunity of resigning, to
attend to his own neglected private affairs. He would have done better
not to. Everything went wrong for him. Aged sixty-four he made a long-
delayed marriage to a relation of the Huyghens family. She was forty-six
and Christiaan Huyghens, the famous scientist son of the poet, had long
before said about her, ominously, "She seems born for adventures." At the
same time poor Van Beuningen speculated disastrously in East India stock.
Whether or not his wife drove him to it, very soon he went out of
his mind. The religious-mystical tendencies of his brilliant youth now returned in manic form. He went out into the streets prophesying the

end of the world and wrote crazy letters trying to convert Jews. His wife left him and he had to be shut up in his own house.

For his royal opponent, on the other hand, things began to go extremely well. Louis XIV helped by revoking the Edict of Nantes, which had given some protection to French Protestants — the trickle of Huguenot refugees into the Republic accordingly now became a flood, bringing textile expertise and capital, as well as still more French influence in the arts and a large number of French tutors and governesses for the children of the rich. Amsterdam benefited and at the same time anti-Catholic feelings were aroused everywhere. There had been English refugees, including Lord Shaftesbury, whose antipopery plotting had been too much for Charles II and who died as an Amsterdam citizen, and the philosopher John Locke, who hid in the city for a time as "Dr. van der Linden." But the prince's great moment was coming. Charles died and his bigoted Catholic brother James II was on the throne. Vastly influential groups in England now looked to the Prince of Orange, whose wife was James's daughter, who was himself Charles I's grandson and who was the self-appointed number-one Protestant of Europe. The intrigues went on, the delicate enquiries were made. Finally the invitation came, secretly, on July 16, 1688.

The prince couldn't wait to accept, but it was not as easy as that — an expedition had to be mounted, backed by the States-General. As a first step Amsterdam's approval had to be gained. Thank God, the prince must have thought, that nobody like Van Beuningen or Valckenier was now leading the "Magnificat." The principal burgomasters now were, once more, Hudde and Witsen.

Both were remarkable men. They were cousins. Johannes Hudde's mother had been a Witsen and he was also a cousin of Valckenier. With his long wig and lace collars and sleeves, and plumpish good-natured face, he did not seem very obviously a first-class brain. But he was in correspondence with the best contemporary scholars, he worked with Christiaan Huyghens on the observation of comets, with Spinoza on the improvement of spectacle lenses, with John de Witt on the mathematical calculation of chance. He produced one of the first actuarial tables and was consequently almost a founder of life insurance. He liked practical problems, like flood control or street lighting. His cousin Nicolaes Witsen, thirteen years younger (forty-seven in 1688), was one of the best known of all the burgomasters. But his interests were philosophy, astronomy, literature and etching — he illustrated Ovid. The Witsen family were famous traders with Russia and a year in "Moscovia" with the Dutch ambassador Boreel was part of his extensive education which also included Leyden, Paris, Switzerland and Oxford. He published a map of "Tartary" and a book he wrote on the history and practice of shipbuilding became a classic and was translated into Russian. (Hudde did some of the loading calculations for it.) With their culture and public spirit burgomasters like this represented Amsterdam at its best and with their lack of pushing commercialism the beginnings of its decay. They were no match for the tough politics of Prince William.

The prince confided in Witsen, and ignored his anxiety. Two of his favorite courtiers, Dijkvelt and Bentinck, and the Grand Pensionary, Fagel, came to the city for soundings and propaganda about the harm to trade which might be done by an alliance between Louis XIV and a Catholic England. Amsterdam's approval was received. This meant that the States of Holland would follow when the Grand Pensionary addressed them in September. After that the States-General approved. The prince was off — he landed in England in November and became King William.

There was great pleasure and pride in the Republic, even amongst the Amsterdamers. But the Republic was soon at war again. Louis XIV was busy pushing eastwards against the German states and the new King of England was able to lead the grand alliance against him.

Meanwhile the spirit of the city began to die.

4.

"WHAT DID YOU THINK of those stupid old Papist ceremonies?" the king asked Witsen after his coronation. For the burgomaster had to go to London with the court "favorites" to work on commercial and maritime agreements to fit the new situation. But the king-stadholder's "Protestant-Dutchness" and familiarity were all he gained. He soon found that the Republic and his city had become politically less important. They had fallen into the trap they had managed to avoid forty years before by refusing Cromwell's invitation to merge and by fighting the first Anglo-Dutch war instead. He signed what he had to sign, under protest, and saved his self-respect by refusing a peerage.

Amsterdam was back in its old posture of resistance to Orange. But its leadership was too weak and the king, especially after his victory in Ireland (still being celebrated), too strong. They tried refusing to submit the names of magistrates to him and to ban the "favorite" Bentinck from the States of Holland. But the king was quite prepared to fan any popular resentment of the regents by all available means. Pamphleteers were discreetly employed to stir things up — asserting, for instance, that "you could always get a job in Amsterdam if you were prepared to marry a regent's discarded whore." Hudde and Witsen were no match for this sort of thing, and in addition a rising influence in the Council was Mr. Joan Corver, a man already over sixty, whose great expertise was in the fields of intrigue and nepotism. He ingratiated himself with the king, constantly assuring him that he did not agree with the other regents, and his star rose all through the decade.

Corver was himself a sign of decay. His face looks both amiable and crafty. What was remarkable about him was that he came so late in life to politics but remained an enthusiast until he was almost ninety. He was immensely rich and owned an enormous double house on the Herengracht. He came from an old family of merchants dealing with Italy and the Levant. He had been one of the patrician boys who accompanied the artists' patron Burgomaster Huydecoper to Berlin, and his late arrival to power was due to a full life. He was very good at moving rivals into out-of-the-way harmless jobs, even those like Rembrandt's old friend Jan Six (also getting on now) whom his own influence had made a burgomaster. He was not the man to get along with Hudde and Witsen; and after Hudde died he managed his pushing-aside trick with Witsen as well. With nephews and cousins, and the results of marriages with allied families, the Hoofts, the Trips, Van den Bempdens, Van de Polls, he set up a power structure which lasted in Amsterdam for half a century. And he himself lasted until he was eighty-eight, when he gave a vast banquet and, perhaps overcome by it, died three months later.

But there was one man, who "arrived" in the 1690's, who at least for a time had his measure. This was Jeronimo de Haze de Georgio, who was a nephew of Hudde (to be a regent one had to be a son, nephew or cousin of somebody) and very rich (if it were possible for one to be a regent, one was almost certainly rich). He was also not very nice. The family derived from the sixteenth-century union of a wealthy Antwerp merchant and the tycoon family Coymans. Jeronimo had married a cousin and all the money had come together. He did various normal jobs; he was a captain in the militia, a magistrate, a representative at the States-General, a director of the East India Company. In 1695 he was a burgo-master for the first time.

The next year when he was not in office came the famous "Under-takers' Riot" in Amsterdam. The cost of the war had led amongst other taxes to one on funerals, which had proved the last straw to many Amsterdamers. The chief rioters were hanged from the windows of the weighhouse on the Dam. Before that the mob had been dangerous, and a good many regents' houses had been plundered. Burgomaster Boreel's house on the Herengracht was wrecked — he was thought to have been too collaborative with the king's men at The Hague. Neighboring houses also suffered, and the mob arrived at Jeronimo's. Here the mob was held at bay with handouts of money while a company of the militia was sent for. When they arrived, shots were fired, two or three rioters were killed, and the crowd ran off fast — to plunder another rich house on their list. All of which proved that Jeronimo de Haze de Georgio knew how to look after himself.

So did another episode, a few years later. In the course of his career Jeronimo had fathered an illegitimate child, Isaac, and had farmed him out to a foster father at Amersfoort, called Eck. Isaac van Eck grew up, came to Amsterdam as an engraver, and in due course wanted to marry Catherina Taelmans. The foster father now told the happy couple the big secret and advised them that if they kept quiet the burgo-master would look after Isaac in the shipping business at Rotterdam. The marriage took place, with a woman chandler called Maria van Eyk, by order of the burgomaster, acting as Isaac's mother. But neither the couple nor Maria could keep quiet. They gossiped loudly and even importuned Jeronimo in the street. He was not the man to stand for that sort of thing. The women were arrested by order of the Schout and the letters from Jeronimo in their possession — the evidence — were taken away. Maria was whipped privately and when she still insisted that the burgomaster was Isaac's father she was whipped publicly. Then Isaac was arrested and both of them were whipped publicly. This was followed by a fifteen-year sentence in the Rasphuis — the Amsterdam men's prison — for Isaac and thirty years in the Spinhuis — the women's prison — for Maria. The wife, Catherina, was simply banned from the city for ten years. It did not pay to be a nuisance to Jeronimo de Haze de Georgio.

He was also prepared to take on his equals. When he was defeated politically and suspected a certain Burgomaster Sautijn of being responsible, he hounded him for years by means of exposing in the courts the corrupt practices of Sautijn's brother which eventually led to ruinous disclosures of the burgomaster's own affairs. It was hardly surprising that Jeronimo had been capable, at least for two or three years, of ousting the deeply entrenched Corver "cabal." He was worth millions of guilders when he died, and one million was in the Bank of England. These were not the sort of men to bring glory to the city.

On the other hand, if the last decade of the seventeenth century and the first decade of the eighteenth were a period when decay took over, it was easy not to see it. The strength of the Republic was oozing away from war demands, but generally it was a boom time for the merchants. Amsterdam touched new heights of prosperity and luxury. But Witsen wrote sadly to a friend about the failure of an expedition of three East Indian ships he had sent to follow the path of Tasman in the South Seas: "Contrary to my instructions they spent nowhere more than three days — the captain drank too much — at the Cape he spent his time enjoying himself — all our people are after is money, not knowledge. . . ." Who did want knowledge was the young Tsar Peter the Great, who arrived incognito in the city — as "Pieter Michaëlof." Witsen looked after him, while he learned about shipbuilding, the burgomaster's own subject. But all the Amsterdamers wanted was money.

Speculation was in their blood. The same share would change hands four or five times in a day. Lotteries had always been a success. It was naturally the place where foreigners in political danger, royal or otherwise, kept their secret escape funds. And if an escape had to be made, the cause of it had probably been helped by a book printed in Amsterdam. Forty presses issued books in all known languages. A future Bishop of Carlisle was shocked to notice at "Widow Shipper's Printing House" that they were printing English Bibles with the title page reading "London" and "Printed by R. Barker and the Assigns of John Bill." And other books were coming out of the widow's thriving establishment supposedly printed in Cologne or Leipzig. What a trading city! The Genoese marble used at Versailles had to be bought at Amsterdam. It remained the one place in Europe where a buyer could always find a seller.

It was easy to be lulled. Most of the world's carrying trade was still in Dutch hands. Their merchant fleet was ten times the size of the French and still twice the English. The Baltic, with the German, Scandinavian and Russian ports, was a Dutch monopoly. All the products of the immense though decaying Spanish-American empire arrived in galleons at Cádiz, where they were off-loaded into Dutch ships. It was profit, profit, profit for Amsterdam. The West India Company had had a somewhat checkered career, with Brazil lost and its few colonies on the Guiana coast in a poor state (though there would be profit from sugar soon), but good business was done — which nowadays everybody fervently wishes hadn't been. The good business was in slavery. The Spanish had no direct connection with Africa and bought the Negroes they needed for their South American plantations. The West India Company had about sixty men on the West African coast, who managed to ship several thousand slaves a year to Curaçao, in cargoes of seven or eight hundred wretched Africans — who were often, incidentally, prisoners of war sold as booty by Africans to the Dutch agents. The rights in this repulsive business were in *"asientos,"* contracts granted by the Spanish government. For four years (1685–1689) all the rights were held by an immensely rich Amsterdam merchant, Balthazar Coymans.

But the East India Company remained the jewel. Its power and prestige in the last two decades of the century were fantastic. Its private government at Batavia ruled over a trading area far greater than the Portuguese empire which had been destroyed. India, Ceylon, Malacca, the Malay Archipelago, all these were extraordinary sources of wealth ultimately leading to Hoeg-straat, Amsterdam. The governor in Batavia ruled the vast territories with the help of vassal princes. The Company's officials and sailors were not paid well and had to make their own fortunes, which they could do by corruption and side trading. The Company tried to keep everything as a monopoly, so that emigration in a general way was discouraged — no energy for colonization, but all for the quick profit. Nor did they encourage missionaries — the Calvinist doctrine of predestination made it clear that colored people could not possibly be eligible for ultimate grace — an attitude which seems to have remained firmly embedded in their descendants of the Cape settlement. However, the thousands of Germans, English, Scottish and French adventurers they hired annually all had to agree to Dutch Reformed worship — except in Japan, where the Company servants were ordered not to practice any religion at all. But the true worship was for the wealth which came back, largely to Amsterdam, to subsidize a life growing more stylish all the time.

The castellated wall enclosed the city in its vast semicircle, resting on the IJ estuary. All the plans so brilliantly made at the beginning of the century had been carried out. There were no suburbs beyond the walls, and inside was an immense population of two hundred thousand. It was Amsterdam in its perfect form. More great houses would be built or rebuilt on the Herengracht and Keizersgracht in the eighteenth century — and that would certainly be the time of the most elaborate interiors — but most of them were up by now. They were not all entirely successful from a practical viewpoint. The high cool passages and high but often scantily lit rooms would have been ideal for a warm, southern land, but for the large family of an Amsterdam merchant they weren't necessarily perfect. What often happened was that the great reception rooms remained empty while he and his family lived in the upper stories in quite limited space. And there was the problem of the entrance. Great domestic retinues were rare. There might be one or two living-in servants plus some daily cleaning women. There was often nobody to answer the monumental front door, which remained a closed decoration. The stately master as well as the chars used the lower, kitchen-level door, and had to bend down or bang his head. Snobbish foreign visitors tended to find this sort of thing amusing. But it was Amsterdam.

There were changes. The poor had not altered. The parallel narrow streets of the Jordaans, now full of French refugees, the tavern-brothel section by the docks, the Jewish quarter, all this was jam-packed with the old color. But the more prosperous Amsterdamers at the end of the seventeenth century, in spite of their glamorous wigs, and the new coffee houses, and the fashion for cognac and gin, had lost some of the joie-de-vivre, the drunkenness of the senses which had led to that mirroring of themselves in their separate moments which was the marvel of Dutch art — as much in Bredero's farces as in the incredible upsurge of painting. And it was the same in business. More and more people were appreciating the pleasures of dividends. Nothing is more easily developed than the rentier mentality and too many Amsterdamers were already developing it. As the rich became richer, class divisions became more marked. Rich young women wore bonnets over high combed hair, great wide sleeves, long gloves and hoop skirts. Luxurious coaches mounted on sleds negotiated the Amsterdam hump-backed bridges, some of them

acting as taxis. Stagecoaches covered the country, and so did the marvelous *trek-schuits* — comfortable horse-drawn canalboats in which you
could go almost anywhere; there was a well organized intertown service,
and all you needed was time and a liking for conversation. The coffee
houses, the taverns, the theater, everywhere public was filled with tobacco smoke from clay pipes. Pipes would even be smoked in church,
though women often refused to allow them in their immaculately clean
houses. Almost everyone took snuff. And another sign of final change from
the old medieval world, when cities were dark at night, was that in 1689
Amsterdam had 2,400 street oil lamps. It was a system backed by Burgomaster Hudde and devised by the artist Van der Heyden, who also inspired a water pump for the fire service.

On the other hand medieval cruelty was always just round the corner.
Every town hall, including Amsterdam's, had its torture chamber. It was
not unusual even for women and boys, if caught thieving, to be branded
with a red-hot iron. Whippings were handed out freely, as we saw with
Burgomaster de Haze's unfortunate bastard. In 1703 a man was broken
on the wheel at Amsterdam for his part in a conspiracy (which didn't
succeed) to sabotage some Friesland dikes. Blasphemy was also a
charge to be avoided, in spite of the city's constant toleration of a maze
of different religious sects — Adrien Koerbagh, a doctor of law and a
physician, was put on trial for his collection of "God less and God-
mocking books" and sentenced to ten years in prison, ten years of exile
and a fine of 4,000 guilders. But the Schout, prosecuting him, had wanted
a sentence of thirty years in prison, plus property confiscation, and this
after his right thumb had been cut off and his tongue pierced with a red
hot bodkin. Thumbs could still be cut off.

Prison cells were available in the Town Hall and at the various gate
towers, and in the *rasphuis* (men) and *spinhuis* (women). These last
two institutions were not medieval, but considered in their time to be
penologically somewhat advanced. They were even tourist attractions,
if of a somewhat kinky nature. Both were housed in former cloisters. The
site of the *rasphuis*, in the Heiligeweg, off the Kalverstraat, is now used
for a swimming bath, but the old entrance on the street is still there, with
a bas-relief by Hendrick de Keyser of a wagon driver whipping the wild
beasts pulling his load of Brazilian hard wood and the inscription "*Virtu-
tis est domare quae cuncti pavent*" — It is right to tame and master what
the people fear. Criminals and idlers were what the people feared, in

this context. It was the concept of the workhouse started at Bridewell in London in 1566. The work done by the prisoners was rasping the hard logs into dust — which could be used in the production of paint. Whipping was applied to those whose efforts were unsatisfactory and for bad cases there was a special cell which could be filled with water — the bad case had the choice of using a pump or drowning. In the eighteenth century this refinement was probably no longer used, but the cell was always shown to the tourists. The whipping block, another sight, was still in use. It was in the courtyard where the work was done, and about the work a German lady tourist said, with blissful horror, "It is like hell — they are half naked, black with sawdust and they sweat so the dust is like a black sauce — you shudder. . . ."

The women in the *spinhuis* — where spinning was one of the jobs done — were there for drunkenness and dissipation, or theft, or street prostitution. As another satisfied German visitor put it, "That's a menagerie really worth seeing."

5.

THE KING-STADHOLDER'S WAR petered out towards the end of the seventeenth century, when it became known that Carlos II of Spain was ill and expected to die. Both Hapsburgs and Bourbons had claims on the throne, and now their overriding aim was to be in a position of maximum advantage when the moment occurred. Louis XIV was suited by peace and accordingly offered favorable terms. So there was an interval, while three or four years of fantastic intrigues went on between the powers. When the death occurred and Louis was able to announce that the Spanish crown would be accepted by his grandson, the Duke of Anjou, as Philip V, King William set about resurrecting the Grand Alliance and a treaty was signed at The Hague in September 1701. It was about the last time the miraculous Dutch Republic was treated as a great power. That winter the king was backwards and forwards between England and Holland, organizing and gingering up the preparations in the camps, arsenals and dockyards. Austria, the German states, England and the Republic were proposing to put 300,000 men into the field. The Dutch troops, like the English, would be thirty percent their own — the rest would be hired from the German states. ("These Dutch merchants," said the German princes, with princely contempt.) But in March 1702 William was thrown from his horse in Bushey Park, England, and died a few days later.

The French hoped that "Messieurs d'Amsterdam" would now act in character and use their influence for quitting. As it happened Burgomaster Corver and friends were too worried about the possible loss of Spanish-American trade to the French, and in spite of opposition from Hudde and Witsen Amsterdam backed the continuation of the king's policy — and the policy of the Council-Pensionary at The Hague, Heinsius. So the Republic was in the War of the Spanish Succession, and declared war on France and Spain on May 8, 1702. The presence of French troops in the Spanish Netherlands made up the minds of the States-General. England and Austria followed soon afterwards.

But the Republic was back in the hands of the town oligarchies. The title of Prince of Orange was now held by the fourteen-year-old son of the late king's cousin. The boy succeeded to the stadholdership of Friesland and Groningen, but the other provinces ignored him. The regents everywhere were free to look after themselves. The great powers of patronage possessed by the burgomasters were used by Corver in Amsterdam in the interests of his family. Sons and nephews aged from four to eleven became, nominally, officers in an Amsterdam infantry company. The trade in sinecures was open and scandalous and remained so for decades. Meanwhile, in the first decade, the Republic bled to death trying to keep up with its commitments to the alliance. The last great Dutch naval effort was at the battle of Malaga in August 1704, which ruined the French in the Mediterranean. On land the English produced a commander of genius in John Churchill, Earl — and soon, Duke — of Marlborough, whose brilliant victories at Blenheim, Ramillies and Malplaquet had taken most of the fight out of Louis XIV. On the way the Sun King, aware of Dutch exhaustion and growing lack of enthusiasm, offered them terms which they would have accepted, but they had to keep going with the English. After Malplaquet in 1709, where losses were heavy on both sides, but especially amongst Dutch native troops, England offered the Republic a secret agreement under which the Dutch would be able to garrison a number of towns along the French frontier. So the southern Netherlands, though under the sovereignty of the Austrian emperor, would or could be an economic colony of the Republic. It was too much for the Dutch to resist and Pensionary Buys of Amsterdam and the other negotiators took the hard line with the French which the English wanted. Unfortunately there were political changes in England, followed by the death of the Austrian emperor, and these two events led to the English doing a deal with the French behind the backs of both the Dutch and the Hapsburgs.

Smarting under this monstrous behavior the Republic made one last effort. They took over the German troops who had been in English pay, in addition to their own, and went it alone with Austria. But within a few weeks, on July 24, 1712, 12,000 men were annihilated in a surprise attack by the French. That was the end of it. They were prepared to accept whatever they were given. Over the next two or three years treaties were made between all the countries involved. The main result was the foundation of British world power. Louis XIV did better than he had expected a few years before. The Dutch gained nothing at all; they did have the right to garrison some towns in the southern Netherlands, and were given guarantees of security but it was all a good deal less than had been promised in the secret treaty.

There had been twenty years of almost continuous war and the Republic was exhausted. The desire to play a big part in the world was gone. It was only realistic. In the previous century both England and France had been held back by internal troubles, which had given the small new neighbor the chance it took so well. But this was no longer the situation. In the new century there was economic nationalism in a world of coal, iron and steel — heavier forces than the spice trade. Because of this it was in industry — especially in the various forms of textile industry, in which Amsterdam had a large part — that real decay made a beginning. Manufacturers received no protection and all raw materials had to be imported. The long war had also forced up Amsterdam wages. But any attempt to get round this by moving to other parts of the country came up against the maze of restrictions imposed by all the other oligarchies. They kept going as long as there was still the impetus brought by the French refugees, but around 1725–1730, when these began to die off, so did the textile business. Poverty and unemployment followed.

However, while industry fell away, the carrying trade, shipping and the money market went on flourishing. In fact this was the halcyon time for the rich and privileged of Amsterdam. Those who felt like it imitated the fashions and habits of Versailles. There were no more Rembrandts, but there were interior decorators. There were no more Brederos, but there was an imitation Molière, Pieter Langendijk. There was a fashion for things English as well as French. A Dutch version of the London *Spectator* came out, English furniture and food were copied. The great canal houses were now more sumptuous than ever, with their painted walls and ceilings by Isaac de Moucheron, gold mantelpieces and scrollwork by the designer Daniel Marot, and stucco everywhere — there were astonishingly exotic interiors behind the sober façades, elegant staircases, little inner courtyards full of pagan gods, and above all the bright colors of the so-called "painted rooms" with dazzling settee and chair coverings and vistas of Italianate palaces and country scenes on the walls. The adventurous spirit shown in bold private enterprise a century before was now sufficiently expressed in lotteries or speculation in bubble companies (the South Sea, the Mississippi) or the risky trade in "futures." The rich Amsterdamers sat back and counted the profits and losses, and filled the smoky Kalverstraat coffee houses, where brokers waited for the early news which could reach them through fishing smacks sent out to intercept the twice- or thrice-weekly Harwich-Helvoetsluis packet boats. The regents of the Corver "cabal," the associated families and friends who ran the city, amused themselves sharing and dividing offices of profit, like the postmasterships, and farmed out taxes. Towards the rough jostlings of the big powers they were firmly neutral. Nobody was prepared to find money for the Republic's defenses, by land or sea. The Dutch had had enough.

The trouble was that the rough world did occasionally insist on intruding. Suddenly the Austrian emperor decided to set up a rival East India Company at Ostend. In order to get rid of this danger to business the Dutch were forced to join another alliance and to commit themselves to support of the "Pragmatic Sanction" which guaranteed the succession of the Austrian empire to the emperor's daughter, Maria Theresa. So they were involved again, and could only hope that nothing would come of it. The Amsterdam banker Deutz lent the Austrian emperor three and a half million guilders. Amsterdam lent money to everybody and made money out of everybody. Things would have to go very wrong before discontent showed against the corrupt, drowsy regime of the regents. A sign that no one was bothering much about anything was the reception, not unfriendly but indifferent, given to the Prince of Orange when he brought his bride, daughter of George II of England, to Amsterdam. Orange meant war, Calvinism, sacrifice, perhaps even patriotism. Amsterdamers were not interested in 1734.

But a commitment was a commitment and eight years later they were dragged unwillingly into the War of the Austrian Succession. The Dutch had managed to keep out for two years, merely making small, nervous additions to their forces. Several countries, including France, had thrown Maria Theresa off her imperial throne; a new emperor, the Elector of Bavaria, was on it and the rising strong man, Frederick II of Prussia, had won Silesia. England, occupied by a war against Spain, had so far not participated. But now George II was worrying about his Hanoverian interests and his peace-minded prime minister, Walpole, had been deposed. So they now asked the Dutch to come in openly on Maria Theresa's side and to fulfill their treaty obligations. The French ambassador at The Hague issued warnings. The Dutch dithered. Their spokesmen represented what was almost a nonentity of town hall corruption everywhere. The power behind them, such as it was, was in the States-General and the States of Holland, and the biggest influence behind these assemblies at The Hague was Amsterdam, where typically one of the burgomasters was now the fat, rich, physically odious libertine Gillis van den Bempden, who had to be helped everywhere by two footmen and was nicknamed "The Crutch."

Dissatisfied with the Dutch hesitations the English acted without warning and suddenly 16,000 men were landed at Ostend to strengthen the Dutch barrier fortresses in the southern Netherlands. So the Dutch were now in, whether they liked it or not. The war proceeded slowly from year to year. The next year, 1743, George II was himself in action and the States-General were finally forced to offer an army of 20,000. The next year their fears were realized and the French declared war on England — who at once demanded naval aid from the Dutch, in accordance with the treaty. The demand was for twenty ships. The extent to which things had been let go was now made even more evident. For they could produce only eight ships. And the admiral appointed to command them had been retired for fifteen years and was seventy-three. It was just as well that French naval intentions were upset by bad weather.

Humiliations and inadequacies like this were stirring the Orangists. And almost at once the French, with a terrifyingly large army, were invading the southern Netherlands. Next May, 1745, there was another humiliation at the battle of Fontenoy, which was lost to the French when it had almost been won by British infantry, owing to the somewhat precipitate withdrawal of Dutch troops. All through 1745 and 1746 the Dutch kept trying to negotiate and the French, though prepared to compromise, kept winning and advancing. They were masters of the southern Netherlands. Louis XV's attitude hardened and he decided to invade the Republic itself.

Faced by a large allied army under the English Duke of Cumberland the French still made progress and would have invaded Zeeland but for the fortunate arrival of an English squadron. This was too near home for comfort. The whole country was erupting — exactly as it had in 1672 and for much the same reason, disgust with the regime of regents. Everywhere people turned instinctively to their one hope, the Prince of Orange. One after another the provinces proclaimed him stadholder, even anti-Orange Holland. When he visited Amsterdam he was given a great reception.

Not that there was much he could do about the war. Things went on going badly and once again it was the Dutch who let the allies down by giving way at the battle of Lauffeldt in July. Fortunately it now suited both the English and the French to make peace. The Republic was saved from invasion and also from a somewhat flamboyant promise it had made to raise 70,000 men.

The sighs of relief in Amsterdam were drowned by noisier sounds. One antiregent movement was the Doelists, who were according to a 1766 dictionary "a set of people at Amsterdam, that kept their assembly in an inn called the artillery yard, or Doelen, in the year 1748, whose transactions are very well described, in the Acts of the Apostles, chapter the XIXth. v.32." (The verse reads: "Some therefore cried one thing, and some another: for the assembly was confused; and the more part knew not wherefore they were come together.") In any case the city was turbulent. Regents' houses were plundered, and there were some bloody scenes on the Dam, the so-called Tax-farmers' Riots. There was no question that there had to be changes and the prince arrived, fully empowered by the States of Holland, to make them. He was an intelligent, religious and kindly man, but these admirable qualities were unfortunately not enough in a political crisis; it was a pity, for his position in the country was so strong that he could have shaken it by the roots. But at least he ended the Corver "cabal." He had a list of names provided for him by a rich patrician called Lestevenon, who was connected by marriage with the Court and therefore in his confidence, and who had not forgotten the way the "cabal" had eased his father out of the burgomastership a few years before.

Amsterdam survived. The English novelist Smollett toured the Republic in 1750. His hero Peregrine Pickle came to the city by post wagon from The Hague for a night in the docks-and-brothels area. He saw a Dutch tragedy, which he didn't care for, and visited an English merchant friend first, and then went to one of the "music houses, which, by the connivance of the magistrates, are maintained for the recreation of those who might attempt the chastity of creditable women, if they were not provided with such conveniences. To one of these night-houses did our travellers repair, under the conduct of the English merchant, and were introduced into another such place as the ever memorable coffee-house of Moll King; with this difference, that the company here were not so riotous as the bucks of Covent Garden, but formed themselves into a circle, within which some of the number danced to the music of a scurvy organ and a few other instruments, that uttered tunes very suitable to the disposition of the hearers, while the whole apartment was shrouded with smoke impervious to the view. When our gentlemen entered, the floor was occupied by two females and their gallants, who, in the performance of their exercise, lifted their legs like so many oxen at plough; and the pipe of one of these hoppers happening to be exhausted, in the midst of his saraband, he very deliberately drew forth his tobacco-box, filling and lighting it again, without any interruption to the dance. Peregrine . . . made up to a sprightly French girl who sat in seeming expectation of a customer, and prevailing upon her to be his partner, led her into the circle, and in his turn took the opportunity of dancing a minuet, to the admiration of all present. . . ."

This view of the Amsterdam scene, with its emphasis on the superior foreigner regarding rather oafish inhabitants, was fairly common — partly because most of the grander visitors had their social life in the aristocratic or royal circles at The Hague or in the country houses of the nobility — and partly because many rich Amsterdamers took pains, in public, to conceal their wealth. It was in character. There was always possibly a profit in your visitors or clients not knowing everything about you. Certainly not many fashionable memoirists penetrated the great houses on the canals.

6.

ONE WHO DID PENETRATE WAS CASANOVA. He came in 1758, when the city was in the middle of a financial boom. Ten more years of the Republic's decay had gone by since the Prince of Orange visited the Town Hall with his list. Soon after this he had been trying to save the country's tottering industries by a limited form of protectionism and by introducing some commercial unity to the overindependent provinces and towns. But he had died in 1751 and nothing was done. The process continued of the gradual death of the sugar refineries, the dye works, the sawmills (hundreds of them going out of action, at Zaandam across the IJ from Amsterdam, which a hundred years before had worked day and night to catch every breath of wind). Shipbuilding declined, and the potteries, and breweries, and hat-making, and book printing, and paper-making. The Republic was in a poor state and becoming poorer. And yet some of the rich went on getting richer. Amsterdam prospered in spite of a few dying industries and in spite of the fact that the great warehouses were not as full as they used to be, and in spite of the fact that corruption was catching up with the East India Company (though its eye for profit was not yet closed — a German visitor noted with some contempt vast stores of common seashells, held "for trading with Africans").

For the carrying trade still bloomed even if, unprotected by Dutch warships, it suffered from privateers — but, then, there was always insurance. And the money market was in still greater bloom. It was an extraordinary fact that in the middle of the Republic's decay a third of the shares in the Bank of England and of the English East India Company and half of the English national debt had been sold to investors on the Amsterdam Exchange.

Meanwhile two burgomasters had come to the fore, Pieter Rendorp and Egbert de Vrij Temminck. They soon found themselves in general opposition to the prince's English widow, Anne, who was both regent and guardian of her small child and now hereditary stadholder, William V. The princess used all the powers she had to assert herself and this led to an

PHOTOS COURTESY OF THE AMSTERDAM CITY ARCHIVES

P. C. Hassalaer — Burgomaster
(1720–1797)

Nicolaes Witsen — Burgomaster
(1641–1717)

Egbert de Vrij Temminck — Burgomaster
(1700–1785)

"Father" Hooft — Burgomaster
(1716–1794)

agreement among the Amsterdam regents, called the "Correspondence," to resist. The few who stayed out received excellent rewards from The Hague in jobs for themselves or their relations. But the royal problems were considerable. A new war among the powers was of course warming up, an agreement between the French and the Austrians suddenly removed all the protection the Dutch thought they had in the southern Netherlands, and while the princess was receiving anxious requests for an increased land force from the country at large, scared of French invasion, she was being pressed by Amsterdam merchants for a fleet to protect their trade with the French, who were offering them special privileges. However, the war did break out and the Republic this time managed to stay neutral. The city financiers could not have asked for more. All the European countries were suddenly after loans, new banking houses were created as if overnight and fortunes were made from speculation.

Casanova arrived in the middle of all this. The attractive Venetian adventurer was then about thirty-four and at one of the heights of his bizarre and entertaining career. He had left Paris with two commissions. One was for a Mme d'Urfé, a rich and aristocratic woman gone on alchemy and the black arts — a field in which Casanova moved with high confidence — they had come together because he had cured her nephew's rheumatic pains by painting a talisman on his thigh and murmuring an incantation. She had a realistic eye for money, however, and spent only about a third of her enormous income. The rest was normally used with great profit on the Paris Exchange — though she would give it all away, she hinted, to change her sex through black magic (she believed there was a way). When she heard that Casanova was going to Holland, she asked him if he would sell some shares in the Swedish East India Company for her, which couldn't be sold on the Paris Exchange owing to the present shortage of money, due to the war. The shortage of money was responsible for the second commission, which was on an official level. The idea was to offer Royal bills of exchange at a reasonable price to "good Amsterdam merchants" for exchange into bills from another country, whose currency was more negotiable. Casanova had put it up. The procedure was that twenty millions worth of bills would be sent to the French ambassador at The Hague, who would carry through the transaction if Casanova brought it off. So with an introductory letter from the duc de Choiseul and a passport from the Dutch ambassador at Paris he set off. Naturally, with a servant.

Two days later he arrived at Antwerp, from where he took a yacht to

Rotterdam, stayed the night, and the next day reached The Hague. He put up at the famous inn Het Parlement van Engeland. Then he went off to the ambassador to give him Choiseul's letter. The ambassador invited him to dinner and wished him luck, but was not optimistic — for success would depend on people's belief that the war would soon end and the Dutch, said the ambassador, had very good reason to think that it would not. Casanova's second call at The Hague was on Tobias Boaz, a Jewish banker, on whom his letter of credit was drawn. He was having a meal, Casanova reported, "with all his ugly and numerous family." However, the banker welcomed him, invited him to stay, and when Casanova lightly asked for ideas on how to make a quick twenty thousand guilders, suggested buying four hundred ducats (which he happened to know were newly minted) for the current price of gold, which was low — then send them or carry them to Frankfurt, exchange them for bills on the Bank of Amsterdam — and it would make a profit of twenty-two thousand guilders.

"Won't the mint find it difficult to trust me with a sum of more than four million francs?"

"They certainly will if you don't pay them in ready money or the equivalent in good bills."

"My dear M. Boaz, I have neither the cash nor the credit."

"In that case you will never make twenty-thousand guilders in a week. One of my children will have to do it instead."

The next day the ambassador gave him an introduction to Hendrick Bicker, head of the financial house Andries Pels at Amsterdam, and sent him to the Swedish minister for help in Mme d'Urfé's shares — there Casanova received another Amsterdam introduction to the banker Thomas Hope (who was a director both of the East and West India Companies). Twenty-four hours later (having also been presented to the regent-princess, and the boy Prince of Orange, and been to the theater to see Racine's *Iphigénie*) he was on his way to Amsterdam in a two-wheeled post-chaise, with his servant. On the way there was an incident, as there very often was with Casanova. A four-wheeled carriage approaching them did not wish to give way, which led to an impasse, with our hero jumping down into the December snow, which came halfway up his boots, holding out his unsheathed sword and demanding satisfaction. The young man inside, an Amsterdamer, smiled down at him, and said that not only had he no sword, but that he wouldn't dream of fighting for such a ridiculous reason. He advised Casanova to get back in his post-chaise, and he would give way. It was a very proper Amsterdam reaction. Two hours later Casanova arrived in the dark and went to the inn De Ster van Oosten.

The next day he found Hendrick Bicker at the Exchange, and the financier told him that he would consider the problem of the French bills. Mynheer Hope was also around and Casanova found him a quarter of an hour later. Hope at once put him in touch with a Swedish agent, who wanted to do a deal on the spot for Mme d'Urfé's shares, and give him twelve percent interest. (Madame had complained that she had received no interest.) But Casanova went back to Mynheer Bicker who told him to wait, because he could get him fifteen percent. He also gave him dinner and the visitor much admired his red wine from the Dutch settlement at the Cape.

Mr. Hope was his host the following day. He was a widower, but a daughter, Esther, was present. She was eighteen or nineteen, possibly much less, and ravishingly pretty, with dark hair, a beautiful skin and large dark eyes. There is some doubt whether she was a daughter, an illegitimate daughter or a niece — in any case she lived there as a daughter, and Casanova was instantly overcome. She spoke French well and played the clavichord with a charming touch. After dinner at three or four o'clock he was shown the house. (It is now 446 Keizersgracht and in use as a library.) He saw a treasure of old china, and half a dozen rooms with marble walls and floors, each room a different color, all with superb specially made Turkey carpets. The great dining room had walls and ceiling in alabaster, with the table and sideboards in cedar wood. Outside, the façade — like so many of the other Keizersgracht and Herengracht houses — was also of marble. (One Saturday Casanova saw four or five servants up on ladders washing it and was highly amused because they all wore large hoop petticoats — which obliged them also to wear protective breeches.) Most of the house was unused, especially since the death of the banker's wife. He and his daughter lived comfortably on the ground floor. And this, again, was a common arrangement in the big houses.

After the inspection Mr. Hope left Casanova alone with the girl, who played the clavichord some more and then hinted that he could take her to a concert.

"I'm sure if you ask my father, he won't refuse . . ."

"You're sure?"

"Very sure — after all, it would be very impolite, since he knows you.

I'm amazed that you're afraid! My father is very polite. I see you don't know our customs in Holland. Girls here have a lot of liberty. They only lose it when they get married! So come on."

Delighted, the thirty-four-year-old guest looked for the father, who was busy writing, and put it to him.

"Have you a carriage?" asked Mr. Hope.

"Yes, sir."

"Good, then there's no need to harness up. Esther!"

"Father?"

"Go and get dressed. M. Casanova is very kindly going to take you to a concert."

"Oh, thank you, Father."

An hour later Casanova was helping her into the carriage. He assumed that her maid would get in, too, but the servant having closed the house door climbed up behind. He was astounded to find himself alone with the lovely girl. It could not have happened under these circumstances in Paris. Esther gaily talked about the program they would hear — there was to be a marvelous Italian singer — and wanted to know why he was silent. He answered craftily that she was a treasure and he was not worthy to be in charge of her. She was amused.

"I know that everywhere else girls aren't allowed out alone with men, but here they teach us to be virtuous and we are not quite sure that we shall be unhappy if we are not."

"Your husband will be happy," Casanova sighed, "and happier still if you have already chosen him."

"Oh, I don't choose him. My father does that."

"Supposing he chooses someone and you love someone else."

"You see, we are only allowed to love someone we know will be our husband."

"So you love nobody," said Casanova, taking her hand.

"Nobody, and what's more I haven't even been tempted."

"So I can be permitted to kiss your hand?"

"Why my *hand?*"

He kissed her lips, bewitched by his introduction to Amsterdam romance. They arrived at the concert, where Esther at once found many friends, pretty and ugly girls, all daughters of rich merchants. There was also another M. Casanova, from a different branch of the family — they agreed to meet, to compare their genealogies — and he also had a blond daughter. Casanova (but, of course) sat between her and Esther and listened to a symphony, a violin concerto and an oboe concerto — the Italian singer came on afterwards as an extra titbit, and Casanova would hardly have been Casanova if she had not turned out, as she did, to be someone from his past. Since she was not on the bill she had to go round with a plate afterwards.

"She does very badly," Esther said, "for after all, everyone has already paid for a ticket. I should think it would be good if she collects thirty or forty guilders."

The singer recognized Casanova, though without words. Mr. Hope turned up at the end of the concert and Casanova delivered Esther to him. He went back to his inn, De Ster van Oosten, and ordered a dish of oysters. But soon the Italian singer arrived, with her small child (also his). They spent the night talking, and the next day without having been to bed Casanova kept an appointment at the Exchange with his namesake. The Exchange amazed him and especially that so many of the merchants and brokers seemed almost peasantlike — yet a man with less than a hundred thousand guilders was so poor that he hardly dared trade under his own name. Later on Mr. Hope offered to buy Mme d'Urfé's Swedish shares, freeing Casanova of brokerage and legal charges, not only at the terms he had promised but with a 3,000 francs bonus, due to some subtle calculation concerned with the value of Swedish thalers at Hamburg. This was one job done, and showed what could be done for a man at Amsterdam, when not only a banker but the banker's daughter liked him.

Next he had an interesting trip with Mr. Bicker in a sailing boat fixed on a sledge. In this they went at great speed across the ice northwards to Zaandam. It was comfortable, firm and safe, and he rather thought he would like to go round the world in this way, if the ice could be arranged — though there was a touch of anxiety when the two sailors on board had to lower the sails at exactly the right moment to stop the sleigh-boat crashing on to land. They returned to Amsterdam drawn by two horses. Mr. Bicker entertained him to supper and he left at midnight, full of friendship, and with the promise from his host that he and Hope would see Casanova through his big deal with the French government.

The following day he was with Mr. Hope and Esther again. All wearing furs, they took a sledge and went to their small house on the Amstel, outside the city, where the blond Mlle Casanova and her fiancé joined them. It was snowing heavily. Later in the morning they decided to go skating — except Mr. Hope. Casanova, no skater, was unable to refuse. He was soon covered with bruises, to everybody's amusement. The two girls skated easily, wearing short skirts with black velvet breeches.

He went back to The Hague for a few days to see the ambassador, who had now received the twenty million from Paris. Then he returned to Amsterdam, having seen his Italian actress, fought a small duel, dined with a princess, and received a poor offer for his French affair from the banker Boaz (who wanted a guarantee of cancellation if there was no peace). He went now to a well-known inn, the Second Byble, in the Nes (there was also a First and Third Byble), and then called on Mr. Hope. The banker was out, but Esther was in. Casanova amused her, purely for romantic purposes, with a fraudulent magic game. He constructed pyramids of numbers which mysteriously gave back answers to questions, and did it with great showmanship — knowing all the proper mysterious little ceremonies. He couldn't have hit a better market. The Dutch were all keen on this sort of thing. Esther was hooked. So was her father, when he heard about it. And for the rest of his stay Casanova had to play the game with them and keep up the pretense that he really had some sort of occult system at his command. According to him it was the greatest possible luck, for the banker relied on one of the magic answers to justify him insuring a ship overdue from the East Indies — and made a vast gain out of it, for the ship turned up. As a result the offer which he made to Casanova, in association with Bicker and some others on the Exchange, for the French bills, was much improved — so that the French received cash less nine percent. (The first offer, which Paris rejected, for the twenty million francs' worth, was ten million in cash and seven million in five and six percent bills, plus a cancellation of a debt to the Dutch East India Company, which doubtless the French did not intend to pay anyway.) All done by magic. It was a great and typical coup for the Venetian.

Not every moment in the city was a triumph. He paid a call one day on the princess with whom he had dined in The Hague — it was the Princess Galitzin, whose husband would shortly be the Russian ambassador in Paris. Casanova dressed himself in high Parisian fashion. (This might have been, typically, a dazzling scarlet red gold jacket, laced ruffles of point d'Alençon, Swiss white silk stockings and glistening pumps.) Afterwards he was going to the Hopes'. He decided to walk and sent his carriage off. To his amazement, far from admiring or respecting his grandee appearance, urchins and common persons shouted and whistled after him all the way. How right and proper this was in Amsterdam. . . . And one night he had another depressing view of the canaille. Coming back from the Hopes' this time he called in at a "musico." "Even the sound of two or three musical instruments plunged one into sadness. The room was full of the stink of bad tobacco and the stink of garlic from the belches of people who were dancing or sitting with a bottle of wine or a pot of beer on one side and a hideous trollop on the other. . . ." It was exactly Smollett's description.

And so the return to Paris, for praise and reward, followed by his usual succession of spectacular ups and downs. But he was back in Amsterdam in hopes of more loot at the end of the year, taking "three fine rooms" at the Second Byble. There was another interesting visitor shortly afterwards, the fabulous M. le comte de St. Germain, who was at the Ster van Oosten. This extraordinarily accomplished charlatan had managed to become a friend, as well as an agent, of Louis XV. He was famous in Paris and Versailles for never eating and always talking, which he did with encyclopedic knowledge. He was a brilliant linguist, a violinist, a chemist. He claimed to be able to make diamonds and to be three hundred years old. He was probably about sixty. He was taken half seriously in that cynical but credulous age, and was just the man to intrigue Mynheer Hope. His presence understandably put Casanova's nose a little out of joint. The Venetian had to use his magic numbers routine to warn the banker against dealing with him.

Once again it came off, for M. de St. Germain, who had his enemies at Versailles, was forced to leave the city abruptly. However, it was not a successful visit for Casanova. There was a series of unfortunate incidents. At cards with some dubious counts and barons at a hotel in the disreputable Zeedyk, he was given a fraudulent letter of credit, which led to someone's reputation going west, and Casanova, having been properly paid after Amsterdam police action, was then robbed in his rooms at the Second Byble. And one evening he went again to a "musico," with a friend — after they had bored themselves for a couple of hours with the popular sport of sleigh-boating on the frozen Amstel (a ducat an hour). The "musico" led to two Italian ladies in a house, and hours of shared enjoyment and debauchery. But even this honest pleasure had a tedious aftermath when a so-called officer and "uncle" of the two ladies arrived at the inn to see him, and demand satisfaction. Casanova packed him off, but it began to seem as if nothing would go right for him in Amsterdam when he was not with the Hopes. Hope was still friendly with him. He invited him to supper once at the "Burgomasters" (Masonic) lodge. There were only twenty-four members. In his honor it was opened in French and according to Casanova, never precisely modest, he went down well with them. Afterwards Mr. Hope told him that the company he had supped with had three hundred million guilders at their command. (Eighteen guilders, at this time, bought forty-five bottles of port.) However, none of it was for Casanova. Conditions were not right for him to make a killing (the French were in bad financial odor). He left for Germany.

Three years later in 1763 the war which had brought such wealth to the Amsterdam financiers and bankers came to an end; and that upset everything. De Neufville, the biggest financial house in the city, crashed, and many others crashed with it.

Boswell's visit to Holland was at this time. He found the country highly taxed, and the towns decayed, with people living on potatoes and gin and poor tea and coffee. He was mostly in Utrecht, studying law, and The Hague, which he found beautiful and elegant but un-Dutch, with too much French style and show and luxury, as "among the rich merchants of Amsterdam" — where the burgomasters were all out for squeezing the population, and not the "old men of honour." (He was thinking possibly of the burgomasters who had signed contracts with his great-grandfather, the Earl of Kincardine, to supply the stones which had been used to build the Town Hall.) Snobbish and full of his young self, he thought Amsterdam "the capital of boorish Holland." It was the typical, innocent, "superior" foreign reaction. Boswell had time only for the nobility in Utrecht and The Hague, but Amsterdam interested him for its brothels and once or twice he caught the "Amsterdam schuit" from Utrecht — making the trip in that leisurely, horse-drawn way along the canals, in the barge which had "a roef, a deck-house, with four oblique windows which go up and down, a table with a drawer full of pipes, a spitting box and a little iron pot containing burning turf for a light." He reports that on May 26, 1764, he went to a bawdy house and was shown upstairs, where he had "a bottle of claret and a juffrouw." Perhaps — it was often the case — there was a little oil painting of her hung outside the room, to facilitate choice (although also possibly to lead to disappointment). Afterwards he called on a Scots minister, whose landlord was an Irish "peruke-maker" (who had known Pope in London), and had drinks at a tavern called Farquhars's, "amongst blackguards." At 11 P.M. he was strolling along, slightly nervous of being knifed, looking for a *"speelhuis"* (or "musico"). Like Smollett and Casanova he found one and "entered boldly." Soon he was dancing a "blackguard" minuet with a woman in laced riding clothes. In Dutch style he kept his pipe in his mouth. But disgusted by the "low confusion" he left. He paid a call on another Scotsman and strolled by "mean brothels in dirty lanes." Then he caught the "Utrecht schuit" and, sharing the "roef" with an Italian musician, and a German officer with his wife and child, he was borne gently out of the city at three miles an hour, his opinion of Amsterdamers unchanged.

7.

WHATEVER young Mr. Boswell thought of them, they were still the brokers of Europe. The stock market was the national sport and the carrying trade was quiet but prosperous. Competition was always becoming more difficult — by now the English outnumbered the Dutch in the Baltic and the Mediterranean. But good money was still being made. The only worry was being dragged into a war, and then having no protection. But for the moment there was no war. The shipowners were happy. The regents never lived more luxuriously. And dividends kept on coming from the East India Company.

On the Kloveniersburgwal a man called Tetje Roen initiated Amsterdamers into the commedia dell'arte. He sent up the rich and powerful and himself died rich (from successful speculation, of course). The least effective of the Princes of Orange, William V, came of age, at eighteen, and two years later brought his seventeen-year-old Prussian princess, Wilhelmina, on a state visit to the city. They sat in a gala box, specially built, in the Keizersgracht theater and together with their retinue and all the notables of Amsterdam watched the famous actor Jan Punt, in heroic costume as Apollo, coming down on a cloud to offer a greeting in richly high-flown language. (That cloud was well known for coming to earth on the stage with a very firm thump.) That was in 1768 and the old theater had not long to go. Its lighting system was horrifyingly dangerous, with chandeliers of candles above the stage, flaming torches in the house and in between the wings boxes of grease in which wicks were stuck. In 1772 a stagehand put in too many wicks and it became so hot that the wing caught fire. In a few hours the whole place was burned down.

A new theater was built on the Leidseplein — on the site of the present city theater, and on the site then of the coach and wagon park inside the Leyden gate. (There was a similar park inside every gate.) It was built of wood in the sober style of the late eighteenth century and called by the populace "the wooden cupboard." A hundred years later it was covered with brick. The inauguration was on Saturday, September 17, 1774, for "the benefit of the Orphans' and Old People's Home," at 5 P.M. sharp. A tragedy was the first offering. Balconies (for six), boxes, or seats in the pit could be reserved. A balcony cost eighteen guilders, a seat in the pit 1 guilder 4 stuivers, and standing room six stuivers.

Soon another landmark, destined to be very celebrated for at least a century, appeared — the classical building on the Keizersgracht, quite close to the burned-out old theater, of the society of "Felix Meritis" — which married social exclusiveness with the fashionable interest in science. It had an observatory, a library, lots of sculptures and physical and mathematical instruments, and an elegant concert hall. It is still there today, looking a little jaded and oddly enough owned by the Communist Party, who lease part of it, upstairs in the old astronomy room, to the excellent little Shaffy Theater. The "Felix Meritis" was in tune with the cultural fashions sweeping Europe — the world of Voltaire and Rousseau and Hume and Joseph Priestley. It opened in 1777.

How agreeable it would have been for Amsterdam to go on and on making money, while keeping up with the trends. But already outside events were once more bearing down on the city. Two years before the American colonists had begun their rebellion, and there was no question at all where Amsterdam stood, although the Republic was still officially an ally of England. They were on the colonists' side first because of fashionable political philosophy and second because, like most Dutch people, they could identify with the colonists in the same situation as themselves, who they felt were in the revolt against Spain. But the third reason was the big one, and the dangerous one — recalling the splendid old Dutch saying, "He who wants the last drop out of the tankard gets the lid on his nose." There were vast profits to be made from smuggling to the colonists via the West Indian Dutch islands of St. Eustatius and Curaçao, plus great prospects for trade in the future if the rebellion succeeded. But they had no, or next to no, fleet for protective purposes and there was much virtuous indignation in Amsterdam when ships were stopped and searched, or taken off to English ports as prizes. French diplomats, who spent much useful time in the city, stirred up these feelings — which were also associated with the new liberalism and antistadholderism.

All this fitted the outlook of the veteran Burgomaster de Vrij Temminck, who was now the undisputed leader of the Amsterdam "Magnificat" (and also, incidentally, the spit of Jack Benny). Born in 1700 he was elected burgomaster twenty-three times, the first time in 1752, when he firmly backed Pieter Rendorp's "Correspondence," the antistadholder and anti-England agreement among the councillors. He was, naturally, rich. They were all rich. But he was the first burgomaster to make himself popular with all classes by a rough-and-ready familiarity (modern politics were approaching and he saw the need early). The second one was his close ally Hendrick Hooft, who learned the trick from him. These two, with the Amsterdam pensionary, Van Berckel, secretly backed the smuggling of war materials. In 1778 after France had joined the war and Benjamin Franklin and John Adams were in Europe looking for friends, it was to Amsterdam they had to turn — after the States-General had turned them down. Van Berckel and Jean de Neufville (who had recovered from the crash of his bank in 1763) negotiated with an American agent, William Lee, a treaty to be operated as soon as England had recognized American independence. Unfortunately during a search at sea two years later the English came across a copy of these proceedings and blew up. The Republic then poured a little oil on the fire, under pressure from Amsterdam, by joining the League of Armed Neutrality, sponsored by Russia. De Vrij Temminck and friends had gone too far. England declared war.

It was disastrous. What could they do without a fleet? They managed one small indecisive battle — the Dogger Bank. The English ruled the sea. No Dutch ship could be sure of getting home — two hundred were captured in the first month, which damped the ardor of the "liberal" merchants who had been so pleased at the stadholder's being forced to ally with the French. Coming back from the East Indies they had to go round the north of Scotland towards Norway. So they began to store the goods in the Indies, where they went rotten. The market for groceries in Germany was lost. Hamburg, Bremen and Emden took advantage (and kept it after the war). The trade which had bloomed happily throughout the century was frizzled and though England made a reasonably generous peace in

1784 things were never the same again. And the war had given the death-blow to the East India Company, though its ruin was half concealed, for its affairs were always conducted in secrecy. A dividend of twelve percent had been paid for the previous ten years and gave a false picture of security. Decades of bad management and corruption were coming to roost. To pay the dividend they had to borrow at high interest rates and depend on next year's supplies to pay the interest. When the war came there were no next year's supplies. The States of Holland gave them leave to freeze payment and set up an enquiry. The war cost the company twenty million guilders. The States of Holland loaned it eight million to prevent instant collapse. The once great company staggered on for a little while longer.

As if war against England were not enough, the Austrian emperor was suddenly threatening to open the Scheldt and restore Antwerp as a competitor to Amsterdam. What with this and his other demands, the Dutch were alarmed and exasperated, and reacted with an unusual unity and determination. Two ships sent out to try the passage were stopped and both sides prepared for war. Meanwhile the political situation was moving against the unfortunate Prince of Orange, who was receiving the blame for all the disasters of the last four years. In Amsterdam De Vrij Temminck, though still a burgomaster, had handed over leadership to Hooft. A new situation had arisen, for many of the regents had become aware that antistadholderism, backed by popular support, was all too likely to mean antiregentism as well. Accordingly a majority of them joined in an aristocratic party, splitting the old states party which had always opposed the Orangists. The rest of the states party now belonged to the so-called Patriot and democratic movement, which was making progress throughout the Republic and was full of Rousseau's ideas about the rights of man and the social contract. It was led in Amsterdam by Hooft, already a most popular figure among the ordinary burghers.

He was no ordinary burgher himself. A member of one of the greatest regent families, he had foreseen the downfall of the closed Corver "cabal" and in 1746, when he was thirty and building himself in the city government in the normal way of an oligarch's son, he had also gone into banking and made himself a fortune dealing with the French. His first wife died and his second was the nineteen-year-old daughter of an English merchant, Jacob Schues, who arrived in Amsterdam with nothing in 1670 and died at ninety-two a millionaire. But the second wife also died soon, not an unusual story, leaving Hooft a daughter, Hester, who grew up and married an immensely rich banker, George Clifford. He died as well, and the twenty-eight-year-old widow managed both the businesses she had inherited (there had been many successful Amsterdam business-women amongst the widows of the past two centuries). Her "democrat" father was therefore not uncushioned in his double-house on the Heren-gracht.

When in 1785 the French came to the Republic's assistance and medi-ated between it and the Austrian emperor, the Patriots' francophilia was unbounded. A banquet was given in Amsterdam to honor the French am-bassador and Hooft welcomed him on behalf of the city. Everywhere in the Republic the Patriots felt things were going their way. Free corps appeared, revolution was in the air. The stadholder was insulted and re-tired huffily to the country with his Prussian princess. While business tried to get back to normal the aristocratic party in Amsterdam, which still had a majority, tried to slip through a number of anti-Patriot measures. They hopelessly underestimated the opposition's backing among the people. On February 27, 1787, a mob besieged the Town Hall.

It was Hooft's moment. Nine councillors were forced to resign and were replaced by Patriot nominees. Both in the great Burghers' Hall inside the Town Hall and outside on the Dam, Hooft was given an ovation. Enthusi-astic militiamen escorted him through the crowd to his coach. He had the right kind of benevolent Santa Claus face. People shouted, "Vivat Father Hooft!" From then on he was "Father Hooft" and there was a similar scene every day when he arrived at or left the Town Hall. He was the most famous and most loved of all the burgomasters. Hundreds of panegyrics were written about him. The triumph went on for several months. In June the remaining aristocratic burgomasters, Willem Dedel and Adriaan Beels, were forced to resign, and the mob, becoming always more revolutionary, plundered and attacked aristocratic houses. Many regents decided it was time to leave.

But also in June "Willemijntje," the attractive but arrogant Princess of Orange, tired of her husband's defeatist attitude to the near civil-war situ-ation, insisted on returning herself to The Hague. She did not get there. At Gouda the commander of a Patriot free corps stopped her and her retinue. She was told that she could not go on without permission from the States of Holland. Wild with indignation the princess stormed back to base, which was Nijmegen. The English ambassador, who had been looking for some means of reasserting the stadholder's authority and, thereby, England's influence, knew how to make good use of the incident. Soon the King of Prussia was furious or pretending fury at the insult to the Prussian princess, and when the States of Holland refused to punish anybody a Prussian army invaded the country. One excuse is as good as another.

The Patriots collapsed everywhere. Most towns surrendered at once and the prince returned to The Hague to enthusiasm and the familiar old football-crowdlike shouts of *"Oranje boven!"* — "Up Orange!" Most leading Patriots had sheltered in Amsterdam, where they were still in a state of defense. However, when the Prussians arrived, armed resistance as always seemed terribly unattractive. Hooft resigned and the Prussians accepted the city's surrender on October 3. Prussian soldiers guarded the Town Hall and Burgomasters Dedel and Beels were back on the job. It was not the most satisfactory of victories. Down at The Hague the princess was crying out for exemplary punishments. Some Patriots were locked up, but very large numbers of them got out — forty thousand were supposed to have left the Republic, mostly for France. After a few weeks' camping on the Dam the Prussians departed, leaving no rosy memories behind.

Amsterdam settled down to its last few years of rule by the aristocratic oligarchs. The last well-known burgomaster was Pieter Cornelis Hasselaer. He belonged to a poor branch of a famous family — Hooft's grandfather, the unwilling ally of Valckenier, had married a Hasselaer. His father had done well enough in the East Indies to buy a country estate and a large house on the Keizersgracht, but Pieter Cornelis felt the need for more and broke off his own career in the Town Hall to make a fortune in the Indies. His first wife, a daughter of the burgomaster persecuted by the terrible Jeronimo de Haze de Georgio, died before he went, and when he got there he married the governor-general's daughter. Before long wife and father-in-law died and Hasselaer returned to Amsterdam with a million. As a burgomaster after the Prussian episode and a firm Orange supporter he acted as a middleman between the prince and some of the still somewhat restless Amsterdam regents. Normalcy was attempted. True to Amsterdam's great charity traditions the Society for Public Welfare (Nut van't Algemeen) was set up on the Kloveniersburgwal, as Baedeker in the nineteenth century put it, "for the promotion of the education and moral culture of the lower classes." But all Amsterdam could really do, along with the stadholder and the Republic, was to flounder on in the hands of England and Prussia. In 1789 the French Revolution began. It was hardly surprising that in 1790 the East India Company owed eighty-five million guilders. In 1791 liquidation proceedings began. In 1791 also the West India Company came to an end. Worst of all symbols of decay in that same year the glorious exchange bank of Amsterdam — the Bank — could not meet any demand for payment in coin or metal.

Doom lay ahead, except for the excited Patriot cells in the city, who formed "reading societies" to cover their activities. In 1792 the French beat the Austrians in the southern Netherlands and by the end of the year the Dutch nightmare had happened, the Scheldt — and therefore Antwerp — had been thrown open. Then in February 1793 France declared war on England, and on the Republic because of the "Stadholder's slavish bondage to the courts of St. James and Berlin." Patriot exiles under a Colonel Daendels made up a "Batavian Legion," which was to be part of an attack on Holland ending up at Amsterdam. The French advanced and reached Breda, but defeats elsewhere forced them to retreat. Bitterly disappointed, the Amsterdam "reading societies" had to go on with their reading for the moment. A year went by with things going wrong for the French. The stadholder and the regents could relax. But then things went right. The French won a battle in which the stadholder's two sons and Dutch troops fought alongside the English and the Austrians. A secret revolutionary committee was formed in Amsterdam and it sent a message to Paris urging attack. The English army withdrew, which helped. And suddenly there was an extraordinary frost which made the river crossings easy and nullified Holland's basic water defense. The French under Pichegru, accompanied by Daendels, now a general, and his Batavian Legion, took the opportunity and advanced northwards without any trouble.

The revolutionary committee in Amsterdam waited. So did the last of the burgomasters — Hasselaer, Huydecoper, Elias and Straelman. They met every day in mid-January 1795 to discuss the hopeless situation, in Straelman's house on the Herengracht, along with high officials like the Schout and the pensionary. The news came that Utrecht had fallen. An Austrian general turned up offering to defend the city with his troops. Nobody was keen. The discussions went on, getting nowhere, over the weekend, the seventeenth and eighteenth of January. Huydecoper went off to The Hague. Hasselaer, not surprisingly, felt ill and stayed at home. So only two burgomasters were there to deal with the arrival of Daendels' representative, a Dr. Krayenhoff. He persuaded them (it was not difficult) that resistance was useless. He promised no violence and they agreed to surrender the city. They summoned the Council for the next day.

COURTESY OF THE AMSTERDAM CITY ARCHIVES

The Freedom Tree on the Dam — 1795

That was Monday, January 19. Weary, ragged French hussars appeared on the Dam, which was renamed the Square of the Revolution. The "reading societies" closed the books and of course everybody else was suddenly a Patriot. A "freedom tree" was brought in and set up with weights and ropes (it couldn't be planted owing to the frost). The crowd were all wearing the Batavian colors — red, white and blue — which were soon also hanging from the Town Hall roof. Inside the surrender went off smoothly. Burgomaster Straelman read out a letter from Dr. Krayenhoff demanding all their resignations. Then the nine members of the revolutionary committee were led in and sat at places prepared for them. Their spokesman read out a speech in which it was politely pointed out that the old administration was finished. The councillors answered by bowing deeply. Straelman thanked the committee for the peaceful manner of the takeover and took the liberty of entrusting himself and his family and everybody else to the committee's protection. While this was going on a balcony door was flung open and somebody shouted to the crowd on the Dam, "Worthy citizens! Our former government has given in to the will of the people!" The Council chamber was cleared, Straelman handed over the keys of the burgomasters' room and then members of the revolutionary committee — now the "provisional representatives of the people of Amsterdam" — escorted the former regents safely through the crowd. It was in the tradition of that other change of power in 1578, when the Catholics had to go.

The Dutch were now Batavians. The same day that ended the "Magnificat" of Amsterdam, the stadholder and his family were being received in England. The extraordinary Republic of the United Provinces had at last been put out of business.

IV

Low Tide
1795–1870

1.

"BE FREE OR BE DEAD — this must be your motto!" cried the official speaker, representing the municipality. "You see this freedom tree — *never* see it without being spurred on and determined to preserve freedom! Children! You have been brought here by your Patriot elders — don't leave this place without an *indelible* impression! The urge for freedom must stay firm in your hearts and be your supreme aim. Old people! How lucky you are in your old age! You approach the grave on unsteady legs, but also with ease in your hearts — for you leave free successors behind! Batavian women! Use your power over your menfolk to inspire them to the defense of freedom! Then tyranny's thunder will have no chance! Mothers! On you —"

And so on and so on — like hundreds of other speeches being made all over the country. The scene was the Dam. It was March 4, the celebration day of the Revolution. The frost had gone and the freedom tree was now properly planted in front of the Town Hall. It was highly decorated and even wore a hat with a red, white and blue cockade. Before the speeches there had been a great procession from the Botermarkt (the Butter Market, which is today's Rembrandtsplein). Taking part were the "revolutionary committee," members of the "reading societies," people who had been locked up for anti-Orange activities, plus leading members of the new provisional administration and symbolic figures like the Amsterdam Maid, children carrying revolutionary slogans and so on. Over two thousand armed burghers lined the route and themselves followed the procession to make a vast crowd on the Dam — or, rather, the Square of the Revolution.

After the speeches there was dancing and general happiness, all with a distinctly French flavor. Militiamen, shopkeepers, wives, high French officers, fisherwomen all enjoyed themselves together in an intoxicating atmosphere of liberty, equality and fraternity. It was true that things became a little less equal when the new leaders of the city and the French officers withdrew for a banquet in the great burghers' hall. But outside the happy shouts went on.

In fact the revolution in Amsterdam was already a triumph for bourgeois ideals. The man who had been made president of the new Council was a thirty-five-year-old lawyer, Rutger Jan Schimmelpenninck — today a face on a cigar box. He had been a brilliant success since youth and he was civilized, moderate and honest. This admirable man told the new Council at once that as soon as the cheers gave way to discontent he would expect them still to operate with "fairness, justice and generosity." And a month later he had them proclaim that punishments would only be carried out for actions which "at all times," aside from politics, were "morally reprehensible." Which meant that as far as Mr. Schimmelpenninck was concerned, property was to be protected.

For the time being too much was going on in the country for the more radical Patriots to notice it. In any case, some other very shabby surprises were just round the corner.

2.

OVERCOME by the general headiness of the revolutionary atmosphere, the Patriots forgot that they were in the hands of a conquering French army. Too easily they assumed their independence and the application of liberty, equality and fraternity; they now discovered that these words — as we all know so well — can have variable connotations. In March they learned that independence was available — on terms. The shock was considerable. In May they agreed to pay a hundred million guilders, allow a French garrison in Flushing, keep and pay for twenty-five thousand troops, and lose various towns and territory. Possibly worst of all they had to allow the circulation of the worthless French paper money, the so-called assignats.

And then, "independent" at last, they signed a treaty of alliance with France, with the almost instant result that their coast was blockaded by the British fleet. Naturally it meant commercial disaster and depression, with more unemployment and poverty, especially at Amsterdam. At the same time, centered in an Assembly at The Hague which replaced the

States-General, the great debate was on between the radical or Jacobin unitarians, who wanted a centralized power on the French model, and the more moderate Patriots under Schimmelpenninck. The moderates won, but events in Paris and an unfortunate sea battle, when the "Batavian" fleet took on the English blockaders at the battle of Camperdown and lost disastrously, made a coup possible for the more revolutionary side. The Jacobins took over at The Hague on January 22, 1798, imprisoning the Committee of Foreign Affairs and twenty-two members of the Assembly. Then there was a straightforward tyranny in the country for several months. A constitution was prepared and imposed on the current French model and in Amsterdam, whose Jacobin club was the chief of the whole network, there was great enthusiasm for these developments. Militant Patriots had been exasperated by the rule of the moderates and had rioted for the confiscation of the ex-regents' property and the dismissal of all officials. Most resentful and eloquent were the smaller burghers who had particularly suffered from the trade depression. The officials were duly sacked and the Jacobin Patriots stepped into the jobs-for-the-boys. The city promptly fell into a chaos of persecution and corruption, with voters' lists (which the revolution had brought in three years before) being ruthlessly pruned of known moderates. It all went against the bourgeois grain too much not to create a backlash. The right people saw the right man — Talleyrand — in Paris. By June the new regime at The Hague was capsized. In Amsterdam the sacked officials got their jobs back, the poor went on being poor, property owners retained their property — it was all a triumph for the bourgeois virtues.

Moderation had won, and that was at least something, but any prospect of a more comfortable life was ruined by the seizing of power in Paris by Bonaparte.

There was a respite, and sudden hope, in March 1802, with the Peace of Amiens. All the old Dutch colonies (which had been lost to England) were handed back. The city came to life again and the merchants' offices buzzed. But the war began again the next year, and all the colonies were promptly lost again. Amsterdam sank back into lethargy, while Napoleon's insistent and ever increasing demands lay over the whole country. The great man believed, rather accurately, that the "Batavians" were not only inefficient but hostile, especially in their undercover but traditional desire to trade with the enemy. He imposed an autocratic constitution, making Schimmelpenninck the head of state, with the old title of Council-

Pensionary. The archmoderate lawyer did some wonderful work (thoroughly deserving his place on the cigar tins) improving administration and with the help of his financial adviser, Vogel, spreading the taxation load — which bore so heavily on Amsterdam. But when he developed eyesight trouble, with cataracts, Napoleon decided that it was a suitable moment to exert total authority. He offered them the choice of annexation direct or receiving his younger brother, Louis Napoleon, as king. After two or three weeks of useless protest they accepted the younger brother.

3.

WHEN LOUIS NAPOLEON WAS IN AMSTERDAM, twice a week a six-horse carriage would set off from the palace stables to bring back M. Chevallier, a pastor of French extraction, from The Hague, to give him his lesson in Dutch. There could be no better symbol of his good intentions nor of the impossibility of carrying them out successfully. His progress in the language, it will be no surprise to hear, was disappointing. On the Dam one should always look up at the palace — it was he who made it a palace — and spare a kind thought for him. For he was a tragicomic but, all in all, most sympathetic figure, unlike his magnificent and dreadful older brother. In fact he was, above all, a younger brother. The emperor, nine years his senior, was fond of him, had carefully watched over his education, made him his aide-de-camp in Italy and Egypt, given him command of a regiment of dragoons and then some not very important political jobs, such as the governorship of Paris. Finally, though his health was not wonderful, he had been given an army command. The older brother had nursed him along. In return he expected, as from everyone else, affection, worship and obedience. From Louis Napoleon came affection, worship and hidden resentment.

He was twenty-eight and at first sight a better-looking, curly-haired version of the emperor. He was intelligent and by now highly trained, but he was also introverted and, by nature, kindly. Conscious of his unsuitability for pomp and circumstance, he could try to make up for it by extravagance or by striking an attitude; but all too easily he would feel silly, and if Napoleon knew about it, he would feel very silly. There was no getting away from his situation. His self-confidence was undermined by a chronic skin condition and by scrofula. No doubt this also helped to make his romantic life distinctly unsuccessful. He was jealous of his wife, Hortense, who was attractive, selfish, and towards him cold and hostile. But she was the stepdaughter of her august brother-in-law — her mother, the Empress Josephine — and she had been forced to marry. Louis Napoleon himself had been in love with one of her cousins, Emilie de Beauharnais, and Emilie had married a M. de Lavalette in one week flat to get away from him. It was trauma, trauma all the way for Louis Napoleon. There was far more rapport between Hortense and the emperor. Neither of them took him seriously. Nor did the emperor understand how seriously his brother took the new job. But Louis Napoleon, having accepted the throne of Holland not very willingly — he was nervous of what the damp climate would do to his health — was determined to be an outstanding king and to serve his subjects. He thought it was a chance of proving himself away from the overpowering shade. It was not what the emperor had in mind.

They arrived in The Hague with their two small sons in June 1806. At once there was a vast increase in the glamour of the scene. Court life began. There were balls and receptions, and minor discords and jealousies when the Dutch felt the French were patronizing them, and flattery and obsequiousness, the "holy water of courts," flowed plentifully. The new king went to work. As a first gesture of independence he asked the emperor to remove all French troops and Napoleon, slightly astounded, agreed to do it; it happened to be convenient, but from then on he subjected the younger brother to an ever increasing series of pin-pricking demands, most of them concerned with the blockade of Britain. Disaster was inevitable, for Louis Napoleon's tragedy was that letting English contraband in was essential to the welfare of his subjects. But it was still a little way off, and he busied himself being a king, and father figure, traveling the country and writing memos to his ministers.

"I want a complete and satisfactory report about the 17,000 souls in Amsterdam who appear to belong to no religion. . . ."

"I have not yet received the report which should have been made about the inspection of the Amsterdam dikes. I am informed that in some places they are lower than they should be. . . ."

"I have received your letter about ———. Get rid of this individual at once and forbid him to return to Holland, unless he wants to be arrested.

See that he never establishes any gaming houses anywhere in the kingdom. . . ."

"Have the house of Hope at Amsterdam informed that I disapprove of the loan demanded by Spain. . . ."

Father of his people, the twenty-eight-year-old monarch wrote conveying the apologies of a brigadier in Italy for the terrible behavior of the brigadier's son to the Schmidt family of Utrecht. The brigadier offered compensation. Louis Napoleon wrote, "It would be agreeable to me to be able to help towards bringing peace and harmony between two worthy families. Make it up with General Darancey and end this affair by the marriage of the two young people. . . ."

"See to it that the Official Journal appears on good paper, with good print and the arms of the kingdom, and that there are always four large pages. It would be a good idea to get the help of some distinguished men of letters, such as MM. Meerman and Bilderdyk. . . ."

"I inform you that conforming to the emperor's wish I have had all communication with England forbidden throughout Holland. No ships may leave any port of the kingdom for a neutral country without a caution and guarantee that it will not go to an enemy country; for greater security permits granted will be signed by me. I have ordered all ships whatsoever coming from neutral countries to be arrested and examined with the greatest care, they will be released only on an order signed by me. All export of gin without exception is forbidden. All letters discovered going to or coming from England must be sent to my ministry of police. . . ."

In January the next year a gunpowder supply ship blew up at Leyden, creating great havoc and damage. The king went there at once and his real concern and practical action on behalf of the victims gave him a very good mark with the Dutch people. Even the queen gave 10,000 guilders, although the kingdom bored her almost as much as her husband. A few months later they had their own tragedy. Their elder little boy went down with croup and died in a few days. They were both heartbroken — and in an attempt to get over it, went off to take the waters in the Pyrenees. Hortense did not come back with him, and kept the other child with her.

Alone now, and lonely, he moved to Utrecht with his court — at no inconsiderable expense — and the queen's absence did not help the balls and receptions. Louis Napoleon was not the sort of man to make a party go. He missed his son, his health was poor. All the time he was under fire from his tyrant brother, who, always critical of the contraband situation, treated him with ironical displeasure; and sent a new ambassador, the Duc de la Rochefoucauld, who was clearly a watchdog. Louis decided to move to Amsterdam. This, again, cost something. The Council had to move out of the Town Hall and take over the old Court of Admiralty. The weighhouse on the Dam was knocked down and removed to improve the immediate view for his majesty. He made an entry into the city, to take up the new residence, on April 20, 1808 — and the population greeted him warmly. He was extravagant, but he did work for them — that message had got through.

In Amsterdam his loneliness and despair grew. He desperately wanted to see his son and he began a long campaign of letters to Paris begging the queen to let him go. Meanwhile there was a new baby, and he was full of suspicion about that. He wrote also to the governess, Madame de Boubers, to his mother, to a lady-in-waiting, Mme de Broc.

"Whatever her hate for me, the evil she does in keeping away from me the one friend I have in the world is too cruel. . . ."

Hortense, of course, apart from any malice of her own, did what her brother-in-law told her.

Meanwhile the lonely king went on doing his job, writing memos to his ministers.

"I wish you to inform the commissioners of the society Felix Meritis that I desire to become a member of this society. . . ." "I am informed that three American vessels which arrived in the Texel on the tenth and twelfth of this month, supposed to be loaded with salt, actually carried English merchandise. . . ." "A large number of condemned men will be executed tomorrow. I desire that some hours before the execution you will see them all, and speak to each. . . ."

There was trouble about the French ambassador's overbearing behavior; there was some double-crossing from one of his own ministers; in Paris they had already written him off. The emperor, disillusioned by his young brother's protection of the Dutch, was determined to ease him out and took every opportunity of humiliating him. And all the time there was the deep personal unhappiness, the child kept from him, his health — treatments suggested by the Amsterdam doctors included arnica and centaury, cold baths, drinking whey, inoculations, while a favorite French doctor gave him urtication. All this and a queen, far from the Dam, to whom he had to write almost hysterical letters of complaint and self-pity, to which she occasionally replied with coldness. He wrote to his own younger brother, Jerome Bonaparte, King of Westphalia, "Tell me if he has spoken of me and of this country, and what he said about it, I know he is not satisfied. Tell me, I pray you, what you know. . . . Tell me also, if you know, why the emperor hasn't asked me to Erfurt and if you think it would have been all right for me to have turned up unexpectedly. Tell me if he has spoken of the demand I made to him to let my son leave Paris. The whole thing is extraordinary, especially his mother's part in it. Tell me if the Emperor Alexander spoke to you about Holland or about me, and how you were treated at Erfurt. . . ."

Poor, lonely Louis, not very much of a king, in his palace on the Dam. But he went on trying, he promoted culture — he was always in touch with the most prominent literary men, such as the highly respected Bilderdijk. "I have received with pleasure your elegiacal poem on the Leyden catastrophe, as well as your collection of Erotica. . . ." (Mr. Bilderdijk!) Early in 1809 he was busy trying to send some promising singers to the Paris Conservatoire. And he made himself popular during some bad floods, and also a smallpox epidemic, by visiting the scenes and showing practical sympathy.

In July the English landed on Walcheren — they were out to destroy invasion preparations. Most of the Dutch troops that existed were away in Napoleon's armies — in Spain and Austria — and King Louis wrote round frantically demanding them back while organizing all forces possible for the defense of Antwerp. Napoleon rewarded him with a scathing, "By your false and petty measures you have lost Holland." Louis was there in the field, doing his bit, commanding a Franco-Dutch force. The emperor contemptuously sent a French marshal to take over. Humiliated, the king went back to Amsterdam.

There had been some slight panic about the safety of the city, for it was quite undefended. However, the English departed, full of fevers. In fact their departure was rather regretted by the population, for the occupation of Zeeland had meant a vastly helpful introduction of contraband goods into the country. But now large numbers of French troops were appearing in Belgium. The takeover would soon take place. The queen wrote, suggesting separation. Louis replied in a long letter from Amsterdam on November 23, 1809:

". . . from the first moments of our union I was convinced that I had made a mistake, that we were in no way made for each other — when I came to Holland the sole consideration which pressed on me was the hope that we would really reunite in a strange country where we would be everything to each other — my hopes were cruelly deceived and I don't need to remind you of the efforts I made, even the self-abasements, to reconcile you to me. . . .

"In that sad period which led us to the Pyrenees, I don't know why I imagined that our sudden dreadful misfortune might change you, just as it had really brought me close to you — when I saw you again at Toulouse on August 12, 1807, I threw myself into your arms and soon I knew perfectly well that everything was finished between us. . . . I left with that firm conviction and I told the King of Westphalia, who was with me, 'That's the end of it — it's finished.' Two years have gone. I am alone, without my son, without my family, constantly embroiled with my brother, who is not just to me — and yet was a father to me. . . . Morning and evening I tell myself that my death will put a good end to my troubles. . . . If your Majesty desires a formal separation, I will subscribe in advance to anything my brother orders, provided that I don't have to live under the same roof or in the same country as you. I add one condition, to have the Prince Royal with me. I also wish that you may find tranquility and happiness. . . ."

So, on the Dam, think of him looking miserably out from his study window. Poor Louis Napoleon. (With a great clattering of hooves the six-horse carriage swings into the square, bringing M. Chevallier from The Hague to give him his Dutch lesson.)

The nightmare soon reached its crescendo. The emperor summoned all his brothers to Paris, and Louis, after much nervous conferring with ministers, but torn by his desire to see his boy, obeyed. A few days after writing to the queen he left Amsterdam. He soon regretted it. Napoleon received him graciously, but very soon Louis found himself, in effect, a prisoner. His son was still kept from him and humiliations were heaped on him — such as excluding him from discussions on Dutch affairs. He was not physically strong enough to try an adventurous escape. Back in Amsterdam, where the French ambassador was more and more overbearing, the rumors flew. After more than three months and various stormy interviews with Napoleon, Louis had to sign whatever his brother wanted — after which the great man became affable and insisted on his presence at his wedding to Marie Louise. After all the strain, Louis felt almost grateful and quite enjoyed the parties.

Then he returned to Amsterdam. The queen (whose plea for separation had not been allowed) followed him. So he saw his son at last. But Hortense merely brought more gloom to the gloomy palace, couldn't stand it, and went off to one of the old Orange seats, Het Loo. Then she left the country again.

The Prince Royal stayed with his father. But soon Louis was in an impossible situation. By the agreement he had had to make in Paris French troops now arrived at The Hague and at Leyden. French customs officers were installed everywhere. In the Amsterdam streets there was a feeling of tension and simple alarm — which boiled over when a citizen shouted something rude at a French ambassador's coachman, who was decked out in full livery, quite close to the palace. Pretty soon there was a large-scale brawl going on and the palace guard had to interfere. Possibly it was a put-up incident. In any case the ambassador made a great thing of it. Napoleon, who had just sent the king a bitter, complaining, reproachful letter — "Your estrangement with France has lost Holland what she would not have lost under Schimmelpenninck or a Prince of Orange" — now fairly sizzled. "I have recalled my ambassador; I shall only have a chargé d'affaires in Holland. . . . I no longer wish to expose my ambassador to your insults. Don't write me any more of your usual cajoling words; you have been repeating them to me for three years and every moment proves their falsity."

For a few weeks he lived in a sort of royal limbo, appointing an ambassador or two, exchanging decorations with the King of Prussia, ordering somebody to make provision that ill or crippled sailors sent ashore "have money to get home without begging, as at present." One of his last letters from the Dam palace was to Madame de Souza, a novelist (married to a Portuguese diplomat; her first husband had been guillotined), asking for information about two passages he found in a notebook: " 'A Child. When you are born everything around you resounds with cries of tenderness, you alone cry. If you manage to have some sort of life, when you die everyone around will be crying and you alone will smile. Mme de Flahaut January 1802.' 'Most of our misfortunes come because we don't know that two and two make four, that is, it's always because of a fault of calculation. Mme de Flahaut July 1801.' " No wonder they rang a bell for him.

He left the city for the Pavilion at Haarlem, a summer house he had bought from one of the Amsterdam Hope family. Here the last scene was played. For he suddenly heard that the French commander, the Duc de Reggio, proposed to set up his headquarters in Amsterdam. At this mortal,

dressed very plainly and the glory was all the more awesome. There he was. He rode by, followed a few yards behind by his famous personal guard, the Mameluke Roustan.

The first impact had been as satisfyingly impressive as anyone could wish, but almost as soon as Napoleon was inside the palace there was an unrehearsed touch which brought a fearful reminder to the crowds. For suddenly a long procession of miserable, half-starved Spanish prisoners passed by in front of the palace, on their way from Haarlem to Utrecht. It was some minutes after the poor devils had trailed away before the festival atmosphere returned.

That night the palace was packed, every window was lit, and the corridors rang with officers and ladies having confused language troubles with the servants. Amsterdamers, not noted for sobriety, got themselves happily drunk toasting the emperor.

And in the morning the usual flattering deputations arrived — the same ones, almost the same people, who had come to greet King Louis and would come again in a year or two — and they received the same warm-hearted thanks. Amsterdam settled down to its guest and master. There was excitement still. People would struggle to put down their own instead of the official carpets on his path from the palace whenever he came out to go by barge somewhere in the city. There was another famous incident for happy gossip. As soon as possible Marie Louise sent a lady-in-waiting around the town to search for English contraband goods and buy them secretly. The emperor's chief valet-de-chambre, Constant, had the same idea — unfortunately the emperor found out and, enraged, ordered him to be dismissed and sent home. But Constant knew about the empress and, accordingly, survived — for the empress confessed and was forgiven. There were nights at the theater, where they were received with wild acclamations. Actors, including the great tragedian Talma, had been brought from Paris and they performed at the Schouwburg — to the great annoyance of the resident French actors of the Théâtre-Français who were ignored — it was supposed afterwards — because they included an actress who had talked indiscreetly.

Napoleon showed the arrogant bad manners of which he was capable on what was supposed to be a great night at the Felix Meritis. A most sumptuous festivity had been laid on by the city. They had enlarged the quay so that the arrival by barge would be more comfortable, the whole interior of the building had been redecorated. It was all elegance and pomp, and all the most prominent people in the country were present. All that was required was the smallest gesture of satisfaction. They arrived. Napoleon was accompanied on his way through the various apartments of the Felix Meritis by various distinguished Dutchmen; he appeared for a second in the packed out hall, but didn't stop there, and went on through the other rooms at speed; and then he said to the empress, "I can't stay in a place that smells of tobacco smoke like this," and he left. Such a fantastic insult stunned the company and led to high indignation. However, that was Napoleon. They were slightly more successful with a water festival for him on the Amstel, with jousting matches between sailors, and races. It all went off well until at twilight they tried a fireworks display — but once more the damp air of Amsterdam won the battle. However, the great man was amused.

When he returned to the palace that evening, a courier had arrived from Paris with important news. The King of Rome had cut his first tooth. Napoleon worked hard every day, dealing with petitions of various kinds, and then departed on a trip round the north, leaving Marie Louise to amuse herself. She went off to Haarlem to admire the flowers. But it was not enough. ("I should die of boredom if I lived here," she told the Duchess of Montebello.) Meanwhile the court at large had a good look at life in Amsterdam, and these were some of their impressions: they admired the 290 bridges, the multilingual capacities of educated citizens, and the luxuriously made oak and mahogany coffins, which were to be seen as if on exhibition in a street of coffin makers one had to pass through on the way to the Théâtre-Français. They refused on principle — simply because Amsterdamers were so proud of it — to admire the old Exchange. (For all the depression of commerce there was still a crowd of brokers and merchants doing business.) They noted that the most distinguished and refined Amsterdamers and the most beautiful women were among the Portuguese Jews. As to Amsterdam society, the women had better manners than the men — who had a tendency to rudeness, which they claimed to be frankness — and were up to date with Paris fashions (the Felix Meritis evening had been very smart). But they did not walk as well as Frenchwomen, perhaps because of the habit of using footwarmers. What the French found most extraordinary — as Casanova had fifty years before — was the freedom with which even well-born girls could go to balls by themselves, and walk alone with lovers. Married women, however, they found much more constant than in France, although the visiting courtiers said to each other complacently that they were now beginning to compare the gallantry and attentions of the French with their cold and methodical husbands. These admittedly worked hard, but they all — those who had not been made bankrupt — ate, drank, and smoked too much. It was normal for an Amsterdam merchant to have a large dinner, preceded by some liqueurs, and then a little later go out and join his friends in a "society" or club, smoke and drink a bottle or two of wine on his own — and return home to supper. At the same time the debauchery in the "musicos" was more advanced than anything in Paris. A Madame de Nicolai appeared at the palace one day to do some salesmanship for her establishment and her young ladies. She was thrown out.

French eyebrows were also raised at the behavior of Amsterdamers at the theater. They ate scharretjes (dab dried in the sun) which smelled disgustingly, bread and butter slices, apples, pears and nuts; and drank punch, coffee, wine and tea; and, of course, smoked; so that it was more like a fairly low tavern than a theater. And lighting was still poor compared to Paris. On the other hand, if the play was at all serious, many people liked to study a printed version — like a score at a concert — while the play went on. It amused them to learn that when there was a need for crowd scenes people sent along their cooks and nursery maids as extras.

And the French liked the botanical gardens, full of exotic specimens, in the Plantage, the city park by the Muiden gate; and beyond that the great flat peaceful countryside called the Diemermeer, forty-four feet below sea level (the flood defense of Amsterdam), and they liked how all round the outskirts of the city solitary people could be seen fishing. But they didn't like those beds-in-cupboards or the feathery-filled balloons which were used as bedclothes.

Napoleon returned from his trip, pleased by his warm reception everywhere — which he evidently thought was the expression of perfect sincerity. He stayed a few days and went off on another trip, leaving Marie Louise to get still more bored. When he came back again, it was announced that they were leaving for France. All the deputations arrived at the palace to pay homage once more. The exalted couple left Amsterdam in mid-October. And then the city seemed very quiet.

5.

Two years passed. Until the end of 1812 — when it was the staunchness of Dutch pontoon engineers which enabled the Grande-Armée to escape at Beresina — the prestige and glory of the French Empire were at their height, and in the "third city" life went on in a fairly subdued way. There was little opposition and even some enthusiasm, for a winning side was a winning side and Amsterdamers saw no particular prospect of not being French forever. Prince Lebrun gave his balls and receptions, as necessary, and everybody came. On January 1, when people exchanged gifts, toys were brought to the palace for the King of Rome. French newspapers, widely read, gave news of French successes and, after May, of the advance into Russia. There were large numbers of French people in the city. They had a kind of quickness, a kind of wit, which Amsterdamers lacked and enjoyed. The French themselves overestimated this. They liked to believe themselves loved. Who doesn't?

But in fact they were the occupying power and every now and then there were uncomfortable reminders of this. The secret and risky contraband business with the English went on, in spite of all the coastguards and numberless customs officers. Some of it was discovered, naturally, and enough to fill warehouses. Napoleon's orders were carried out rigidly, even when the confiscated goods could have been useful to the army or distributed to the poor. Everything was removed to an open space on the eastern extension of the Herengracht, towards the docks, and publicly burned. What couldn't be burned was taken out and dumped in the water. Quite apart from the unlucky merchants who had taken the risk and lost, Amsterdamers in general were bitter about this procedure. As a matter of principle they would almost have preferred to lose blood rather than merchandise.

They also had no inclination to lose blood and there was a vast dismay amongst the richer classes when their young men were called up to join the "Gardes-d'Honneur." This changed the views of many influential people who had become quite favorable to the French. It annoyed them that they couldn't buy their sons out. A Mr. Hosthuis offered to arm, mount, and equip a whole company at his own expense to keep his son free from a military career. Some of them prudently joined a French Masonic lodge, which had been started a year or two before at Amsterdam, in the hope of endearing themselves to Marshal Oudinot, who was its Master. Apparently this did them no harm. But they all went in, including young Mr. Hosthuis.

Then came Beresina and the beginning of setback. Because of their close connections with the Baltic, merchants in Amsterdam were quicker than anyone in Paris to appreciate what a catastrophe could be in store for the Grande-Armée. But nobody dreamed of the empire falling apart. Then from the end of 1812 the rumors began and through the months of 1813 as the Grande-Armée retreated and allies defected, the many French in Amsterdam became sick with anxiety. When the censored newspapers did not mention the battlefields, the letters or messages back from the Gardes-d'Honneur spread their own news around the city. It was still difficult to believe. But the French were all too aware of the ever more ironical expressions on the faces of Amsterdamers. Gradually hope was given up of some great counterstroke by the emperor. In the city everything was tense and quiet. Very little business went on. The most important French official now became the director of the postal service. There was a crowd constantly outside his office, waiting for news.

The defeat at Leipzig was the beginning of the end. Amsterdam remained apparently quiet. But Van Hogendorp, an Orangist leader, and some other nobles and regents at The Hague, were secretly organizing a coup. Falck, the commander of the Amsterdam civic guard, was one of them. Then came a November evening, on which Garnier, the author of *Mémoires sur la cour de Louis-Napoleon et sur la Hollande,* recalled that there was a grand dinner party given by M. Scitivaux, the military paymaster-general. The guests were French and a brave atmosphere of gaiety was achieved. The disasters were ignored or put aside as grossly exaggerated, and they all talked cheerfully about literature and music. All at once, however, they became conscious of distant noise. They listened tensely. There was no doubt what it was, and it could not be more frightening. It was the mob. The batman of a military commander who was one of the guests now arrived at the house, scared and breathless, to inform his master that a crowd shouting angrily against the emperor had broken into various administrative offices. Pillaging and fire-raising were going on and

French people were being molested or worse. For the first time in years the old cry *"Oranje boven!"* was being heard. The party broke up. Those who had no duty to go to hurried home as discreetly as possible and locked themselves in.

The noise went on all night. The withdrawal of the few troops of the line to Utrecht — to face the advancing Prussians and Russians — had been the opportunity for the underground plotters to get things stirred up. An Orangist sea captain called Job May had successfully begun the Amsterdam riot. The crowd had a good time. They forced the prison to open its doors. They burst into the prefecture and tore up everything. The very unpopular prefect de Celles and his much more unpopular assistant Dubois were lucky to escape — the plan was to throw them into the canal with stones tied round their necks, but a loyal officer snatched de Celles to safety and Dubois got out dressed as a woman, arm in arm with a friendly Amsterdamer. The most disliked Frenchmen of all were the customs officers, and several of them did go into the canal. French policemen who were trapped also had a bad time. There were plenty of cruel incidents, but the mood on the whole was lighthearted. The most enjoyable and furious onslaught was on the Rokin office of the tax collector — the place was wrecked, records burned, and the large quantities of money found were not looted but thrown magnificently into the Rokin canal. (A good deal was recovered a few days later.)

Things were a little quieter the next day but there was no question that the French power was over. Prince Lebrun was still in the palace, but having ordered a general evacuation of government offices to Utrecht, he also made his way there — unmolested, for he himself remained well liked — and then back to Paris. Less exalted French people did not enjoy themselves. Many were arrested, all were trapped. The city was all at once stranded — there was no government and a restless mob. But order was reasserted by the civic guard commander, Falck, and as soon as the news of this reached The Hague Van Hogendorp and his associates marched to the Town Hall and read out a proclamation declaring the Prince of Orange the head of state — and the news of this, in turn, then went to Amsterdam. There was no instant support in the city, except for the Orangist faction — Amsterdam's tradition, after all, was anti-Orangist. And for several days there was a state of chaotic uncertainty. There was an outburst of incendiarism. The palace was threatened by looters. But then suddenly a company of Cossacks arrived at the Muiden gate, on November 24, and the first reaction of people was to welcome them extravagantly as liberators and allies. The Cossacks, however, showed themselves even more convincingly as pillagers and rapers. Fortunately their officers arrived and were able to control them, but the short experience of them while they were on the loose did more than anything to turn Amsterdamers in a firmly Orangist direction. *"Oranje boven!"* now was the general cry, the Orange color was suddenly everywhere — and as soon as this happened in Amsterdam, the rest of the country followed, and a deputation could be sent by Van Hogendorp's provisional government to London, where the Prince of Orange was waiting.

His position was very solid. Most of his time away had been spent in Prussia — the king was his brother-in-law — but he had been in London since April and had made good arrangements with the British government. Though there were still some French garrisons in the country he could accept the invitation confidently; and six days after the arrival of the Cossacks at Amsterdam he landed at Scheveningen, and went first to The Hague.

He was received with enthusiasm, but the next two days were absorbed by discussions with Van Hogendorp and others in which it was made clear that the old form of government was out. On December 2, 1813, he made his entry into an Amsterdam hung everywhere with the Orange color. Anyone expecting great pomp was disappointed. It was all very calm and businesslike. He arrived in a simple carriage, which he shared with three doubtless eminent men, with three or four security police following. He was wildly cheered but only stayed a few hours — long enough to be proclaimed Sovereign-Prince of the Netherlands, to receive the magistrates and the usual deputations. His Prussian mother, now the Dowager Princess, who had hastily left with his father in 1795, made her entrance into the city the next day and was given a guard of honor and an all-is-forgiven friendly reception. A few days later the princess and her son came, with some ladies-in-waiting. It was all very quiet, and successful, and Dutch.

The Hague now returned to being the center of government and there — while elsewhere the emperor's trail of disaster was leading towards abdication — work was done on a Fundamental Law to act as a foundation for the new Dutch state. But the culmination of it all took place in Amsterdam on March 29, 1814, when an assembly summoned to the Nieuwe Kerk on the Dam voted overwhelmingly (448 out of 474 present in the great church) for the law's adoption. The next day, also in the

Nieuwe Kerk, the Prince of Orange took the oath. But in fact all this was very temporary, for in January the British foreign secretary Lord Castlereagh had visited the prince at The Hague, and a project was being developed for joining Belgium to Holland. The Austrians approved, forgetting their claim to the former Austrian Netherlands — which was Belgium — in return for dominions in Venetia. Everything was agreed, although no one asked the Belgians what they thought. The prince — who was now to become a king — formally took over the Belgic provinces in Brussels in August 1814. Various difficulties had to be ironed out at the Congress of Vienna — such as arranging to give his former principalities of Nassau to Prussia in exchange for Luxembourg. During May 1815 — in the middle of Napoleon's hundred days — the powers recognized him as William I, King of the Netherlands. The political problems of the next two or three decades were largely concerned with the attempt to absorb Belgium into a unified country — which turned out to be impossible. But the centers of action were Brussels and The Hague. Amsterdam was now purely a commercial city.

6.

AND NOT a very throbbing commercial city, either. Even the money market had faded and was now being taken over by London. Money flowed from London to Amsterdam rather than the other way round, as in the great days. Much later in the century, when boom times returned, Amsterdam money flowed again — notably to the American southern states after the Civil War and then into American railroads and farm mortgages. But there was no boom now. There were still East Indian interests, for the British had handed back the Dutch possessions. But it was almost symbolic when in 1822 the great corn magazine originally built for the East India Company subsided quietly into the Amsterdam mud, for the piles had given way. So had the piles under the greatest of the city's institutions, Hendrick de Keyser's Exchange. A temporary wooden structure was put up on the Dam instead. There were symbols of decline everywhere. However, in 1824 the Netherlands Trading Company was formed to put life back into the carrying trade. The king underwrote a $4\frac{1}{2}$ percent dividend for twenty years (which cost him four million guilders in 1831). But for Amsterdam an unfortunate fact of life was that for bigger ships it was inaccessible. The shallow Zuyder Zee had only just been able to cope with the old flat-bottomed "Indiamen." A fifty-mile canal through North Holland was constructed. It was a help, but not enough. Again, better approaches made Rotterdam the natural go-between for English trade and the traffic of the Rhine. That meant loss, and so did the fact that the Scheldt was now open and Antwerp once more competing as a port.

Lethargy could hardly be avoided. Amsterdam was more and more an onlooker. The great Dutch event was the successful ten-day invasion of the southern Netherlands, which had just become the Kingdom of Belgium, in protest against the terms imposed by the great powers. Twenty-five years later a perfectly appalling monument (nicknamed "Naatje" from the symbolic female figure which crowned it, the "Netherlands Maid"), commemorating this event, was put up in front of the palace on the Dam. But the Dutch, though not the king, adjusted fast to the halving of the Netherlands kingdom, which brought it back more or less to the size of the old Republic.

Business went on, of course, at Amsterdam. In size at least it was still a great city, even if it seemed to have become a dinosaur. The lively poorer districts like the Jordaans in the west and the Jewish quarter in the east retained their old atmospheres, but the middle and upper classes lived dull and stuffy lives in pale imitation of the past. It was cozy, it was not unenjoyable. Though the descendants of the former regents still were likely to be rich and to live in the big canal houses, the absence of the old power made for a more bourgeois, less patrician air. Aristocracy stayed in The Hague (its place in Amsterdam was at the Grote Club on the Kalverstraat corner of the Dam) and King William only came to the city on his annual visits, which were strictly limited; for almost all the year the palace was empty. (Already the opinion was being expressed that it should go back to being the Town Hall again. The argument went on for more than a hundred years, but eventually ceased because socialists felt that the Town Hall of the golden era was too much associated with rampant capitalism. Which indeed it was.)

Amsterdam's *gezelligheid* — the "cozy-sociable" syndrome — showed itself in the increasing number of "colleges" or clubs. Some arose from the old Patriot clubs, like the very grand Doctrina et Amicitia in Kalverstraat, which eventually was to amalgamate with the Grote Club. Some arose from charity like the Zeemanshoop — members who were sea captains had their own personal flags, and could signal to each other at sea. But there were dozens of more modest associations, which earned some criticism for desecrating Sundays. Billiards and drinking Madeira were the sins they encouraged. They led to wives being left alone in their beautifully clean houses, but they also organized balls — even masked balls. Behind the dull-looking, often black-painted façades — it was said that the whole city was held together by paint — two or three impoverished housewives would club together for a dancing lesson from a still more impoverished French dancing master. (*"Queu de chat* — right foot more forward, jufvrouw — very good!"*) In winter there was the Italian opera, the Théâtre-Français and the Amsterdam theater on the Leidseplein. It was a romantic period, with a partiality for moonlit scenes. On Friday evenings there were cold and drafty concerts at the Felix Meritis, strictly for the privileged classes. But hoi polloi who wanted to mix with their superiors could join the afternoon promenade which always took place, in fine weather, alongside the Keizersgracht. Especially on Sundays. For more rowdy entertainment there were the coffee houses and wine houses and the Salon de Variétés in the narrow old street called Nes — now just a dull alley full of warehouses. At the most respectable coffee house, the Café de l'Etoile, they played billiards and dominoes all day amidst the cigar smoke, and it was usually full up.

That was Amsterdam — a cozy backwater in a long-drawn-out post-eighteenth-century hangover. Anything of cultural interest was likely to happen at Leyden or Utrecht. However, as Bredero said, things can change. A writer and poet, Evarhardes Potgieter, headed a group of romantics haunted by the lost greatness. They started a shortlived literary review, *The Muses,* in 1834 and then in 1837 a much more famous monthly called *The Guide — De Gids —* which at last injected a little aestheticism into a dreary society. A young Reformed Church minister, Nicolaas Beets, was inspired to write *Camera Obscura,* a book of sketches about country life, done with seventeenth-century realism, which became a Dutch classic.

It was a sign of revival. So, more sadly, was the gradual end of the *trek-schuit* — the beautiful and civilized way of traveling by canal in a horse-drawn barge. A stagecoach service everywhere almost put an end to it and then came the first suggestions about a railroad from Amsterdam to

Cologne. The argument went on throughout the 1830's. People were quite reasonably afraid that the engines would frighten the cows. Amsterdam-Cologne was turned down and the first line was the modest stretch Amsterdam-Haarlem, which had to be laid out with a temporary quite substantial bend in the route, to cheat the land speculators. A bigger project for a line going southeast to Utrecht and Arnhem was turned down by the States-General, but pushed forward by King William — who guaranteed a debenture — where would the Dutch have been without their royal family? — and on November 2, 1842, the line to Utrecht was opened. The journey of about twenty-four miles took an hour and eight minutes, the engine had a high funnel, and the driver wore a top hat and something like a frock coat. The king, William II now, ran the company, appointed the officials, and fixed the tariff. Financial problems soon became too much and a new company was set up. Of the 100,000 shares 67,000 were placed in England — a fact which would have been inconceivable to the eighteenth-century financiers of Amsterdam.

Highly taxed and almost bankrupt, the country was rescued by a skillful finance minister, Van Hall, a former Amsterdam advocate. He proposed either a once-and-for-all extra tax on property and income or a voluntary three percent loan. The States-General plumped for the loan, which was natural enough. What was slightly startling, and encouraging, was that it was a huge success. The royal family subscribed eleven million guilders and Amsterdam backed it. Things began to look a little better and profits were now coming in from the East Indies again, a happy reminder of the golden past. As if in celebration a new Exchange was built in Amsterdam. It was a fine representative of an architecture which had become, to quote a sad professor writing somewhat later (H. Brugmans), "utterly illogical in the use of materials and distinguished above all by a complete lack of taste and inspiration." The new Exchange was large, imposing and rather like something out of *Aïda*. To make room for it the end part of Damrak, which had brought ships right up to the Dam, had to be filled in. And the old fish market had to go. (The fearful Exchange lasted just into the twentieth century. In its place now is the great store, the Bijenkorf.)

But 1848 was approaching, the year of revolutions in Europe, and even this backwater could not be untouched. A bad potato famine stirred things up. For some years liberal, antiautocratic feelings had been showing themselves and now produced an outstanding politican in Rudolf Thorbecke (modestly remembered in Amsterdam amidst the night-life pleas-

The Harbor — 1870

ures of the Thorbeckeplein, which leads out of one corner of the Rembrandtsplein). He was no dashing revolutionary but a professor of law at Leyden. He was backed by Potgieter and the *De Gids* writers, but he was pedantic and overbearing and William II, though a kindly man, didn't take to him. He refused to consider any constitutional changes as suggested by Thorbecke, but he became suddenly nervous in February 1848 when Louis Philippe lost the French throne. There are times when panic is sensible. A revising commission was set up, with Thorbecke one of the members.

Meanwhile Amsterdam suddenly came to life. An obscure workers' movement arranged a meeting on the Dam on March 24, and because the authorities warned people away, they naturally came in large numbers to see what was going on. The movement — "The Union for Moral Culture — All Men Are Brothers" — was extremely startled by its success, but the meeting never got going. Gangs of youths appeared. The Dam was crowded out, general pandemonium ensued, and large-scale rioting, which

[260]

the police and volunteers from the militia put down with enthusiastic firmness. The Town Hall, very happy and relieved that its authority had been upheld, issued a smug announcement: "You have seen the attempt of those who wished harm to you and to the Fatherland put to shame in a most efficient manner. . . . May God's indispensable Blessing be bestowed on King and country." But authority was so scared of revolution that no doubt the episode helped the new constitution to go through at The Hague. At least it showed the city breathed. And it was nearly forty years before there was an equally good riot — the "Eel Riot" of 1886, sparked off by lower-class indignation about the banning of a rather obscene traditional sport — eels hung on a line across a canal pulled at by contestants in boats.

So there was no revolution. For the next fifty years the hottest political issue was religious education in primary schools. Should denominational schools be state subsidized? The social climate, stuffy, worthy and humanitarian, was set by Thorbecke, whether in or out of power — and King William III, who succeeded in 1849, kept him out as much as he could. The great lake between Amsterdam and Haarlem was filled in ("empoldered") and turned into good pasture land, the weight of taxation on the poor reduced, some more of the population enfranchised, the Vatican allowed to set up a Dutch hierarchy — which brought down one Thorbecke government when the king accepted a Calvinist protest petition at Amsterdam. Slavery was abolished in the East and then the West Indies, though not for the time being the semi-slavery cultivation system in Java, which was the subject of the fiction best seller of the period, *Max Havelaar* by Multatuli, the pseudonym for an ex-colonial official, Douwes Dekker. The book sketched Amsterdam merchants in what was their common image at the time, as spiritually dead, cunning and grasping. Alas, the bourgeois virtues seldom have a good press. But the merchants were having more and more to be happy about. Business was improving.

The city was at last waking up. One sign was that great former burghers were being celebrated. A plaque was put on Rembrandt's house in the Jodenbreestraat and a statue of him put up in the Botermarkt, or Butter Market, which became the Rembrandtsplein. A statue also went up of Vondel in the new seventy-five-acre park which became the center of a new fashionable district across the Singelgracht, south of the city wall, and the park was called Vondel Park. Suddenly there were entrepreneurs with vision. The most remarkable was a physician, Dr. Samuel Sarphati, who had high energy and a burning private motto: "Amsterdam advance!" (*"Amsterdam vooruit!"*) His medical interest in hygiene led him to start a private refuse disposal service. That was in 1847, the year gaslight came to Amsterdam. A few years later, dissatisfied with the way bread was made, he started his own flour and bread factory, which improved the hygiene and cut the cost. Next in the sixties he was responsible for an enormous and extraordinary building on the Frederiksplein, an exhibition palace for industry (Paleis voor Volksvlijt). Domed and pinnacled, what was most remarkable about it was that it was largely built of glass, like London's Crystal Palace — and like it, too, it would be burned to the ground in a famous fire about seventy years later. Finally the doctor produced the splendid and luxurious Hotel Amstel, which stands on the river. With justice is the neighboring bridge Sarphati bridge, and nearby a Sarphati street, a Sarphati quay, a Sarphati park — the doctor deserved them all.

But Professor Thorbecke possibly deserved more gratitude from the city than anybody, for it was under his second administration of the country that the project was set in motion for the building of a canal by which ocean liners could reach the city directly from the North Sea. The work, which involved the construction of a dam and enormous locks, began in 1865. The canal opened eleven years later. It revolutionized the city's prospects.

V

Recovery
1870–1940

1.

A Frenchman, and Amsterdam-lover, Henri Havard, left behind some glimpses of the early seventies. On board one of the little steamers which could always be seen busying about the shallow water, he made the old sea approach to the city from the Zuyder Zee into the IJ estuary. He saw fields of colza on the north shore, a great source of oil for lamps, and little black and red houses, and in the distance the hundreds of black windmills of Zaandam, "like an army of insects with their yellow and red sails." Then there were the great brown sailing barges, the "*tjalks*," plowing along. He could see steamers noisily entering the canal which went up through North Holland. There were red painted boats loaded with milk and vegetables making for the city, which first of all looked like a line of black lacework slowly coming out of a mist.

The estuary was silver calm. They passed the East Dike, still with the "forest of masts" of the ships it sheltered. And now Amsterdam was suddenly there, real and life-size. In the foreground there was a flotilla of little boats and steamers, busy loading or unloading or hooting for late passengers. There was noise and activity everywhere, cranes creaked, dockers worked, the quay was alive with people, horses, wagons, omnibuses. Behind them were the tall, tapering, narrow, gabled houses, painted in somber colors but with hundreds of white framed windows like eyes watching the port's activity, and beyond the rooftop line there was a vague impression of towers and domes shaped in Oriental or Spanish fashion. Amsterdam!

It was like nowhere else, bourgeois and yet romantic. In another dozen years, however, the splendid approach view from the water would be blotted out by the Central railway station. Meanwhile M. Havard stepped on shore, deeply satisfied. He stayed in the narrow old Kalverstraat, which was the busy center of the city, full of cafés, restaurants and the best shops. His hotel could have been the Keizerskroon, or De Oude Graaf, or the Neuf (Bed and Breakfast 1 guilder 90, Dinner with Wine 2 guilders

50). There was no street in Holland like the Kalverstraat, said M. Havard. It was perpetually crowded. There were ladies in bustles, gentlemen of course in black, beggars masquerading as shoeblacks and matchsellers, and a poet with long gray hair who would recite for you. It was noisy. There were carillons at each end, street organs and street singers — on one corner could even be heard the sound of a dance band (trombone, violin, drum and cornet). Its peak times were during the business hours of the Exchange on the Dam, when brokers filled the cafés, and between eight and nine in the evenings. High-class boulevard ladies were in residence in the narrow side streets. There was always something going on, said M. Havard. On Saturdays, he noted, smart Jews joined the promenade. On Sundays when the shops were shut there was a parade of carriages — the social world on its way to show off in the new Vondel Park.

Oh, dull and comfortable city, now so happy to be making money again. On the Dam he watched the merchants and brokers and shippers making for the Exchange. They walked straight ahead, silently, hurriedly, intently, with the absorbed seriousness of men carrying out some religious cere-mony of importance. Splendid Amsterdamers — but M. Havard, as a socia-ble Frenchman, allowed himself to be a little critical when he saw them at private parties smoking among themselves while the women, many of whom were capable of discussing anything at all in three languages, had to chat to each other about domestic things. He also disapproved the re-placement of so much elegant eighteenth-century furniture. But the spot-lessness of everything remained beyond praise. The varnish and the door-handles gleamed.

The traditional cosmopolitanism remained. He noticed in the houses that books on tables were mostly in French, and also in English and Ger-man and "sometimes" in Dutch. It was the same in the jolly-night-out center, the smoky café-concerts in the Nes, where the singers were French, English, German and "occasionally Dutch." Coarse German songs were especially popular and the customers liked to join in. Notices read: "Please do not bang the table with your canes."

M. Havard went everywhere, to concerts in the park on the east side, the complex of gardens which included the Zoo — like most European zoos begun thirty or forty years before — and in winter at the chilly, ex-clusive Felix Meritis and in Dr. Sarphati's glass Palace of Industry, which was a popular place for promenading. (The acoustics were terrible.) He heard opera companies from The Hague and Rotterdam performing to rapt audiences in the municipal theater.

He was also able to see one of the last Amsterdam kermises. The *kermis,* or fair, was the annual time for fun and games in the Netherlands and the Amsterdam version had always been one of the best — that is, the most enjoyably drunken — but this relic of medieval lustiness was a little too much for late nineteenth-century respectability. The main center was the Rembrandtsplein — the former Botermarkt — which was normally full of secondhand booksellers, mostly Jewish, with cartloads of books. During the *kermis* the square was occupied by fairground booths and such simple pleasures as giant ladies, bearded ladies, jugglers, fortune-tellers, panoramic views and war spectacles. There were stalls for pickled cucumbers and gherkins and onions and beetroots, and especially for waffles and fritters, which were called *poffertjes* and were the great *kermis* treat. The smell of the frying *poffertjes* was distinctive and not for the sensitive. There were open-air taverns and everybody was busy throwing off a year's comparative restraint. To M. Havard's amazement girls from rich and respectable backgrounds seemed to be perfectly prepared to be accosted and kissed by happily drunken young men below their social station. It was also a big time for servant girls. *Kermis*-time went on for two weeks and traditionally they were allowed out from their household duties on the second day of the second week — this hardly luxurious right was sometimes even written into their engagements. But they looked forward to it passionately and were quite ready to spend all their year's savings on one wonderful day. An escort could be hired. M. Havard reported touchingly that a little more had to be paid if he wore a hat, and a little more still if he also had an umbrella.

If the more fastidious could do without the *kermis,* nobody really disapproved of the second great Amsterdam traditional pleasure — skating on the Amstel, on the canals, on the IJ. Summer brought some dazzling sights — like the eerily beautiful mass of flowers on a barge slowly making for the flower market — but it brought some dazzling canal smells as well on the really hot days, which could even reach into the Kalverstraat cafés. But winter was the time for Amsterdam, when with ice and snow the canals were lovely beyond belief. Everybody skated, and if the ice lasted stalls and fires appeared on the frozen Amstel, wine and brandy could be bought, and then the waffle makers arrived — and suddenly, said M.

Havard, it was a winter *kermis*. When this happened it was like a nostalgic leap back into the glory days.

2.

NOT EVERYONE who came to Amsterdam in the seventies enjoyed himself as much as M. Havard. There were two brothers, one who ran an art gallery in the Leidsestraat, the other who was a vice-admiral and the commander of the Navy Yard. They had a brother-in-law, a celebrated minister of the Dutch Reformed Church, with a house (number 8) on the Keizersgracht. The three men were unaware of a peculiar distinction they shared; they were uncles of the greatest Dutch artistic genius since Rembrandt. In May 1877, he arrived. He was to work for an examination in classics, required for the university's seven-year course in theology.

Vincent van Gogh was twenty-four. He was red-haired, sturdy, curiously peasantlike, morose, eccentric and solitary. He was the family's awkward one. After a quiet start in another uncle's art business at The Hague he had been sent to London. He was interested in art and all went well. Unfortunately he fell in love with his landlady's daughter. He discovered with horror that she was secretly engaged. He was persistent. She refused him. But his capacity for intense feeling and for bitter disappointment was quite abnormal. The happy life was ended. He moved to other lodgings and was in despair. And he did not get over it.

The firm sent him to its Paris branch for two months. Then he was back in London, living a wretched, lonely life when he was not at work. Religion began to absorb him. The next year they sent him to Paris. He was already solitary and eccentric and obsessed by a private need to achieve some great end — not a material one — but what? It was a typical young man's ferment. He loathed the Paris gallery and spent all the time he could reading the Bible with a friend. (There was always a friend. And his younger brother loved him, his family worried about him. "He stands in his own way," his country pastor–father wrote. It was true. He seemed to choose misery.) The gallery resented his going home for Christmas in their busiest time and he was sacked. He went back to England and took a job at a school at Ramsgate, and then at another school under a Methodist preacher. But it was no good. Morbid and sensitive and more and more religious, he began to see no future except somehow within the Church. He went home. He took a job in a Dordrecht bookshop. That was no good either. The torment, the brooding went on. Destruction of self and spreading the word of God seemed more and more the only way for him. It was agreed. The family would help.

In Amsterdam he stayed with his Uncle Jan, the admiral. Uncle Stricker helped with the Latin lessons and found him a classics teacher, Dr. Mendes da Costa. But the task before the strange and intense young man was hard — for he had done no regular study since he was a schoolboy. His only desire was to lose himself in saintly work amongst the poor. The drudge of Latin grammar was a torture.

But he began hopefully. He bought prints and Greek and Latin books from a Jewish bookseller, no doubt on the Rembrandtsplein. Uncle Cornelius from the Leidsestraat supplied him with paper. Every day he went for a long walk. He watched men working with sand-carts on the site of the new Central station. He liked the little narrow streets round the docks, with the lithographic and printing offices, the shops for sea charts, and stores for ship victuals, and the forges and coopers' shops. He loved the interiors in the Jewish quarter — wood-choppers, carpenters, grocery stores, druggists. Once he came on an open wine cellar, a dark vault in which men with lights were running about, and the sight made an extraordinary impression on him. Everywhere he was reminded of Rembrandt's etchings.

Work alone in his room, lessons, solitary walks and work again were his life. It was slightly interrupted when the admiral's house filled with aunts and cousins for a day or two or there was a family wedding at Utrecht — Vincent was there on the outskirts, the oddball fish out of water, belonging and not belonging. He had no contacts outside his uncles and the teacher, and the strain of doing something hopelessly unsuitable soon began to tell: "My head is sometimes heavy and often it burns and my thoughts are confused. . . ."

He had to try to convince himself that God would help. His long, wonderful but garrulous letters to his brother were full of religious bromides; he felt himself destined only for the work of God — and yet in all of them his obsessive interest in pictures and artists comes out. Here he is, walking at night beside the IJ, "the ground dark, the sky still lit by the glow of the setting sun, the row of houses and steeples against it, lights in the windows everywhere and the whole mirrored in the water. And the people and the carriages like little black figures, such as one sees sometimes in a Rembrandt." He walks in the afternoon along the canals and notes the sun in the dark water — it "reminds him of *Winter* by Thorwaldsen." He is up at five to work in the admiral's summerhouse with his exercise books, and watches workmen coming in through the yard gates in the pouring rain of a thunderstorm; he notes the poplars and elderberry bushes bowed down and the way the rain falls on the piles of wood and the ship decks; he sees boats sailing and a little steamer, and in the distance across the IJ the swiftly moving brown sails, and "the sky is a picture by Ruysdael." Or in winter, when the admiral had gone out one evening to visit Uncle Cor in the Leidsestraat and a letter arrived from Brussels. It was from Vincent's father, who was there at the bedside of another brother, painfully dying. Vincent hurried out to take it to his uncle, and caught him up on the Dam, where he found him waiting for a bus "under a lantern." His mind was full of the possible sad news and perhaps also of the religious significance of suffering, but true to form as he saw his uncle standing there he was reminded instantly of Landseer's *Highlander*.

It was extraordinary how his real interest was hidden from him. What he thought was important was to hear Uncle Stricker preach in a crowded church and "to see the faith on so many faces." And the impossible, lonely Latin grind went on. His reading, apart from work, was *The Imitation of Christ*. He found words in it so deep and serious "that one cannot read them without emotion and almost fear." A break for him was a visit from his young English friend in Paris, who brought him a highly suitable present, Bunyan's *Pilgrim's Progress*. They went to the Trippenhuis together to see Vincent's favorite pictures, and also to Uncle Cor's gallery, and to Uncle Stricker on the Keizersgracht, and when alone they discussed the love of Christ. One wonders what Uncle Jan, the admiral, thought.

But Vincent was becoming more and more oppressed by his difficulties. Uncle Stricker found time to give him two lessons a week. A panic-making discovery was that he must also learn algebra, mathematics, geography and Dutch grammar. That meant another teacher had to be found for private lessons. Vincent went home to the country in south Holland for Christmas and then came back to the grind. His father arrived in February, met his teachers, and soon realized that Vincent had not the faintest chance of passing any examination. But the poor obsessed young man struggled on for a few more months. A letter to his brother in April was full of concealed anxiety — he was desperately trying to keep his courage up. In July he had given in. There would be no seven years' theological course for him.

He left Amsterdam and went to a training school for evangelists at Brussels, where the academic requirements were more modest. The next year he lived in a mining district in southwest Belgium and there, forever doing nothing by halves, he upset the committee which sponsored him as an evangelist by giving away everything he owned (which was, of course, not much) and following Jesus' teaching too literally. He was dismissed. He lost his faith and felt helplessly alone and useless. Then he began to draw, and ecstatically found himself.

After a time he went to Brussels, where he worked and studied. When he was twenty-eight he went home to his father's country parsonage for economy's sake. Everything at first went well. He went out every day into the fields and worked at drawing. Achievement, even happiness, was possible. Unfortunately another visitor at the parsonage that summer was a cousin from Amsterdam, Uncle Stricker's daughter, K——. She was a recently bereaved widow, young and attractive, with a small son. For the second time in his life Vincent fell heavily in love. It was even more disastrous than the first, in England. K—— was glad to be friendly with him, but did not suspect his feelings at all. She was grateful for the purposive attention he gave her little boy. It was all for nothing. She was still grieving for her lost husband. When Vincent at last declared himself the reaction was a horrified "No!" and a speedy departure. The second taste of unrequited love destroyed his happiness for good.

The family were shocked, disapproving and entirely against him. Life at Etten became difficult for him. The family could hardly be blamed. They themselves were the poor relations, and Vincent was emphatically the poorest of all. How could he keep K——, even if she accepted him, and the child as well? It was ludicrous. He explained to his brother serenely, "He who loves lives, he who lives works, he who works has bread." It was not convincing, and not likely to appeal in the bourgeois city. But he was not prepared to give up without a struggle. He did not, he could not believe that he was permanently rejected.

He wrote to her in Amsterdam. She refused to read his letters. He was urged to send no more letters, even to her parents, but he would not agree. He sent his Uncle Stricker a registered letter instead. He complained to his brother that his mother had prayed for him to be resigned. He *could not* be. His love obsessed him. All he wanted was somehow to earn enough money to buy a railway ticket to Amsterdam. At the end of November his brother sent him his fare — it remained only for a sister who was acting as a friendly spy to confirm that the loved one was at home. He went in December.

The evening found him, with God knows what emotion, ringing the bell of his Uncle Stricker's house on the Keizersgracht. When it was answered he was told that the family were at dinner. But he was asked to come in, and as he went through the door he thought himself within a few seconds of seeing her. He was soon disillusioned. There was no sign of her at the table.

He had to go through the farce of greetings and small talk, although they all knew why he was there, and at last he brought himself to ask, "Where is K——?"

"Mother, where is K——?" said Mr. Stricker, gazing at his wife.

"K—— is out," she said.

The battered lover nervously talked about an art exhibition. But after dinner the rest of the household disappeared and his uncle and aunt spoke to him alone. Mr. Stricker told him that as a clergyman and father he would read him a letter that he had been proposing to send to him. But Vincent interrupted.

"Where is K——?"

"K—— left the house as soon as she heard you were here."

It was horrible. But after a few shattered moments his pathetic lover's need to rationalize suggested to him that it could even be a good sign. Then his uncle read him the letter. It was like a sermon. It urged him to stop his own letter-writing and to try to put the whole affair behind him. Unaccustomed to argument, the eminent clergyman was startled when Vincent said he would do neither. Soon all three lost their tempers. Vincent suddenly put his hand in a lamp and exclaimed, "Let me see her for as long as I can keep my hand in the flame!" Hastily one of them put the lamp out, but they were shocked by the act though still insisting that he could not see her. What now made things worse was that conscious of his despair they became kind to him. They even invited him to stay the night and when he refused they both put coats on and walked with him to some cheap lodgings.

He spent two more days of misery in Amsterdam, seeing his uncle again, but with no glimpse of K——.

He never got over it. He wrote to his brother, "Eating strawberries in spring, yes, that does happen in life, but it is only a short period of the year and we are now far from it. . . ."

Years of sublime achievement lay ahead — the nine years left of his sad, offbeat life. He was in Amsterdam once more, in the autumn of 1885. Wearing his fur cap and old ulster he came with some Eindhoven friends to see the new Rijksmuseum, which had taken over from the unsuitable Trippenhuis as the national gallery. He stood for a long time in front of the supreme picture of married love, Rembrandt's *The Jewish Bride,* and it was as if he could not bear to leave it.

3.

THERE BEGAN in the last decades of the nineteenth century a kind of Indian summer for the city. Suddenly it was no longer a backwater, and did not feel itself a backwater. The population was bounding up. The city felt right again, like a champion regaining a title. With the North Sea canal for the oceangoing ships and, a little later, a canal to the Rhine to get the benefit of the huge German industrial expansion, Amsterdam was once more a center of international trade — especially in tobacco, coffee, copra, cocoa, tea, rubber, quinine, kapok, tin, spices and teak. Diamond-cutting and polishing, the Jewish specialty, supplied the whole world. The merchant fleet grew. The money market and the stock exchange had reestablished themselves.

The uplift spread in all directions. From 1880 there was a second university. It was founded by the redoubtable Dr. Abraham Kuypers, a theology professor and fervent Calvinist politician who would in due course head the country's government. At the municipal theater on the Leidseplein outstanding players had emerged. There was Maria Johanna Kleine-Gartman, a regal lady who in the interest of naturalism no longer declaimed to the audience but totally lost herself in the part. The leading actor was Louis Bouwmeester, and his wife, Theo Mann-Bouwmeester was a great name in Amsterdam at the end of the century, and until 1939 when she died at eighty-nine (of her it was said that she never, never underacted). In 1890 the theater had gone up in flames and been replaced four years later by the present Stadsschouwburg on the same site. Eighteen ninety-eight saw *Ghetto*, the first antiromantic realist play of Herman Heijermans, who had begun his career with sketches of Jewish family life in the Amsterdam paper *Handelsblad*. A new Heijermans play became almost an annual Christmas event.

A concert hall, the Concertgebouw, was built and its orchestra would soon become world famous — especially from 1895 onwards, when the twenty-four-year-old Willem Mengelberg became conductor. He took over from Willem Kes, who had had seven successful years. The orchestra's first concert had been in 1888. Before this, in spite of the society of Felix Meritis and of a general enthusiasm for music, standards had not been high. In 1883, Brahms had visited Amsterdam to introduce his Second Piano Concerto and when the moment came for the cello solo in the third movement, *three* cellists began to play, each of them refusing not to be the soloist. It would never, never happen in the Concertgebouw.

The new neo-Gothic Rijksmuseum, which had attracted Van Gogh back to the city for a day, was the work of Cuypers, a Roman Catholic architect, who filled the Netherlands with neo-Gothic churches (six in Amsterdam alone) after the mid-century Catholic freedom, and also built the neo-Gothic Central Station. But he left more than a neo-Gothic mark on the city, for he lived until he was ninety-four (1827–1921), was always influential and set off a new generation of architects, who excited world interest. Berlage had more of the Damrak filled in to put up his uncompromisingly solid Commodity Exchange. It stands up in front of you on the left when you walk down from the Central Station and always seems an emblem of Dutch modernity. Kromhout built the Hotel American at the end of the century. De Klerk specialized in apartment houses, or rather apartment streets, for he liked to treat a whole street as a single building, and the decorative pieces which might look rather odd at your particular number had to be considered in relation to the rhythm of the whole. It was hoped that the residents felt the same satisfaction as the architect. His visions began to appear from 1913 on, and at the same time Van der Mey put up the Scheepvaarthuis, the merchant shipping building which used bricks as decoration against a concrete skeleton.

Some of the building expansion in the late nineteenth century was as bad as the Jordaans had been in the seventeenth — like the "Pijp," south of the Singelgracht, a district full of long, narrow, lightless and depressing streets. And not everyone liked Berlage's Exchange. E. V. Lucas, the English essayist, wrote with masterly self-control, "For a permanent public building something more classic is probably desirable. . . ."

However, modern times had come. The new prosperity made it possible to stir the still somnolent working classes. There was now a socialist party, led by a former Lutheran pastor, Domela Nieuwenhuis. He wrote an article in a periodical called *Justice for All* about William III's annual visit to Amsterdam in which he expressed astonishment that so elaborate a celebration and so much homage was given to a man who made so little of his job. He was promptly locked up, but released as an act of grace on the sixth birthday of the Crown Princess Wilhelmina — who was the old, illiberal but careful king's last gift to his country. (All the male heirs in the Orange family had died, and at sixty-two he had married again, to Princess Emma of Waldeck-Pyrmont; and Wilhelmina's birth in 1880 caused great celebrations.) Nieuwenhuis went on to be elected the first socialist member of the States-General. The king survived for a jubilee in 1889, when the enterprising founder of the Krasnapolsky Hotel dazzled the city by illuminating the Dam with five thousand electric lights.

Meanwhile the face of Amsterdam was being changed more than in any other way by the new forms of transport. Firstly there were the bicycles with the enormously high front wheels which were popular in the eighties, but disappeared after 1890 when the air tire arrived and Amsterdam became one of the great bicycle cities. Similarly the horse-drawn bus service had reached its full flower, shaking and jerking over the cobblestones, when trams arrived and were at once realized to be ideal. They were horse trams, of course, to start with. One of them can be seen on the Dam, along with the terrible "Naatje" statue, lovingly painted by Breitner (1857–1923). His pictures caught precisely the cozy, bourgeois, prosperous nature of the city.

Then came steam trams, which could offer a local railway service. E. V. Lucas was in one of them when he witnessed an incident which seems somehow just what ought to have happened around an Amsterdam steam tram in 1904. At a stop the driver, the stoker and the guard all got out and posed in a group for a photographer who had set up his tripod. Heads of passengers protruded to watch. Great care was taken. Success. But the photographer "was preparing another plate when an incoming tram dashed up so unexpectedly as to cause him to jump, and, in jumping, to overturn his tripod and precipitate the camera. . . ." The passengers could not have had a more hilarious show. But there was no rage, no furious argument. (Imagine it in France.) The photographer simply busied about picking his things up and a few minutes later was arranging a group picture of the second tram crew. E. V. Lucas rightly saw great significance in all this. It showed the national equability. We can add that it also showed an Amsterdamer's attention to the profit motive and his typical, sublime unselfconsciousness, characteristics Lucas found when he visited the Oude Kerk and heard of its popularity for weddings. "The *koster* (verger) deplores the modern materialism which leads so many young men to be satisfied with the civil function; but the little enclosure, like a small arena, in which the church blesses unions, had to me a hardly less businesslike appearance than a registry office. I saw on one Thursday three bridal parties in as many minutes. The happy bride sat on the back seat of the brougham, immediately before her being two mirrors in the shape of a heart supporting a bouquet of white flowers. Contemplating this simple imagery she rattles to the ecclesiastical area and the sanctities of the five, ten, fifteen, twenty or twenty-five guilder carpet. After, a banquet and jokes."

Amsterdam, 1904.

However, things were not cozy all the time. The year before, there had been a railway strike in January, which began with men refusing to move some "tainted goods." At the end of the month the companies gave in, a taste of blood for socialists and trade unionism. The government at The Hague, headed by the Calvinist Dr. Kuyper, promptly brought in a law prohibiting strikes in the public services. The socialists called for a general strike, which began in April and was widespread in Amsterdam. Dr. Kuyper brought troops in, employers staged lockouts and, though the well-organized Amsterdam diamond workers stayed firm, the strike collapsed on April 9. Many railwaymen lost their jobs and plenty of iron and bitterness was left behind. And the Dam had another memory of a turbulent crowd.

The old square suddenly increased to its present size with the demolition of the militia commandant's house, an eighteenth-century relic which stood where once, in the golden century, there had been taverns by the fish market including the famous "House under the Sail." With the old Exchange also going the whole place was a terrible mess for several years.

But all this was against a general background of rising prosperity and a rising population — six hundred thousand when the Indian summer was interrupted by World War I.

4.

HOLLAND was not in the war, but in that summer of 1914 the Dutch scene became as military as anywhere else. The reserves were called up (conscription had been brought in at the end of the nineteenth century) and an army of almost half a million was mobilized, and kept available for the next four years, while The Hague government steered along the delicate path of neutrality. It was not a happy time for the Dutch. To be neutral is to win enmity from everybody who is not. And though the Scheldt was closed and Antwerp fell to the Germans it was not to be 1585 all over again. There were a million Belgian refugees, but this time they brought no prosperity to Amsterdam. Nor was neutrality profitable as it had been so splendidly in the Seven Years' War of 1756–1763, though there was an inflow of large amounts of capital which in due course helped the money market. But the city depended on world trading facilities and especially the immense imports from the East Indies. Though the Concertgebouw and the Stadsschouwburg could go on as usual, and a new big store appear on the Dam (Peek & Cloppenburg — the Bijenkorf was already where the old Exchange had been), and De Klerk in 1917 could put up one of his large "intuitively controlled" housing blocks, underneath what seemed enviable normality commercial life was breaking down. What with U-boats and minefields, the need to obey first German and then Allied restrictions, and finally the Allied ban on all imports which could go to or replace anything sent to Germany plus unrestricted submarine warfare, Dutch sea trade died. At the same time the country was hopelessly dependent on Germany for coal and had to export food in exchange. In the end they were almost as badly off for food as the Germans.

It was not an easy ride. On the other hand they could recover quickly and the first two postwar years were boom years. Western Europe's troubles intervened but the East Indian trade, so important for Amsterdam, kept on increasing. As a money market the city gradually established itself as third in the world, after London and New York. Then they joined in the benefits when Europe's condition improved after 1924. Economy and rigid orthodoxy kept the guilder strong. The city's population was up by another hundred thousand. On the north side of the IJ, facing the city, there were dry docks and the petroleum dock, and on the south side vast new quays. The building of the world's biggest lock went on at the entrance of the North Sea canal. There were plants for the chemical and dye industries, oil, sugar refining, soap manufacture, glass. There was an increase in shipbuilding. There were tanneries, distilleries and breweries. By the late twenties the recovery which had begun at the end of the last century was still in full swing and there was something of more or less everything in twentieth-century industry. And the Jewish diamond-cutting and polishing industry remained the world center. In certain cafés dealers could always be seen turning over little mounds of stones with their specially grown fingernails. Old Amsterdam scenes like this went on with the new; the new was typified by the vastly successful Olympic Games of 1928. Jan Wils, influenced by Frank Lloyd Wright towards functionalism, built the stadium. Modern architecture remained very much in flower. Fashionable south Amsterdam was full of it. Functionalism, Expressionism, the New Objectivity, the Amsterdam School — all these architectural nuances were displayed. The newest scene perhaps was at Schipol. Already in 1920 a London-Amsterdam air service had been started, using two converted De Havillands with room for two passengers; and in 1921 the world's first booking office for air travel was opened. Schipol, the airfield, was a hundred and fifty acres of reclaimed land — from the old Haarlem lake — to the south of the city. (There was now a plan in being to reclaim the Zuyder Zee.)

Willem Mengelberg was still conducting the Concertgebouw orchestra and Amsterdam had become outstanding for its choral societies. The theater worked hard to follow the latest trends, like German Expressionism. But the city, though fatter and busier, was very much what it had been before the war. The canals were still restful and beautiful, though the great houses on the Herengracht and Keizersgracht were becoming too difficult to live in. Cars occasionally fell into the water and the fire brigade learned to rescue them. An old debate continued, without result, about returning the palace to its original use as the Town Hall. Morning and evening the cyclists swarmed. The great elaborate barrel organs went round, and their appearance in poorer streets would open every window. Once a year the flags would go up at fishmongers and street-corner stalls to announce that the fresh herrings were in — *"Hollandse nieuwe"* — a celebration, not quite unconscious, of the fish which had really been the cause of the city's existence. St. Nicholaas, or Sinterklaas, or Santa Claus, made his annual festive entry into the city from the harbor, on a white horse and attended by his black servant, Peter, at the end of November. There was a good deal of poverty in the back streets, but it was far away from the cozy cafés of the Kalverstraat. And every January 1 *Gijsbrecht van Amstel* was played at the municipal theater, the Stadsschouwburg.

Bourgeois, comfortable, civilized, the women a little frumpish, the men a little overweight, still clinging to neutrality and the strength of the guilder, this was Amsterdam coming into the danger-laden thirties. But the world depression hit hard — naturally, with so much dependent on international trade. Unemployment rose, with The Hague government concentrating on economy and balancing the budget. Public works helped a little (the marvelous Amsterdam Wood, and its rowing course, was begun at this time). In 1934 there were bad riots in the Jordaans. But over all was the ever more looming shadow of the neighbor to the east. There was a small but noisy Dutch Nazi movement. In 1936 a meeting at the exhibition center to support a countermovement, "Unity through Democracy," was attended by 12,000 people. Something of the strain showed in the queues for and the emotional reception of the British film *Victoria Regina* in 1937 — there was a clear connection with Queen Wilhelmina, who had reigned since 1890 and was so infinitely respectable and solid. She represented the qualities in which Amsterdamers placed their hopes.

Hopes were not enough, and yet it was still possible for a foreigner to envy the apparent placidity, the island feeling of cozy security, which seemed to be the atmosphere of Amsterdam. Neutrality in World War I had meant missing not only a share of the blood and suffering but also the experience. The result was a certain stuffiness, an old-fashionedness which no amount of trendy modern architecture could alter. There was something in the air which was pre-1914 and not to be found in the air of London, Berlin, Paris and Brussels. The prospect of another interruption by war was a nightmare, but there was a vague expectation that they would be able to stay out again.

However, nerves were stretched tight as the crisis developed in August 1939. Hitler attacked Poland and the show was on. The Dutch reserves had been called up, as in 1914. The Concertgebouw was used as an assembly point and was full of troops and equipment. It was a gloomy sight.

VI

The Nightmare
1940–1945

1.

ABOUT FOUR in the morning on Friday, May 10, 1940, people in south Amsterdam heard a sinister rumbling from the direction of Schipol — the sound of bombs. The long nightmare had begun.

During the next few days nothing much else was heard or anything seen of the battle, except for the planes high over the city and the searchlights at night. For Amsterdam the battle was a long-drawn-out agony of tension and contradictory rumors, and all the time the radio issued a stream of ghastly news flashes — "German aircraft over —" — "Large numbers of parachutists —" The old defense of flooding, which had protected the western provinces in the past against opponents like Louis XIV, was no good against sky invaders dressed in Dutch uniforms and backed by a strong fifth column of the Dutch Nazi party. Even so the Dutch fought successfully enough to upset the German program, "necessitating" the terror bombing attack on Rotterdam. It was all over by May 15. Queen Wilhelmina, the royal family and the Government crossed to England — necessarily and rightly — leaving behind the unfortunate, unhappy, shattered Netherlands.

Amsterdam, untouched, waited. The Germans arrived. On the Raadhuisstraat which leads from the Westertor towards the back of the palace and into the Dam the crowds seemed curiously placid, with children neatly squatting in the gutters, and everybody so well dressed, the comfortable citizens of a great city, as if it were a show, while Wehrmacht contingents passed by in cars and trucks decorated with camouflaged tree branches. The sight had a kind of terrible fascination.

There were suicides and attempted suicides and a rush of calls on the fire brigades due to people burning books and papers too hastily. Unhappiest were the many German Jews who had settled in Amsterdam in the past six years after escaping from Nazi persecution. But a tenth of the population was Jewish. What would happen to them could only be conjectured. The natural fright in everybody's mind was of course covered very

[283]

soon with a veneer of hope that perhaps nothing would. As for the other nine-tenths of the population, dazed by the appalling situation in which they suddenly found themselves, an early reaction was of a certain relief that the days were passing very much like days had passed two weeks before. The departure of the queen and of the Government had inevitably left many people with a sense of being let down. There was some comfort in the surprisingly correct behavior of the German troops. It was even friendly. So was the red-bordered proclamation of power by the country's new ruler, Dr. Arthur Seyss-Inquart, which was stuck up on the hoardings. "I have today taken over civilian authority in the Netherlands. . . . The magnanimity of the Fuehrer and the efficiency of German soldiers has permitted civil life to be restored quickly. I intend to allow all Dutch law and general administration to go on as usual, so I expect all judges . . . [etc.] . . . to remain in their places. . . . There is no reason why we should not respect one another." It was in two columns of five or six hundred words, German on one side, Dutch on the other. Meanwhile a few people were being rounded up, the unfortunates who happened to be on a Nazi blacklist — in particular, Jews known to be politically active. Of course members of the Dutch Nazi party — the NSB — often found themselves being promoted in their careers. Enemy occupation had come once more to Amsterdam.

Soon certain new things became familiar sights — German army traffic signs, or hospital signs: "Stadtmitte," "Lazarettsperrbezirk," "Feldgendarmerie," "Marschverpflegung," "Umleitung." Then there was the sound of German military bands, of German boots and German marching songs sung in fearful unison. There would be the NSB man in his dark uniform selling Nazi newspapers on the street corner. Nothing openly ghastly happened — though there was a Gestapo headquarters now — they had taken over a school in Euterpestraat in south Amsterdam. People shrugged their shoulders and it seemed to be generally decided that the only thing to do was to try to adapt to the situation.

After a time, when the first shock was over, Amsterdamers could find a certain wry amusement in the Wagnerian posturings indulged in at German or NSB ceremonies. But Dr. Seyss-Inquart on his trips around went out of his way to be agreeable. The behavior of the troops remained exemplary. But now and then there was a glimpse beneath the skin. For instance a German army car halted at a street corner, where there was a man with a flower stall. He was asked for a direction, and gave an answer. The car went on. Suddenly it stopped again, then turned round in the road and came back to the corner. A German soldier got out, went up to the flower seller, and slapped his face. That was observed in June 1940, in south Amsterdam. Very funny, of course, if one thinks of the scene in the car as the flower seller's words sink in. (What can he have said?) But also, of course, not very funny.

By the end of June Amsterdamers were recovering their spirit a little, along with the rest of the Dutch. On the twenty-ninth, which was Prince Bernhard's birthday, thousands of people put on the white carnation which he was famous for wearing. Later on in the year when the Battle of Britain showed that the war was not over yet the numbers listening to Queen Wilhelmina's radio broadcasts from London increased vastly. Now the Germans began to act against selected, fairly eminent people, sending them off to Buchenwald as hostages for the population's good behavior. And in Amsterdam the Jews were experiencing the first tastes of real unpleasantness.

From July the Germans began to pile on orders and restrictions. All firms owned by Jews had to be reported. Jews were dismissed from all government and public offices. Jews were not allowed to enter cinemas. All Jews must report to the police. Every week something odious was published — a weekly Jewish paper was even licensed because the German authorities felt it would help with the communication of orders. The Amsterdam police — those who were not NSB members — were sometimes able to send out warnings. (For them ghastly problems of conscience would arise when they were forced to help the SS carry out arrests.)

People were nauseated by the treatment of the Jews. Otherwise things were generally quiet; there was a sort of fake normality. There were minor incidents of protest on the lines of the white carnation — there was the use of the color orange in various overemphasized ways, which particularly annoyed the NSB chief, Mussert. There was some minor sabotage, with damage to wires and cables and notice boards. Then on February 22 and 23, 1941, the Germans carried out the first sizable roundup of Jews, seizing four hundred men and youths and herding them on to the Jonas Daniel Meijerplein, one of the squares in the "Jewish quarter." The poor devils were lined up in their pathetic overcoats and scarves and trilby hats, feeling God knows what horror and fear and pain. The occasion was photographed. One can see the peak-capped officer in his long greatcoat and the helmeted bullies and the victims standing with their hands up, squatting with their hands up, lying face down on the cobblestones. While this agony went on for hours transport trucks waited in line beneath the great seventeenth-century Portuguese synagogue. Finally the four hundred were loaded into them and driven away. Inside a year almost all of them were dead.

Those pale bewildered faces in the photographs haunt one on the Jonas Daniel Meijerplein. But nowadays there is also a statue there, the figure of a burly Amsterdam docker, which commemorates what happened two days later. For the shock of the episode went through the city and from the twenty-fifth to the twenty-sixth of February there was a general strike. Almost everything stopped. It was the city's "day beyond praise," when fear was conquered by the senses of outrage and contempt. At one point German "green police" went through the streets in trucks shooting at random, as a threatening demonstration. But the demonstration which mattered was the Amsterdamers'. It was the first gesture of resistance.

Notices signed by the German air force general Friedrich Christiansen were posted up ordering the total resumption of work, public and private, on Thursday the twenty-seventh. "There will be no meetings or gatherings of any kind, nor any political party activity. Anybody disobeying will be proceeded against under German military law. Hereafter anyone who strikes, or who agitates for strikes, will receive up to fifteen years and, if defense industry is involved, death."

The general honeymoon, so far as there had been one, was definitely over. And the horror treatment of the Jews continued. Jews were forbidden to use bathhouses or to go into public parks. There were more roundups. Jews in Amsterdam lived with ready-packed knapsacks, waiting for the sound of the trucks screeching to a halt and the banging on the doors. Jews could be forbidden by law to hold any job at all. Non-Dutch Jews had to report for "voluntary emigration." All the Jews in Zaandam, across the IJ from the city, were expelled. Jewish patients had to leave hospitals. Jews could only cross the Amstel by the ferry. A six-pointed yellow star was introduced, black bordered and bearing the word "*Jood*" in black. They had to wear it on their coat or overcoat — even in the garden, on a balcony or at a window. A curfew was introduced. Jews had to be at home from 8 P.M. to 6 A.M. — and during this time they were not allowed to pay or receive visits, and all windows had to be shut. They were forbidden most public transport, they could not own telephones or use public telephones. And much of the city was out of bounds to them.

Naturally thousands of Jews, as well as "Aryans" who were on the wanted list, went into hiding or, as the phrase went, "dived." They became *"onderduikers"* — divers. Resistance groups helped them. The need for food coupons was one of the main problems. There was of course a black market in them — but that needed money and most Amsterdam Jews, contrary to Nazi propaganda, were not well off. A whole industry sprang up in false identity papers. More people joined the resistance groups. But most people, being neither Jews nor heroes, were shielded from all this and merely suffered in the general depression and the decline in living standards — apart from the enthusiastic collaborators and smart boys who were able to use the extremely expensive black market restaurants. All the familiar Nazi paraphernalia was used to drum up support — there were NSB youth movement parades on the Dam, with swastika flags hanging from the palace, and mini-Nuremberg rallies at sports grounds. And the roundups went on. Everyone in the city became used to the awful sound of them. Almost everyone had seen huddled figures in trucks or some luckless group being marched along.

2.

WHAT HAPPENED if you were caught up in it? If you had dived or were wanted politically, there might be a visit to the Euterpestraat Gestapo headquarters. People who had not dived, after being assembled, would be taken — possibly even by tram, making a last, overcrowded journey through the familiar streets — with no one bothering to look at them, for anyway Jews weren't allowed to go by tram — to a railway siding in the docks. Here a long train waited. The carriages were normal. The only difference was that once the passengers were in, the doors were locked. The Dutch policemen in charge of the train signed for the numbers as if for a goods consignment. Then there was a long wait. Another special tramload would arrive, consisting of Jews who had dived, or of cases where there was a "punitive element" — Jews, for example, who had been caught catching a tram — for them one of two cattle trucks were attached to the end of the train. They, too, were handed over and signed for. They

The Jewish Quarter — 1943

climbed, often with great difficulty, into the trucks. After which there was another long wait and then the train moved. They would all get out in the wooded country of the province of Drenthe to the northeast, close to the German border. This was Westerbork camp — where, Jews in Amsterdam were encouraged to believe, life was not too bad. It was, of course, very much too bad. However, those who managed to stay a few months were lucky, for it was a transit camp and before all of them there was another train journey ahead, by cattle truck to Auschwitz. *Of the 130,000 Dutch Jews, most of whom lived in Amsterdam, 100,000 did not survive.*

A similar statistic was that out of eighty-seven young Jewish pupils who had to leave a Montessori school on Niers-straat in south Amsterdam, by an order in 1941, only twenty came back at the end of the war. One of the sixty-seven was Anne Frank. The extraordinary thing was how normal and pleasant a life she and the other children were able to live against the nightmare background. Not that they were at all unaware of it, but they could take it more naturally than their unfortunate parents. The twelve-year-old Anne was a gay, small, intelligent and energetic child wholly absorbed by her friends and by her school life. The neighborhood was one of wide attractive streets and comfortable modern houses. The Franks had money. Anne's father was a refugee German Jew who had set up a good business in Amsterdam and was now, of course, living very discreetly. He was a man of high quality — who incidentally had been commissioned in the field as a German army lieutenant in 1918. Sometimes the telephone would ring with a warning that the Germans were looking at the district, and he would sleep away from home for a night. To avoid the confiscation of his firm he had handed over to his "Aryan" partners, known to us as Koophuis and Kraler. These were middle-aged men, one a Dutchman, the other an ex-Austrian. Both turned out to be credits to humanity.

The office and warehouse were in an old house on the Prinsengracht, close to the Westertor. The business concerned spices and there were spice mills in the warehouse. As things became more unpleasant for the Jews, Koophuis and Kraler suggested that Frank and Van Daan, who was another Jewish associate in the business, could go into hiding with their families in the building itself, for the upper part at the back was unused. The front of the house, facing the canal, was typically all windows, three rows of three, over the ground-floor warehouse. There were two small entrances, both opening onto steep Amsterdam staircases — one up to the first-floor offices, the other straight up to the second floor. Here on one side of the landing were storerooms to the front and on the other the entrance to the rear section, with another little staircase going up; and this entrance could be concealed by a swinging bookcase, its shelves loaded with box files. This top back portion of the house contained four or five rooms or compartments and a W.C. The suggestion was accepted. Week by week carpets and pieces of furniture were moved discreetly first to Mr. Koophuis's home and then at weekends to the Prinsengracht.

Two girls worked in the office, Miep, an Austrian married to a Dutchman, Henk; and Elli, who was the daughter of the warehouseman downstairs. They had to be brought into the secret. Both girls turned up trumps, then and to the end of the extraordinary story. The new residents were to be Mr. and Mrs. van Daan and their son, Peter, and Mr. and Mrs. Frank with their daughters, Margot, the elder, and Anne. It was the beginning of July 1942, and they planned to move — and become "*onderduikers*" — on the sixteenth. Mr. Frank told Anne that she must enjoy herself while she could.

She did. She had her boyfriends at her new school, the Jewish Lyceum. There were various best girl friends. There were her examination results. There was the diary she had received on her thirteenth birthday a few weeks before, which she began to write up assiduously. Then suddenly things had to happen more quickly than had been anticipated. On Sunday, July 5, a card arrived at the Frank house on the Merwedeplein calling up Margot, the elder sister, aged sixteen, for work at Westerbork. It seemed to be the moment for a change of address. Mr. Frank happened to be out. Mrs. Frank went over to see the Van Daans, who lived nearby. The girls packed their private belongings. They did not know where the hiding place was to be. It was a hot day. They felt very excited and strange.

Their mother and Mr. van Daan came back. A boyfriend arrived to see Anne and was sent away. Then Mr. Frank turned up and heard the situation. Mr. Koophuis was rung up. He came in the evening and so did the office girl, Miep, and her husband — they took shoes and clothes away with them, and later on came back for more. The Franks had an upstairs lodger, Mr. Goudsmit, who made things difficult by staying at home that evening. The next morning, unlike the day before, it was wet. They were up at five-thirty, and dressed themselves in double layers of clothing — Jews could not dare be seen with a suitcase. Miep was there and Margot cycled off behind her. Anne said good-bye to Moortje, her cat. They left a note for Mr. Goudsmit, asking him to take the cat to some neighbors.

COURTESY OF THE AMSTERDAM CITY ARCHIVES

Occupied Amsterdam — 1942

Then, all three heavily stuffed up with clothes, Anne and her parents set out to walk in the rain, at about seven-thirty. It was a long walk as well as a wet one. Owing to their yellow stars they could not catch a tram or be given any sort of lift. However, they reached the Prinsengracht house safely and disappeared inside. The Franks had dived.

An hour or so later at the Merwedeplein house the lodger, Mr. Goudsmit, came downstairs and saw that the whole place was empty and in a mess — with the breakfast things left as they were. In a panic he rang up Mr. van Daan, who came round at once pretending astonishment. They found the note about the cat and a plate of meat which had been left. The two men then busied about tidying things up and making sure that nothing incriminating had been left around — and in fact Mr. van Daan, who knew perfectly well it had been left on purpose, found an address in Maastricht which enabled him to suggest to Mr. Goudsmit that there had been talk months before of an army officer friend spiriting them away to Switzerland — so perhaps it had come off. Later that morning Mr. Goudsmit, as requested, took the cat to a neighbor, the mother of one of Anne's friends. Within a few days other friends had accepted the Switzerland story. According to Anne Frank in her diary Mr. van Daan said that one woman spoke definitely of an army car picking them up in the middle of the night.

Then, warned of German roundups starting the next day, the Van Daans also dived, on July 13, 1942, and joined the Franks. The two families settled down to live, unseen, unheard — and Anne, living and watching, wrote her diary.

This child, happy by nature, "normal" though talented, was made by extraordinary circumstances into a genius. It is hardly believable, when one reads through this amazing document, that its author was *thirteen* at its beginning and only just fifteen at the end. Its great impact comes from the extraordinary mixture of mood — one is plunged from nightmare horror to domestic comedy to adolescent romantic troubles and all the way back again. It is, of course, world famous — or perhaps one should say was world famous for a time after the war, and the fame was assisted by the success of the play *The Diary of Anne Frank*. Time passes, there are other troubles. But anyone, for a long time to come, who fails to read it, is missing something very precious. A great service was done by a German writer, Ernst Schnabel, in interviewing survivors and witnesses for an exceptionally moving book, *The Footsteps of Anne Frank*, which puts the whole episode into context and should be read with the diary. It goes on to the terrible ends of the secret inhabitants, with Anne dying in Belsen concentration camp and only Mr. Frank surviving.

Yet they had come to think they would get away with it, for the strange hidden life in the *"achterhuis"* — the back premises, which is the title of the diary in Holland — lasted over two years. Fear kept coming, but you cannot go on being frightened for two years. And meanwhile, all around this still small center, Amsterdam life went on. Mr. Koophuis and Mr. Kraler, and the girls Miep and Elli, came to the office every day, all of them showing enviable guts and loyalty. Other Amsterdamers also had to show these qualities. The secret inhabitants had to be fed, and since food was rationed coupons had to be bought on the black market. But a baker whom Mr. Koophuis approached understood at once, asked no questions, and supplied bread without coupons for months, at great risk. Then there was the greengrocer, who had a shop close by on the Leliegracht, but every day went round himself with a handcart, delivering to certain addresses. Miep, the office girl, bought remarkably large quantities from him. The greengrocer asked no questions. He belonged to a group of 105 Amsterdamers organized to supply people in hiding. In due course all were picked up and sent to concentration camp — and most of them froze to death in a cattle truck at the end of the war. Five of the 105 survived, and the greengrocer happily was one — with his legs crippled by frostbite.

In November 1942, an eighth guest was invited to join the party in the *"achterhuis."* It was Mr. Dussel, a dentist. He was, of course, amazed to find them there. A former neighbor, he had accepted the Switzerland story. Miep went on seeing Mrs. Dussel, who was not Jewish, but never gave her a hint where her husband was. Keeping secrecy was a great strain — it had always to be watched. There was a bad moment when Mr. Koophuis mentioned the Franks indiscreetly to his wife, and then realized that their young daughter, who knew nothing, had overheard. A few days later the girl let him know by an indirect remark that she had understood — but it was never mentioned again. The strain on all their nerves can just about be imagined. Or, perhaps it cannot be. There were dreadful moments — especially when Elli's father fell ill and a new warehouseman was employed, who was untrustworthy and had to be watched all the time. One moment was when the landlord sold the house and brought the prospective buyer round to inspect. Mr. Koophuis, taking them round, sweated ice and managed to concoct a story of a lost key to keep them out of the hiding place. It was close. The great fear was of some accidental visit by police, because of fire or air-raid damage or burglary.

Sometimes, after dark, when work was over and the house silent, one or two of the hiders would creep down into the offices and perhaps take a very cautious peek into the street. Mr. Frank or Mr. van Daan could use the rear office for work, and could telephone any necessary report — as of burglars — to Koophuis. Both the office girls on different occasions spent a night upstairs, as a demonstration of friendship. Both were utterly terrified by the experience. The building made ghostly noises, the heart froze every time there was a sound of a car outside in the city, and every quarter of an hour the bell of the close-by Westertor would sound. Of course, neither girl slept at all. All the others, however, apparently slumbered away without any trouble, as if they were in a hotel and there was no war.

Outside, in Amsterdam, life went on becoming more dangerous. Jewish districts were cordoned off by warning notices. On May 26, 1943, 3,000 Jews were arrested and on June 20, 5,600. Apart from Jews the Germans were increasingly concerned with their "political opponents." Resistance groups became bigger, underground newspapers flourished — *Vrij Neder-land, Trouw (Loyalty), Het Parool (The Password)*. Young Dutchmen especially were "diving" in thousands to avoid the call-up for labor camps. There were resistance triumphs, such as the March 1943 burning of the building in the Zoo park containing the Amsterdam register — this was carried out by the group of the sculptor Gerrit Jan van der Veen, one of many rounded up and executed. Most nights the city shook from antiair-craft gunfire.

Meanwhile the sheltered, hothouse existence went on in the *"achterhuis,"* observed and reported by the extraordinary little girl. She could be moody and unfair, as well as vivacious, but she was always candid. A natural writer — and a natural best-selling writer — she produced her diary in the form of letters to an imaginary friend, a fortunate idea, for it encouraged her to be descriptive and factual. To begin with she is very depressed by not being able to go out, she is frightened at night, frightened when they creep down to listen to the radio in the back office. When the Van Daans come the extra faces are a comfort. She and Mr. van Daan upset each other easily, but Mr. van Daan gets on very well with her sister, Margot. Anne is not impressed by Peter van Daan, the teen-age son. She has a continuing annoyance when her mother treats her as a small child.

The families coexist — eat together — but also remain apart. Anne is amazed and horrified when she hears Mr. and Mrs. van Daan quarreling angrily — she has never heard such a thing. There are also quarrels between the ladies about sheets, about whose dinner service is to be used. Anne breaks one of Mrs. van Daan's soup plates and catches it from her. Parents remain parents, and children have to be brought up — there are discussions about which books they should be allowed to read, and Peter van Daan gets into trouble for reading the wrong one — he is sent to bed without his supper. The three children keep the school terms, and work away at French irregular verbs and so on in a normal way. After two or three months everybody is getting rather touchy. Mr. Frank, whom Anne worships, is calm and above it. The others argue and lose their tempers easily. But they have birthday celebrations — and Anne is annoyed when Mrs. van Daan flirts with her father.

Then depression and fear over the concentration camp news, about shooting hostages, about Elli's boyfriend being sent to work in Germany is followed by happiness that she and her sister and her mother are all suddenly on very good terms. She asks Margot if she thinks her ugly and Margot says she is quite attractive. She has given Peter van Daan an apple.

Then there is the night when Miep stays with them — and her husband, too, who belonged to a group helping other *"onderduikers."* It was, Anne says, great fun (though, as we know, Miep didn't think of it quite like that, nor did her husband). But the next day they have a few moments of terror. Suddenly from the landing in front of their false bookcase entrance there is a sound of hammering — but that's all right, she knows it's the man who has come to deal with the fire extinguishers. Then the hammering stops, and after an interval there is a knock on the bookcase door. They all turn white. Anne feels she is fainting. Then there is a pulling and wrenching at the secret door. All that has happened is that it's jammed and they hear Mr. Koophuis's voice saying, "It's only me." And so, relief. But there ought to be some other word for that sort of relief.

It is November 1942. Peter van Daan is given a game of Monopoly, a razor and a lighter for his sixteenth birthday. (Koophuis and the others are able to buy things for them in the shops, of course.) They have 150 tins of vegetables in store, and 270 pounds of dried peas and beans. They become excited over good news from North Africa. Mr. Dussel arrives — he is a cultivated, agreeable, middle-aged man, but Anne never gets on with him. For one thing he sleeps in her room. Dussel is full of the horrors going on outside — they are all a little upset, and even feel guilty. The guilt feelings persist. She sees two Jews in the street through the office curtains on a Sunday evening and feels she has betrayed them. She worries about the children now begging for bread in the streets, and the stories of women returning home from shopping to find their families vanished in some new roundup — while the Franks, the Van Daans and Mr. Dussel are in their comfortable shelter. But soon she has forgotten it all in rage at being picked upon and criticized by the grown-ups.

And the months go by. They get the news that the Van Daans' house has been stripped of its furniture, but they keep it from Mrs. van Daan. Rows and arguments are really the main occupation — Anne is usually in the thick of it, but her older sister Margot and Peter van Daan are more passive. The quarrels shock Mr. Dussel, but he gets used to it. Anne gives an instance of one. Mr. van Daan jokingly teases Margot with eating little in order to be slim, upon which Mrs. Frank tells him sharply that she can't bear his stupid chatter, upon which Mr. van Daan colors and stares straight ahead, in silence. Peace, of course, returns. In a way they are so deeply united, deep down, by their circumstances, that they are more free to react openly to every emotion than in ordinary life.

In 1943 the air raids increase, the house shudders. No air-raid shelter for them. Anne is always terrified and at night hurries to her father's bed while the noise is on. There is a horrible panic one evening when thieves, or intruders, are heard in the warehouse. Mrs. van Daan hurries up from the private office where she has been listening to the radio. Mr. Frank and Peter go down and are unnerved by the sound of a door shutting. Up at the top they are terrified because Mr. van Daan has a cold and can't help coughing. They remember that the radio is still tuned to the BBC. They all listen desperately. When the ordeal is over, and whoever it was has gone, perhaps frightened by an unexpected sound of life, they all have a pressing need for the lavatory. They still dare not pull the chain. The smell is awful, Anne says.

They hear the bombing of North Amsterdam, and of Schipol, the city's airport. There is the good news that the Carlton Hotel, a large luxurious hotel by the Muntplein, in use as a Luftwaffe H.Q. and a German officers' club, has been hit by British bombs. They hear about the Resistance group's attack on the city registry in the Zoo park and how the fire brigade, in dealing with the fire, made sure of saturating any unburned documents. There is the news of Turkey joining the Allies, and they hear how a

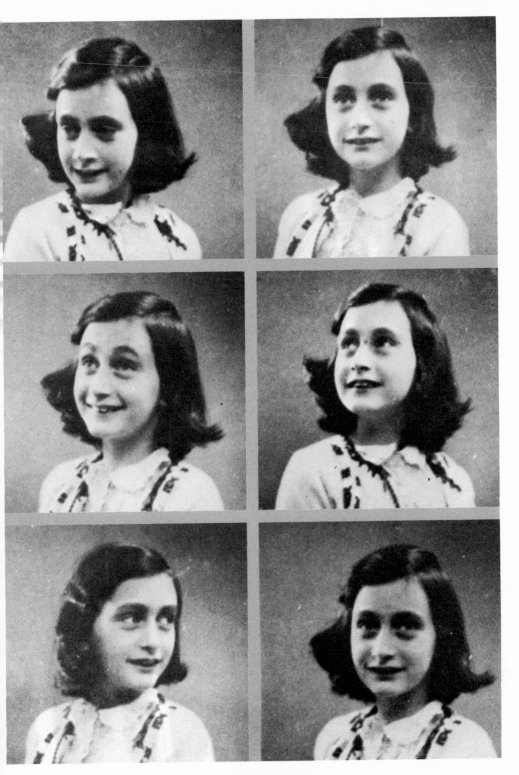

Anne Frank — 1944

newsboy shouting it on the Dam has his papers almost snatched out of his hands by eager readers. Good news is needed. Anne doesn't care for the endless diet of kidney beans and haricot beans, and she is growing out of her clothes.

However, there can be a moment of high amusement. One night during an air raid, with Anne lying terrified beside her father, they hear Mrs. van Daan jump out of bed and then a nasty seemingly nearby explosion. They all get up hurriedly. The Van Daans can see a glow, and she thinks the house is on fire, while he doesn't — and it isn't. So they all go back to bed. But after a quarter of an hour the noise of the raid starts again. Mrs. van Daan, finding no sympathy, at once leaves her husband, and the Franks hear her going into Mr. Dussel, who says to her, "Come into my bed, my child!" The Franks collapse with laughter.

The marvelous domestic rows continue as more months go by. Koophuis and Kraler, Miep and Elli keep them going. There is occasional nervousness about the warehouseman. Mrs. van Daan's fur coat is sold, and she makes a screaming row when she finds the money must be used on the household. It is 1944 and Anne, enthusiastically and self-analytically in the middle of puberty, starts a love affair with Peter. It takes her until April to get a kiss. People outside are talking about the coming invasion and what will happen if parts of Amsterdam are flooded, or if the city is evacuated. Inside the political discussions and rows are continuous. Anne notes that when Churchill makes a speech, which they all listen to, huddled round their small illegal radio (the one in the office had to be given in), the "grown-ups" can hardly wait for the speech to end so that they can begin discussing it.

On Easter Sunday evening they are petrified by a break-in down in the warehouse. The men go down. Mr. van Daan shouts "Police!" and scares the intruders off. But there's a hole in the door. A couple come by and shine a torch through. They can now expect the police to come. The men go back upstairs and they all wait tensely. Later that night steps are heard in the house, and the secret bookcase entrance is rattled. When it's over they all need the lavatory, as always after fear, and they have to use a tin wastepaper basket. Mrs. van Daan gets some chlorine to help with the smell. They all try to sleep, still in terror. The next day they are able to ring Koophuis.

That panic subsides, but everyone is very much on edge. Their protectors also have problems. Mr. Koophuis is often ill, Mr. Kraler is called up like other middle-aged Amsterdamers for digging anti-invasion trenches (but he manages to get out of it). Miep tells them about a black market engagement party. The chestnut tree in the courtyard is green and they have been nearly two years in their hiding place. Whitsun is hot and unbearable, for since the office is on holiday no window can be opened. They swelter, and brood on their situation, and quarrel. Though Anne, as she becomes older, becomes more interested in herself and her romantic problems, she still lets us hear the voices of the others — we can still hear poor Mrs. van Daan complaining about almost everything. At last D-Day comes, and hope and excitement. But Mrs. van Daan is soon depressed again.

A few days later the main interest is strawberries, for an agent of the firm has managed to bring some back from the country. At half past twelve the house is locked, and inside are the four from the office and the hidden families. They are all busy stalk picking, and freely going up and down the stairs for supplies. It is all a curiously confident performance, for after all it's the middle of the day and no effort is being made to be quiet. Suddenly the street doorbell rings and everything changes. They are all upstairs in a second, the bookcase door is shut and they have to wait until the all-clear is given. (It was the postman.) It's July and the attempt on Hitler is another encouragement. Anne writes at length about her relationship with her parents, and the generation gap and so forth. July goes. On August 1, still in a mood of gloomy, youthful self-analysis, she ends what she does not know will be her last entry in the diary, "I . . . keep on trying to find a way of becoming what I would so like to be, and what I could be, if . . . there weren't any other people living in the world."

There were other people. Friday, three days later, was a fine, sunny day, with the canal trees making patterns on the office walls. Office and warehouse were functioning normally. Suddenly, quietly, a car drew up. A fat German "green policeman," a sergeant, got out with about four middle-aged Dutch plainclothesmen. They came in and went up the stairs to the inner office, where Mr. Kraler was at his desk.

"Are you in charge?"

"Yes."

"Come along. We want to see the storerooms."

So it was over. A fat plainclothesman looked in the main office and told Mr. Koophuis and the girls to stay in their places. Mr. Kraler led the party upstairs. The front storerooms were searched and then at the bookcase

Hunger Winter — 1944:
A starving boy

landing the revolvers came out. He had to open up. He went up the little stairs with a revolver in his back and saw Mrs. Frank. He told her, "The Gestapo is here." She stayed quite still. Mr. and Mrs. van Daan appeared, and the two girls. They all had to put their hands up.

It was all very quiet and grotesquely unexpected. Mr. Frank was helping Peter with an English lesson, which was interrupted by a man with a revolver. They had to join the party. The last was Mr. Dussel. There were no hysterics. They were all absolutely quiet and knocked out. The sergeant asked for their valuables and was given the cashbox. He filled Anne's briefcase with the contents, having first emptied it, so that all her diaries and writings were scattered over the floor. Then he told them that they had five minutes to get ready. But he was not really in a hurry. They went off and packed their knapsacks, silently.

Down in the office Mr. Koophuis had managed to ring up his brother, so his wife could be told. He knew he was in for it. He wanted the girls to try to get out, but Miep refused, for Henk, her husband, was expected for lunch. Elli was shaking and crying. Koophuis finally managed to persuade her to take his briefcase, and see if she could leave it at a nearby chemist for his brother. With her legs like jelly she went off with it, and found no one outside to stop her. Then Henk arrived. Miep met him at the office door with a whispered "Gestapo!" and pressed money and the ration cards into his hand. He shot off into the street, and went quickly back to his own office, where he disposed of that day's list of *"onderduiker"* addresses.

Then he returned to the Prinsengracht and watched the house from the other side of the canal. By now there was a police van outside. Soon he was joined by Mr. Koophuis's brother. In the office itself Miep was alone, for both her employers were, of course, arrested. She heard them all pass the door and go down the stairs. From the window she had a glimpse only of the Van Daans, deathly pale and calm. The two men opposite saw the van start off, cross the bridge, and come down beside them on its way to Euterpestraat, the Gestapo H.Q. Henk went off to tell Mrs. Dussel where her husband had been for the last two years, and where he was now.

All ten were locked up together. There were no fierce interrogations, or torture sessions, it was all a very bureaucratic end to Amsterdam's most famous war story. In due course, the "Aryans" were dealt with separately, and happened to survive. Of the eight Jewish prisoners from the *"achterhuis"* only Mr. Frank came through. Oddly enough when they rode from the city towards the hells of Westerbork, Auschwitz and Belsen it was in a locked compartment of an ordinary train and the thrill of being able to look out at the countryside made it seem almost like a holiday.

3.

FOR AMSTERDAM the last and worst war winter lay ahead. But during this August there was a growing optimism in the city — which had really begun with the July 20 attempt on Hitler. There were wild hopes and rumors. Those people who had been able to patronize black market restaurants all through began to feel more nervous, and to consider how it might be possible to change sides. NSB members became very nervous indeed. Then on Sunday, September 3, Brussels was freed and on Monday, Antwerp. That evening they heard on their forbidden radios that the Allies were in Breda — Dutch soil at last. The next day was *"dolle Dinsdag"* — crazy Tuesday. Everybody went mad with anticipation. They were all getting ready to greet the liberators. People were suddenly braver about listening to the radio. Orange favors were rashly displayed. A good many Germans and NSBs were beginning to behave like fugitives and planning to journey eastwards. But then it was Wednesday, and things settled into the old depression. Ten days later there was excitement about Maastricht, but disappointment that the Allied armies were moving east towards Germany rather than coming up through Holland. But three days later there was the thrill feeling again, with Prince Bernhard's voice coming through from London on the evening of September 17 to announce the airborne attack on Arnhem. For a few days the city waited while that crucial and terrible battle went on only fifty miles away. As their contribution railwaymen obeyed the call from London and went on strike.

But the battle was lost (and my brother* with it) and the Dutch faced the winter still under their occupiers. The *"Moffen"* (Dutch for Kraut or Boche) paid them out for the railway strike by deliberately slowing the transport of food to the west, which included Amsterdam, and since there

---

* Major Anthony Cotterell, Royal Fusiliers, writer and War Office reporter, attached to 1st Parachute Brigade. Wounded by SS in a shooting incident after capture, and subsequently missing.

PHOTO BY EMMY ANDRIESSE — LEIDEN UNIVERSITY COLLECTION, COPYRIGHT © BY JOOST ELFFERS

Hunger Winter — 1944:
Handcart burial

was in any case a transport problem, the effect was appalling. At the end of September they blew up the harbor installations of the city — and of Rotterdam. In the country as a whole there were 300,000 *"onderduikers"* in hiding — mostly young men. The industry of forging or stealing identity papers was at its peak. There was very little food in Amsterdam in October and November. Everything was looking bleak and depressed. There were few cars about, just a few bicycles. Clothes were becoming shabby. Large numbers of people began to look like tramps. In December it was worse; everything came to a halt with the intense frost. The authorities did what they could. Central kitchens were set up which offered meals made up of sugarbeet, offal and scraps — one of them was at the Port van Cleve on the Spuistraat, before and since a splendid center of happy overeating, but here people queued for hours in the snow for some watery soup. There were more call-ups for older men to go digging — such as Mr. Kraler, now in a forced labor camp, had once avoided. At Christmas there were bad signs of tuberculosis and hunger oedema. People with swollen limbs haunted the dustbins. The desperate shortage of fuel — there was no gas or electricity — brought people into the pathetically empty Jewish quarter, where floorboards and roof beams were sawed out of houses, and anything that could be burned was taken. There were street-corner black markets where one could see a row of women all holding out their little trays or cartons of goods — such as reels of cotton.

With the new year everything became worse. The one trade which was extremely busy was the undertaker's, for thousands of people were now dying from hunger and cold. Coffins were made of cardboard or were often simply paper sacks. Funerals were a constant sight, with a sort of open coffin, which could be used again, mounted on a tricycle, but still accompanied professionally by men in tall black hats and black coats. The city could not be run properly; all services faltered, the canals began to smell — probably as they used to two or three hundred years before, when people didn't notice. Hundreds left the city with tireless bicycles and handcarts, going on foraging expeditions into the country, trying to get food directly from the farmers. Meanwhile the *"Moffen,"* with the war now definitely lost, were ransacking the country, removing rolling stock, cars, and buses. And they were trigger-happy. It was the most dangerous time of all. There was more suffering through transport or bureaucratic breakdowns than through any deliberate cruelty. But there was plenty of cruelty. Whenever a resistance coup was brought off the Germans hauled

PHOTO BY EMMY ANDRIESSE — LEIDEN UNIVERSITY COLLECTION, COPYRIGHT © BY JOOST ELFFERS

Hunger Winter — 1944:
Amsterdam undertaker

The Canadians arrive — 1945

a few men out of prison, took them to a convenient public spot, and shot them; and anyone passing was roped in and compelled to watch.

Visitors to the Rijksmuseum can walk a little farther round the Stad-houderskade alongside the waters of the Singelgracht until they see a small park on the other side. Here twenty prisoners were executed on April 3, 1945. Photographs were taken which show us those bodies on the Weteringplantsoen and the bleak street scene opposite. It was one of many such incidents. An anonymous Amsterdamer wrote that they were left there for twenty-four hours, and described how under a cold sun people came and gazed, and couldn't bring themselves to leave the sight of it, and how there were children, overawed and curious, whom no one thought of sending away.

"God, let me never forget these twenty, whose names we don't know, who lay like old rubbish. . . ."

The last weeks were exciting but nerve-racking. With the Canadians invading westwards the Germans opened sluices, blew up dikes, and finally the great sluices at IJmuiden, so that there was water on all sides of Amsterdam. In the city the level was rising at an alarming rate. With the sewage system no longer working there was also a plague of rats.

But suddenly there was the news of Hitler's death, suddenly the sight of Orange flags appearing and food dropped from the air by the "enemy" over the half-dead, hungry city. There were some cruelly unlucky victims of shooting across the Dam from a few Germans trapped in the Grote Club. The next day, May 8, was Amsterdam's liberation day. It was an odd fact that then and for some time afterwards many resistance-group survivors who for months or years had taken appalling risks and who now logically had the greatest reason for rejoicing felt instead a strange and terrible sense of anticlimax. But ecstasy was the general rule. Barrel organs appeared, people danced and jostled, there were posters everywhere about thanksgiving services, portraits of the royal family. On the Dam they put up a large maypole in front of the palace.

VII

A Forum Atmosphere
1945–

1.

A QUARTER OF A CENTURY has gone since the liberation. And how is Amsterdam? Well . . . for one thing it's the fourth tourist city of Europe (after Paris, London and Rome), where hippies can hold love-ins in the Vondel Park on Sunday afternoons. For square bourgeois headline-readers and televiewers Amsterdam's image has become excitingly tinged with decadence. Who would have thought it? The London *Times,* startled by the various stories of riots on the Dam, has enquired in a raised-eyebrows leader, "Is this Holland?" *The Times* wanted to know what had happened to the solid satisfaction of Rembrandt's burghers, and noted with mild irony, "It is odd, to say the least, that at the municipal elections in June five seats on the Amsterdam city council and eleven percent of the total vote should have been won by gentle nihilists who are opposed to authority, motor cars and war, and in favour of wholemeal bread and helping old people." It is all quite true and mildly comic, and as always with Amsterdam unpretentiousness creeps in. Ah, such a cozy city! A few weeks after the riots I recall a nihilist Amsterdamer, a dropout history student, who informed me from his corner in an old, tiny, crowded bar on the Damstraat, "In America, in California, it's real." He meant the general revolution of youth. "In Amsterdam it's a phony. It's not really serious. Here it's an act. Hippie capital of the world — no, no, no."

As the nihilist finished speaking a commotion broke out. Two yards away, happily, there was a fight, two men barking like dogs, blows, a shattered end to conversation, blood, and a man sitting down, holding his head. Conversation resumed.

"That was unpleasant," I said, but the nihilist insisted that the fight had been phony, too. He said that the couple were always fighting, it meant nothing.

"Everything is phony here. In California it's real."

"Would you suppose," I asked him, "that in California, or in London, you could walk into a bar and have a native dropout student talk to you in good Dutch? Of course not. Why are you all so good at languages? Because of history. Because of the carrying trade. You're still part of the golden century —"

He used a friendly obscenity, with idiomatic correctness, and I left him, with questions unanswered. What on earth did he do all day? Who supported him? And what would he do when he was thirty? What would other people do, whom I had met, when they were thirty? For instance, the white-faced drug addicts living in squalor on a barge alongside the Amstel. Or perhaps they would never be thirty.

It was hard not to keep on thinking about these things. But a great deal more had been happening in Amsterdam than the revolution of youth. The silent majority had also been busy.

2.

AND THERE WAS PLENTY OF NEED FOR IT, for after the war there was an immediate crisis confronting Amsterdam. The East Indian empire was about to go, and with it possibly the basis for the carrying trade which had been at the back of the city's greatness. There would also be a large number of ex-colonial Dutch who would now have to make a living at home. With more people to feed and no empire, the only answer was to expand in every possible direction. When Amsterdam had been getting over occupation by the French, the attitude had been very different — resignation to mediocrity. But that had been at the end of the great eighteenth-century decline. World War II on the other hand had interrupted the recovery which had been going on with ups and downs since the 1870's, when the North Sea canal was opened. In addition the experience of the war, horrible as it had been, somehow put a shot of adrenalin into the Amsterdamers — three-hundred-year-old adrenalin. It was already working, perhaps, in the long line of pale, underfed, shabby but formally dressed Amsterdamers who queued for the reopening of the Rijksmuseum.

The whole nature of the port had to be changed. Tobacco, coffee, tea, rubber and spices, all tropical products, had largely been the business of the docks — not much in the line of bulk products. But in 1952 the Am-final insult Louis exploded. There was a feverish meeting of ministers and generals in the Pavilion, at which for some time the king was all for total resistance, even to flooding the city. But it was always "easy to appease his anger by appealing to his good nature" and "the prudence inspired by the ownership of property had more voice in the council than outraged glory." So he decided to abdicate. He had tried to be a good king, and he had tried to be independent; it had not worked out.

A proclamation was posted up in the Amsterdam streets. The news was sent to the emperor. Louis slipped out — having to leave his son once more — on the night July 1 and 2, 1810. He went off to take the waters in Bohemia. Subsequently he lived in retirement in Italy until he died in 1846.

On the tenth of July Napoleon incorporated Holland with France and named Amsterdam as the third city in the French Empire, after Paris and Rome.

4.

THOUGH THE GENERAL BUSINESS of the city was still carried on, the effect of all the draconian measures against trade with England was grim. By the end of Louis's reign grass could be seen growing between the stones on the quays. About forty thousand people in a population of at most a quarter of a million lived more or less on charity. Many of the more prosperous Amsterdamers also suffered badly. Interest on the national debt had not been paid for three years. Napoleon dealt with this by cutting the rate by two-thirds — admittedly, the remaining one-third was paid, so the price of the stock actually went up on the Exchange, but it was not a solution to intoxicate the investors. Then the new measures of conscription, the vast number of French officials and army officers who came intruding into the new part of "France," the prevalence of customs officers and the imposition of strict censorship of the press — all these were unpleasant features of the new regime. The country was divided into French-style "departments," with prefects and subprefects. The *"préfet"* of the Zuyder Zee department, to which Amsterdam belonged, was the Count de Celles, who was noted for being equally ignorant of administration and of human nature. One of his staff, in charge of the military department, was a Monsieur Dubois, who was still more disliked — so much that in due course a plan was made to get rid of him. Partly because they had had so much influence in politics, art, fashion and society it did not seem to occur to the French that anyone might resent their presence. M. Dubois one night went happily to a masked ball at the Théâtre-Français — which had existed for some years. They were waiting for him when he came out wearing his domino, followed him and at a convenient point, seized him, and threw him into the Amstel. Unfortunately it was not the detested M. Dubois, but it was almost the end of a most kind and agreeable man called M. Prévot — who managed, after some time, to save himself and reach the bank. Things were always going wrong nowadays in Amsterdam.

The governor put in charge of the country during its process of absorption by France was a moderate and kindly seventy-two-year-old Frenchman "of good family," Charles-François Lebrun, Duke of Piacenza. His modesty and good sense kept the temperature down. He did not live in the palace but took over the French ambassador's house, where following his own taste the necessary banquets and receptions were comparatively free of pomp. The French attended but so did the usual Dutch court followers — who had paid homage to the old stadholder and to King Louis and were happy to dress up again. People in general were subdued. There was no active resistance movement. The Code Napoléon was introduced without raising a murmur — and in fact the general unification the French brought did the country a useful service. Most of the domestic staff at the palace went off to serve the emperor in Paris. A large sum of money from a quick fifty percent tax on the value of all "colonial goods" found in the warehouses of the city also went to Paris.

That there was a touch of depression in the air, unnoticed by the happy French, was hardly surprising. But everybody celebrated — prudently — the emperor's birthday on August 15. There were flags, flattering statements from authorities, and free performances at all the theaters, which included the city theater, the Théâtre-Français and a German theater, where, rather inexplicably, Italian actors performed. There was also, to give heart to the citizens, a firework show. Thousands lined the Amstel to watch and the governor's daughter-in-law, the Baroness Alexandre Lebrun, lit the first one. Instead of the gay pyrotechnics expected, the excitements of crackling and banging, and marvelous flowers in the sky, hers was the first of several halfhearted failures. It was all due to the damp in the air. The crowd, disillusioned, went home. Things were always going wrong nowadays in Amsterdam.

Twelve quiet months passed. The governor, pursuing his careful way, and well aware of the secret trade which in spite of all obstacles still went on with the English, managed to persuade a good many merchants to give it up — in return for the hope of various commercial freedoms being restored. On March 20, 1811, Marie Louise bore Napoleon a son. In Amsterdam, as in the rest of Europe, the news seemed to give an absolute solidity to the emperor's regime — and this again helped the governor's efforts. The birth of the King of Rome was a great excitement. The first announcement in Amsterdam was by the commissioner-general of police, M. Duvilliers-Duterrage, who cried from a box at the Théâtre-Français: "The hero of the century, Napoleon the Great, has a son — who one day will be his worthy successor!" The next morning delegations began arriving in Amsterdam from all over the country bringing congratulations to the governor. Seeing that their future was irremediably tied to Napoleon, more and more people became pro-French. For days Amsterdam blazed with lights from all the private and public festivities.

Soon there was a greater excitement. The news came that the emperor and empress were to tour the country. It was instantly the one subject of conversation. His intentions were endlessly and fruitlessly explored by everybody from the country nobility and the owners of Herengracht houses in Amsterdam downwards. Every town and village on the itinerary, which was sent two months in advance, was overcome by the thrill of the occasion — no matter what private political opinions might be held. But the greatest problem was where on earth everyone would stay on the journey, for almost the whole court was coming. Amsterdam itself had problems, though the palace was large. The stables were hopelessly inadequate and too far away. The flower market had to be converted, and put under canvas. Then there were the two guards of honor, richly equipped, one marine, the other of the militia, both competing for the exclusive guard of the palace. A troop of the line, contemptuous of them, also demanded the privilege. So it was shared and everyone was annoyed. All those who were in a position to be invited to the coming banquets and receptions were highly animated.

At the end of September Napoleon and Marie Louise made their slow way north, to Antwerp, to Berg-op-Zoom, to Breda and then Utrecht. It was a triumphal progress. From everywhere rumors of "amusing" royal incidents flew ahead. There was the pro-English mayor of Breda whose city keys were kicked away by the imperial boot. There was the unlucky valet at Utrecht who went into the wrong room and woke guess who. In Amsterdam the flags were up and the ceremonial route magnificently prepared with posts between which the French colors were suspended. Every private house was also decorated, often splendidly. And the day arrived — much more fortunate than Utrecht's, where it had been raining hard.

The first procession, a long way ahead, was that of the empress — who was not yet twenty. (Napoleon was forty-two.) She arrived in a dazzling carriage and the air resounded with vivats and applause. When she stopped the carriage to admire the arches of triumph and to read the loyal inscriptions and was seen to be smiling happily there was delirium. And then there was the pomp and circumstance of the accompanying court, the dignitaries, the ladies-in-waiting, the ladies of the bedchamber, the chamberlains, the equerries, all rumbling by to happy cheers, after the beautiful young empress had disappeared into the palace.

And then a silence. The crowds waited. "He" was evidently a long way behind, and after an hour or two people became tired, or impatient, or bored. But not too much. The build-up was superb. All at once there was the sound of horses. A large body of cavalry suddenly appeared, and went by, clip clop, clip clop, and the crowds, who wanted to be impressed, drank in the marvelous uniforms, and the richness of the equipment. This was the real thing. Power was in the air. Suddenly a distant noise told everybody that "he" was coming, and the excitement became vast, and hearts thumped, for a glamorous moment was a glamorous moment — there are not too many in life. It was all deceptively simple, and yet magnificent. After the cavalry had passed (they formed up on the Dam, now, of course, the Place Napoléon, facing the palace) there was an interval, and then what seemed to be another troop approached, until they came nearer and the splendor of their various uniforms, in quite another and superior category, and some of the middle-aged faces and less rigid dressing of the horses made it obvious that this was the general staff. Clop clop clop clop on the cobbles. The general staff passed, full of splendor, tension mounted unbearably, and there was a vast murmured whisper of anxiety. It was as if they were suddenly afraid "he" wasn't coming or that they had missed him in the middle of the generals. And then hearts swelled, eyes filled with tears, and the crowd went mad. No fancy uniform for him. He was sterdam-Rhine canal was opened and this offered a whole new role — notably the supply of ore for the Ruhr furnaces. An immense, automated installation for the transshipment of all bulk cargo was built. As a result, for example, grain imports went up in this postwar period by eight times. Meanwhile the bulk carrier business had started and the North Sea canal had to be widened and deepened, and the IJmuiden harbor mouth enlarged to take the new giant ships. The thrust to become bigger and better was going on all the time, and still goes on. A consequence is that a line of vast installations stretches across the northern horizon of the old city. And the city feels the pressure of this.

In addition there was the purposeful recovery of old trades. The tragic mass murder of the Jews might have put an end to the diamond industry, but it was reestablished brilliantly. There was the same intensive effort in another business where the Jews had been very active, especially as a result of the immigrant refugees from Germany after 1933 — the ready-to-wear clothes industry. Probably the vast increase in tourism helped another revolution here, a vast upgrading of Amsterdam as a fashion center. Elegant little boutiques mushroomed. The reception rooms of decaying Herengracht houses were beautifully restored to their old colorful grandeur and became impressive showrooms. Twenty-five years after the liberation, trendy foreign models found it natural to live in Amsterdam. There was a Men's Fashion Fair. To meet and help on the expansion an international ready-to-wear sales center, the world's biggest, with fifteen acres of floor surface, was being built close by Schipol Airport — now used by thirty-seven airlines and four and a half million passengers — and close to the junction of various inland motorways to the continental hinterland. It was adding another monument to Amsterdam's coming to profitable terms with the latter part of the twentieth century.

Many other monuments to the same happening added to the skyline of the city, the great complex of storage tanks at the Jan van Riebeck harbor, the Mobil refinery, the colossal RAI Congress and Exhibition center. Two magnificent tunnels under the IJ were built, and a bridge over it. The city became the European headquarters of enterprises like IBM. Mobil's refinery offered vast possibilities for petrochemical industry on the banks of the North Sea canal. Bonded warehouses both in the port and at Schipol were attractive to foreign industries needing to store products and spare parts duty free. Amsterdam was chosen to be one of the links in the coming chain of World Trade Centers. It will be one more monument, another

complex of high white buildings with dramatic curves and rectangles, surrounded by marvelous motorways. The Japanese are building a large hotel
to look after, among others, Japanese business visitors. Twenty-five years
after the liberation Amsterdam's future looks sky-high.

To cope with all, of course, the city has had to expand. In fact a plan of
expansion to take in the needs of the year 2000 had been approved just
before the war and it went ahead in 1947. But by 1970 all the land projected for use by 2000 had been absorbed, most remarkably by the "garden cities" — beautiful, well spaced and elegant (or nightmarishly futuris-
tic, depending on one's point of view), with their enormous artificial lakes
and woods and parks and shopping centers, the whole thing in the tradition of the great seventeenth-century expansion, planning the good life.

A metro is being built and the first line to be completed will serve the
newest of the "garden cities," Bijlmermeer in the southeast, where 130,000
people will live. Here there will be traffic on three levels, every block will
have its own parking garage, eighty percent of homes will be within 550
yards of a metro station, nowhere will be more than 440 yards from a bus
stop, and every bus stop will be reachable by a subway; there will be a
network of traffic-free cycle and footpaths, and superb children's play facilities, and space for the recreational needs of different age groups, pri-
vacy at home and yet ease of communication. Oh, dear. Perhaps it will be
wonderful. It ought to be wonderful.

3.

NOT EVERYBODY in Amsterdam has been utterly delighted with all this. The
fact that the old city was an increasingly popular international tourist attraction was at least a guarantee of survival; and that was a comfort, for
thousands of Amsterdamers felt that some of the new monuments of success were leaning too heavily on the city's heart, were enemies with smiling faces about to stifle everything that was worthwhile. Many were won-
dering what life was about, anyway. The Amsterdam tradition of freedom
for minority groups was deeply engrained and as strong as ever. In the
general world-ferment of the late fifties and sixties, the general syndrome

of anarchism — anti-American-imperialism — drugs — sexual revolution — youth revolution — and so forth, the city offered a naturally sympathetic breeding ground. John Lennon and Yoko naturally came first to the Hilton in Amsterdam to hold court in bed. As the burgomaster told the Crown Princess Beatrix and her fiancé, Claus von Amsberg, when the couple visited the city in July 1965, "Amsterdam is known as a difficult city, and Amsterdamers are difficult people. . . ."

Friction between the House of Orange and Amsterdam was traditional. The aims of the burgomasters and merchants had rarely coincided with the aims of the stadholders, and the only prince who had actually lived in Amsterdam had been a Bonaparte. After him both William I and William II had made Amsterdamers conscious of a certain reluctance on their part to stay long in the city. All this could change into fervent loyalty at times. The old queen Wilhelmina had been extremely popular; she liked the city and was always welcome. It was she who had said in reference to the great strike of 1941, "For me Amsterdam will always be the city where the people's resistance to the usurper first spread abroad like a flame." When she abdicated and Juliana was crowned in the Nieuwe Kerk, on September 7, 1948, a period of less frequent visits to the city set in, official and informal, and possibly a shade of the old coolness between Amsterdam and the House of Orange returned, largely through overanxiety on the part of authorities. In any case a socialist council was not likely to show itself overwhelmingly royalist. This is delicate ground, for the cords which bind the House of Orange to the Dutch, including the Amsterdamers, are very strong; the subtleties which affect the relationship are also — very subtle.

Only the other day, as I write, there was plenty of informality when the queen was visiting Bijlmermeer, the garden city of the future, and broke from the official party to investigate personally a refuse smell complained of by the wives in one apartment block. The episode was replete with evidence of warmth, affection and admiration. All the same Orange obviously represents, above all, the establishment. In 1965 the recovery from the war had taken place long since, the students of the two universities, both in the heart of the old city, could not remember the war at all, labor was restive after a long period of wage restraint (some of the unrest being against its own traditional leaders), the Common Market had attracted great international companies to establish headquarters which were symbols of the prosperous but terrifyingly impersonal life of the future. People who loved the old city of bars and canals were less than enthusiastic about skyscrapers like the Netherlands Bank which now rose above the Frederiksplein, where the old exhibition palace had been, instead of — what had been the rival possibility — an opera house. All this with the new freedom and permissiveness sweeping the Western world made Amsterdam a place more than slightly bubbling with irritations and frustrations. So the visit of the newly engaged royal couple came at a sensitive time. In addition there were also, of course, many Amsterdamers who did remember the war, and some of them were not too keen on the idea of a marriage between the crown princess and a German.

Actually it went off fairly smoothly. Pamphlets were thrown into the boats which took them on a trip through the canals. People with placards which demanded "Republic!" or made reference to one aspect of the German occupation with "Give me my bike back" were quietly arrested. But it was after this day that the celebrated "Provo" movement took seed and the problems of the police grew. "Provo," an inspired name, came from the word for provocation — *provocatie.* The movement was, to begin with, more or less philosophical and literary. Success made it political.

Its support came from Amsterdam's always plentiful supply of young artists and intellectuals, dropout artists and intellectuals, from the student left, discontented with the left-wing parties, and the general radical, pacifist, anti-Vietnam, anti-NATO youth-opinion areas. It was anti–middle-class culture, anti the "indifference" of the welfare state and the growing powerlessness of the individual, anti motor cars, air pollution and smoking. It was for improving the quality of life (by, for instance, supplying free white-painted bicycles to replace all the traffic in the city center). It was for long hair, worn-out clothes and free sex, for more playtime and less work. Illustrative pop art "happenings" were often staged by a magician, Robert Jasper Grootveld. In other and not necessarily happier days the image of all this might have been orthodox youthful idiocy, touched by a pleasant crankiness. What made the Provos matter was their discovery that the "happenings" could not only make a point, but "provoke" the authorities — the police — and make them look fools or bullies.

Then the royal wedding took place the following March in the Westerkerk — the Nieuwe Kerk being in the hands of the restorers — and all Europe's televiewers could watch the smoke bombs exploding among the coaches of the procession. The police handled it capably, with some tough use of the baton — and some wrong heads being hit (Provos had the great knack of getting out of the way) — and the marriage went off success-fully. But the incidents left the atmosphere simmering a little. Nine days later there was an unfortunate example of public relations when the police put on a photographic exhibition of their hard-line action. There was trouble at the opening, which was filmed and shown on TV that night. Burgomaster van Hall also appeared on the screen, asking for feelings to cool off. The same evening there was a Provo "happening" on the Dam, with fires being started in front of the palace.

Names of the young Provo leaders became well known, like Roel van Duyn and Rob Stolk and Luud Schimmelpenninck. In June Provo Bernard de Vries (the inventor of the white bicycle idea) was elected to the coun-cil. But feelings were not cooling, and the police-baiting continued. On the Spui, the busy little street which crosses the middle of Kalverstraat, there is a statue of a little boy, called the *"Lieverdje"* or "Little Darling," which was presented to Amsterdam by a cigarette company. The Provos had condemned it as a monument to the slave consumer of tomorrow and every Saturday evening a dozen of them assembled there, shouting what-ever seemed appropriate or staging a scene. Every Saturday evening thou-sands of people were out on the town and the "happening" at the *"Lieverdje"* was always the focal point for a big crowd. Soon the police would arrive and break it up, getting bad marks from the public, who in Amsterdam are always, at least to start with, automatically against them in almost any situation. The fact was the police simply did not know what to do about the Provos, whose provocations were often subtle — though the movement, not entirely without its encouragement, was becoming mixed up with the rougher sections of the city's youth, who just enjoyed police-baiting without ideological considerations (they helped Provos to leave a scene which needed, prudently, to be left). The police tried being tough and they tried being lenient. Nothing worked and either way they were criticized.

So the year went on (1966) and the tourists came, and the round-trip boats went round the canals, the puppet show was in business on the Dam. On a hot Saturday night in June there was trouble again. Down on the Leidseplein, the biggest center of night and theater life, the whole place was in a state of siege. The terrace of the American hotel, normally crowded, was empty. Close by the police were making baton charges on a largely youthful crowd in front of the Weteringschans prison. However, Sunday came and all was quiet. But on Monday the Communist paper *De*

Waarheid managed to start an agitation about the payment of holiday money to building workers. The affair hinged on a cleverly inflated triviality. A minute sum (two percent) was to be deducted from each man for administrative costs. Union members would get it back, but "unorganized" men would not. As seventy percent were "unorganized," the Communists happily denounced the arrangement as theft.

That evening, a warm evening after a hot day, a thousand building workers arrived outside the building where the unions had hired a room to make the payments. It was on the Marnixplantsoen, a square in the Jordaans, the west side working-class district famous until the war for its convivial street life — but now just a depressed area, though the myth of the Jordaans exists still in sentimental songs.

The police watched and were slightly nervous. The crowd grew, and many of them were in the mood for a good riot. Traffic came to a halt. A police Volkswagen was surrounded. A chief inspector arrived and was roughed up. He ordered batons to be drawn and there was a five-minute battle which seemed to satisfy all customers. The atmosphere became more peaceful. But very soon it changed. There was a group round a man on the ground, a fifty-one-year-old bricklayer, Jan Weggelaar. He had had a heart attack and he was dead. Of course the rumor now spreading through the crowd was that the police had killed somebody. Stones began to fly.

The chief inspector, who had a face wound, retreated. So did most of the police, with difficulty. There was nothing else they could do. Shouting "Murderers!" most of the crowd set towards the city center, making for the Town Hall, the old admiralty building on the lovely and disgraceful (because of the red-light district) seven-hundred-year-old canal street, the Oude Zijds Voorburgwal. This was between eight and nine o'clock. Back at police headquarters they contacted Chief Commissioner van der Molen and reported events. Burgomaster van Hall was out for the evening and unreachable. Next Van der Molen arrived and took over. He looked at the chief inspector's wound, stopped armed forces being sent out and, magnificently, called for his sword. He changed into full uniform, put on the sword, and went off in a car. It seems a wholly admirable and splendid reaction. His car plunged into the crowd, which was already close to the Town Hall. He got out at a corner and was promptly surrounded by a threatening crowd. But Van der Molen was equal to the situation. He persuaded someone to go and find the workers' leaders, and ask them to meet him, and meanwhile the angry but fascinated crowd round him grew larger. By midnight a meeting had taken place. It was decided that the workers would assemble the next morning by the Dockworker statue on the Jonas Daniel Meijerplein, and decide whether to strike or not. The Amsterdam police chief had brilliantly avoided violence.

Meanwhile at the hospital where the dead man, Jan Weggelaar, had been taken, it had been a slightly protracted business making certain that heart failure and no sort of physical injury had caused death. So the police press conference did not end until 2:30 A.M. This unfortunately meant that only one morning newspaper, *De Telegraaf*, would carry the definite news that it had been a natural and not a police-caused death. Amsterdam was quiet, except for a few Provos shouting "Murderers!"

In the morning Van der Molen arrived at HQ before nine, somewhat exhausted, and left at once for a conference with the burgomaster at the Town Hall — ordering, just in case, that no mobile units should be used without his permission. Since they knew where he was going, this hardly seemed to matter.

Meanwhile thousands of building workers were streaming towards the Daniel Meijerplein. Plainclothes police were present and, in error, one uniformed adjutant, who was soon surrounded. There were encouraging shouts of "Trample him dead" and so on, and a struggle took place to rescue him. Speakers were heating up the crowd about *De Telegraaf*, a paper which is regarded as having a right-wing bourgeois image, accusing it of lying — for the crowd still believed that the police had caused Jan Weggelaar's death. Soon a march was being made on a nearby office of the Building Industry. Its assistant director, noting with concern the approach of hundreds of shouting workers, wrapped himself in a curtain to avoid broken glass and rang for help, only to learn that the police on the square were themselves barricaded in. However nothing happened worse than broken windows, for the main body of the crowd was on its way to *De Telegraaf*.

Most of the press in Amsterdam are situated on the Nieuwe Zijds Voorburgwal, a filled-in ancient canal street. At the bottom of it, on the Spui, there is a large and busy bookshop, concerned with social revolution, and marked by a concentration of earnest, bearded young men. The *Telegraaf* building is large and modern, and the paper's circulation is the biggest in Holland, well over six hundred thousand. It was a suitable enemy and now it awaited attack. A reporter had rung up with the news. The news chief promptly told the porter to bolt all the doors. The porter rang the police, who very shortly rang the editor to assure him of support.

It was all very exciting. The staff felt themselves back in the sixteenth century. Defense preparations went on. When the first workers appeared and began shouting, the siren sounded inside, the iron gates were shut, the rolling screens came down to protect the presses. But where were the police? Stones obtained from a nearby building lot began to be hurled against the shutters. There were several street entertainments. A tram was stopped and its windows broken, a car burned, a photographer injured, and meanwhile the attack was being pressed on the building. Where *were* the police? Leading building worker troops broke in and set about making a mess of the ground-floor reception area. Then there was an old-time battle on the barricaded stairs. *Telegraaf* employees fought with fire extinguishers, chair-legs and stair-rods. The editor rang through to the burgomaster, who was still in the middle of his conference and who pointed out that more rioters had arrived in other parts. "But not in the building!" cried the frustrated editor, getting nowhere.

And next door in the *Telegraaf's* Color Supplement section they had succeeded in getting through to the Minister of Justice in The Hague, Dr. Samkalden — the present burgomaster of Amsterdam.

"Samkalden here."

"Your excellency, do you know that we are besieged?"

"Yes, yes, meneer van Loon, I've heard about it."

"Do you also know, your excellency, that we have been besieged for half an hour and threatened and there's no sign of police, although we have constantly asked for help?"

Naturally the minister could not help. But why weren't the police there? It was all because the commissioner in charge at HQ was a man with strongly traditional upbringing. He had kept on trying to get in touch with the Amsterdam police chief, Van der Molen, who had forbidden the use of the mobile force without his personal permission and who was in conference with the burgomaster. Every time the commissioner rang the Town Hall, the normal procedure was adopted. A member of the legal department took down the message and brought it to his superior, who also was in the conference. Then the latter had to bring it to the attention of the burgomaster.

It wasn't a system designed for quick decisions, even if it has a certain charm. So it was only after a substantial delay and when the commissioner found out that he could ring through direct to the burgomaster, and through him to Van der Molen, that the newspaper could be relieved.

In fact by the time the police did arrive the attacking workers were already on their way. The main action was now on the Dam and Damrak, and they had been joined by anybody who was in the mood for a good riot. The big stores on the Dam lost their windows. It was a youth battle as well as an industrial battle now. Provos and young roughs — the "Nozems" — were joining in, parking meters pulled out, kiosks knocked over, police tires burst by nails — and police reinforcements were coming in from outside the city. At teatime there seemed to be an interval, for the workers tended to go home and stay there, but by about eight in the evening the Dam was full again and the Nozems were everywhere, the more subtle Provos keeping out of the way but offering encouragement. A truck came along supplying stones to rioters, the roadway of course was broken up for more munitions, the police fired thirty-one shots, purposefully hitting nobody, cars were burned, and there was a sympathy hooting procession by taxi drivers. Finally there was a charge against a barricade in front of the hotel-restaurant Port van Cleve, home of excellent rump steak and pea soup. Everybody went home. Twenty-nine of the police and thirty of the public had been injured.

Amsterdam was slightly stunned and shocked. For two more days there were mild outbreaks of trouble. Then the weather changed; the hot spell was over and it rained. The city relaxed. It had been like a fever, and the burgomaster addressing the Council had no doubt at all whom to blame: the Provos.

4.

LATER ON IN THE YEAR there was a different and longer-drawn-out agitation. It was really an old war being stoked up again. When Amsterdam suddenly began to expand beyond the Singelgracht in the latter part of the nineteenth century, there was a traffic problem. There had been five main streets radiating across the canals towards the city gates, around which most heavy traffic parked. Now they had to bear a heavier load, and it meant street widening or filling in parallel canals to ease the strain — either solution infuriating to lovers of the old city. Fervent defense campaigns in the early 1900's had saved two beautiful canals, the Leidesgracht and the Reguliersgracht. But the charming little Warmoesgracht had gone, and so had eleven Herengracht houses and fifteen on the Keizersgracht. And some streets came into the traffic business for the first time. One of these was Vijzelstraat, which runs southwest from the Muntplein. The Carlton Hotel stands on its corner. This end was sixteenth century and barely twenty-three feet wide; the next, longer part crossing the canals was seventeenth century and thirty-three feet wide. It was decided to knock down the west side, which included about fifty of the canalside houses, one of them belonging to Professor Jan Six, namesake of his ancestor who was Rembrandt's friend. There were already worries that what had been, historically, a busy shopping street would be filled with large office buildings — and the worries were immediately justified, for the council leased the ground between the Heren and Keizersgracht to a bank, the Netherlands Trading Company, and by 1926 the two canals were connected by an enormous, very uncozy, if admirable office building. Ten days before the opening the president of the bank gave his house, Herengracht 502, to the city as an official home for the burgomaster. Then came the Carlton Hotel, built overhanging the pavement in an attempt to keep some intimacy in the street. The third empty plot, between the Keizersgracht and Prinsengracht, became a great apartment block, with a shopping arcade. A street which ran parallel and in between the two canals, Kerkstraat, went through the middle of it. This was the cause of the 1966 affair, for on March 23, 1955, while some repair work was going on several floors above, the shopping arcade collapsed. After some time it was decided that the building was unsafe and in 1962 the demolition gang went to work. So there was a large vacant lot between the two historic canals.

The need for demolition had been controversial, but the landlords had proposed to put up a complex of shops, apartments, offices and a hotel. Four years later the shopkeepers of the former building and those nearby in the Kerkstraat who had been forced to put up with temporary premises at the bottom of the street were informed that a new company had taken over, that it would be some time before they could return, and that when they did, rents would be much higher. Next came rumors that the new company had financial difficulties and was selling out and that the buyer was a bank, the Algemene Bank Nederland. Then it became official, though nothing was said about any alteration to the shops-and-apartments project.

Then in September the bank published a sketch of its proposed building in its house magazine. There was no sign of any shops or apartments. Uproar broke out amongst the old-Amsterdam lovers. The proposed bank's architect had also designed the great glass Netherlands Bank on the Frederiksplein. The word "bank" was emotive. Their great headquarters were like enemy strongholds, threatening to turn the living old city into another dreary metropolis for commuters.

The press was stirred. Protest letters were signed by hundreds. A typical newspaper cartoon showed an immense safe rising up and dwarfing the gabled roofs. Posters said: Ban the Bank. The society Europa Nostra sent a telegram of protest from Rome. However, the burgomaster and aldermen submitted the proposal on November 16, agreeing roughly with what the bank's house magazine had said, that Amsterdam was the financial center of the country, and the bank should be in the center of the center, furthermore noting that no one else but the bank could afford it. Every sort of Amsterdam society now joined in the protests, historical, academic, artistic and, of course, anarchistic. Socialist Youth and the Provos organized a Teach-In. "Regents! Hands off inner Amsterdam! . . . Once again the living qualities of Amsterdam are being cynically sacrificed to what is thought to be the interests of business. Because of the lack of all round vision. . . ." The idealistic wordiness reflected a much primmer and more respectable movement than the Provos' "happenings," but it amounted to much the same thing.

It was the conflict, if there really was one, between the new wealth and the high white buildings of the end of the century and the quality of personal life.

That was what came out at the Teach-In, held in the Hotel Krasnapolsky on the Dam, in December, three days before the Council debated the matter. Over six hundred people packed into the room and there were thirty-seven speakers. About the only friend of the bank was Professor Delfgauw, who advised them all not to be afraid of Mobil Oil, or large banks, or mammoth tankers or jumbo jets, and reminded everybody that in order to keep up old gabled houses money was necessary. Dr. W. F. Heinemeyer of Amsterdam University put the case against the bank as well as anybody. "As far as the inner city is concerned, most Amsterdamers want a closely mixed-up network of streets and squares . . . where there's a great variety of possibilities for doing things one doesn't have to do, shopping, going to films and plays, sitting on terraces, in cafés, looking around, wandering about . . . a place where one can be *out* and at the same time *at home*, where it's a pleasure simply to *be*. . . . One can call it the 'forum' nature of the inner city, and this is something so precious that no administration must be indifferent about it."

It was an evening of cries from the heart. Three days later the Council debated the proposal — taking time off to watch a football match on TV between Liverpool and Ajax, Amsterdam (a team from whose fortunes many Amsterdamers not at the Teach-In obtain the meaning of life) — and voted for it by 30 to 14.

The ban-the-bank movement had lost. "The regents" had won. All the same the strictly emotional movement had made news in Holland for months, and it had shown how quite stately and respectable and eminent people could find themselves collaborating with the anarchistic Provos. They had demonstrated that the quality of life and the preservation of beautiful old buildings and streets, while not identical concepts, were all the same absolutely mixed up with each other.

The battle would go on being fought. The metro was coming, and the new tunnel under the IJ, which would bring vast upsets to the area between the old St. Antonies–poort, where Rembrandt had painted Dr. Tulp's anatomy lecture, and the Portuguese Synagogue . . . clearly a movement to ban all cars from the city center could be the next enthusiasm . . . and the concept of the Forum. . .

Small things? In a way. Amsterdam is a cozy city. But also, of course, certainly not. For more and more people saw that that marvelously planned network of canals centered round the Dam offered a chance that here could be, in the year 2000, a sublimely agreeable place. If only bankers and industrialists would stay outside the Singelgracht.

The Anne Frank Ho
COURTESY OF K

Golden era houses

5.

IT WAS THE TIME of Flower Power, Lennon and McCartney, Vietnam, drugs, long hair, the international, noncommunicating, but everywhere the same youth movement. Nowhere was more suitable for it to feel at home than in Amsterdam, with its historically implanted instinct for toleration and the "Forum" quality which had been noted at the Teach-In. The Dam became a part of the forum particularly favored by the young. So did the Central Station. It all depended on the point of view, and for some the beautiful people were standard-bearers of a new and lovelier world, and ornaments to the hall and surrounds of the railway station, while to others they were a squalid nuisance, badly needing to wash and probably to be deloused. Among those inclining to the latter opinion in 1967 were a group of marines and sailors who suddenly appeared to carry out a voluntary cleaning up operation. Some long hair was forcibly cut, and so on.

Naturally this was an event to give immense pleasure to the square silent majority of Holland and elsewhere, but it also gave Amsterdam more publicity for its role as a center for the hipsters. In succeeding summers they came from everywhere to sit around in the city. Those who approved of the "Forum" quality could only approve, and on the whole did. The freedom was real. Notices everywhere proclaimed student revolutionary activities. Pornographic books and magazines still looked a little odd calmly displayed in the many excellent bookshops. The neon signs outside the rubber goods, unusual helps and special-film-show Sex-Shops added a garish note. But the traditions of a former age were kept going by the plump ladies who sat on view, in hospitable mood, behind some of the windows of the Oude Zijds Voorburgwal and nearby. Often the prevalence of long hair and beards and fancy clothes made the seventeenth century seem to be back again in extraordinary reality.

Meanwhile the working city went on working. In October 1968, the IJ tunnel was opened, linking the city with Amsterdam-North and forming part of the great ring road system being created. In the docks eight thousand ships were bringing in twenty million tons of goods a year. Eight million tons left by canal. At the container terminal the two largest container cranes in Europe could each deal with four hundred tons an hour. . . .

And on the Museumplein, the great green square which was the center of the late nineteenth-century expansion, pop groups and folk singers performed with radiant success to packed houses in the Concertgebouw, and so on other evenings did the peerless Concertgebouw orchestra under its marvelous new conductor, Haitink — the great Van Beinum's successor. Close by on the square over 400,000 people went in a year to the Stedelijk (Municipal) Museum to see its modern art collection and the Van Goghs, which would soon have a museum of their own in the next block. At the city end of the square, on the Singelgracht, there were over 800,000 visitors to the Rijksmuseum.

One and a half million people went on canal round-trips. "This is the Herengracht, ladies and gentlemen, where in the seventeenth century the rich merchants —" Ah, we know, we know. Though according to opposition anarchist mini-posters the "regents" are still with us.

On the Leidseplein at the Stadsschouwburg (the Municipal Theater), where the symbol of industriousness above the stage, the beehive, was the same emblem which Coster's Academy had used in 1618, there were plays, like *Wie is bang voor Virginia Woolf,* opera and ballet — and the national ballet in particular was making its mark in the world, unhindered by the world's ignorance of Dutch. On the stairs the pictures of Amsterdam actors and actresses looked down from the past and from the previous theater, which burned down in 1890 — names like Louis Bouwmeester, Marie Johanna Kleine-Gartman and Theo Mann-Bouwmeester from the nineteenth century and Eduard Verkade, Louis van Gastern and Else Mauhs from the twentieth. In the streets around the square — and round about the other entertainment square, the Rembrandtsplein — topless ladies pranced innocently in bourgeois nightclubs, transvestites bloomed in their little corners, in the dozens of all sorts of bars people drank, mostly gin and beer — *"een borreltje," "een pils"* — with whiskey and sherry always becoming more fashionable, and more expensive. Elsewhere in the city, as at Tingel Tangel on the NZ Voorburgwal — the street of the newspapers — traditional political satire cabaret flourished, with a very intimate and attractive, very Amsterdamish atmosphere and, to foreigners, highly obscure jokes. Other theaters were in business, from the huge vari-

SY OF VERENIGING "DE AMSTERDAMSCHE HAVEN"

Bridge over the Leidsegracht

Seventeenth-century gables

ety house Carré on the Amstel to the experimental theater-in-the-round De Brakke Grond off the Rokin.

Forty cinemas showed films from everywhere else — only rarely a home product. The world's ignorance of Dutch and the Dutch tendency to speak other people's languages, so useful in business, make things difficult for Dutch writers and film-makers. Their market is inevitably restricted, and especially with films the capital needed seems to make them an impossible venture. Yet there is no shortage of film directors in Amsterdam. The Netherlands Film Academy was founded in 1958, and gives four-year courses. Companies like Scorpio Films produced some wonderfully impressive low-budget feature films in the sixties, like *De verloedering van de Swieps,* with a lay-about disturbing an Amsterdamer's normal suburban household, or *De minder gelukkige terugkeer van Joszef Katús naar het land van Rembrandt* (*The Not-so-fortunate Return of Joszef Katús to the Land of Rembrandt*) which was filled with current local problems and controversies, the Provos, attitudes to the Monarchy, and so forth. A Dutch Film Production fund now subsidizes producers. In fact all artistic life in the country is heavily state-subsidized — Amsterdam itself spends twenty million guilders (slightly more than $6 million) a year. Few writers anywhere can be self-supporting, and the number is minimal for the Dutch. All the same there is no shortage of writers in Amsterdam. They are mildly subsidized in one way or another — and so are artists, some of whom have a sort of minimum-wage guarantee. There is no shortage of artists, either. Official attempts to help them include a twenty-five percent subsidy for works bought by Dutch citizens. It seems to work — I can think of places where it wouldn't — but even so there have been confrontations. Artists have even staged sit-ins in the Rijksmuseum (in front of the *Night Watch*) as well as in the Stedelijk, protesting about their conditions.

It could be treated as part of a more general symptom, the crying for breath at the end of the sixties against the all-intrusive, enveloping welfare shield. Not that the authorities were showing any crude lack of understanding. After all in Amsterdam they had been in the welfare business for hundreds of years. For instance a youth advisory center which was set up during the Provo troubles of 1966 and found itself overwhelmed with clients, who could remain anonymous, ever since — drug troubles, pregnancy, trouble with police, money — has always been openly antiestablishment, antiauthority. It has also been state subsidized. It is the kind of comfortable paradox that Amsterdam can produce with beguiling ease.

6.

HOWEVER, Amsterdam's fame and attraction to youth were beginning to become slightly too much of a good thing. The sight of so many thousands of expressionless faces had a good deal of fascination. But the mass sleep-out in the Vondel Park and the Amsterdam Wood, as well as the tendency to use the Dam as a warm summer night dormitory, had hygienic-aesthetic aspects which did not appeal to squarer citizens. Even the well disposed were apt to find the beautiful people less beautiful. The Burgomaster of Amsterdam was Dr. Samkalden, a man of extremely civilized and liberal views. He was faced with the old, old problem of how to maintain toleration when dealing with the illiberal and intolerant. The city government went to remarkable lengths to set up cheap extra-sleeping accommodations, in hostels, converted houses, noncommercial youth hotels. To deal with the marijuana problem the famous Paradiso was started, a psychedelically painted old church building close to the Leidseplein, where the young could unofficially smoke pot without risk of arrest and sit around grooving to a musical noise background rather like a continuous mass bombing raid. It was an immense success. At the end of the 1969 summer a bylaw was passed, but not enforced, forbidding anyone to sleep on or around public monuments.

This concerned the Dam, and was in answer to protests. Many of the protests were heartfelt. It was a long time now since the war, but there were many reminders of it. The most famous was the Anne Frank house, with its pathetic pencil marks on the doorpost showing the changes in her height. And everywhere in the city one would suddenly come across a plaque in a wall, stating that on this spot so-and-so had been shot for Holland. There were street and square names, like 40–45 Plein in the brand new, wonderful suburb Slotermeer on the west side, or the Mr. Visser Plein on the tragic and half-flattened-out territory of the old Jewish quarter (he was a burgomaster who had tried to help them). There was

Gerrit van der Veenstraat, named after one of the best-known Amsterdam underground heroes. In the middle of this long and comfortable-looking residential street in Amsterdam-South, once called Euterpestraat, was a pleasantly designed building with a tower — the Gemeentelijke Middelbare School voor Meisjes, the City Middle School for Girls. This had been the Gestapo HQ. There were lots of people who did not forget the Gestapo HQ. And there was the Holland Theatre near the Zoo, which had been the assembly point for the deportations, and there was the monument to the 1941 strike. But *the* monument was on the Dam, the national monument to all the deaths and murders and sacrifice.

It had also been a splendid solution for the great old square, which earlier on in this century was in a considerable mess. The terrible stock exchange was knocked down, and the commandant's house which faced it, and the two great stores appeared — one hardly dares to think what the ban-the-bank movement would have said — and for years efforts were made to think of something suitable to fill the increased space opposite the palace. After the war the choice was all too simple. Four hundred thousand certificates were sold, each entitling its owner to a symbolical, minute part of the Dam, and this pleasantly helped to meet the cost of the national monument unveiled by Queen Juliana on May 4, 1956. Circular brick steps went up to a white column, decorated with figures, behind which was a curved wall containing twelve urns, eleven with soil from each of the provinces and the twelfth with soil from Indonesia. But to the masses of young tourists and hippies the monument had an insidious attraction. It was like a phallic symbol and the steps were extremely suitable for lying on. It was quite entertaining on a warm day just to sit down on the Dam, whether on the monument or not, and let the world go by. The sight of people doing this became in itself a tourist attraction. Numberless interviews took place in which the young and long-haired, speaking in a dreamy monotone, offered variations of, "This is a groovy scene, man, this is where it's at, man. . . ." Many of them preferred the steps of the monument to the dormitories and hostels, and the Central station was close at hand with all mod. cons. for anyone who felt like a wash and brush-up. To those Dutch people whose patriotic feelings were outraged — and this was certainly a very large proportion of people, especially in the rest of the country, where Amsterdam was growing a Sodom and Gomorrah reputation — others would say that the national memorial was a monument to freedom rather than to old-fashioned patriotic militancy. The police

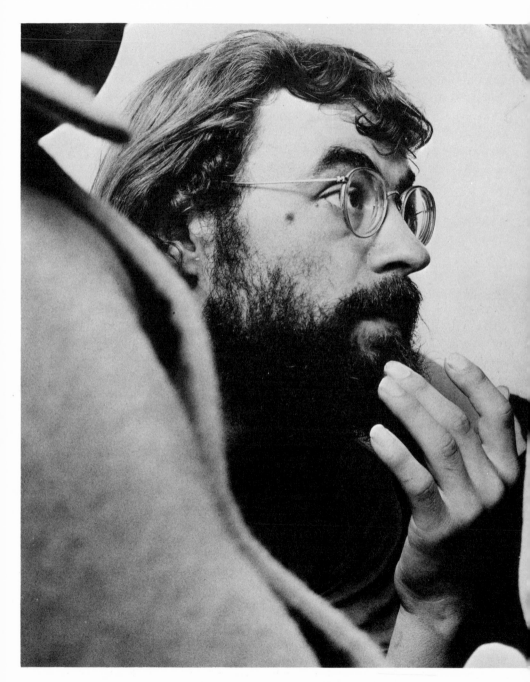

Roel van Duyn: prominent "Kabouter"

remained tolerant. The monument remained a hippie totem pole. And then it was winter again and the problem was over.

In February 1970, the beatnik Provos, who had officially disbanded themselves in 1967 "to avoid bloodshed" but had not lost their nausea for middle-class life or their liking for the paradoxical, emerged again. They were now the Kabouters, which can be translated as gnomes or elves, and were led by a slightly built, agreeable and highly intelligent sociologist, Roel van Duyn, who had the typically "student" appearance of a vague mix-up of John Lennon and Groucho Marx. He had the Provo — or ex-Provo — seat on the Council. Since leadership is anathema to the movement perhaps one should say that he was the nonleader not leading them. The Kabouters offered a combination of whimsical dottiness and a sprinkling of good sense, plus plenty of nuisance and publicity effects. With his paradoxical, humorous, didactic approach Van Duyn was rather like a young Bernard Shaw. In fact the Kabouters often seemed like a regiment of Bernard Shaws. They came, predictably, from students and artists and the cultured dispossessed and they were for freedom and the beautiful life and nonprofit-making industries and the poor and the old and, as the London *Times* had noted, wholemeal bread. They were against bankers, industrialists and any motor cars at all in the city center.

The Kabouters issued a proclamation. "How does a new society arise from an old society? Like a toadstool on a rotting tree trunk. Out of the sub-culture of the order-in-being grows an alternative communal life. . . . Left and right the toadstools of the new society will spread. Fairy circles of elf-cities will join together in a world-encircling net: the Orange Free State." The Town Hall was to be regarded as an embassy, with Van Duyn as an ambassador between the two states.

The new society would be socialist . . . "no longer the socialism of the clenched fist, but of the intertwined fingers, the erect penis, the escaping butterfly. . . ." The proletariat was now the provotariat. A dozen "Ministries" were set up to deal with the Kabouters' major interests, for example the Ministry of Public Works, which would be concerned with the planting of vegetables and the breakup of motorways; or the Ministry of "Milieu-Hygiene," which would fight against pollution and for "biological balance," or the Ministry of Defense, or Offense, which would specialize in sabotage. On proclamation day Kabouters wearing pixie hats attended a ceremony on the Dam, where a tiny orange tree was planted as a "new

COURTESY OF "DE TELEGRAAF"

Hippies around the National Monument on the Dam — 1970

national monument." They were furious when authority (order-in-being) had it removed shortly afterwards.

It was to be an eventful year. Kabouters were always in the news, especially when they were occupying empty houses, on behalf of the homeless — until police interruption. On April 30, the queen's birthday, there was a mass youth sit-down in the Rokin, blocking all traffic — until police interruption. On May 4 homosexuals tried to place a wreath at the Memorial Day ceremony. Women's liberation appeared in the shape of "Dolle Mina's" — "Crazy Mary's" — girls getting up for men in buses and campaigning for abortion and so on. Then at the June city elections something remarkable happened — the Kabouters polled eleven percent of the votes and five candidates were elected to the Council. (The movement had also spread over the rest of the country.)

All this helped to ensure the reappearance of international youth in the summer. They arrived, white faced, long haired, grimy, monosyllabic, occasionally beautiful and always enviably free of rheumatism. It was the hippie capital of the world and the Dam was the place to sleep. The hopes that they would all go off to the dormitories and hostels were not realized — although large numbers did go. But for people with shops and hotels and businesses around the Dam the joke had gone far enough. When in August a thousand of them were sleeping in the square, and cluttering it up all day, the burgomaster at last decided to enforce the bylaw about public monuments. The order would apply from six o'clock on Monday evening, August 25.

That morning the Dam was jam-packed with Amsterdamers and tourists gazing at the spectacle of the hippies lying around the memorial. It was a terribly zoolike experience, but fascinating also to see people fascinated by people doing almost nothing at all. The true hippies who were not dozing gazed about with nothing but benevolence. There was an incident during the morning when a Kabouter, spectacled and bearded, suddenly showed himself on the memorial steps, holding a poster above his head. In Dutch and English its message was "Sliep Uit — Sleep Out." Several more Kabouters followed him, carrying the same advice. That was all and the warm day passed quietly. Six o'clock came and the hippies still sat and lay about the steps.

There was no sign of any police until a quarter to ten, and they began by being very gentle and tolerant. But as well as the hippies and Kabouters, there were groups around like the Socialist Youth and Red Youth, who were interested in playing up the ban and creating a riot — they had the specific interest of upsetting the Indonesian President's visit to the city, scheduled for the following week. Also present were youths who simply liked a nice riot. And so there was one. It was quite as bad as in 1966. In due course the police charged, wearing white helmets and carrying basket-like shields. Shots were fired and rioters wounded. Cobblestones made excellent ammunition. The windows of the great store De Bijenkorf were smashed and their contents looted. Fighting and looting spread to the streets around, Rokin and Damrak and Nieuwendijk. Oddly enough it spread no farther. Within a half-mile radius of the Dam one suddenly saw a gang of youths rushing by but for what purpose was not clear. Down on the Rembrandtsplein and Leidseplein nobody heard anything.

But in the morning the country at large was fairly well horrified. People sent flowers to the wounded policemen. The burgomaster, Dr. Samkalden, came in for bitter criticism, for putting the ban on, for not putting it on earlier. There was resentment because it seemed that action had only been taken because a VIP was coming. The burgomaster defended himself firmly, insisting that what he had done was in the interests of tolerance. People were appalled by the pictures of the mess left behind on the memorial.

In spite of everything there were fifty or more hippies lying in the usual place on Tuesday evening, with the police keeping clear. But the peaceful scene was not to last. Just as in 1967, when some marines and sailors had taken it upon themselves to "cleanse" the Central Station, a hundred more of them now arrived. They came charging down the Damrak in rows of ten and, cheered enthusiastically by guests on the balcony of the Hotel De Roode Leeuw, burst enthusiastically on to the Dam, truncheons at the ready. There was immediate proof that in an emergency hippies could move fast. Only two or three were caught and ejected personally by the marines, who then set about cleaning the memorial of all dirt and rubbish. When they were satisfied they marched away to the station, via Warmoes-straat, singing the war song "Zorg, dat je erbij komt." ("Make sure that you're there.") At the station a large number of Amsterdamers sang it with them. Behind them there was some mild rioting, but not much, and there were three hundred policemen around the Dam.

All square and patriotic Dutchmen were delighted by the episode. The

COURTESY OF "DE TELEGRAAF"

Hippies in flight, chased by marines — 1970

leader in *De Telegraaf* the next morning said benevolently that such things must *not* happen, and added, however, the marines must be treated with the utmost leniency.

That night again, things still rumbled. There were Molotov cocktails in supply and crowds of youths on the warpath on the Dam. Not, of course, hippies. A boy shouted that there were police buses on the Rokin — *"Kom op, bij de bank op het Rokin staan busjes met smerissen."* The youths swarmed off to throw their bombs. The first one arrested was a nineteen-year-old German from Wuppertal, who was advancing on the police with a bottle of benzine in hand. Meanwhile on the Nieuwendijk, bar and shop owners paraded up and down with sticks to protect their property.

The next morning a headline said: Amsterdam a Sad City. And the waiters at the Roode Leeuw were threatening to sue the Council, for all the guests had gone.

7.

IT WAS NOT REALLY A SAD CITY. It was a famous, wonderful and tolerant city. But it's right and proper to end with Amsterdam in a mood of questioning. For nothing became it so splendidly — though quite normally, also — as the fierce debate which went on for the rest of the year. To begin with, for days after the affair was over the Dam itself was crowded with people discussing it — which excellently demonstrated the forum quality of the city center which was brought up in the ban-the-bank campaign. (The building of the bank, incidentally, after some years of technical trouble, goes ahead.) The riots, though they had received a good degree of international publicity, were hardly worthy of it from their actual seriousness; they were puny by other nations' standards. But the nature of Amsterdam gave them significance. It had been a confrontation of ways of life — forgetting the thug fringe element. The arrival of the marines pinpointed this. They were so healthy and clean-cut, but the glow and pleasure they brought to the silent, or not so silent, majority was tinged with a slight disquiet that there had been something just a little storm-trooperish about the exercise. On the other hand, from the most liberal point of view, were there not limits to toleration? The marines had perhaps played the part of the stern Calvinists of the seventeenth century, the counter-Remonstrants. It was the same old Amsterdam.

While the ring-roads went on developing, and the petrochemical plants, and Ajax, the football team, and the metro, and the newest wonderful suburb, fit for the twenty-first century, and while the Amsterdam money market kept its fourth place in the world rankings, the Kabouters also kept on going, working for a society with no loan slavery, more trees and psychiatric clinics where there would be no difference between patients and doctors. But there was a mishap to a Kabouter paper run by the "Min'stry of Offense of the Orange Free State," for it enclosed in its first number of 2,500 copies an envelope in each issue containing a small quantity of what the police called poor quality marijuana. "We are going underground — good-bye!" the paper cried in its last number, and forecast an ecological disaster in 1980. "Get used to eating grass, fatten your dogs, develop a taste for insects, learn to make arrowheads. . . ."

The next Kabouter campaign was about the coming census. They complained about the intimate questions and the information about everyone which would be available by computer; and they complained about the use of old-age pensioners for collecting the answers, and about the stairs they would have to climb, and the extra tax they would pay on the extra money they earned. "Don't do the work, pensioners. Everybody else, don't answer the questions."

St. Nicholas Day on December 5 is the Dutch day for giving presents, preceded a week or two before by the arrival in Amsterdam of the saint, Sinterklaas or, as others put it, Santa Claus. This year the Kabouters were attacking Santa on account of his services to luxury shops and also because they thought he should come every day. But there he was as usual on a Saturday in November, coming into the quayside in his Spanish boat (he spends the rest of the year in Spain) with his horse and his black servant, Peter, to a salute of guns and bell-ringing from his own nearby St. Nicholas church. As usual thousands of Amsterdamers and their children were there to applaud him on his way down the Damrak and into the Dam, where he was welcomed before the palace by a city alderman. The procession ended with a feast at the Hilton Hotel.

And the summer seemed a long time ago. On many walls there were half-torn and out-of-date posters, mostly with some sort of revolutionary motif. It all seemed rather sad and nostalgic. How young they had been.

And how touching was the earnestness of it all. "School for violence." "*Re-volte* — a magazine produced by one of the groups who misuse their freedom." And how had I missed the beguiling Cineclub festival in July? Every evening had been a treat: Monday *May Revolt*, Tuesday *Strike Film*, Wednesday *Renault Strike*, Thursday *People's Park* and Friday *Draft Avoidance in the U.S.A.* In a few more months, no doubt, it would all be starting again, but for the moment there were ghosts about.

There are always ghosts, of course. A favorite winter journey of mine is the early-morning train trip to Amsterdam after the night ferry crossing from England. (I like to travel in a civilized way.) Holland is so splendidly compact and on this short run every place name is evocative of the famous past — Rotterdam, which was Erasmus's town; and Delft, where William of Orange was assassinated; and The Hague, still with the glory of the stadholders' courts; and scholarly Leyden, where there was one great siege; and Haarlem, where there was another. But the train is full of dark-suited businessmen on their way to the office and all one sees of the history-laden towns are high apartment blocks close to the railway line, all of them lit up — and in a peculiarly Dutch way, endearing but also a little frightening, for quite open to the view are the massed vertical heaps of sitting rooms, which all look well furnished and comfortable and tasteful, and all seem so exactly the same. After Haarlem the winter daylight is emerging and I remember that these last miles to Amsterdam over the Haarlem dike were the original stretch of railway in Holland. Somebody took down the dialogue on one of the early rides in the 1840's and I hear those ghost voices in the carriage full of late twentieth-century businessmen.

A funny man insists on calling the engine a horse, and someone else is nervous.

"The horse has got a cold."

"Now it's beginning to go! This is what I like."

"Nonsense! This is just child's play. It's something else in Belgium, they turn an hour into five minutes."

"How terrible! They wouldn't get me on it —"

"Look! There goes the *schuit* and there's nobody in it. But it's going pretty well —"

The voices fade. That anonymous reporter went on to complain bitterly about the passing of the *schuit*, the wonderful system of horse-drawn canal boats. He deplored the loss of the wit and good conversation, and

COURTESY OF AERIALPHOTO KLM AEROCARTO N.V., THE NETHERLANDS

Amsterdam from the air — 1971

recalled how one used to dress up for the journey and take better tobacco than usual, and the freshness of the air, and the scenery and the villages, the whole thing giving one a feeling of being "out" — and one went wherever one wanted to go with a calm that suited the Dutch character. Where else was this emphasis on being "out"? Of course — it was in the cry from the heart in the ban-the-bank campaign, the desire to be "out" and "at home" in the forum atmosphere of the city center.

They should never have stopped the *trek-schuits*. Maybe the Kabouters can bring them back. But we are reaching the city now. On the left are the vague shapes of great dock installations and on the right the high apartment houses, carefully spaced, splendidly planned, of the western "garden city" Slotermeer. And then a closing up, some late-nineteenth-century streets slanting in on one side, a sudden glimpse of old gables on the other — and we are there. I pick up my bags and go out of the Central Station. Full daylight now, taxis, buses, trams, bicycles, St. Nicholas church with scaffolding round it — its red-neon cross won't be shining in the dark for the moment — and in front of me the Damrak leading down to the Dam. The old city is there and, yes, I feel that I am "out" and "at home."

Bibliography

Algemene Geschiedenis der Nederlanden [General History of the Netherlands]. Utrecht: De Haan, 1952.

Amstelodamum Jahrboek [Amsterdam year book].

Barbour, Violet. *Capitalism in Amsterdam in the Seventeenth Century.* Baltimore: Johns Hopkins Press, 1950.

Bientjes, J. *Holland und die Holländer im Urteil deutscher Reisender 1400–1800.* [Holland and the Dutch in the judgment of German travelers 1400–1800].

Brugmans, H. *Geschiedenis van Amsterdam* [History of Amsterdam]. Haarlem: Uitgeverij Joost van den Vondel, 1930.

———, ed. *Het Huiselijk en Maatschappelijk Leven onzer Voorouders* [The domestic and social life of our ancestors]. Amsterdam: Elsevier, 1914.

Burke, Gerald L. *The Making of Dutch Towns.* London: Cleaver Hume, 1956.

Carter, Alice Clare. *English Reformed Church in Amsterdam in the Seventeenth Century.* Amsterdam: Scheltema & Holkema, 1964.

Casanova, Giacomo. *Histoire de ma vie* [History of my life]. Paris: Plon, 1962.

Couvée, J. H. *De Dam* [The Dam]. Utrecht: A. Oosthoek, 1968.

D'Ailly, A. E. *Historische Gids van Amsterdam* [Historical guide to Amsterdam]. Amsterdam: Allert de Lange, various editions.

de Balbian Verster, J. F. L. *Burgemeesters van Amsterdam in de 17e en 18e eeuw* [Burgomasters of Amsterdam in the seventeenth and eighteenth centuries]. Zutphen: W. J. Thieme & Cie, 1932.

de Boer, M. G. *Een Wandeling door oud-Amsterdam* [A walk through Old Amsterdam]. Amsterdam: Meulenhof, 1952.

Delta Magazine, vol. X, nos. 3 and 4. Amsterdam, 1967.

de Parival, J. *De Vermaechlijckheden van Hollandt* [Les délices de la Hollande; The delights of Holland]. n.p., 1660.

de Roy van Zuydewijn, H. J. F. *Amsterdamse Bouwkunst 1815–1940* [Amsterdam architecture 1815–1940]. Amsterdam: De Bussy, n.d.

Duboscq, André. *Louis Bonaparte en Hollande* [Louis Bonaparte in Holland]. Paris: Emdi-Paul, 1911.

Edmundson, G. *History of Holland.* Cambridge, England: Cambridge University Press, 1922.

Fahrenfort, Janszen, Sanders. *Oproer in Amsterdam* [Uproar in Amsterdam]. Amsterdam: H. J. W. Becht, 1966.

Frank, Anne. *Diary of a Young Girl.* London: Constellation Books, 1952.

———. *Het Achterhuis* [The back premises]. Amsterdam: Contact, 1947.

Garnier, Athanase. *Mémoires sur la cour de Louis-Napoleon et sur la Hollande* [Memoirs of Louis Napoleon's court and of Holland]. Paris: n.p., 1828.

[349]

Amsterdam

Geyl, Pieter. *History of the Low Countries*. London: Macmillan, 1964.
———. *The Netherlands in the Seventeenth Century*. London: Benn, 1964.
Gosse, E. *Studies in the Literature of Northern Europe*. London: Kegan Paul, 1879.
Havard, Henri. *Amsterdam et Vénise* (Amsterdam and Venice). Paris: Plon, 1876.
Huizinga, J. H. *Dutch Civilization in the Seventeenth Century*. London: Collins: 1968.
Lucas, E. V. *A Wanderer in Holland*. London: Methuen, 1905.
Lugt, Frits. *Een Wandeling met Rembrandt in en over Amsterdam* [A walk with Rembrandt in and around Amsterdam]. Amsterdam: Van Kampen, 1915.
Motley, J. L. *Rise of the Dutch Republic*. London: Routledge and Sons, 1889.
Physiologie van Amsterdam [Physiology of Amsterdam]. Amsterdam: Leepel & Brat, 1844.
Rosenberg, Jakob. *Rembrandt*. Cambridge, Mass.: Harvard University Press, 1948.
Schnabel, Ernst. *Anne Frank: Spur Eines Kindes* [The footsteps of Anne Frank]. Amsterdam: Fischer Bücherei KG, 1958.
———. *The Footsteps of Anne Frank*. London: Longmans, 1959.
Temple, Sir William. *On the United Provinces of the Netherlands*. Cambridge, England: Cambridge University Press, 1932.
ten Brink, J. *De Werken van G. A. Bredero* [The works of G. A. Bredero]. Amsterdam: Binger, 1890.
ter Gouw, J. *Geschiedenis van Amsterdam* [History of Amsterdam]. Amsterdam: Van Holkema & Warendorf, 1891.
Valentiner, W. R. *Rembrandt and Spinoza*. London: Phaidon Press, 1957.
———. *Rembrandt und seine Umgebung* [Rembrandt and his background]. Strasbourg: Heitz, 1905.
van Duyn, Roel. *Schuldbekentenis van een Ambassadeur* [An ambassador's confession of guilt]. Amsterdam: Meulenhof, 1970.
van Gogh, Vincent. *Letters of Vincent van Gogh*. London: Constable, 1927.
van Lennep, J. *De Werken van J. van den Vondel* [The works of J. van den Vondel]. Leiden: Sijthof, n.d.
van Thienen, F. W. S. *Op't hoogh toneel* [On the stage]. Amsterdam: Stadsdrukkerij, 1969.
von Dunin-Borkowski, Stanislaus, S.J. *Der junge de Spinoza* [The young Spinoza]. Münster: Aschendorffsche Buchhandlung, 1910.
Wilson, Charles. *Holland and Britain*. London: Collins, 1946.
Wolf, A. *The Correspondence of Spinoza*. London: George Allen & Unwin, 1928.
Zunthor, Paul. *Daily Life in Rembrandt's Holland*. London: Weidenfeld & Nicholdson, 1962.

Index

Index

Index

Index

Maria Theresa, of Austria, 209, 210
Marie Louise, wife of Napoleon, 243, 247; visit to Amsterdam, 247-251
maritime interests, 35, 203
Marot, Daniel, 209
Mary, daughter of Charles I of England, 144, 148
Mary, wife of William III of Orange, 198
Mary of Burgundy, 31-33
Matelief, Cornelis, 84
Matthias, Archduke of Austria, 66, 69
Mauhs, Else, 328
Maurice of Orange, Stadholder, 77, 79, 92, 110, 121; and religious controversy, 102, 105, 110-112
Mauritius, 84
Maximilian, Archduke of Austria, 32-35, 140
May, Job, 254
Mazarin, Jules Cardinal, 148, 151
Mechlin, in Brabant, 35; superior court at, 26
Medici, Cosimo de', 178
Medici, Maria de', 137-140
Mediterranean, 224
Medway River, 183
Mendoza, Diego Hurtado de, 105
Mengelberg, Willem, 274, 278
Mennonites, 45, 46, 158, 163, 164
merchants, 27, 33, 36-37, 52; and the Sea Beggars, 60; at onset of 18th century, 202
metro, 314
Meuse River, 17
Meyer, Lodewijk, 193
Michelangelo, 166
Middleburg, 72
Milton, John, his *Paradise Lost,* 155-156
missionaries, 16, 203
Mississippi Company, 209
Militia, 25, 39-40, 94
Mobil Oil refinery, 313, 323
Molière, 184
Molucca, 84; Amboina incident, 112
monasteries, 23
money market, 80, 208, 213, 256, 273, 342; and World War I, 277-278
Montebello, Duchess of, 250
Montelbaans-tor, 34, 177
Moors, 28
morality, 116-118
Morteira, Rabbi, 161-162, 164-165
Moucheron, Balthazar de, 82
Moucheron, Isaac de, 209
Mozambique, 84
Muiden, 63, 92; castle, 21, 92, 187; literary circle, 101, 102, 105, 120, 122, 125, 133, 146, 147, 175
Multatuli (Douwes Dekker), his *Max Havelaar,* 261
Municipal theater, 267; Stadsschouwburg, 19, 274 277, 279, 328; Keizersgracht, 134-135, 184, 224-225; Leidseplein, 225, 258, 273, 274
Münster, in Westphalia, 42; Treaty of, 147, 148; Bishop of, 186
Munt-tor, 10, 34
Muses, The, literary review, 258
Museumplein, 328
Musicos, 222-225
Mussert, Mr., NSB chief, 285

Naarden, 61-62

Napoleon I, 237-245, 247, 256; visit to Amsterdam, 247-251
Napoleon II, King of Rome, 247, 250, 252
Napoleonic Code, 246
Navigation Act, England, 151, 183
navy, 79, 148, 151, 152; in Second Anglo-Dutch war, 183; in French invasion (1672), 186, 187: by mid-18th century, 210, 226
Nazi movement. *See* Dutch Nazi party
Netherlands Bank, 7, 316, 323
Netherlands Film Academy, 331
Netherlands Trading Company, 256-257, 322
New Amsterdam, 183
New Bridge, 36, 85
New Side. *See* Windmill Side
Nieuwe Kerk, 18, 24, 27, 47, 56; in fire of 1452, 28; and Calvinists (1578), 68; and building of new Town Hall, 175, 176; wedding of Princess Beatrix and von Amsberg in, 316
Nieuwendijk, 62
Nieuwenhuis, Domela, 275
Nieuwezijd. *See* Windmill Side
Nieuwezijd canal, 22
Nijmegen, 61, 63
Nil Volentibus Arduum, Francophile society, 184, 193
North Sea, 16, 27; canal, 262, 273, 278, 312, 313
Novgorod, 27
Nozems, 321

Occu, Pompejus, 38, 41, 62
Occu, Sybrant, 62, 63
Oetgens, Franz, 85, 87
oil industry, 278
Old Chamber. *See* Chamber of Rhetoric
Oldenbaarneveldt, Jan van, 78, 83, 105, 110; and West India Company, 111; and Vondel's *Palamedes,* 121
Oldenburg, Mr., 193, 194
Old Side. *See* Church Side
Olympic Games (1928), 278
opera, 258, 267
Orangists, 69, 70; and Spanish rule, 59-69; and Amsterdam, 67, 315
Orleans, Duchess of, 186
Ostend, 210
Ostend Company, 209
Oude Kerk (Old Church), 19, 23, 24, 46, 47, 85, 119, 276; in disorder of 1566, 56
Ouderkerk, 18, 165
Oudezijd. *See* Church Side
Oudezijds Voorburgwal (Velvet Canal), 52
Oudinot, Nicolas C., 253
Ovens, Jurriaen, 178
Overlander family, 144
Overyssel, 78
Oxenstjerna, Axel, 114

Paget, Reverend, 102
painters, 119, 204
Palace, 18, 247; and Louis Napoleon, 238, 242; Napoleon's stay, 247-250; and King William I, 257
Palace of Industry (Paleis voor Volksvlijt), 262, 266
Palma Vecchio, 166
Pankras, Gerbrand, 138
paper-making, 213
Paradise, the, Kalverstraat, 38